At the Bend of the River Grand

*One Hundred Thirty Years of the
Passionate Pursuit of Holiness at
Eaton Rapids Camp Meeting (1885-2015)*

David & Marybeth Baggett,
with Joelee Bateman

The Asbury Theological Seminary Series in Pietist/Wesleyan Studies

EMETH PRESS
www.emethpress.com

*At the Bend of the River Grand: One Hundred Thirty Years of the
Passionate Pursuit of Holiness at Eaton Rapids Camp Meeting (1885-2015)*

Copyright © 2016 David and Marybeth Baggett
Printed in the United States of America on acid-free paper

All rights reserved. No part of this book may be reproduced, or stored in a retrieval system or transmitted in any form or by any means, electronic, mechanical, photocopying, recording, scanning or otherwise, except as permitted by the 1976 United States Copyright Act, or with the prior written permission of Emeth Press. Requests for permission should be addressed to: Emeth Press, P. O. Box 23961, Lexington, KY 40523-3961.   http://www.emethpress.com

Library of Congress Cataloging-in-Publication Data

Names: Baggett, David, author.
Title: At the bend of the River Grand : 130 years of the passionate pursuit
   of holiness at Eaton Rapids Camp Meeting (1885-2015) / David & Marybeth
   Baggett, with Joelee Bateman.
Description: Lexington, KY : Emeth Press, 2016. | Includes bibliographical
   references.
Identifiers: LCCN 2016015260 | ISBN 9781609470982 (alk. paper)
Subjects: LCSH: Michigan State Holiness Camp Meeting Association--History. |
   Camp meetings--Michigan--Eaton Rapids--History | Eaton Rapids
   (Mich.)--Church history.
Classification: LCC BX8476.E28 B34 2016 | DDC 277.74/23082--dc23
LC record available at https://lccn.loc.gov/2016015260

To John Oswalt, 19th President of ERC
Teacher, Mentor, Friend

When I consider how my light is spent,
Ere half my days in this dark world and wide,
And that one talent which is death to hide
Lodged with me useless, though my soul more bent
To serve therewith my Maker, and present
My true account, lest He returning chide;
"Doth God exact day-labor, light denied?"
I fondly ask. But Patience, to prevent
That murmur, soon replies, "God doth not need
Either man's work or His own gifts. Who best
Bear His mild yoke, they serve him best. His state
Is kingly: thousands at His bidding speed,
And post o'er land and ocean without rest;
They also serve who only stand and wait."

— John Milton

Contents

Foreword by Dennis Kinlaw / ix

Preface by David Baggett / xi

Acknowledgments / xv

Introduction / 1

Prelude: Camp Meeting 2015 / 9

Part I—The Second Great Awakening and Camp Meetings in America

Chapter 1
    Christianity in 19th Century America, 1790-1900 / 27
    Spotlight on Camp Meetings / 38
    1865-1884: Postbellum America / 41

Part II— The Turn of the Century

1885-1914: *Fin de Siècle* America / 45
Chapter 2
    The Forest City, 1885-1894 / 47
    Spotlight on Marshall M. Callen / 59
Chapter 3
    A New Century, 1895-1904 / 63
    Spotlight on Joseph H. Smith / 70
Chapter 4
    Eaton Rapids *Is*, 1905-1914 / 73
    Spotlight on George Bennard / 80

Part III— Between the Wars

1915-1944: America between the Wars / 85
Chapter 5
    War Years, 1915-1924 / 87
    Spotlight on E. Stanley Jones / 90
Chapter 6
    Depression Years, 1925-1934 / 95
    Spotlight on Henry Clay Morrison / 100
Chapter 7
    The Golden Jubilee and War Again, 1935-1944 / 103
    Spotlight on Lloyd H. Nixon / 109

Interlude: Fourteenth Decade Underway / 111

Part IV— Post World War II

1945-1984: Cold War America / 129
Chapter 8
    Scene by the River, 1945-1954 / 131
    Spotlight on J. C. McPheeters / 137
Chapter 9
    Camp Ground, 1955-1964 / 141
    Spotlight on Clarence Hutchens / 147
Chapter 10
    Who among These Sturdy Oaks? 1965-1974 / 149
    Spotlight on Hayden Carruth / 173
Chapter 11
    Dappled with Sun and Shade, 1975-1984 / 175
    Spotlight on Wallace Haines / 194

Part V— Contemporary America

1985-2015: America in the Information Age / 235
Chapter 12
    The Centennial Celebration, 1985-1994 / 237
    Spotlight on Samuel Kamaleson / 259
Chapter 13
    A Third Century, 1995-2004 / 261
    Spotlight on Dennis Kinlaw / 265
Chapter 14
    Walking with God, 2005-2014 / 267
    Spotlight on John Oswalt / 282

Postlude: Thy Kingdom Come / 285

Conclusion / 297

Appendix 1 / 305

Appendix 2 / 307

Appendix 3 / 333

Bibliography / 339

Foreword

Camp Meetings

Dennis Kinlaw

When Abraham Lincoln was elected president of the United States, he was in New York City. As he journeyed to Washington for installation, he stopped in New Jersey to give greetings to the two houses of the state legislature. In brief greetings to the legislative bodies of a state that had not voted for him, he introduced to the world the intellectual concept that was to determine his leadership of his country in its time of crisis. He referred to the United States as "the almost chosen people." It is clear that Lincoln felt that the United States had a divine mission to show the world what a free nation should look like. Echoes of that perspective live with us now when political leaders in a secularized version of Lincoln's conviction refer to the *exceptionalism* of the American nation.

What was the source of Lincoln's conviction? It was clearly a religious conviction for him. It was, specifically, a Christian conviction. Lincoln, however, was not officially known as being in any sense actively involved in the Christian Church. The United States was remarkable among the nations of the Western world in that it had no state church. The anti-slavery conscience in America was not the result of the pronouncements of institutional religion or even the result of political decisions handed down from our political leaders. It was a public conscience that arose from the people themselves of which Lincoln was a sensitive part. What most people do not know is that the American camp meeting movement was a major factor in all of that. Our current historical amnesia is costing us dearly.

We are indebted to our authors here. This volume should help us recover some sense of national destiny. It is a needed work and, I trust, will be read widely.

Preface

The Best Is Yet to Come

David Baggett

Eaton Rapids Camp Meeting has touched my life profoundly. One of my earliest memories, in fact, was looking high into the air at the windows near the top of the tabernacle. It was after an evening service, if my faint memory serves, and I must have been herded back to the main auditorium after the youth service was done. People were milling about and darting in various directions. I still recall seeing some tables set up with various advertisements (likely from Bible schools and the like) at the back of the tabernacle, and the outstanding impression I experienced at that age was the sheer enormity of the structure. It was simple but elegant—it seemed well-nigh ornate to me—with doors propped up all around its perimeter. Its capacious wooden canopy was enough to mesmerize my imagination for quite some time. I am guessing I was around five or six years of age. I didn't know it at the time, but I was smack dab in the center of a vintage piece of classic Americana. This was camp meeting, in Eaton Rapids, Michigan, and it was, to my best guess, 1971 or 1972.

From my earliest days, I heard preaching in church each Sunday morning (and evening, and most Wednesdays), but come summertime my five siblings and I would ready ourselves for an extra special dose of it. We would disappear from our suburban home outside Detroit—where my mother grew up; my dad was from Tennessee—and materialize at camp meeting, a couple week-long intensive church-on-steroids event, a vestige of the holiness movement about which I would learn quite a bit more later in life. In those early years of my life, this was part of the air I breathed, and I didn't imagine things could have been different.

We attended various church camps through the years, but the Eaton Rapids grounds were, in many ways, the most quintessential and central. Bath houses, an ice cream parlor, cottages, a cafeteria, meeting rooms, and walking trails physically defined the grounds, a place ubiquitous with leaves and flowers, punctuated by trees, bathed in shade, and half encircled by a gently flowing little river at two adjacent edges. I still remember my first images of that river as my dad drove our family the final leg of the 75-minute pilgrimage from Dearborn Heights. Once there, time seemed to stand still. To this day, life slows down when I enter the grounds—now over forty years later. Even from my time as a youth, the refreshing retreat and reprieve it afforded from the rest of life seemed well-nigh surreal, yet still somehow normative, life as it should be; going home would almost make me think the magical place where the river bends and such peace pervades had all been a dream.

Yet I knew the experience had been all too real, wielding a powerful influence on me, determining how I saw (and continue to see) the world from very early on. Eaton Rapids shaped me, and mine is but one story among many that can be told. The story of the Eaton Rapids Camp Meeting is made up of thousands of narratives, both like and unlike mine, but together they all make up its story. Not only that, the story of Eaton Rapids Camp Meeting is also part of a yet larger collection of stories—of the town, of the state, of the country, of evangelical Christianity, of the Holiness Movement, and, most ultimately, of the greatest Story of all.

My parents and siblings' treks to Eaton Rapids weren't just idiosyncratic features of my childhood or an inexpensive vacation for a working class family—they were a large reason I grew up thinking faith in God is as natural as breathing. The place forged my mental strictures and structures, stamping the tenets of historical Christian faith deep into my guiding vision of reality. It simply never seemed a realistic idea to me that God doesn't exist. Evangelical Christianity, biblical and holiness Christian faith, was the heritage in which I was steeped, becoming entrenched in my psyche, with Eaton Rapids playing a central role in my spiritual formation. As I grew into adulthood and pursued my vocation as a philosopher, my past shaped me, defined me, and charted my future. My professional interests in ethics and moral apologetics, I have little doubt, are closely connected to the holiness sermons I imbibed as a child, often in rapt attention, the words sinking into my heart and forging my view of the world and understanding of the human condition.

When I was 27, I lost my father to acute lymphoblastic leukemia. More recently I lost my oldest sister when she was only 53, and yet more recent still, in 2013, I lost my mother, less than three months after she turned 82. These losses make me want to cherish each day, and they also inspire me to relish, protect, and preserve the past—not to nurse a nostalgia that's debilitating, morose, or macabre, but to remember that God is the same yesterday, today, and tomorrow, that nostalgia rightly understood is as much about the future as the past, and that the best is yet to come.

This history was born of such a desire. The summer my mom was diagnosed with cancer, I was walking the grounds of Eaton Rapids and thinking of her and her love of the place and people. She was the daughter of a violent alcoholic, which affected her deeply; she and my dad were of modest means, but they were good people and gave their six kids a solid upbringing. Church camp was always a vital part of that heritage, and in her last twenty years, after all but a few of her kids had moved from the state, Eaton Rapids had become only all the more special—a healing place, a safe and loving context, a family. She owned a cottage there, contributed liberally of her time and money, stayed active teaching kids, volunteering in numerous capacities during Camp, and was a friend to many. When, for health reasons, she had to come live with me in Virginia the last few years of her life, her love for Michigan and for Eaton Rapids never waned. My United Methodist Virginia pastor preached her funeral and, having heard so much about ERC, felt compelled to mention it: "Blessed by our conversation, hearing about the Eaton Rapids Holiness Camp Meeting that I had assumed was a thing of the past, but she assured me that that tradition was alive and strong as the Holy Spirit was still very much at work within such gatherings."

So as I walked the grounds, she seemed to haunt the place; in my mind's eye I could see her everywhere—sitting in the tabernacle, walking the paths, eating in the cafeteria, holding an ice cream cone. I was half convinced that, if I inclined my ear, I could nearly hear the echo of her laughter emanate from her cottage. She was part of the place, and it her; she loved the grounds, and what the place and people represented: people of God converging together to fellowship and find inspiration to walk uprightly and faithfully in this world. Most of all she loved the sermons, good solid biblical preaching delivered by men and women anointed and called to the task of delivering messages at once biblical and timely, by turns challenging and inspiring.

For me the chance to work on this history, relishing its twists and turns, its local flavors and universal themes, has been a labor of love, one small way to pay homage to my mother, to explore what the grounds she so loved represent, and to recount an ineliminable and deeply formative part of my story and that of so many others. In writing this account, I've been able to visit some old haunts and wax nostalgic, to convey a sense of what this tradition has meant to me, to savor a wonderful yarn with many distinct and variegated but intimately related parts, and to honor what Eaton Rapids Camp Meeting has always stood for, still does, and will continue to represent—which is something of eternal permanence and infinite value, however the camp meeting tradition fares in the future.

A word on the organization of the book: one challenge posed by researching the history of Eaton Rapids was the abundance of material available. Over the course of the camp's 130-year existence, tens of thousands have attended, hundreds have preached, and a multitude have served. This history is the story of all of these participants; their stories make up ERC's story, as tesserae compose a mosaic, individual forms combine into a collage, single threads are woven into a tapestry. In the same vein, Eaton Rapids itself is but part of a larger story—of camp meetings, of Christianity in America, of the church universal. The particulars matter, for without them no larger pattern can emerge; as such we were determined to capture and present to you, the reader, as much of this rich detail as possible. We have arranged these elements, we hope, in an accessible manner, cutting through what might be otherwise dense material in a variety of ways to reveal connections and to illuminate ERC's charms.

Primarily the story is arranged chronologically—in five major divisions that track key eras in American history: (1) background to the camp meeting tradition with coverage of the Second Great Awakening, (2) the turn of the twentieth century, (3) the period between the world wars, (4) America after World War II, and (5) contemporary America. Punctuating these historical eras are summaries that attempt to locate the happenings of camp meeting within larger cultural trends. These five primary divisions are then subdivided into fourteen chapters—the first devoted to the historical context of the camp-meeting tradition and the remaining thirteen each recounting a decade of Eaton Rapids history. Additionally, we offer what we have called "spotlights" on select figures whose contributions to Eaton Rapids encapsulate the spirit of the camp—evangelists, missionaries, presidents, song leaders. These spotlights come in a variety of forms including biographical sketches, tributes to the figures, and articles written by or about them; the titles of each will signify what readers should expect to follow.

Another feature of this book is a detailed account of camp meeting 2015, with a daily log that covers every major event and service. This account is separated into three sections interspersed throughout the book—a prelude, an interlude, and a postlude—with headers marking the inclusion of notes from each sermon and Bible study. We conclude the history with some analysis, giving a rundown of the lessons and encouragement that we believe this story has to offer us today. The voices of ERC's past speak to us still, and in this conclusion, we hope to amplify their message. Finally, we include an abundance of enchanting photographs culled from ERC's archives and three appendices: (1) a record of the association presidents; (2) a year-by-year roster of camp officers, platform speakers, and other camp workers; and (3) the transcript of a sermon delivered by President W. G. Nixon in 1926. Readers should feel free to process through the book as they wish, depending on their interests and needs, feeling free to pick and choose and revisit often.

Whether the tradition fades away or roars back, it will forever be the case that it played a huge role in the history of our nation and in the lives of many. Whether you play a part in this vaunted tradition or not, either at Eaton Rapids or elsewhere, it is our hope that this history will bring some of its blessed texture and richness to you, that this temporal and eternal story, this particular and universal narrative, will minister to you and bring edification to your soul.

Acknowledgments

When I (Dave) undertook the task of writing this history, I was unaware of the work that had already been done by others, which was considerable, although I figured that there would be plenty of material to work with. I expressed an interest in working on a History to Dr. John Oswalt, a former professor of mine at Asbury Theological Seminary and the President of the Camp Meeting at the time, and before long he made me part of the Historical Committee and entrusted to us the task of writing this history.

The History Committee, especially Betty Uithoven, would prove invaluable to the work, as would the labors of past historians of the camp meeting, like Beth Nixon Carruth and, most recently, Joelee Bateman, a friend of mine and my mom's and a cottage next-door-neighbor (if you see red, you know you're close). What further facilitated the task were various compilations of historical materials from years past, and the time many took to pass along stories, share documents and pictures and mementos, and help in ways big and small to bring the project to fruition. Faithful chroniclers have recorded relevant facts, dates, anecdotes, mission statements, committee minutes, and a wealth of other relevant data that proved a treasure trove of useful insight and helpful information as my wife and I worked on this snapshot of the camp meeting's history.

Walter Eschtruth dutifully mined his historical collection of materials and unearthed a wealth of valuable resources for us to use; he's one shining example of many whose help was invaluable. We were especially grateful for his timely help because, by the year after he provided it, he had gone to his reward. It was both a happy and sad occasion to hear of Walter's passing before this project was completed.

Thanks to all those who have expressed enthusiasm and support for and abiding interest in this project, including (but not limited to) Ellie Bartlett; our Liberty colleagues Roger Schultz, Emily Heady, Matthew Towles, and Donna Donald; and our son and budding historian Nathaniel. We are grateful, too, for the proofreading completed by Lindi Rigg.

Many thanks to Emeth Press and Dr. Larry Wood in particular for an abiding passion for campmeetings, believing in this project, and seeing it through to completion with such professionalism and skill.

In all of these ways this is a deeply communal effort made possible only by the diligent work of ever so many, to whom we are deeply indebted and of whom we are most appreciative.

Introduction

Listen for the Buzzing

When you read a work of history, always listen out for the buzzing. If you can detect none, either you are tone deaf or your historian is a dull dog. The facts are really not at all like fish on the fishmonger's slab. They are like fish swimming about in a vast and sometimes inaccessible ocean; and what the historian catches will depend partly on chance, but mainly on what part of the ocean he chooses to fish in and what tackle he chooses to use.

—Edward Hallett Carr

This book chronicles the history of the Eaton Rapids Camp Meeting in Eaton Rapids, Michigan, spanning from 1885-2015—130 plus years. Needless to say, much has transpired in that time. Through the years, many have passed through the camp's gates, making its story both an aggregate of many smaller stories and a microcosm of a much larger story.

An important part of this narrative was the work necessary to make the campground and to keep it up, to carve it from the forest, to "chop out a place to worship" and provide the beautiful and functional context in which subsequent life-changing preaching and fellowship could happen. This means that part of the story involves raising funds, paying bills, exerting toil to construct buildings—none of which is particularly glamorous, and all of which is penultimate at most. But in this corporeal world in which we're called to be co-laborers with Christ, it's crucially important nonetheless, and rightly construed it is altogether spiritual as well. What follows then is an account of trustees and pastors, laypeople and grounds workers, altar calls and sawdust trails, theology and experience, prayer and work, septic tanks and electric lines, human depravity and divine grace, salvation and sanctification—the story encompasses all of these things and more.

Reading these pages, one immediately recognizes the ties that bind us to the past. Despite all the cultural changes that have taken place over the course of Eaton Rapids' history, human nature, biblical truth, and the essence of Christian salvation have not changed. The needs and hungers that stirred the first attendees in 1885—women garbed in their big-bustled, shoulder-covered, high-necklined dresses; men clad in all-black suits while donning their stiff-crowned hats—are much the same as the needs and hungers of people today. Styles may change; the human condition remains constant. This makes the story of Eaton

Rapids Camp Meeting, despite its particularity, universal in its themes, expansive in its scope, and more relevant now than most would think.

Drawing out those connections was our challenge in writing this history. In the 19th century, when Eaton Rapids Camp Meeting began, many if not most historians operated with a simplistic idea, namely, that facts speak for themselves, that little interpretation of historical events was required. Like Mr. Gradgrind in *Hard Times* put it, "What I want is Facts. . . . Facts alone are wanted in life." As historian Edward Hallett Carr has written, "This was the age of innocence, and historians walked in the Garden of Eden, without a scrap of philosophy to cover them, naked and unashamed before the god of history." He continues, "Since then, we have known Sin and experienced a Fall; and those historians who today pretend to dispense with a philosophy of history are merely trying, vainly and self-consciously, like members of a nudist colony, to recreate the Garden of Eden in their garden suburb."[1]

Carr's point is that the question of what constitutes history is a difficult one, and, on his view, it involves "navigating delicately between the Scylla of an untenable theory of history as an objective compilation of facts, of the unqualified primacy of fact over interpretation, and the Charybdis of an equally untenable theory of history as the subjective product of the mind of the historian who establishes the facts of history and masters them through the process of interpretation, between a view of history having the cent[er] of gravity in the past and the view having the cent[er] of gravity in the present."[2]

But he doesn't consider the historian's task any more precarious than the same dichotomy of fact and interpretation that we regularly encounter in other guises: the particular versus the general, the empirical and the theoretical, the objective and the subjective. In this way he thinks the predicament of the historian is a reflection of the nature of man. There is both an objective reality out there or back there, *and* various subjective responses to those objective realities. We see the world through various filters—some more accurate and revealing than others—but there really is an objective world we see. Historians shouldn't pretend to have anything like complete objectivity, and that's quite alright. Historians interact with the facts, and out of this dynamic dialogue, good history can be done. "The historian without his facts is rootless and futile; the facts without their historian are rootless and meaningless."[3]

We emphasize this challenge at the outset because we wish to be transparent about what will serve as the unifying theme in this study, the lens through which we will conduct this particular investigation. The central idea and unifying thread is this: *Eaton Rapids Camp Meeting has, with remarkable consistency in the course of its history, refused to privilege the pursuit of happiness above or apart from the pursuit of holiness.* Perhaps this has always been rather countercultural, but never more so than today when the Gospel of Happiness, of whatever deflationary variant, seems to reign supreme, not just in public discourse, but even among many professing Christians.

---

[1] Edward Hallett Carr, *What is History?* (New York: Vintage Books, 1961), 21.
[2] Ibid., 34.
[3] Ibid., 35.

The word "holiness" today invariably invokes the specter of images of dour piety, lectures about chastity, and stern facial expressions. In many contexts, including many Christian churches in the United States, it's a term much less common than it used to be. When it *is* used, its connotations are not infrequently quite negative, bespeaking false sanctimony, rigid legalism, or stifled impulses that are better set free to find expression and guiltless manifestation. It is a word that, for many, reflects a bygone era best left behind, when repression reigned, natural desires went unsatiated, and happiness was sacrificed at the altar of capricious rules and stultifying moral regulations.

That this is the prevailing perception of holiness is especially interesting in light of the primacy of such a category in biblical teaching, the general history of the church, and the specific narrative of American Christianity. Holiness is not optional for the Christian. The Bible is replete with admonitions to walk uprightly, resist sin, be led of God's Spirit, and undergo transformation. Christian salvation isn't just a ticket to heaven; it's a process of becoming entirely conformed to the image of Christ, of being made new, of experiencing a revolution of the will—and a transition from salient concern for self to a character of self-giving love. To become able to love God with all of one's heart, soul, mind, and strength, and one's neighbor as oneself, *is to be made holy*, to be radically changed. Ultimately, salvation culminates in nothing less than such complete transformation.

Salvation, from a Christian perspective, involves being saved *from* something *for* something. We are saved from sin and self-consumption, from bondage that keeps us in darkness and from God's best for us. Into a sinful condition we are born, but we were made in God's image and meant to know God and love Him and others. We were also intended to be used of God, to find our God-given vocation, to serve God and others, to do good works—not to earn salvation, which is impossible, but out of gratitude to God for the salvation He has provided for us in Christ. To be used of God, however, we must be filled with His fullness, His power, and His holiness. We are to be "set apart"—the etymological significance of *holiness*—to be changed to be like Him, to be holy as He is holy. And to know God in this way—to love Him and know we are loved by Him, to be inwardly changed and transformed, to be filled with His presence and power, and equipped and anointed to serve Him—is to experience our *telos*, to live as we were meant to live. And to experience such kingdom life is to experience joy. To be happy and holy, ultimately, according to the Christian story of salvation and anthropology, are one and the same.

C. S. Lewis described this convergence in *The Great Divorce,* in a scene in which he imagines meeting George MacDonald in heaven:

> I tried to tell how a certain frosty afternoon at Leatherhead Station when I first bought a copy of *Phantastes* (being then about sixteen years old) had been to me what the first sight of Beatrice had been to Dante: *Here begins the New Life.* I started to confess how long that Life had delayed in the region of imagination merely: how slowly and reluctantly I had come to admit that his Christendom had more than an accidental

connexion (sic) with it, how hard I had tried not to see that the true name of the quality which first met me in his books is Holiness.

Lewis had seen that his quest for joy was the same as his quest for Holiness. Rather than holiness standing at odds or in tension with happiness and fulfillment, they were inextricably tied together, organically inseparable.

In a 1953 letter, Lewis wrote, "How little people know who think that holiness is dull. When one meets the real thing (and perhaps, like you, I have met it only once), it is irresistible. If even 10% of the world's population had it, would not the whole world be converted and happy before a year's end?"[4] Lewis considered it a deception that moral goodness had come to be confined to the region of Law and Duty, which never lets us feel in our face the sweet air blowing from "the land of righteousness," never reveals that elusive Form which if once seen must inevitably be desired with all but sensuous desire—the thing "more gold than gold."[5]

A desire for such holiness undergirds the camp meeting tradition. Camp meetings, in America and elsewhere, involve being literally set apart for a season, in order to focus on truths that don't change, on a God who is the same yesterday, today, and forever. Eaton Rapids Camp Meeting began two decades after the end of the Civil War, as part of the second grand epoch of camp meetings in America. The first epoch had been forged in the spirit of the Second Great Awakening, between around 1790 into the first few decades of the 19th century. The Civil War resulted in the loss or diminution of many of those camps, but the end of the war also fomented a renewed interest in starting such camps again. Begun in 1885, Eaton Rapids was one of the most significant of such camp meetings, and, while others have withered away, dissipating or disappearing, Eaton Rapids has endured, faithfully proclaiming the message of justification and sanctification for over 130 years.

The undiluted message of holiness and full salvation, like the aromatic, picturesque, idyllic tree-lined environs of Eaton Rapids, has been a most compelling and beautiful attraction to attendees all these years. In its heyday, Eaton Rapids Camp Meeting could boast of thousands in attendance, swept up in its proclamation of the Good News of Christ and promises of deliverance from the power of sin. When Eaton Rapids began, in the aftermath of the War, America was, in the estimation of many, in a state of spiritual malaise if not outright decline. The need for moral renewal and transformation was acute, and the Wesleyan and Holiness message of entire sanctification found receptive ears. While Presbyterian and Congregationalist participation in camp meetings

---

[4] *Yours, Jack,* 211.

[5] Scott Burson and Jerry Walls, *C. S. Lewis & Francis Schaeffer: Lessons for a New Century from the Most Influential Apologists of Our Time* (Downers Grove: IVP, 1998), 264. As Burson and Walls write, "One of the most pressing assignments for the twenty-first century apologist is to strip away the deception that keeps people from seeing the heart of the Christian faith—the biblical doctrine of holiness—in all of its golden glory and spectacular splendor. This means we must consciously reject today's dominant, stifling legal grid in favor of one that is profoundly liberating and richly relational."

declined in the 19th century, Baptist and especially Methodist participation skyrocketed. What drew the crowds and animated the speakers was the call to holiness and the victorious Christian life. The message is powerful and compelling, wild and beautiful, challenging and stirring, and it's a message needed as much today as it was needed in 1885.

John Wesley taught that Christianity fulfilled all of a person's deepest, truest desires, making the Christian a happier, more productive person. When pressed to define "the character of a Methodist," he answered, in a 1742 tract of that title: "God is the joy of [the Methodist's] heart. . . . He is therefore happy in God, yea, always happy, as having in him 'a well of water springing up into everlasting life,' and 'overflowing his soul with peace and joy.'" Chris Armstrong has written, "Just as their founder had experienced having his 'heart strangely warmed' in 1738 at a meeting on Aldersgate Street, Methodists practiced a religion of joy. Frontier Americans cracked jokes about the 'shouting Methodists,' but the Wesleyans wore the label as a badge of honor. They felt their own joy was one of the best advertisements for the truth of the message they preached."

Happiness, fulfillment, deep joy—these were among the earmarks of those in the Methodist movement and Holiness circles, and they were seen as attendant experiences of biblical holiness. From the start of Eaton Rapids, a recurring refrain has consistently been that happiness and holiness are natural dance partners. Intimacy with God and victory over sin are vital parts of fullness of joy. The notion that happiness and joy are goals natural for human beings to pursue is an old one, of course. In his *Nicomachean Ethics*, Aristotle sought an answer to the question, "What is the ultimate purpose of human existence?" What is the end or goal to which we should direct all of our activities? We tend to seek a variety of things—pleasure, wealth, a good reputation. But none of these can occupy the place of the chief good for human beings. To be an ultimate end, an act must be self-sufficient and final, "that which is always desirable in itself and never for the sake of something else," and it must be attainable by man. Aristotle claims that nearly everyone would agree that happiness is the end that meets all these requirements. We seek other things to make us happy; they are thus means to an end. But happiness is always an end in itself.

Those in the Holiness Movement, like all human beings, cared deeply about happiness; but what animated their quest wasn't the pursuit of happiness, primarily, but rather the pursuit of holiness, even while deeply convinced that (the deepest) happiness and holiness were profoundly consonant, indeed ultimately one and the same. What philosophers call the "hedonistic paradox" is this: pursuing happiness usually tends to be an ineffective way of finding it; happiness tends instead to show up when we seek something else, something that produces the happiness, the deeper source, which isn't happiness itself, but rather that of which happiness is the byproduct or natural accompaniment. To find our life we must lose it; to achieve our deepest joy, we have to seek something else—God himself. This is the paradox at the heart of the Christian message and the Holiness Movement, a truth that powerfully inverts and subverts the prevailing plausibility structures of our society today.

Among some of what has changed in American culture during the thirteen decades of Eaton Rapids Camp Meeting is a significant shift in focus away from holiness. Even among many professing evangelical Christians, other considerations and emphases have eclipsed the historical focus on holiness. The Holiness Movement has given way to the Happiness Movement—happiness construed in a far less robust way than the deepest joy for which we were intended. Rather than hearing about self-control or submissive obedience to God's commands as the path to joy, psychological categories of self-fulfillment and self-actualization have of late more often assumed priority.

What has happened here was the result of a great many historical antecedents and cultural influences, but one colossal contributor is the estrangement, if not outright divorce, of happiness and holiness. Orthodox Christian teachings and moral strictures are increasingly cast as inconsistent with human fulfillment. This is a profound departure from the sort of teaching that's been consistently proclaimed at a place like Eaton Rapids Camp Meeting for the past 130 years. There the airtight connection between holiness and happiness has been a central teaching; to be holy is to be happy, to experience the fullness of joy for which we were designed. Ultimate joy and happiness, it was taught, can be found only in a redeemed relationship with God as we submit to His Lordship and sanctifying grace. Happiness wasn't thought to be the product of *assertion of self*, but of *dying to self*; not in insisting on one's own way, but in yielding to God's way; not in satisfying each and every desire, but in submitting our desires to God.

The Holiness Movement itself did not always get this balance right. At times its preachers and teachers emphasized too little the joy in Christ, the fulfillment that can come only from relationship with God. Holiness at times was preached in ways that reinforced perceptions; it was more about following rules and enforcing codes of conduct than a vital, life-imparting relationship with God. On occasion rigid and pharisaical legalists held sway over those who rightly saw in Wesleyan theology a call to be perfected in love. On other occasions the joy to which we're called in Christ was thought to involve fanatical emotional displays rather than more authentic inward experiences of peace and happiness.

As part of the Holiness movement, Eaton Rapids also sometimes fell short of its goal, but its history is replete with those who strove, often with success, to remain faithful to the historic faith, to proclaim biblical holiness rightly understood, to wed happiness and holiness—as a 1940 brochure read, "Happy the persons who find God here." Fulfillment and joy were seen as natural byproducts of reconciliation and harmony with God, but happiness wasn't touted as the ultimate goal. What could give people such joy and happiness was the larger focus, and that Source of true joy was God alone—the God who is holy, and calls us to be holy as He is holy.

It would be a paradigm of historical naivety to imagine that the changing context of Eaton Rapids hasn't exerted its effects in 130 years of history. What used to be a place notoriously free from distractions is now no longer so useful for getting away from it all; smart phones and internet connections are ubiquitous; in 1885 America was recovering from a Civil War, whereas in 2015 America is a superpower; in 1885 the camp meeting tradition, after its precipitous decline around the Civil War, was on the increase, while the camp meeting tradition in 2015 is, in the estimation of many, petering out, if not teetering on its last leg; in 1885 Eaton Rapids was a camp meeting that had found a piece of property to operate on and whose future was altogether open-ended, whereas in 2015 it's a longstanding institution, a programmed annual event, whose history and glory days are well-established and documented. It's a different time, a different world. And those are just a smattering of examples of relevant contrasts.

Despite such changes, however, Eaton Rapids has been remarkably consistent in its message. To this day Eaton Rapids Camp Meeting upholds and trumpets its compelling vision—a call for holiness, a reminder that fullness of joy accompanies the sanctified life, a message of God's power to redeem, heal, transform, and save to the uttermost. A message just as true, good, and beautiful in 2015 as it was in 1885. It is a message that has touched countless lives, and will doubtless touch many more.

For an example of a touched life, consider Charles Ives (1874-1954). Here is a little known and rather surprising fact: The 20th-century American composer used the camp meeting phenomenon as inspiration for his Pulitzer Prize winning Symphony No. 3. The symphony—which is very short, lasting just twenty minutes—was not premiered until 1946, almost forty years after its composition. Symphony No. 3 is notable for its use of a chamber orchestra, rather than the complete orchestra Ives used for his other symphonies. The symphony is scored for a chamber orchestra of a flute, oboe, clarinet, bassoon, two horns, trombone, bells, and strings (violins, violas, cellos, and double basses).

Through its instrumentation and arrangements, its harmonies and melodies, the piece evokes memories of country meetings during Ives's childhood, when people gathered in fields to sing, preach, and listen—the iconic camp meetings of early America. It is a nostalgic piece, as the modern composer glances back at a 19th century childhood of hymns, bells, and children's games throughout the three movements filled with complex harmonies and meters. He incorporates hymn tunes and American Civil War-era popular songs, which are closely related to camp meeting songs, as part of the symphony's musical material. The three movements whisk listeners back through time to experience collectively the rhythms of camp meeting—from the old folks gathering, to the children playing, to the worshipers communing.

Such is our hope for this book, to welcome readers into this tradition—both current camp meeting participants and interested parties. To conjure up the voices of the past and recapture the best of the tradition.

We invite you to hear the organ strain, come down to the river, gather at the tabernacle. This is camp meeting.

Prelude

Camp Meeting 2015

My wife Marybeth and I rolled into Eaton Rapids in the early afternoon. Three nights before we had stayed in Wilkes Barre, Pennsylvania, and enjoyed dinner with Bill Irwin and his wife Megan Lloyd, who teach at Kings College, where I taught for four years. Bill started the successful Philosophy and Popular Culture series, first with Open Court, now with Wiley Blackwell.

The next day we drove over 500 miles and stayed at the Chelsea House Victorian Inn in Chelsea, Michigan, after taking in a play on a zombie apocalypse at the Purple Rose Theatre begun by Jeff Daniels, of *Terms of Endearment* and *Newsroom* fame.[6]

The next day we visited Frankenmuth, stopping on the way to see the gravesites of my dad and sister at United Memorial Gardens in Plymouth, Michigan. At Frankenmuth we took a carriage ride, enjoyed a chicken dinner with an extra side of giblets and homemade bread—all served by a curtsying waitress—and stayed at the Bavarian Inn with a lovely third floor balcony view of the meandering Cass River.

We got up the next morning, July 17, and made our way to Eaton Rapids, first stopping in Lansing to pick up an order from Kinko's, and to enjoy lunch at P. F. Changs. The print order consisted of 150 copies of a short biography I wrote of John Oswalt, who's stepping down from the presidency of Eaton Rapids Camp Meeting (ERC) this year, and 200 copies of highlights from the book we're writing on the 130 year history of the ERC—the volume you hold in your hands.

Within an hour or two of arriving at camp, the Historical Committee convened. In attendance, in addition to my wife and I, were Betty Uithoven and Kathleen Ray, both members of the Board. Kathleen is also Vice President of the Association. Betty has been our main point person on the Board as we've labored on the history book; she made the case to the Board we needed a scanner for old pictures, ensuring that we were able to secure a quite good one. Marybeth's been busy scanning, already in just a matter of weeks scanning nearly 400 images since we got the scanner delivered to our home in Lynchburg,

---

[6] And *Dumb and Dumber* infamy.

Virginia. At any rate, the Committee met in my cottage to discuss plans about upcoming activities and events of the Committee.

Various matters were discussed in the Committee meeting. I told them we hoped for a draft of the History to be finished by summer of 2016, and Kathleen mentioned that she wants to do a number of activities to build up to its publication. Among events planned for this year will be a talk on the book-in-progress, scheduled for Friday, July 24, at 2 p.m. in the back of the ice cream parlor. We discussed ways to make the talk interactive, like by my asking those in attendance various questions about the history of the camp and giving them the chance to answer. After the meeting I also thought about the possibility of a poetry contest about ERC, since the History is filled with poems and it's been quite a while since anyone wrote a new one.

Among other items discussed: the need to think of other events the Historical Committee can sponsor, and our plans to digitize all the ERC records eventually.[7] A robust revision and expansion of the History for the 150th (nineteen years from now—obviously this is a long-term goal). We also need to be very intentional to save and carefully preserve every document generated by ERC—from Board Minutes to brochures to daily handouts, and more. Since I took over the Historical Committee about three years ago, I've been remiss at doing this, and I need to rectify that.

Kathleen encouraged me to speak with several particular folks, among them Bruce Moyer, one of the speakers this year, and someone associated for a long time with ERC. David and Helen Jones, too, are people I should see, since each year they produce a CD of Camp pictures that could prove very useful. Larry Holley had been an active person at ERC, but he's gone now; his son David is still around, and I should pick his brain too. Larry had been in charge of the Eaton Rapids Historical Committee.

Miller Farm, adjacent to the Campground (the original ERC land was purchased from the Millers), houses several museums that are significant for Michigan generally and Eaton Rapids more particularly. The farm is a state of Michigan historic landmark, and is owned and maintained by the Eaton Rapids Area Historical Society. In one of those museums is a section on the camp meeting; Larry Holley was, from what I understand, largely responsible for that. After the Committee meeting, Marybeth and I went to visit that museum (and of course enjoyed some ice cream while we were at it—the rigors of research!), and saw the ERC section of the museum, featuring a picture of the *Stirling* and some old ERC brochures and the like.

Tours, field trips, property and building rentals, special events, and an ice cream parlor make up the cluster of buildings. The dairy farm and ice cream factory of Dennis and Minnie Miller are located just blocks from downtown Eaton Rapids. Tourists and locals can visit their stately home, built in 1864, along with the Miller Barn #1, the Wright One Room School, the Plains Church, and the Jean Kline Building—a collection of Eaton Rapids storefronts and

---

[7] Secretary John Werner has tirelessly worked to digitize decades worth of Board minutes.

businesses throughout the years. Jean Kline, by the way, was a local historian who did excellent work; an article of hers I got hold of a year or two back was very helpful in fleshing out some details about ERC history. I wish I'd had the chance to know her.

After dinner and a short wait, the first service was upon us. The message from camp president, Dr. John Oswalt, had been printed in a camp meeting announcement and reminds us of the purpose of the Camp that's about to start: "In the days before radio communication, ships required three instruments in order to know their location: a compass to know the direction they were heading; a chronometer to know their east-west location; and a sextant to know their north/south location. It was absolutely necessary that these instruments be precisely calibrated, and that was something that was done every time the ship was in port. For each of us, camp meeting is our port. Here we get our spiritual instruments recalibrated and reset. Then when we are on the high seas again, facing all the conflicting claims and demands that would blow us off course, our instruments will not fail us, but point us straight toward our final harbor. Come to Campmeeting!"

The old tabernacle, named after President Callen, who to this day remains the longest serving president of the Association, began to fill and buzz with anticipation. Carol Zink was at the piano, for something like her fifteenth year running, and Elizabeth West, after a one-year hiatus, was back at the organ, an eleven month old in tow. Scott Crecilius and his daughter Amy led the singing, and Hayden Carruth accompanied with music. Hayden is the son of Hayden Carruth, Sr. one of the truly great presidents of the Association. Hayden's grandfather on his mother's side was also President, as was *his* father, giving Hayden Carruth, Jr. quite the ERC heritage! It was a pleasure speaking with him and his wife after the service. Hearing from Hayden stories about his parents from his perspective, as their child, was nothing less than fascinating. The Association knew them in their formal roles—him as President, her as Camp Historian and Children's Worker—but Hayden knew them as mom and dad, yet without any less sense of how special they were.

LaVerne Davenport, the President-Elect of the Association, welcomed everyone to camp. He's a Presbyterian minister who has been associated with the Camp for 34 years. After spirited songs like "Wonderful Grace of Jesus" and "Leaning on the Everlasting Arms," David Gallimore gave a message. David was a Nazarene pastor in Oklahoma for twenty years, before moving back to his wife's native Georgia to start a full-time evangelism ministry. David was originally from West Virginia, going to college at the University of Cincinnati, transferring to Ohio Christian University at 19 after an encounter with Christ.

God, Change Me (Acts 1:4)

Sermon by David Gallimore

Gallimore preached from Acts 1:4, which instructed the early believers after the ascension of Christ to wait for the promise of the Father. Revival in medicine often involves just life support, and David challenged us along these lines: Has the concept of revival in the church turned into spiritual life support? Just more services, or enough to get by until the next infusion of strength? Rather than a truly life-transforming experience? Our prayer should be for a radical revival. When we consider Acts, we can see what this looks like:

First, it's a great down pouring from above. It's an act of God that comes from our response of obedience, most of all prayer. Let's pray not just *for* revival, but *until* revival comes. Let's pray, "Lord, are my hands clean and heart pure?"

Second, that produces a great uprising of the people. Be obedient to what He prompts us to do. Camp meeting, David told us, was where he was saved, sanctified, called to preach—even where he found a wife! There's no telling what God has in store.

Third, that produces great outreach to the community. In the American church, church is often seen as one more consumer product—and all about me. Self-centeredness prevails. "Feed me, preacher." We get spiritually fat. We need to exercise our faith outside the church.

Acts 1:4 says not to leave Jerusalem, but wait. They waited for ten days—sounds like camp meeting. We've lost the spiritual discipline of waiting. Waiting is countercultural. At camp meeting we get away from the rush, and can practice waiting.

Fourth, there's a great ingathering back to the church. A mighty harvest. Acts 2:41 features the invitation, and 3000 believed.

Is this for today? Acts 2:17-18 says that in the last days God will pour out His Spirit on all people.

Our ultimate prayer isn't "God, bless me," but "God, change me." But we must want wisdom as badly as we want air; be desperate for it!

The next morning, on Saturday, was a prayer service at 7 a.m., the "Morning Watch." President-Elect Davenport encouraged for the focus of our prayers this set of concerns: Dr. Oswalt's safe travels to camp Saturday night, the speakers, safety in the predicted heat (90s), and, most importantly (in accord with the message from the previous night), openness to God's Spirit.

The first Bible study convened at 9 a.m. The Bible teacher this year was Bruce Moyer, an evangelist commissioned by the Missionary Church, and author of *Those Contemplative Cats*, *Daily Thoughts on Holiness*, *Daily Thoughts on Victorious Christian Living*, and *Name Him Jesus*. The study will cover 2 Corinthians, more of a book-centered study rather than a lot of meticulous verse-by-verse analysis.

Introduction (2 Corinthians) & A Comforting Ministry (2 Corinthians 1:1-11)

Bible Study by Bruce Moyer

2 Corinthians is unique, by showing Paul as a man. Paul was the author of the book, and the date was likely around 56 or 57 AD. It's an early epistle (rather than one of Paul's prison or pastoral epistles). Corinth was flattened around 146

BC, then rebuilt by Julius Caesar about a century later. Geographically in Greece, but it was culturally Roman. It was a major slave-trading location, and hosted big sporting events of the time honoring Poseidon. It was quite prosperous, but some were very wealthy and others very unwealthy. There were many temples, the most important dedicated to Aphrodite, the goddess of love. To be "Corinthianized" was to be sexually immoral. It was a place full of racial and social-status diversity, and a strategic location for a church, since it was a major destination for travelers. For Paul it was an ideal place to make tents, awnings, and sails for boats. It was also a magnet for immigrants.

Why would Paul write such a letter? He had been there a few times, but his absence seemed to have caused a vacuum. And some criticized Paul a great deal, so his interactions when he'd visit had been stressful. They didn't take too kindly to his corrections. So lots going on when Paul wrote 2 Cor. Paul had an unpopular message: this isn't a time for self-exaltation, but for self-emptying; not for pride, but for humiliation. Understandably, other teachers had more attractive teachings.

In terms of an outline for the book, chapters 1-7 feature a defense of Paul's Character and Ministry; 8-9 an invitation for an offering; and in 10-13 Paul pours it on about his authority.

Today, 1:1-11: A **Comforting Ministry**, which biblically is related to stress and distress. Paul used 5 of 10 words for suffering. Most of such words relate back to being squashed, pressured. We will face all sorts of suffering. Suffering helps bring comfort in four ways:

First, *Strength* (3-5). Strengthening is proportional to the pressures. Paul isn't trying to minimize our afflictions, but to maximize our perspective. Second, *Solace* (6-7): our suffering isn't punishment for our past, but preparation for future ministry. Third, *Selflessness* (8-10): Learn that we are not to rely on ourselves, but on God. Notice blessing and result in v. 10. Fourth, *Sharing* (11): Unique Christian support system, where fellow laborers together get under a burden and help carry it.

Jesus Passes By (Mark 9:1)
Sermon by David Gallimore

The 10:30 service featured David Gallimore. From Mark 9:1: Jesus passes by a man blind from birth. "Jesus passes by." The light of the world—who will enable us to *see*. Light is about to penetrate the darkness. Jesus used his spit to heal the man—the man was desperate. (Recall how this resonates with David's first sermon that culminated by reminding us to be as desperate for God's blessing as for air.) We are vitally dependent on God. The man was healed, but several missed the blessing:

First, the disciples were blinded by the *problem*. Every miracle starts with a problem. The disciples wanted a theological discussion about why the man was blind.

Second, the neighbors (v. 8) were blinded by the *past*. They knew this blind man and didn't think he was very special. Don't let your past rob you of the miracle God has for you. Don't give up on anyone. Don't get frustrated with people who struggle with their faith.

Third, the Pharisees were blinded by their *perspective*, because they couldn't get past the fact the healing happened on the Sabbath. At the same time, the Pharisees had conjured all sorts of ways to fit in work on the Sabbath, by the "law." Just because something is the law doesn't make it right. Even a great heritage can become a great hindrance if we're not open to what Jesus wants to do today.

Fourth, the parents were blinded by *pride*. They didn't want to be ostracized by the Pharisees, so they ducked the question. But the healed man boldly proclaimed in v. 25, "I was blind but now I see." Quite a powerful service and altar call!

A few activities, like the Camp picnic, had to be cancelled early Saturday afternoon because of the inclement weather. Normally there's a huge cookout in front of the cafeteria and a variety of accompanying entertainments. Weather this year has been a bit of a challenge—unusually hot, numerous downpours, and, as a result, ubiquitous mosquitoes. None of this is dampening spirits too much, but it does make matters a bit more challenging. The Cottage Owners meeting scheduled for 2 o'clock did take place; by then the sun began to reappear.

Saturday evening's service featured Jack French, Executive Director of Evangelism and Outreach for World Gospel Mission. Jack has been here before, most recently in 2010 and 2012, but, before that, in 1958 and 1959! In those early years he came as part of a college quartet when he was around 20. He still remembered some of the preaching he heard way back then.

Spiritual Blindness (2 Corinthians 4:3)
Sermon by Jack French

French took as his text 2 Cor. 4:3, but then, more importantly, Mark 10:46 and following, prefacing his sermon by saying that when God has our attention, He can do more in 15 minutes than what might otherwise take years. The earlier sermon on blindness made Jack think about other stories about blindness, and forms of spiritual blindness, of which there are all sorts. Among the kinds of spiritual blindness are blindness to the Word of God, blindness to the will of God (especially the lie that God's will isn't what's best for us), blind spots, microscopic vision (preoccupation with minor theological squabbles turned into huge ones), and telescopic vision (just thinking about heaven and not this life).

From the biblical text French then inferred several lessons about healing from spiritual blindness:

> Be dissatisfied about blindness.
> Be alert to Jesus walking by.
> Forget about the crowd.
> Throw off anything that stands in the way.
> Know what you want when you get there.

His sermon was accessible and homespun, testimonial and anecdotal, warm and inviting. Much of what goes into the experience of listening to camp meeting preaching, or doing camp meeting generally, doesn't make it into an official History—and it probably shouldn't, as it's tangential at best, even incidental. But knowing I was to keep a journal of this year's meeting made me meticulously mindful of little details that, though we're cognizant of them at the time, are later painlessly excised from the record. The songs sung, the temperature and humidity, the rumbling thunder, the ominous sky, the technical difficulties that interrupted the sermon for several minutes, the inspiring organ play, the weather advisory that Michigan was under this evening—all were constituents of the service and parts of its lived experience.

As I considered the speaker in particular, not only did I ponder the words spoken, but I was mindful of style too: the colorful illustrations and telling anecdotes, the cadence in his sentences, idiosyncrasies of his enunciation and diction, his pacing and tempo, the relative depth of his voice. All of these combined and blended to contribute to a holistic and integrated experience filled with quite objective facts, but facts that usually don't get written down for posterity. Recording history is like taking a picture of the Grand Canyon or Pike's Peak. Try it and see for yourself; take a picture while there, and then compare the picture with the reality. The picture captures but a hint, an echo, a sliver of the experience, and, though it's something you'll be glad to have later, it's no substitute for the real thing. Likewise, retelling the story of what happens at camp meeting is worthwhile, but is never a match for the experience itself.

The service ended with the congregation singing "Open My Eyes, that I May See."

Then my wife and brother and I respectively enjoyed fellowship over a Mud Slide, Chocolate Milkshake, and Root Beer Float in the festive and friendly ice cream parlor. Again, words fail to capture the ensuing enjoyment.

Sunday Morning Watch: About thirty people—men and women, young and old—gathered in the Tabernacle at 7 a.m. for prayer. It was a beautiful morning as the day came alive, birds chirping all around for background music, the air cool and comfortable. Some knelt at the altar while others sat in the front pews, and those who felt led took turns offering their praises and intercessions. Prayers ranged from pleas for strength and healing and transformation to revival in and blessing on churches, the camp, the city, and the country. Among those kneeling was Dr. Oswalt, who made it to camp the night before after having served as the Bible teacher at Indian Springs Camp Meeting in Georgia. He prayed a powerful and passionate prayer for our eyes to be open to the ravishing holiness of God, and spent time praying, too, for those in each age group of the Camp—from the youngest to the oldest.

A Candid and Compassionate Ministry
(2 Corinthians 1:12—2:24)
Bible Study by Bruce Moyer

About an hour later the 9 a.m. Bible study got underway. The speaker, Bruce Moyer, joked he wanted the Camp secretary to put into the minutes that he himself was wearing a tie and Dr. Oswalt wasn't. The passage to be discussed was 2 Cor. 1:12 – 2:24. The first part of this lesson was about having a **Candid Ministry** (recall that the first Bible lesson was about a **Comforting Ministry**). Paul was confronting accusations against him because he had to effect a change in plans. His trustworthiness and authority were called into question. Paul had said he'd come to visit in a certain way and time, but it ended up he didn't, so some said what he spoke, and thus wrote, couldn't be trusted.

Verse 12 shows that a candid ministry is based on a life that is unreproachable. We should ask if there's anything God is speaking to us about, remembering that actions speak louder than words. God wants to make us holy—moral purity and integrity. We are to be blameless, spotless.

Verses 13-14 also show a candid ministry is based on a message that's understandable. We are to say what we mean. Paul's message contained no hidden meanings or agendas.

Verses 15-17 reveal that a candid ministry is based on motives that are unquestionable. Paul's motives were pure even if his plans had to change.

Verses 18-20 show another basis to such a ministry: words that are believable. We need to be consistent, true to our word. Drawing from Oswalt's book *Called to be Holy*, Moyer says to be holy is be right (to act rightly), to be true (to your word), pure, and filled with self-giving love.

Verses 21-23 reveal that such a ministry is verifiable. God does it, through His Holy Spirit. Three words are used here: (1) *Anointed*: furnished with necessary power to do the task; (2) *Sealed*: authenticity, a ratification of ownership, the genuine article; and (3) *Spirit as Deposit* or earnest, initial down payment. By means of these three things the Holy Spirit provides the verification.

The second part of this lesson was how to have a **Compassionate Ministry**. Characteristics of a Compassionate Ministry:

First (1:24): Willingness to focus on others. Be a helper of the joy of others; partners working alongside others. Compassion doesn't mean we don't face problems head on, but it's hard to be compassionate when we're the object of our own affection.

Second (2:1-3): Willingness to confront. Paul had sorrow in sharing what he had to say. But the wounds from a friend can be trusted. Confrontation can be as painful for the confronter as the confronted. Confront in compassion and love.

Third (2:4): Willingness to express compassion. Truly compassionate ministry expressed by both declaration and demonstration. With anguish of heart and many tears Paul shared his concerns. We need to be able to cry with people over their struggles and lostness. There's no replacement for genuine empathy.

Fourth (2:5-11): Willingness to forgive the repentant. There comes a time to pour on the love. Three words here: (1) Pardon: give freely, cancel guilt; (2) Comfort: encourage, strengthen; (3) Reaffirm love. When repentance happens, it's time to stop the discipline. Remember God's continuing purpose for the person.

What were some of the reasons Paul gave for why it was time to forgive? (See verses 6-7.) The punishment was sufficient; its purpose was to elicit repentance. It was necessary as long as the person persisted in the sin. Another reason was so that the person wouldn't be devoured by sorrow. (Verse 11.) Also: in order that Satan might not outwit us. Remember that he's the accuser of the brethren. Satan is happy for us to ignore sin or dole out punishment for too long. Either mistake will do.

A Call to Diligence (Hebrews 6:9-12)
Sermon by Jack French

Sunday 11:30 service: Jack French. Hebrews 6:9-12 (a bit from 4 and 5 too). The scripture says we are not to be lazy. Consider this word "lazy." The book of Hebrews is filled with strong, sturdy theology, and then followed by strong imperatives.

Laziness nowadays often gets cast in various ways: indolent, slothful, lacking in zeal, indifferent, negligent, sluggish. In terms of the Greek word, etymologically it most means "dull." The word is transliterated *notros*. In the Bible there's a different word that sometimes gets translated "dull" or "slow," but its connotation is often positive. *Notros*, though, indicates an inborn sluggishness bound up in the very life of the believer. It's not a personality type, being tired, overworked, and so forth. Rather, it's a deep spiritual problem, involving slowness of learning.

Chapters 4-6: What are the causes or results of this dullness? First, it's an unwillingness to eat solid food, and a corresponding failure to distinguish good from evil.

Second (5:11): We can come to the Lord with confidence because He's experienced all we have. Dullness involves this: rather than running to God, we listen to the accusing voice of the enemy.

Third, dullness involves loss of diligence and staying power. Comfort in church often turns into laziness.

On Sunday afternoon, it was time for the Memorial Service, presided by Dr. Oswalt, who reminded those gathered that we don't grieve as those without hope. The names of seven deceased friends of the Camp were mentioned, and those in the crowd could stand for any of the persons mentioned with whom they shared a special connection.

Stand Firm (Ephesians 6:10-18)
Memorial Service by John Oswalt

Oswalt then preached from Ephesians 6:10-18. The mystery of God's salvation will be demonstrated to the principalities and powers. The Church is God's plan to show that God can save His work, despite those voices that insist He can't. We're in a battle, Oswalt preached, and we have enemies within and without.

Oswalt was careful to avoid saying the real battle was elsewhere; no, this is a real world, with choices that have important consequences. But the battle isn't a physical one, but rather a spiritual one. The enemy loves lulling us into a false security, resulting in our removing our armor. The passage tells us to take up the whole armor of God, so that we might stand. To *stand* is the recurring motif. With this in mind, Oswalt elaborated on each piece of armor:

The *belt of truth*: Roman soldiers carried their weapons in their belt. In terms of truth, what matters here is truth about reality (today people think they can make up their own reality—they're not past Genesis 3 and the tree of the knowledge of good and evil); truth about the gospel; and truth about the Christian life—that God wishes to take up residence in us.

The *breastplate of righteousness*: protects the vitals, and especially the heart. Biblically, the heart is the seat of our thinking, feeling, and deciding. The dichotomy between head and heart isn't biblical. We're a unity. Regarding righteousness, two aspects commend themselves: imputed righteousness is the righteousness of Christ credited to us, whereas imparted righteousness is God's enabling us to live righteously. We can be what we're called to be.

Shoes of the Preparation of the Gospel of Peace: This pertains to settled foundations; the "hob nails" in the shoes of Roman soldiers were like golf cleats, making firm footing possible. Not only do we have peace with God the Father, we can have peace within ourselves, wholeness, even if we find ourselves in outward conflict. Shoes of such a solid foundation of peace can enable us to stand.

Shield of Faith: The offensive infantry used large round shields, but the shield of faith here refers to the defensive body shields. Such body armor, when a line of them would form, would constitute a solid iron wall. Such soldiers could *stand*. The shield of faith can guard against fiery arrows—faith grounded in God's Word and that's been proven in life.

In this connection, Oswalt distinguished carefully between *questions* and *doubt*. Questions are fine; they express "I believe, help my unbelief." Real doubt insists on not taking up the armor, not believing until it's proved my way. We can have deeply settled faith that we have eternal life, and if we know where we'll spend eternity, we can endure anything. Oswalt related the tale of his own struggles with assurance while growing up until, at Taylor University, the assurance came.

Helmet of Salvation: the Romans took helmets seriously, for obvious reasons. Likewise should we, concerning our salvation, both salvation past and confidence in God's present and continuing ability to save us and deliver us—in His way. Even regarding death, don't be afraid of it.

Sword of the Spirit: the Word of God. When Jesus was attacked, he responded with scripture. So how should we respond when we're attacked?

Is this a Memorial sermon? Yes, indeed. For all of those commemorated were examples of those who stood, and in whose places we can now stand in their place. The final hymn was "Soldiers of Christ, Arise."

Memorial Service for Marguerite J. Bartlett

Shortly after that service was a special Memorial Service, at 3:30 p.m. on July 19, 2015, for Marguerite J. Bartlett (1921-2014), something of a Camp Matron. The Bartletts have been a strong presence on the Campground from early in its history, and Marguerite's family was well represented on this day, convening from all over the country. Oswalt began the memorial with a welcome and scripture reading, then James E. Bartlett III read the following:

Marguerite ("Margie") Johnson Bartlett was born on her family's pioneer homestead in Osprey, Florida on August 7, 1921. She grew up with two brothers, Clifford and Alva Johnson, and attended Sarasota High School.

At age 17, Marguerite married Allen E. Bartlett, who became a Methodist minister in 1941, and together, they served churches in Michigan for 6 years. Marguerite's role as a minister's wife was one she cherished. In 1947, they returned to Florida and for the next 25 years, they served churches in Florida, moving every three or four years, as Methodist ministers were required to do at that time.

During those years, Marguerite raised a stepson, Allen Bartlett, Jr. and three more children: Beth, Jim, and Nancy. Margie attended college with her children, becoming an L.P.N. and R.N. and earning a B.A. and M.A. in education, and finally a B.S. in nursing, magna cum laude, at age sixty. Her career included nursing jobs as director of education at W. T. Edwards Hospital in Tampa and coordinator of nursing at the Florida Mental Health Institute, also in Tampa. She retired in 1988 after twenty-eight years of service, and was widowed in 1989.

Marguerite was 18 when she spent her first summer at Eaton Rapids, and never missed a campmeeting afterwards for 75 years. She passed away on August 21, 2014, at the age of 93, leaving a legacy of Godly love to her family and all those whose lives she touched. She is survived by her brother, Alva; her three children; eleven grandchildren; and ten great-grandchildren.

Kris Hole then read a poem written by Linda Stevenson (niece of Marguerite):

Do Not Weep for Me

If you could only see me now
You'd never shed a tear;
If you could only listen to
The melodies I hear,
You'd never wish for my return
You'd never ask God, "Why?"
For there's no pain or sorrow here,
No tears to dim the eye.
Just lasting peace and perfect joy
Unlike I've ever known.
And oh the glory I have seen
As I look to Heaven's throne.
For there is Christ, my Lord and King,
With arms outstretched to me
Who says, "My child, I'm glad you're home;
I've waited patiently."
Now He enfolds me in His love,
I worship at His feet.
Oh, glorious, amazing grace
Flows from His mercy seat.
So do not mourn or weep for me.
Please do not despair,
For with the joy God fills my heart
There's nothing to compare.
I'll wait for God to call you home
And one day we will be
Together, never more to part,
For all eternity.

Beth Bartlett Ingalls then read her reflection called "Mom, the Mighty Oak," prefaced by a poem called "Success": "You can use most any measure/ When you're speaking of success./ You can measure it in fancy home, expensive car or dress./ But the measure of your real success/ Is the one you cannot spend./ It's the way your kids describe you/ When they're talking to a friend."

Not long after Mom's death last August, preoccupied with my sorrows, I mistakenly turned down an unfamiliar street. Since it was going in the same general direction as the intended route, I decided to keep going. I began to notice the massive oaks which were everywhere—their huge branches overlapping in the middle of the road to form a "tree tunnel." As I drove amidst them I was awed ... not merely by the beautiful scene, but by the calm I felt—the sense of comfort, security, and being loved which I always felt in Mom's presence. It was like she was there, sitting beside me.

In my amazement at the change of mood I was experiencing, I exclaimed out loud, "That's what you were Mom, a mighty oak!" Then, amused at the irony of her tiny 4 foot, 7 inch frame being proclaimed "a mighty oak," I grinned and tried to understand the riddle of why I would say such a thing. It certainly wasn't associating her with the oaks where she lived, or her long-time relationship with Eaton Rapids Campmeeting where we spent most of my childhood summers. That was a mere coincidence. This feeling within me was much more personal—like a personification of her character. Majestic and commanding (as these oaks were), she was a Tree of Life, a center of strength and nurturing, an example of one whose "trunk" was so strong, she could weather the storms of life, adapt and grow to meet the challenges. She wasn't afraid to stand alone and speak out, if need be, for what she believed was right and she tried to teach her children that same independence she exhibited.

Her roots reached deep into her faith in God, which influenced the decisions she made and the attitudes she displayed in her daily life—decisions like her career choice in nursing, and the love and concern she emanated for the lives she touched. She was determined to let God's love shine through her to others.

I'm sure that a lot of the comfort I was feeling related to the canopy of branches over and around me, like Mom's arms enveloping me with the unconditional love she always displayed—ready to step in, in whatever manner you needed. She offered the gift of herself—her interest, encouragement, even advice if you asked for it. It didn't matter if you'd made mistakes in your decisions; she always had your back.

When they speak of a family, the descendants are portrayed as the branches. (I preferred that to imagining myself an acorn.) Her tree, at her death, contained three branches for her children, eleven for her grandchildren, and nine for her great-grandchildren, to which, several months later, another great grandchild was added. Then, there were grafted-in branches of a step-son and his progeny, several sons and daughters-in-law, and "adopted kids" along the way. As the many branches have matured with the support of the strong trunk and nourishment from the roots, the reach of this mighty oak is becoming ever wider.

Speaking of a mighty oak … I did think of one very special oak tree in her life. At her original home, on a piece of her family's 1867 homestead in Florida, an oak began to grow when she was a very small child. She used to tell us stories of the fun she had jumping over it and watching it grow. This oak was the scene of many outdoor Thanksgivings when the tables were placed in its shade. As the number grew, the celebration became a "family reunion" and the tree grew larger, to accommodate the additional tables (I'm sure).

I like to think that Mom and this special oak tree grew simultaneously as they matured, weathering the storms and providing shelter for others. . . perfect examples for us to see the beauty and joy in life and the manifestation of God's blessing to us all. And the tree? Its trunk is now about 15 feet in circumference and it has a span of over 120 feet. You can see why I called her a Mighty Oak!

It wasn't such a riddle after all. Just as a mighty oak endures for years, we are left with her memory and the legacy of love that she embodied. May those that she touched and inspired continue to branch out. . . spreading her love and faith to others. Who knows? We could honor her precious memory by producing a few saplings of our own.

Following three verses of the hymn "He Lives" came family remarks, including from James, reminded of Capra's classic *It's a Wonderful Life*, imagining for a moment what the world would have been like without his mom; and Beth saying that she never remembered her mom saying a negative word about another. Notable too was Emily Bartlett Walsh, who said everything about camp meeting reminded her of her grandmother, and whose stirring memories were punctuated by a poem she shared that she'd written when she was just sixteen years old:

To Grammie

I'm sitting at a living room table,
in a lovely old rickety cottage,
laughing and playing Skip-Bo with a grey-haired, blue-eyed woman,
who loves nothing more than to do just that with anyone
who happens to be interested.
I'm sitting with a woman who puts the leftover corn
in the front yard for the birds,
and wakes up early,
so her grandchildren can open their eyes to the smell of bacon
and the warmth of a pot-bellied stove.
I'm sitting with a woman who has bounced
three generations of sweet babes on her knee,
and softly sung them all to sleep:
"...and if that mocking bird don't sing, Grammie's gonna
buy you a diamond ring."

I'm sitting with a woman who is known by all her grandchildren to be the
best back-scratcher and the best story-teller in the world,

and is provided with plenty of chances to prove both.
I'm sitting with a woman who fried up my brother's first fish,
and taught us that blackberries were ready to eat when, at a touch,
they fell off their stems into our hands.

I'm sitting with a woman who helped me memorize my first Bible verse,
and taught her family to give God thanks before every meal.
I'm sitting with a woman who makes a mean "garbage soup,"
and always has a full table,
since she never turns away anyone who wants to have a bite.

I'm sitting with a woman who showed God to me,
singing high and clear the hymn,
"Jesus, Jesus, Jesus, sweetest Name I know!"

I've often thought there's nothing so beautiful as a person who is loved.
A person who, to earn that love, first spread it around,
and made others more beautiful, too.

I'm sitting at a living room table,
in a lovely old rickety cottage,
playing Skip-Bo with my Grammie.
She gives me a smile, I give one back, and I think,
This is the most beautiful woman in the world.

After remarks by Dr. Oswalt and the song "God Be with You 'Till We Meet Again," the service came to close.

Part I

The Second Great Awakening and Camp Meetings in America

Chapter 1

Christianity in 19th Century America, 1790-1900

In *Christianity: A Social and Cultural History*, a section entitled "Evangelical Mobilization" helps set some of the historical context for the emergence of the camp meeting tradition in America. The book argues that the Second Great Awakening was the most influential revival of Christianity in the history of the United States. From about 1795 to about 1810, there was a "broad and general rekindling of interest in Christianity throughout the country. This movement in turn provided a pattern and an impetus for similar waves of revival that continued through the nation until after the Civil War."

The state of Christianity in the country after the American Revolution was lamentable. The conflict of war had wreaked havoc in many local congregations, particularly where the fighting had been most intense—in places like New Jersey, New York City, the Philadelphia area, and the Carolinas. The revolution had been especially deleterious to the Episcopal Church, whose ties with England made it particularly suspect. Moreover, "the disestablishment of the churches in the southern states and attacks on the tie between states and the church in New England also led to uncertainty."

Interest in religion more generally seemed on the decline; concern for nation-building, developing the western regions of the country, strengthening the economy, and avoiding international disputes consumed the population's attention, leaving little room for religious activities or reflection. Additionally, the increasingly popular deistic belief system had swayed many against the faith of their fathers. Indeed, several prominent patriots—such as Ethan Allen who captured Fort Ticonderoga and Thomas Paine whose "Common Sense" galvanized support for the revolutionary cause—embraced this anti-supernaturalist take on theism, which lent deism even more credence. As a result of these various influences, allegiance to the churches wavered.

There were, to be sure, scattered outbursts of Christian revival that continued during the war and afterward. As more European immigrants arrived, they continued practicing their varieties of faith brought from the Old World. Scattered throughout New England, the Congregationalists followed in the tradition they inherited from Jonathan Edwards and others. In the middle states,

Presbyterians kept alive their religious traditions, as did Baptists in the South. And while no major revival sprang forth from these movements, some individuals were roused from spiritual slumber to come forth as new leaders, such as Barton W. Stone in Virginia.

One of the earliest antecedents of the camp meeting movement happened in North Carolina in the 1790s when Presbyterians there began to get together in the late summer after harvest for so-called "Sacramental Meetings." John Oswalt writes, "While it is not known exactly the format of these meetings, they do seem to have been outdoors and did involve preaching and communion."

The western phase of the revival movement had its genesis in the dedicated work of Presbyterians like James McGready and itinerants from the Baptist and Methodist churches. As the writers of *Christianity* put it:

> McGready's church in Logan County, Kentucky, began in 1797 to pray regularly "for the conversion of sinners in Logan County, and throughout the world." In 1801 the efforts of McGready and like-minded leaders bore spectacular fruit. In August of that year a great camp meeting convened at Cane Ridge, Kentucky. Thousands streamed to this gathering, as several preachers—black and white; Presbyterians, Baptists, and Methodists—fervently proclaimed the Good News.
>
> The results were electrifying. Some of the unusual bodily effect—the jerks, dancing, laughing, running, and the "barking exercise"—may be attributed to powerful psychological release. Isolated families, subject to a hard and perilous life, were responding with their emotions to a message from stirring, charismatic leaders. Other effects—such as the rapid organization of churches that followed the camp meeting—were more clearly religious.

Oswalt explains that as people pushed farther west, over the Allegheny Mountains into Kentucky, they continued the practice of meeting together late in the summer, but these get-togethers were more challenging to convene in their new territories due to wilderness conditions and threats of Indian attacks. As the year 1800 drew near, these challenges subsided, making way for the first great camp meetings. Details about these meetings are limited; what remains often conflicts, but it seems that the first major camp meeting took place in 1800 at the Red River Cumberland Presbyterian meeting house near Adairsville in southwestern Kentucky. The Holy Spirit moved throughout the camp meeting, and attendance soared in the hundreds and, in some accounts, thousands.

The next year witnessed the monumental Cane Ridge meeting north of present-day Paris, Kentucky. Oswalt writes that upwards of 50,000 people—or a fourth of the population of Kentucky at the time of the revival—attended the meetings at Cane Ridge and Red River in 1801. At both locations, concurrent services were held, as numerous evangelists preached simultaneously and listeners would move from location to location to listen to their favorites.

Oswalt notes, too, that if the preaching was marked by great "unction," it produced great conviction, and many were "deeply moved, shouting, crying out and falling to the ground. While there were unquestionably great outbreaks of what was then called 'enthusiasm', it has been shown recently that the reports of these outbreaks were often exaggerated, both by friends and by opponents of the meetings."[8]

Dr. Leigh Eric Schmidt writes about these meetings in Cane Ridge in his book *Holy Fairs*, suggesting that the people were likely observing a ritual with origins in the Scottish Communion festival that poet Robbie Burns satirized. In Scotland, communion had become a political issue. Every Scot was a member of the church, and thus entitled to communion. So certain ministers began to fear administering the sacrament to unrepentants unworthy of it, a serious biblical mistake. So they began "fencing the table," not letting persons in open sin take part in communion. Five-day communion festivals began to be held in order to ready people for communion. This was much of the impetus behind many early camp meetings in America, too—and the way something that was originally designed as a renewal movement within the church transitioned into an evangelistic outreach, and eventually into a major civilizing force on the frontier.

Cane Ridge was the tipping point for the rise of camp meetings at the start of the 19th century. Dr. Marlin Hotle, editor of *The Holiness Digest*, explains that "[f]rom this point the camp meeting spread so rapidly that by 1805 Francis Asbury called the summertime meetings 'Methodism's harvest time' and encouraged the Methodists to have six hundred of them by 1810. According to W. W. Sweet, there were almost one thousand camp meetings by 1820."

The renewed interest in the faith touched off at Cane Ridge and similar camp meetings led to a rapid growth in Presbyterian churches in the South. By comparison, however, Presbyterian efforts paled beside the accomplishments of the Methodists and Baptists. Methodist circuit riders and Baptist farmer preachers fanned out throughout the South and the opening West in unprecedented numbers. By the 1830s these groups had replaced the Congregationalists and Presbyterians as the largest denominations, not only in the South but also in the whole country.

One reason for the denominational shift seems to have been theological. The theology of the Second Great Awakening, particularly in the expression of one of Yale's Timothy Dwight's pupils, Nathaniel Taylor (1786-1858), differed from the theology of the colonial revival. "To preserve God's sovereignty in

---

[8] Deborah M. Valenze is one who accentuates, likely in hyperbolic fashion, the transgressive nature of Methodist camp meetings in the later eighteenth and early nineteenth centuries: "The camp meeting made public the worst private experiences of lower-class life. Middle-class refinement and oratorical skill seldom tempered this unembarrassed admission of past degradation. Primitive Methodism thus elevated the debased to the realm of the sacred and upset the hierarchy of experience essential to conventional social order." See Deborah M. Valenze, *Prophetic Sons and Daughters: Female Preaching and Popular Religion in Industrial England* (Princeton: Princeton UP, 1985), 90.

salvation, Edwards and Whitefield had stressed the inability of sinful people to save themselves. The theology of the leading revivalists in the South and of Taylor stressed more the ability that God had bestowed on all people to come to Christ. The Second Great Awakening thus played an important role in the process by which the dominant Calvinism of the eighteenth century gave way to the more Arminian faith of the nineteenth."[9]

Stylistic reasons may have also played a part in the Methodist presence. However exaggerated were some of the claims of hysteria, the wild enthusiasm in the early years of camp meetings meant they would acquire a bad reputation among some of the more conservative and staid churchmen. Popular minister Edward Irving asserted in 1828 that Methodism privileges "feelings" and "fancies" over the objective, real "sacraments and ordinances of the church." Wesley himself is easily misunderstood on this score. He emphasized the inward aspects of Christian conversion—his heart being "strangely warmed" at Aldersgate a paradigmatic example—and he accorded pride of place to religious experience; but at the same time, he was notoriously anti-emotional, which arguably caused him a few theological troubles. The new birth, for Wesley, was most assuredly not primarily a matter of an effusive, emotive display. However, his emphasis on experience—particularly when it's not remembered that, alongside religious experience, he privileged scripture, tradition, and reason in his quadrilateral—might help explain some of the more physical displays of emotion among his followers. Wesley himself said that a preacher ought to avoid the possibility of driving crowds into mass hysteria, "loud shouting, horrid unnatural screaming, repeating the same words twenty or thirty times, jumping two or three feet high, and throwing about the arms or legs both of men and women, in a manner shocking not only to religion, but to common decency." Dr. Emily Heady, a Victorian scholar, suggests that "Wesley discouraged such

---

[9] Timothy Dwight was a grandson of Jonathan Edwards who became president of Yale College in 1795 and helped greatly to contribute to a resurgence of interest in classical Christianity. When he arrived at Yale, he noticed many of his students adhered, to at least some degree, to the Deism of the French Enlightenment. To battle this trend, he launched a two-pronged effort: by forthright argument he strove to restore confidence in the Bible, and he began a four-year cycle of sermons designed to communicate the essentials of the faith. "In 1802 revival swept the Yale campus; one-third of the 225 students were converted, and many of these became agents for revival and reform in New England, upstate New York, and the West. From Connecticut, concern for revival spread up and down the East Coast. Soon there was hardly a locale in which Christians were not praying for revival or thanking God for giving them one." Besides Taylor, another pupil of Dwight's was Lyman Beecher (1775-1863), who was particularly active in organizing the forces of the revival into permanent organizations designed to evangelize and reform America. Through the efforts of Beecher and people with his vision, the country saw the founding of the American Board for Foreign Missions (1810), the American Bible Society (1816), the Colonization Society for Liberated Slaves (1817), the American Tract Society (1823), the American Sunday School Union (1824), the American Educational Society (1826), and many more. These agencies gave the Second Great Awakening the kind of long-lived institutional influence that the first had never enjoyed.

displays because for him they signaled not the self-emptying moment of conversion but rather a self-aggrandizing desire to enact religious experience."[10]

Perhaps because emotional displays figured prominently at camp meetings, many Presbyterians refused to participate after 1805; nevertheless, they remained an important part of the frontier ministries of the Methodists, Baptists, Shakers, Disciples, and Cumberland Presbyterians. Methodism profited the most by their popularity and gradually institutionalized them into its system of evangelism. So another reason for the emergence of Methodist leadership on this score was logistical and historical. Because Methodism was characterized by its itinerant preachers, the Methodist movement provided the impulses that fueled the type of revivalism that marked the camp meeting tradition.

Francis Asbury (1745-1816), one of the first two bishops of the Methodist Episcopal Church, reported in his journal that by 1811there were over 400 camp meetings held annually along the frontier from Georgia to Michigan. He visited the meetings and their offshoots as he itinerated throughout the areas of North Carolina and Kentucky, and "he was greatly impressed by them and by their potential for real spiritual growth in the places they occurred. He was enough impressed that he exhorted all his district superintendents (presiding elders, as they were known at the time), to start camp meetings in their districts. Many took the exhortation seriously, and the number of meetings increased exponentially through the second and third decades of the nineteenth century."

This was the first epoch of growth for camp meetings in the 19th century— roughly from 1800 to 1840. Ron Smith, past president of the Francis Asbury Society, writes that Dickson Bruce perhaps best captures the history of these meetings in the first part of the 1800s in his book, *They All Sang Hallelujah*, which won the prize for anthropology from the University of Tennessee.

The documentary *God in America* outlines how these camp meetings played a significant role in shaping the American character during this time. After its founding, America went to work constructing its identity. By 1800, 200 wagons a day were heading west. But when the people got there, they would have to carve out a new world. The expanding frontier was a dangerous place, the sense of isolation profound, and churches were sparse.

One of these early pioneers, James Finley, traveled with his family from North Carolina to the Ohio frontier in the late 1790s. In later life he would become a leading figure in America's religious life, but as a young man he struggled alone with his faith. He explains, "Sometimes my faith wavers, in spite of all my efforts to hold it up, and my conscience stings me with remorse." He wondered, for example, what the point of praying was, since if he was one of the elect he would be saved in God's good time, and if he was one of the nonelect, praying would do no good because Christ didn't die for him.

With the rise of camp meetings, there was a gradual collective shift away from the old Calvinist idea that God had made these choices before we were ever born. Now it was becoming more common to think people were conferred

---

[10] Emily Heady, "Flutters, Feelings, and Fancies: John Wesley's Sentimental Sermons and the Spirit of the Age," *Christianity and Literature* 53:2 (Winter 2004): 152.

by God's grace a meaningful choice. In 1801, Finley left Ohio, heading for Kentucky where thousands had been drawn to a religious gathering in the town of Cane Ridge. He had heard of the meeting and that such revivals, or camp meetings, were springing up across the frontier. Hundreds, sometimes thousands of ordinary people would gather, drawn by the message of new, charismatic preachers seeking to save souls.

Finley knew of the growing perception that the new republic was in moral decline. Ministers warned that fewer people were going to church than before the Revolution. America, they feared, faced a spiritual crisis. A sense of urgency in bringing people to Christ prevailed, because it was not just about saving *them*, but *the nation* as well. Somehow many considered the nation to have lost its moral underpinnings—religion no longer occupied a central place.

As Finley drew closer to Cane Ridge, he grew nervous at what he was walking into. He told his companions he, unlike others succumbing to hysteria, wouldn't "fall down." When he reached Cane Ridge on August 8, 1801, as many as 20,000 people had gathered there. He walked into a clearing in the woods, and people all around him were crying and on their knees begging for God's forgiveness. These were people who had never seen such gatherings before. The preachers towered above people in their stands, preaching day and night, and everything was announced by trumpets blowing.

Finley saw people screaming and shouting, slaves co-mingling with masters. The cacophonous gathering made a noise, some thought, like that of the Niagara, a vast sea of people agitated as if by a storm. 20,000 people tossed to and fro like the waves of the sea in a maelstrom. People were rolling, others fainting. Finley himself felt his knees nearly give out. In time he would weep copiously, shout out, and be converted. He described a sensation of streams of love; he thought he would die for excess of joy.

News of Cane Ridge and other meetings like it spread. Over the next few decades there would be thousands more, as a wave of revivals swept through South Carolina, Tennessee, and Georgia. Delaware, Maryland, and Virginia began to host yearly camp meetings that were wild with enthusiasm, and revivals burned across New York. The revival spawned new denominations and made Baptists and Methodists flourish; even older denominations became more evangelical in response. By 1811, more than a million Americans were attending at least one religious revival a year. Methodists attracted more converts than any others. The Methodist flavor of the camp meetings lent to its populist appeal. Because Methodism is perceived as the faith of the heart and emotions, adherents felt welcome, no matter their education or economic status. They needed only a right heart of penitence before God. People were thus urged in unapologetically passionate terms to turn to God's love.

Another important reason for Methodism's growth is that they sent out itinerant preachers and circuit riders who organized churches and the like, imposing an order on an unruly landscape: a system ideally suited to frontier life and appealing to normal folks. Methodism's circuit riders became a focal point of people's lives. They didn't just bring Methodist sermons, but books. Sunday school taught people how to read and write, class meetings generating infrastructure and moral stability on the frontier. In 1850, over a million Methodists dotted the landscape. Two thirds of churchgoers at the time were evangelical Protestants. Religion had come back to the center, and with it a strong push for social reform. Evangelical Christianity went to work building a new America. Orphanages, prisons, poor houses, schools, hospitals, women's rights, and more became part of its ambitious, bottom-up agenda.

Some well-known preachers at the time included Richard Allen, Peter Cartwright, and Charles Finney. Allen started the African Methodist Episcopal Church in Pennsylvania. Finley himself felt called to preach, becoming a Methodist preacher in 1809, dedicating his life to preaching and social reform. His is but one person's story; a plethora of others could be adduced.

Unfortunately, though, by the 1840s the sectionalism and political furor that was eventually to explode in the Civil War began to take its toll on the camp meetings. As Oswalt explains, "The divisions within the Methodist Church leading to the birth of the Wesleyan Church and eventually to the Methodist Episcopal north and south denominations contributed to this decline. Many camp meetings continued on, but the early flourishing was greatly diminished. Then came the War, and that signaled the end for many camps, especially those in the South, where many areas were drastically depopulated, especially of men."

Hotle, too, argues that the Civil War provided fresh challenges and opportunities for the holiness movement generally and the camp meeting tradition more specifically:

> While the holiness message had been a vital part of many of those early camp meetings, most of them had been broad in their ecumenical base and had thus majored prominently on the conversion of sinners. Thus, to this point, the camp meeting had been more of a tool for evangelism than for revival and discipleship. But the Civil War created a climate of disarray from which the church world was not exempt. By this time many of the early established camps had either died or degenerated to simple social gatherings. Opposition to the message of holiness began to develop.

Into this void stepped leaders like J. A. Wood, W. B. Osborn, John S. Inskip, and George Hughes who sought to revive the church at this crisis moment. Together they organized the National Camp Meeting for the Promotion of Christian Holiness and coordinated camp meetings in the Northeast. Hotle explains that their efforts reignited interest in the camp meeting tradition and "during the last two decades of the nineteenth century many state and local unions began to develop after the order of the National Association," so much so that "[b]y 1892, there were forty-one different holiness periodicals being produced, most of them monthly."

If the war marked the end of many camps, it also marked a new beginning, a burst of new life for the movement, leading to its second epoch of growth, beginning at the close of the Civil War. In the 1870s and 1880s there arose in the United States a new concern for social righteousness. At least one social analyst suggests that the scandals that plagued the Grant administration, the reconstruction of the South, and the rapid industrialization of the North raised questions about the possibility of a faith that could change the way a person lived and behaved in society. Christian leaders began anew to encourage people to look to Christ for grace that would enable them to live lives characterized by love, integrity, uprightness, and humility—in short, what the Bible calls "holiness."

This is exactly when camp meetings were reborn. People who had attended Phoebe Palmer's Tuesday Meeting for the Promotion of Holiness in New York City founded the National Camp Meetings for the Promotion of Holiness. Dr. Melvin Dieter, a religious historian who taught at Asbury Theological Seminary, has written the most significant work exploring the camp meeting resurgence of this period, namely, *The Holiness Revival of the Nineteenth Century*.

Oswalt conjectures that part of the impetus for the new movement may have been the result of seeds sown before the war: the great revival of 1857-58 coming out of those New York noon prayer meetings and also the 1858 publication of William Boardman's *The Higher Christian Life*. In any case, Oswalt writes, "In 1867 a meeting was called in Vineland, New Jersey, for all those interested in the promotion of Christian holiness. The meeting was a great success, and out of it came the National Association for the Promotion of Christian Holiness and the decision to hold a camp meeting for that purpose in Vineland the following year. Delegates who had come from other parts of the country were encouraged to return home and start similar events. They did so and between 1870 and 1900, literally thousands of holiness camp meetings sprang up."

Once more, the Methodists led the way. Indian Springs Holiness Camp Meeting in Georgia—which had such a life-altering effect on long-time Asbury College president and popular Eaton Rapids speaker Dennis Kinlaw—had its beginnings among like-minded Methodist preachers supported by Methodist evangelists. Another camp meeting, Hollow Rock, at Yellow Springs, Ohio, began in 1838, and with a possible year or two hiatus during the Civil War, continued on and received new life in the holiness movement. And in 1885, the Michigan State Holiness Camp Meeting Association, which sponsors the Eaton Rapids Camp Meeting, had its beginnings as the Lansing District Holiness Camp Meeting Association.[11]

Camp meetings filled an ecclesiastical and spiritual need in the unchurched settlements as the population of the young nation moved west. As the name

---

[11] Oswalt adds, "Although these camp meetings never became quite the 'phenomena' that Cane Ridge and Red River had been, they were still remarkably popular. Like the earlier ones, most were held in August, after grain harvests were complete, and folks came to live in very primitive surroundings for as long as two weeks. They came to hear gifted orators proclaim the good news that Christ had died not only to bring us forgiveness for our sins but also to make it possible for Christians to live in victory over sin. Stories are told of as many as 5,000 people gathered in some of the locations and of great movements of the Holy Spirit."

implies, those who attended such meetings came prepared to camp out, gathering at the prearranged time and place from distances as great as 30 to 40 miles away. Families pitched their tents around a forest clearing where log benches and a crude preaching platform constituted an outdoor church that remained in almost constant session for however many days the camp lasted. People came partly out of curiosity, partly out of a desire for social contact and festivity, but primarily out of their yearning for religious worship. Activities included preaching, prayer meetings, hymn singing, weddings, and baptisms. From camp meeting to camp meeting, theology varied, but a sudden conversion experience was usually emphasized.

Camp meetings affected the religious and social life of the frontier in various ways—with mixed results. The emphasis on a sudden conversion tended to reduce doctrinal preaching to a minimum, break down the old creedal standards, and undermine the concept of a learned pastoral ministry. Camp meetings stressed the individualistic and activistic attitudes of Protestantism, which resonated with the frontier life and eventually pervaded the religious outlook of rural America. Camp meetings often lingered as summer Bible conferences into the 20th century, but even as frontier society waned in significance, camp meetings were still to exert considerable influence into the 1900s.

Camp meeting, at least at Eaton Rapids, remains both an individualistic and communal affair, and always has been. It involves immersion in and participation with the community, and strongly emphasizes the church; at the same time, however, it accentuates, in classical Protestant fashion, the importance for each person to get in right relationship with God, as well as providing a visible reminder that the Christian church involves more than merely local churches.

Eaton Rapids is also strong, and probably not anomalous in this regard, in bringing in speakers who are accomplished scholars, and juxtaposing them with seasoned practitioners, thereby reducing the perception that Christian dedication is an anti-intellectual exercise. The current president of ERC, John Oswalt, to cite but one example, is a significant Old Testament scholar and prolific writer. Camp meetings tend to be heavily experiential, it's true, but when done well they need not undermine the life of the mind. Quite to the contrary: in my own experience as a Christian philosophy professor and ethicist, I have little doubt that it was my experience in the holiness tradition, breathing the air of camp meetings as a child, that helped inspire my vocational pursuits. And mine is but one of many stories to tell, all testament to the ways camp meetings have made a huge impact on people's personal trajectories, spiritual lives, and vocational callings.

In light of the example of John Wesley himself, it would make sense that a tradition following in his footsteps would grasp that authentic Christian experience can be integrated with a rigorous mind. My wife and I were privileged to spend our first anniversary in Oxford, and after dinner we attended evensong at Christ Church, capping a magical day of visiting such sites as C. S. Lewis's Magdalen College and the Inklings' hangout *The Eagle and Child*. As the early evening service ended and we quietly started to exit the chapel, we looked down and saw, engraved in the tiles beneath our feet, the names of two famous graduates of Christ Church: John and Charles Wesley. It was another very special moment for us, and, among other things, it reminded me that the Wesleys (like Lewis later!) had rigorous minds and weren't afraid to think hard. Wesley, who tutored logic at Oxford, had a passion for education, insisting that all his preachers could read and equipping each of them to sell the books produced by the massive Methodist publishing enterprise.[12]

All that said, the camp meeting movement is not merely a history to be learned. As Ron Smith explains, "For many, many Christians across the nation, camp meetings are places renowned for dynamic singing and a kind of preaching that calls people to repentance for the forgiveness of sins and cleansing of hearts yearning for the higher life in His Spirit. I have personally prayed with two different governors of varying states and a State Supreme Court Justice—among many others—at altars of prayer as they sought God for His help in their daily Christian walk."

Such accounts remind us that important parts of the story of camp meetings in general, and certainly of Eaton Rapids in particular, are the individual and quite personal accounts of those on whom those meetings have made such an impact. Smith himself, who's preached at Eaton Rapids, writes that, for him,

> Camp meetings go beyond my experiences as preacher and teacher—and beyond my historical research. For it was at an altar of prayer at Delanco Holiness Camp Meeting I found God's pardon for sin and a heart cleansing that has been an anchor point for my walk with God. While struggling with a particular situation caused by sin in my life, I simply could not get past the defeat precipitated by my transgression. After all, how does one get past the grip of sin and death? Even though I had begun to live as a Christian, I found myself in the agony of failure and heard only the scornful voice of the adversary of my soul say, "You can never undo what has been done." My soul was empty, my mind was horrified, and my spirit was defeated. The heavens were like brass as my wounded, paltry prayers bounced from a despondent heart. As I kept trying to plead my case for forgiveness, a need wrought by my own stupid choice for sin, I heard the voice of the Spirit say, "Ron Smith, I

---

[12] Wesley once wrote to aspiring ministers lest they were ever tempted to drive a wedge between reason and devotion: "Suffer me now to add a few plain words, first to you who under-value reason. Never more declaim in that wild, loose, ranting manner, against this precious gift of God. Acknowledge 'the candle of the Lord,' which he hath fixed in our souls for excellent purposes. You see how many admirable ends it answers, were it only in the things of this life: Of what unspeakable use is even a moderate share of reason in all our worldly employments, from the lowest and meanest offices of life, through all the intermediate branches of business; till we ascend to those that are of the highest importance and the greatest difficulty! When therefore you despise or depreciate reason, you must not imagine you are doing God service: Least of all, are you promoting the cause of God when you are endeavoring to exclude reason out of religion." The Christian message is for the educated and uneducated alike—human beings all, afflicted with the same malady only God's grace can heal.

don't remember what you are talking about. Your sins I have removed as far as the east is from the west, and I remember them no more!" His sacred heart of pardon purchased my freedom. And at an altar of prayer, He shared His victory over death, hell, and the grave with me. I was 19 years old.

Two years earlier, at Taylor County Camp Meeting in Butler, Georgia, an almost twelve-year-old little girl responded to the evangelist's call to the altar for people who desired to receive Christ as their Lord and Savior. Jesus gloriously saved that little girl's soul, and ten years later she became my bride for life. So Dorena and I find it a sacred privilege to be on the camp meeting circuit today. Not only did camp meetings alter the course of American history, they were used by God to shape our very lives. Who knows the rest of the story for that person I will call to an altar of prayer this summer? But one thing is sure, the eternal victory for his or her very life may be found in a sharing Savior who still rides the circuit. Hallelujah to the Lord who is the same yesterday, today, and forever!

The story of camp meetings in America is the story of thousands of changed lives and transformed husbands, wives, and children, and of a nation revived and purified, preserved and seasoned.

Spotlight on Camp Meetings

Article by Henry A. Ginder

The Holiness Camp as an institution must ever keep the Great Commission in proper perspective. The Great Commission gives the Church her assignment in two specific areas. They are the *evangelization* of the world and the *edification* of the Church. Thus the objective and purpose of every camp meeting should center in this two-point assignment. Our pastors, our people, our churches, and our communities should feel the impact of the camp meeting in the areas of evangelization and edification.

Evangelization

The campers and camp meeting attendants should be impressed with the importance of being a part of the prayer organization of the camp. Every person should be involved in a *prayer cell* or a *prayer chain*, or at least be a *prayer partner*. By this we train our people to readily serve on the *prayer team* in the home congregation.

The preaching should confront every attendant with his "sins" and his "sin" and make clear how to achieve pardon and purity, which will produce peace and power. The message of heart cleansing and Holy Spirit Baptism must be the theme of every holiness camp meeting. The place, purpose, and power of the Holy Spirit as a Person in the life of the believer, must be expressed, exalted, and experienced.

Edification

The daytime sessions of the camp meeting are great days of opportunity for the preacher to fulfill the latter part of the Great Commission, "teaching them to observe all things." This is the time for inspiration, instruction, and indoctrination. Here is the nurture ministry of our camp meeting. There should also be opportunity for personal testimonies and prayers as an exercise for the development of our people.

Involvement

It is important to have the pastors of our constituency participate in the camp meeting. This will naturally bring the people.

Each camp meeting should plan for a special ministry to children and teenagers. If possible, they should have separate meeting places and operate their program simultaneous to the adult camp. If this is not possible, they should have special sessions somewhere, sometime during the camp meeting. They should, of course, all be a part of the great evangelistic rally in the evening.

Camp meetings and colleges should be brought closer together. Heartfelt religion and higher education are *neither* mutually exclusive nor incompatible. Our colleges and our camp meetings should complement and support each other.

Camp meeting administrators should speak at our colleges and college administrators and instructors should speak at our camp meetings. There may also be the interchange of administrators serving on the Boards.

Congregational growth should ever be the concern of camp meeting administrators. The camp meeting has not fulfilled its role as an institution in the structure of the church if it has not contributed to congregational growth. After the camp meeting there should be an inspired pastor and instructed people. There should be new conversions and new consecrations. Our good men should return from the camp meeting as God's men.

World missions must be a part of the program of every camp meeting. The mission program around the world should feel the strength of the annual camp meeting. This should be reflected in new recruits for the mission field and renewed support both by prayer and purse, for the mission program around the world.

The purpose and objective of the holiness camp meeting may be further stated by presenting six reasons for conducting camp meetings one hundred years ago, taken from the book *Days of Power*. In note form we present these reasons with application to our present day situation.

> The influence of Civil War. Bitterness—hatred—distrust. The camp meeting stimulates love and confidence. (If camp meetings were needed then, they are surely needed now for the same reason.)
> The absence of the Class Meeting. There is a tendency to omit prayer meetings, etc. Self-examination and tarrying in the presence of God are often missing. (For this reason camp meetings are needed today.)
> The operatic type of singing is coming into vogue. (The trend today also is toward heavier music. Here the camp meeting meets a need. We need Christian experience songs and deeper life and holiness songs.)
> Inordinate ambition in style of church architecture. (Today also we need the rugged touch of a camp meeting setting with its simplicity and closeness to nature. This provides a spiritual release.)
> Increased emphasis on the Liturgical form of service. (The church today also experiences danger in being tied to certain forms. We need the informality and freedom of camp meeting.)
> Sermons are shortened and characterized by doctrinal indefiniteness. (The camp meeting provides opportunity for doctrinal definiteness and full-length sermons.)

Atmosphere

The atmosphere of the camp meeting will be remembered by those who attend our camps long after they have forgotten the sermons and songs.

Holy Ghost anointing on the camp meeting is the camp meeting imperative. It is not only to be preached but to be practiced. During the camp meeting it should be practiced by everyone from the director to the dishwashers. There must be an atmosphere of love and fellowship, of holiness and helpfulness, of composure and confidence, of goodness and Godliness.

The Future

The future for the holiness camp meeting is bright. I believe they will continue until Jesus comes *if* we keep them properly related to the Great Commission, and *if* we involve our boys and girls, our teenagers and college youth, and *if* we present, without apology, the clean, clear message of Bible holiness.

1865-1884: Postbellum America

America in 1865 was in flux. It had just concluded a costly war, with the highest number of casualties of all America's armed conflicts—620,000 or 2% of the total population. The Civil War, too, brought the American experiment to the testing point, and its aftermath continues to reverberate today.

Beyond the devastation wrought by the war—in loss of life, financial burdens, and destruction of land and property—the outcome shifted the country toward a more centralized, and empowered, federal government. The Southern agrarian way of life, too, was diminished, both in actuality through the abolition of slavery and the requisite restructuring of the workforce that followed and in public estimation since the industrialized North emerged victorious over their Confederate counterparts.

However, while the war left a traumatic legacy, its resolution also opened up new possibilities for the nation. Western expansion increased exponentially it seemed, as questions about slavery in new territories were finally settled and the land America had accrued during the nineteenth century, through the Louisiana Purchase and from the Mexican-American War, could more readily be settled. Prospective pioneers were urged on by the Homestead Act of 1862 that promised 160-acre land grants for people meeting certain qualifications.

Newly burgeoning industries also benefited from unencumbered access to the frontier, mining it for natural resources like coal and oil to be transformed in factories in the East and returned as products to people throughout the country. This process made possible the massive fortunes of men like Andrew Carnegie (Carnegie Steel Company) and John D. Rockefeller (Standard Oil Company), two of the most notable late nineteenth century industrialists—known disparagingly as robber barons because public sentiment found certain of their business practices unscrupulous and exploitative.

Still, technological development flourished—the transcontinental railroad (completed in 1869), the telephone (1876), celluloid (one of the first plastics invented, 1869), the carbon-filament lightbulb (1879), improvements in photography development (1879), to name only a few. These technologies brought an optimistic spirit to a nation mourning a great loss. As expansion continued westward and the country grew through increased immigration, it also became more intellectually united through newly laid telegraph lines and railroad track. Newspapers and magazines, too, connected people across large distances, and Joseph Pulitzer and William Randolph Hearst demonstrated the power and influence of the written word with their competing media conglomerates.

1865 to 1884 America truly was an age of extremes in many ways. Mark Twain captured this contrast with his co-written novel *The Gilded Age* (1873), the title of which has been adopted to characterize the era in which they were writing. Gilding is a decorative technique whereby a thin coat of gold covers a less valuable substance like wood or stone. So, too, for the country, Twain explains in this quote from the novel: "The external glitter of wealth conceals a corrupt political core that reflects the growing gap between the very few rich and the very many poor."

The nation was optimistic for improvement and recovery after its lowest point yet. And the westward expansion, technological developments, and powerful public figures of the 1860s through 1880s embodied and encouraged that optimism. However, such materialistic successes didn't satiate or answer the deepest human needs, and the time was ripe for spiritual renewal.

Part II

The Turn of the Century

1885-1914

Fin de Siècle America

By 1893 the American frontier, which had for so long symbolized the country's optimistic spirit and embodied its romanticized possibilities, was declared closed. So said Frederick Jackson Turner in a paper presented to the American Historical Association, basing his conclusions on the census of 1890 that reported no fewer than two inhabitants for every square mile within the nation's borders. As the nineteenth century wound down, then, America faced new challenges: among them, what was the country's position on the world stage, where did Native Americans fit in their culture, and how could society prevent exploitation of its most economically vulnerable by the increasingly prevalent and powerful corporations?

The first global test of American solidarity and reunification after the Civil War came by way of the country's intervention in Cuba in 1898. Spain had been steadily losing world power, and its colony in Cuba—a mere ninety miles from the Florida Keys—was challenging the mother country's authority. Goaded by the journalistic efforts of William Randolph Hearst and Joseph Pulitzer, and catalyzed by the sinking of the USS Maine, Congress declared war on Spain, in defense of Cuba, on April 25, 1898. The aftermath of the short-lived war left America with territories in the Philippines, Guam, and Puerto Rico and national uneasiness about the country donning an imperial role.

As American expansion extended farther west over the course of the nineteenth century, it increasingly encountered Native American nations whose ways of life and understandings of land ownership clashed considerably with theirs. As the more powerful of the two, the American government dictated the terms of their engagement, and most often did so without consideration of the disastrous effect on Native American values and mores. The Dawes Act of 1887 epitomized this disregard, as it sought to disrupt and disband tribal nations by assimilating individuals into American society apart from their Native American loyalties and identity.

While homogeneity was being sought in the prairie lands, ethnic diversity was on the increase in the East and West. Spilling over from the pioneer-movement enthusiasm, European immigrants flocked to industrialized Eastern cities, most famously through the Ellis Island immigration station in New York. In the West, immigrants came primarily from China and Japan, lured by the possibility of railroad work and, for some, the California Gold Rush. This immigration boom well illustrates tensions at the heart of America—its promise of a better life and its sense of exceptionalism. The Statue of Liberty was dedicated in 1886, with Emma Lazarus's welcoming words, "Give me your tired, your poor, / Your huddled masses yearning to breathe free," etched into its base. And come they did: 1.25 million people were processed through the station during 1907, a record that held for eighty years. Yet against this backdrop were calls for restrictions on admittance, much of it communicated acerbically; these voices wielded some influence with the passage of the Chinese Exclusion Act and the Alien Contract Labor Law and implementation of a literacy test for new immigrants. Still this immigration swelled the American population to seventy-five million in 1900, up considerably from five million in 1800.

There was much work available for Americans. Corporations continued to produce, with industrial cities of the mid-West becoming increasingly influential. Chicago, for example, hosted the World's Columbian Exposition in 1893, an event that both celebrated the city's accomplishments and importance to American culture and elevated it further in the popular imagination. Ten years later, Henry Ford boosted Detroit's economic and cultural standing when he established the Ford Motor Company in 1903. But opportunity for some did not ensure financial security for all; many in urban and industrialized areas faced low wages and unsafe working conditions. Still others lived in substandard tenements, surrounded by crime, alcoholism, and violence. The labor movement was birthed from such conditions, with its calls for living wages and the end of worker exploitation, but often these strivings for justice ended in violence themselves—with the Haymarket Riot of 1886 being a prominent example.

But help for the urban underclass also came from another source, a source whose mission and method were governed by a biblical model of servanthood, meeting physical and emotional needs and proclaiming the gospel message in word and deed. Christian groups like the Salvation Army, true to its historically Wesleyan heritage, stood in the gap between the haves and the have nots, ministering to society's most vulnerable: the poor, the desperate, the alcoholic, the hungry, the homeless, the untouchables. The Salvation Army, in particular, demonstrated their mission on the world stage through disaster relief after the Galveston Hurricane of 1900 and the San Francisco earthquake of 1906. Forthcoming help from these groups depended on human need, not political expediency or social standing, and was motivated and sustained by Christian charity, not financial gain. In many ways, groups like the Salvation Army and those who shared their theology participated in American culture and contributed to it. But their religious convictions and spiritual resources enabled them to transcend the economic, racial, and political quarrels of their day, and to bring some measure of redemption to them.

Chapter 2

The Forest City, 1885-1894

Saratoga of the West

Eaton Rapids is on the northward course of the Grand River as it flows from Jackson to Lansing, Michigan's capitol, where it turns westward, at its confluence with the Spring Brook. Founded in 1838 by Amos and Pierpoint Spicer, Samuel Hamlin, and C. C. Darling, the city is named after John Henry Eaton, who at 28 was the youngest member ever to join the U.S. Senate, despite the Constitution's requirement that members be at least 30. It gained city status in 1881.

The Only Eaton Rapids on Earth tells the story of this community, and the book's title offers up another interesting tidbit of its history. The book's intriguing title can be attributed to E. E. Horner. While president of Horner Mills and on one of his frequent trips abroad, Horner wrote home, addressing the card from England to only "Eaton Rapids." The card reached Eaton Rapids, and the city became "The Only Eaton Rapids on Earth."

Historically it was a thriving community located in a region with lush farmlands. Its waterpower, furnished by the shallow clear waters of the Grand River, ran grist, wool, and lumber mills. The city's nickname, the "Island City," derives from the island located downtown, with a public park, in the Grand River. The area constituting Eaton Rapids was first settled by pioneers around the year 1835, mainly for its timber and waterpower. The following year, a sawmill was constructed near Spring Brook in Spicerville that would provide the lumber used to start Eaton Rapids. In 1837, the mill company built the Old Red Mill and used the power from the stream to grind corn. The mill company later used wood from Spicerville to construct their own sawmill along the Grand River, as well as a wool-carding mill.

In 1852, mineral water was first discovered by E. B. Frost, earning Eaton Rapids worldwide fame and (a third) nickname: *The Saratoga of the West*. Fourteen wells were drilled in total, most of which no longer remain. Immense subterranean water tables were of superb mineral quality and gave rise to the artesian wells. This water was in huge demand and led to a large influx of people seeking mineral water baths as well as cures from all types of ailment. So famous was the quality of these mineral springs that sixteen daily trains brought health seekers to the two mineral bathhouses within the city.

Another draw to the area was its Chautauqua, making Eaton Rapids a center of culture for the region. Chautauqua was originally a Christian undertaking that would become an adult education movement in the United States, highly popular in the late nineteenth and early twentieth centuries. Named after Chautauqua Lake in New York where the first meeting was held, organized by Methodist minister John Heyl Vincent, Chautauqua assemblies expanded and spread throughout rural America until the mid-1920s. The Chautauqua brought entertainment and culture for the whole community, with speakers, teachers, musicians, entertainers, preachers, and specialists of the day. Former U.S. President Theodore Roosevelt was quoted as saying that Chautauqua was "the most American thing in America."

An important feature of Eaton Rapids' downtown area, Island Park, was owned and operated by J. D. McAuliffe from 1872. It was hailed as a "shady retreat for pleasure seekers . . . (with) a fine collection of animals and a museum of rare specimens." In 1897 Eaton Rapids bought it to use as a city park. From 1908 to 1929 the Eaton County Battalion of the G.A.R. held its annual encampment there, then named Grand Army Park. Summer concerts, reunions, and picnics brought many to the park over the years. A group formed in 1973 to save the island from erosion served to refocus attention on this idyllic spot.

Another interesting tidbit about the town: Harlow Curtice, *Time Magazine*'s 1955 Man of the Year due to his leadership at General Motors, was from Eaton Rapids. He was born near Eaton Rapids on August 15, 1893, the son of Marion Joel and Mary Ellen Eckhart Curtice. He obtained his early schooling at Eaton Rapids, where classmates recall him as a freckled, serious boy who—in the words of one of them—"was quiet, modest, and blushed easily and often." He graduated from high school at Eaton Rapids and went on to become President of General Motors in 1953.

Interestingly enough, a 1935 article in the *State Journal* reported that very soon after the first families settled on the banks of the Grand in 1836 and 1837 and formed a little community that became Eaton Rapids, they began to think of religious activities. On a tombstone in the cemetery one may read the following: "Tryphesa B. Conklin died June 26, 1840, age 21 years, 8 months, 24 days. She was a devoted Christian. In her house was held the first religious service ever held in this place." This young woman had invited all the settlers to come to her home and bring their children. Three times the number came that the house would hold, so they spread out into the yard. Mrs. Conklin read the Bible, prayed, and preached, and they sang. She held regular meetings and organized a Sunday School.

The First Methodist Church was organized in the town in 1840. This was the fourth church in the county, the Griffith Methodist in Hamlin Township having preceded it by two years. The very first in the county was Methodist, founded in 1834, presumably in Bellevue Township. In 1842 the Rev. W. W. Crane, a circuit rider, preached in this community, and there is a record of a funeral on September 19 in that year held in the schoolhouse, at which he preached the funeral sermon for three: the mother of James Gallery, John Bently, and the child of the local blacksmith.

The Congregationalists organized the second church in Eaton County, at Vermontville in February 1838. The Eaton Rapids Congregational Church, the second in town, was founded in July 1834, by the Rev. Joseph W. Smith. Two of the recognized great preachers of their day served as pastor of this church, and both came here for the benefit of the Eaton Rapids mineral water, the curative and magnetic qualities of which were becoming widely known. These were the Rev. J. S. Edwards, a descendant of Jonathan Edwards, and the Rev. P. R. Hurd.

The Eaton County Courthouse Square is a rare example of an intact nineteenth-century Michigan government complex. The showpiece of the square, the stately Renaissance Revival courthouse built in 1883-85 was designed by D. W. Gibbs & Company of Toledo, Ohio. The interior features several elaborate marbleized slate fireplaces, stained glass, and native butternut and walnut trim. A cast zinc statue of *Justice* crowns the building and towers above the city. On July 4, 1894, fire destroyed much of the courthouse. The structure was rebuilt almost exactly to the original plans. The 1873 Second Empire sheriff's residence, built with an attached jail, is one of only a few of its age remaining in the state to this day. The courthouse square is listed in the National Register of Historic Places.

Lansing District Camp Meeting Association

Camp meeting came to Eaton Rapids by way of the Lansing District Camp Meeting Association. The first meeting of the Trustees of the Association was held at the Lansing fair grounds June 20, 1885.[13] The Rev. Mr. C. E. Holbrook of Charlotte was elected as president and the Rev. Mr. George L. Mount as secretary. A committee was given the task to search for "suitable grounds for camp meeting purposes." For about $900, thirty-three acres of land, located on the banks of the Grand River within the boundaries of Eaton Rapids, were purchased from Mr. Solomon C. Perrine to give the newly organized association a site for a camp meeting.

The Only Eaton Rapids on Earth describes the campground's chosen location as follows: "From a religious standpoint, one of the institutions that is known, not only throughout the state but nationally, is the Camp Ground, situated one mile south of this city, beautifully nestled at the bend of the Grand River which leads to the old historic Perrine's dam."

A book called *A History of Our Churches, In the Eaton Rapids and Springport Areas of Michigan* reports that an initial $455—collected through gifts ranging from $5 to $20—was raised among those present to apply on the $900 cost of the property. Preliminary work was started at once; the directive was given that half of the ground be cleared or underbrushed, a well dug, and fencing provided.

In early 1886 or so, work began on the first Tabernacle on the south side of Tabernacle Drive with its enclosed pulpit end toward the river. In a very short

---

[13] Reports vary a bit here. Another source says the Lansing District Camp Meeting Association was formed on July 27, 1885.

time the 55 by 100 foot structure was built with provisions for expansion, and before long it was too small, so 12 feet were added on each side at the cost of $115.00.

The first lots on the subdivided grounds went for ten dollars apiece with two years to build. After 1885 the cost for lots was $15.00. If no cottage was erected, the lot would revert to the Association at the end of that time.

Necessary clearing of roadways was authorized, and by March 1886 a hotel to accommodate twenty-five persons was built, along with a dining room utilized primarily by the speakers and transients attending the meetings. An office was needed at the gateway for admission by ticket.

Some cottages were going up, a few complete. To aid in caring for the people in the summer of 1886, twenty-five tents were secured from the supply depot of the state troopers and placed on lots along the roadways where cottages would one day stand. These were available for rent at three and four dollars with an extra dollar for a raised wooden floor. Six gasoline lamps or torches furnished the lights for the evening meetings.

The owner of the Morgan Hotel in town leased a plot inside the gate on which to build a boarding house. Board at the hotel was set at five dollars per week, or one dollar by the day, four in a room, with individual meals available at 25 and 35 cents. It still stands today as a remodeled home. The boarding house accommodations were inadequate for the attendance, so tents were provided for many of the overflow, and still many slept under the cover of their farm wagons.

On July 24, 1886, the opening day, the people came. They filled the hotel, and all the tents. Some brought empty mattress ticks and filled them with straw at the corral, sleeping beneath their farm wagons. Six gasoline lamps provided illumination for the night services. Breakfast and supper were 25 cents each, and dinner 35 cents.

Life centered in what was happening on these grounds for ten days with very few distractions. Of the real illumination that occurred in the lives of men and women, we have no written record. *Retrospect and Prospect: The First Eighty Five Years*—reprinted at the beginning of the Benson Publishing Company's songbook *Power and Praise*, containing songs both lively and spirited, or slow and worshipful—recalls this camp meeting as follows, "Yet every action recorded in the months immediately following that first encampment breathes encouragement, an optimism about the project that had been undertaken. At 10 cents per day per person, or 50 cents per season, receipts from all sources had been $2,351.83. In spite of an untended fire that had swept the grounds after camp and destroyed over 100 trees, the buildings were untouched."

The first meeting of the camp was held for ten days, and this length of time has prevailed through the present time. The original idea of ten days has remained in place, but the opening date was changed to the evening of the last Thursday in July with the closing date the first Sunday in August.

The next year the Ticket Booth was reshingled, and a dormitory was ready with thirteen first floor rooms, the second floor in two large chambers that could accommodate 25 to 30 persons. This helped manage the crowds somewhat, but owners of cottages were urged not to let rooms stand empty, to double up with cots and bunks, and to provide both room and board for as many extra people as they could possibly handle. Some tenters even boarded extras. Another twenty-five tents were ordered, and all were rented. So at the end of what was then little more than a country lane grew the "Forest City." Transportation was made available at the daily trains, a dime a passenger, a nickel a bag.

In laying out the grounds and establishing the roads, those in charge were thoroughly imbued with religious fervor as they executed their vision in every minute detail: the roads spelling "Holiness"—accounting for why the road twisted as it did among the "SS" around the old corral—and the tabernacle erected inside the letter "O." This job was contracted to a townsman. On the large arch to the entrance of the grounds there was inscribed, "Holiness unto the Lord." The first caretaker of the campgrounds was O. M. Wilkes, who gave about half time to the Association. He had living quarters in the hotel. This arrangement, a 1960 brochure said, has prevailed, with slight variation, ever since.

1886 marked 390 registrants in the Association, and by the next year that number had grown to 630. In 1887 the appraisal of the grounds and Association-owned buildings was $8,000.00; individual cottages were appraised for $6,000.00.

Because the camp was organized during the horse and buggy days,[14] it seemed advisable to charge an entrance fee to the grounds for horses as well as people to help with the finances of the camp. Season tickets were $.50; single admission was $.10; entry for a single horse was $.05; a season ticket for a horse was $.25; and a season ticket for a team was $.50. A corral was furnished at the extreme southern part of the grounds. When tickets were sold, individuals were told to retain them throughout the camp and present them upon departure. If tickets were lost, admission was charged again, a ruling in force because of the numbers of people who came in by boat. The first session receipts amounted to $4,351.83. During the presidency of Dr. W. G. Nixon the gate fees were removed and a budget set up to care for the finances of the camp.

Elizabeth Rogers Kellogg's Michigan-based novel *Into the Harness* describes what it was like in those earliest years: "They've cut roads through and cleared some of the underbrush. Wilbur (Rocky Canedy) has worked on several of the cottages and the wooden floors for the 50 tents they plan for this season. They've got the tabernacle up and the grounds fenced. No telling what it may mean for Eaton Rapids in the future. They certainly are dedicated and some are coming from other states. Methodists sing at their meetings. The street that

---

[14] John Oswalt, in 2013, wrote that the advent of the motorcar both helped and hindered the camp meeting movement in that it made it possible for people to come from farther away but also to engage in other activities that had previously not been available. "Thus," he concludes, "many would say that the heyday of the holiness camp meetings was in the 1920s. It is truly amazing how many still continue, nearly one hundred years later. Some are struggling, to be sure, and some have transformed themselves into more of a Christian entertainment center, but many remain true to their original mission of being a place to which people can come to re-focus their lives on what matters, a place where God can regain the center of their lives."

went out to the campgrounds from Eaton Rapids, Plains Road, was well traveled. A man stood at the entrance gate to collect the 10-cents-per-person fee and to direct the drivers to the corral back in the woods where the horses could be tied out."

She adds, "The Eaton Rapids Campgrounds have been a place of happy associations both spiritual and festive ever since," and a place where many a marriage has been solemnized.[15]

Jean Kline was a long-time Eaton Rapids resident who spearheaded a great many projects for the Eaton Rapids Area Historical Society. She passed away in 2010, but she wrote a wonderful article about ERC three years before in the July 15, 2007, *Eaton Rapids Community News*. Basing her glances into the past of Eaton Rapids on historical research and personal accounts as shared with her, she too helps flesh out those early days. "Get the chores done early 'cause we're going to camp meeting tonight," she imagines was a phrase that's echoed each summer in Eaton Rapids since 1886 or so. "Folks came by the thousands," she writes, pitching tents or sleeping on straw. "It was a ten-day event starting the last week in July after harvest was finished and before fall plowing began—with stirring music and gripping preaching," the same schedule today. "At that time," she adds, "most of the residents were farmers who left their fields early to attend to the livestock and evening chores. Mother prepared an early supper, corralled the children, scrubbed their hands and faces and threatened them if they did not stay clean at least until they left for town. Even those who lived in town had a cow to milk, chickens to feed and eggs to gather as well as attend to at least two horses."

She continues, "Once in town, they tied their horse to the hitching rail near the Grand River and rode the Stanley Steamer to the camp grounds. If you lived on the west side of the river, this saved about five miles in travel. Others drove directly to the campgrounds. Some came on horseback, some walked and still others were met at the train depot and were charged ten cents for each passenger and a nickel for each bag to be delivered by horse-drawn taxi. Women in large hats and bustled skirts that swept the ground made sure their children were properly dressed with long cotton stockings, girls in white and boys in black, no matter how hot and humid the weather might be. The men dressed in proper black suits and derby hats that were removed upon entering the Tabernacle. They found their way through rows and rows of tents making their way to the huge, three thousand-seat Tabernacle in time for the evening service."

From time to time, as mentioned, a ferry operated across the river, saving the long five-mile drive to the campgrounds via town. The colorful excursion boat—the *Stirling*—made the trip up river several times daily, docking where provision was made for the purchase of entrance tickets. It provided transportation from the railroad depot. The steamer was a flat bottom side-wheel

---

[15] Kellogg wrote a series of historical novels, of which *Into the Harness* was just one. *Across the Deep Threshold*, *Them Days of War*, and *I Don't Cry Much* were others. Many thanks to Charlene Skinner for allowing us to see her copies of all of these; Charlene is the wife of the current ERC groundskeeper and a relative of Kellogg.

craft owned and operated by John H. Stirling, navigating the Grand River between its docks located near the dam and the entrance to the grounds.

A gentleman by the name of Coller from Flint put a screw wheel boat on the river that carried about twenty people. His boat would make about three round trips to the *Stirling*'s one, but because it drew too much water and weeds collected on the propeller and retarded the speed, and because it came in contact with stones that broke off the propeller blades, the boat did not prove very profitable for its owner, and he did not return another season.

Mr. Frank Rice was given permission to operate a ferry from the present Ed Buechler property across the river to the Camp Ground in 1886. This was quite a saving to those living south of the city, as their teams could be left on the south bank of the river, and by using the ferry, they could save approximately five miles in travel for the round trip.

These practical steps facilitated attendance by many throughout the area. They came to participate in worship and share in the message proclaimed. The Rev. Sam Jones, a nationally known evangelist, was one of the speakers in 1887, and the following year the Rev. Sam Small, another eminent divine, attended the entire meeting. Renowned speakers started to come from all over the United States and considered it an honor to be invited to conduct one or more of the ten-day sessions. Dr. James Hamilton was elected president in 1888, and at the annual meeting the name of the Association was changed to the Central Michigan Camp Meeting Association.

From the first, the campground was very popular. The meetings had gained in popularity to such an extent that not only the bus lines but several other persons with their carryalls met all trains, serving effectively all those in need of transportation. It was especially attractive to many from the metropolitan centers who moved their families here to get away from the perennial turmoil of the city and to give their children the advantage of the great open spaces. Boating and swimming were quite popular, and it's reported there was no record of a single accident from either sport across all the years. Many local people as well as transients built homes on the grounds and resided there during the summer months. Most of the cottages on the grounds were built before 1940; most of them have been remodeled from what was referred to as a "wooden tent" with four walls and a floor. Many are updated homes complete for year-round use, with all the necessities for comfortable, modern living.

1889 brought another name change, to the Michigan State Holiness Camp Meeting Association. During the brief years of its existence as the Lansing District and then the Central Michigan Camp Meeting Association (1884 – 1889), the Worship Committee was composed of the pastor of the Eaton Rapids Methodist Episcopal Church, the District Superintendent of the Lansing District, and the pastor of Lansing Central Methodist.

With the change to "Michigan State Holiness Camp Meeting Association" came other changes de-emphasizing its local character. The presiding elder was no longer automatically president. Local ties, particularly with the city of Eaton Rapids through the many local trustees and businessmen and the pastors of the Methodist Church, remained strong. Yet the wider ministry of the camp emerged. A tally of the entries in the gate registry for 1895, while showing solid support from Lansing, Jackson, Grand Rapids, and even Detroit, as well as the many smaller towns nearby, also revealed an astonishing number of entries from beyond the Straits, Canada, New York, Pennsylvania, Ohio, Indiana, Illinois, and Wisconsin. A few were even from beyond these nearby states, including Iowa, Colorado, California, and Washington.

What drew attendees from so far was the gospel message, proclaimed by a variety of evangelists and preachers. *Retrospect and Prospect* explains the quality of the speakers of these early years: "Within a half dozen years the 'general favorite,' Joseph H. Smith, then conference evangelist from Philadelphia, had come to managing the speaking schedules. In addition there would be listed one 'general evangelist of national reputation,' at least one Bishop, and a list of perhaps a half dozen local men 'to preach, teach, and assist.'" The very best in the country were sought. To hear them and to speak themselves came the bishops of the denomination from all over the country.

At the peak of the missionary movement came the great missionary bishops: Bishop Walden from Africa, again and again Bishop Oldham (once a government surveyor) from China and South America, Bishop Werne from India, Bishops Ninde and Mallalieu, and, in the year of his refusal to become bishop, E. Stanley Jones. The following biography of E. Stanley Jones comes from the United Christian Ashrams website:[16]

> Stanley Jones was born in Baltimore, Maryland, January 3, 1884. He was educated in Baltimore schools and studied law at City College before being graduated from Asbury College, Wilmore, Kentucky in 1906. He was on the faculty of Asbury College when he was called to missionary service in India in 1907 under the Board of Missions of the Methodist Episcopal Church. He began his work among the members of the very low castes and the outcastes. He did not attack Hinduism, Buddhism, Islam, or any Indian religion. He presented the Gospel of Jesus Christ, disentangled from western systems and cultures, and their sometimes non-Christian expressions. "The way of Jesus should be—but often isn't—the way of Christianity," he said. "Western civilization is only partly Christianized."
>
> Brother Stanley, as he was familiarly called by thousands of people, attracted wide attention among the high castes, the students and the intelligentsia. He was invited to speak at ancient universities and before learned societies. Soon he was set aside by his church to interpret the Christian Gospel especially to educated men and women. In 1919, with foresight and great-heartedness, the Board of Missions of the Methodist Episcopal Church offered him the wide-ranging role of "Evangelist-at-large" to India and to wherever else he

---

[16] "Stanley Jones," *United Christian Ashrams*, accessed December 29, 2015, http://www.christianashram.org/e-stanley-jones.html.

might feel led, which subsequently proved to be to the far corners of the earth. Dr. Jones conducted great mass meetings in leading Indian cities. At one such meeting, their leader said, "We may not agree with what Dr. Jones is saying, but we can certainly all try to be like Jesus Christ." He inaugurated "round table conferences" at which Christians and non-Christians sat down as equals to share their testimonies as to how their religious experiences enabled them to live better. Thirty years before the United Nations came into being he proposed a Round Table of Nations.

Theodore Henderson, first as pastor, then head of "aggressive evangelism" for the denomination, and finally as a beloved bishop, came repeatedly. Sometimes as high as 300 pastors fed on the rich fare in his School of Evangelism. The quaint old brochures would announce: "If they get here, they will speak." And often, as the gate registry testifies, they did indeed "get there."

Retrospect and Prospect provides the following overview of the speaker list of those early years:

Only a few of the men who wove their ministry into the life of the camp over the years can be mentioned here. We would begin, of course, with Joseph H. Smith who, as "conductor of the meeting," then expositor, and finally as teacher in his unique School of the Prophets and quizmaster of the Question Box, left his stamp on three generations. E. N. McKaig, a repeated favorite, early ranked near him in popularity. M. C. B. Mason, Secretary of the Freedman's Aid Society, one of the most representative colored ministers of the South, returned again and again whenever he had the date free. C. F. English, C. J. Fowler of Boston, C. W. Winchester, and Henry Clay Morrison were frequently co-workers in the early 1900s, some of them speaking from this platform over a span of thirty years. Beverly Carradine was on call to come whenever he could. E. F. Walker of San Dimas, California, a particularly able expositor, came first a year or two later. With him in that especially fruitful encampment was C. W. Ruth, the "speaker to the conscience." John L. Brasher, Will Huff, and George Ridout, orators who used their voices to bring the glory down, came often to the great and growing camp. With them, in the ministry of song, are associated the names of E. R. Akin and Frank Arthur, with Emma Perrine at the piano.

By 1890 the many functions of auxiliary groups for children and youth required a place of their own, and the spot was chosen for constructing Epworth Chapel. Seth Fowler designed a handsome building with an elevated floor, a closed north end for a platform, windows, porches, and steps surrounding the other three sides. It was attractive and functional for a time, but early pictures show that it required groups carrying their chairs outdoors to have enough room. In 1900, it was decided to rip out Epworth Chapel's floor, porch, steps, and windows, and redesign the building along the lines of the Tabernacle, with raised doors, increasing the capacity to 150. Some of the windows were reinstalled in the four upper peaks of the roof structure for light.

Services in the Chapel were largely for the younger groups and conducted by people especially suited to that line of work. It had a seating capacity of 150 and had always been a very popular meeting place. The knowledge those attending received during the meetings was of vital importance, and in many instances on their return they took up work in the Sunday School and became leaders in that branch of the church. Very often those in charge hailed from the Chicago Evangelistic Institute, an outstanding seminary.

The Recording Secretary Book of the Eaton Rapids Camp Meeting Auxiliary of the W.F.M.S., 1891-1926, begins with this entry from July 20, 1891: "At a meeting called in the cottage of Mrs. M. J. Barnard on Eaton Rapids Camp Ground, an Auxiliary known as E.R.C.M. Aux. of the W.F.M.S. was organized, the object being to gather in the women scattered over the Conferences, who have no Aux. at their own home, and yet are moved to farther (sic) the Redeemer's Kingdom through this Society, which has been signally blessed by God."

Four days later Epworth Hall was dedicated, on Friday, July 24, 1891 (the second day of Camp). Camp Meeting that year ran from July 23 to August 2— "for the Sanctification of Believers and the Conversion of Sinners." A small pamphlet advertised the occasion, promising "famous workers" and a "great meeting." It made mention of Bishop W. F. Mallalieu, D.D., of New Orleans, "our great revival bishop," and Rev. James H. Potts, D.D., Editor of *Michigan Advocate*. Other speakers identified were Rev. David B. Updegraff, "The Quaker Methodist," scheduled for General Supervision and Rev. Enoch Stubbs, of Philadelphia, scheduled to preach every day. "It is confidently expected that Major Cole, noted evangelist, will assist in the evening services. Rev. D. F. Barnes, D.D., Rev. J. I. Buell, D.D., and Rev. R. W. Van Shoick, D.D., and others would be present a part of the time, the brochure reported, and Rev. M. M. Callen, D.D. would conduct the singing. Tuesday, July 28, was scheduled for Missionary Day, led by Women's Foreign Missionary Workers. Miss Sarah M. DeLine, of Bombay, India, would be the attraction for the day.

Other features of camp meeting included the "League Hour," which was held at 4 o'clock each day under the direction of Epworth League workers. Special services by and for young people, in the new and attractive Epworth Hall. Prominent leagues would be present, and everyone was invited to this "great spiritual feast," encouraged to bring Bibles and songs of joy and gladness.

The pamphlet listed the various expense fees for board, lodging, and meals. A 25% discount on entertainment applied to ministers and their wives. Sleeping accommodations were free to all ministers who brought their own bedding, and straw for beds was free for everyone. Feed for horses was available at a reasonable rate. The *Stirling* was advertised, and it was announced that omnibuses met all trains, and that travelers were to take the one marked, "This Bus Enters the Grounds." Admission fees were delineated, and this further announcement provided: "Desirable building lots now in the market at small prices. Now is the time to build a cottage. Ten new cottages since our last meeting." The back of the brochure listed twenty rules and regulations of ERC, pertaining to Gates, Horses, Teams, the Corral, Cottage Owners, and a catch-all category of miscellany—and one final warning: "Beware of Pickpockets."

At this time, in 1891, the Association Secretary was L. DeLamarter, and the President was W. I. Cogshall. It would seem this was the first year that renowned national holiness preacher Joseph H. Smith was a platform speaker. He would go on to be a platform speaker at ERC for nearly forty years; as Oswalt put it, "He owned this camp."

Dr. Marshall M. Callen became President of the Association in 1892, a position he held until 1919 when he died suddenly. During the early years of his tenure, he was also song leader on several occasions.

In 1893, the painting of the hotel (Unity Boarding House), grocery, and ticket office, along with moving the corral cost $77.80. The next year, in 1894, the Association's name would be changed again, this time to the Michigan State Holiness Camp Meeting Association, the name it still retains.

In those early days, the trustees were very reluctant to incur any debts and made just such improvements from year to year as they were able to afford. The great D. L. Moody (1837-1899) and Ira Sankey (1840-1908) were in their heyday at this time, and it was suggested to the trustees that they secure their services for the ten days' meeting. The astounding amount of $1,000 for the entire meeting baffled them; they were reluctant to take the chance. Had they dared to make the venture, it's been suggested, the railroads would have run excursions, and the coffers of the Association would have been filled to almost overflowing.

By the end of this first decade of the Camp, in 1894, about fifty "elegant cottages" could be found on the grounds, and "new ones are being built every year." These were paying property, as they rented well during the meetings. "Desirable building lots" were marketed at "small prices," as "Every year adds beauty to the grounds." But the 1894 brochure noted that this wasn't a "fashionable resort with expensive rates of living, but a quiet rest-place, where one can live as cheaply as at home. With safe boating on a shallow river, it is a paradise for children," and "[p]ure, healthful drinking water in abundance."

Camp meeting workers for 1894 were Rev. Jos. H. Smith of Indianapolis, the "able and popular preacher of the last two years' meetings," who would have charge of the first few days of the meeting.[17] A nationally famous holiness preacher, Smith preached at ERC for 38 consecutive years. Apparently he had a good sense of humor. One evening some young people were making noise after hours. The President leaned out of his window and shouted to them to be quiet and go to bed, whereupon Dr. Smith leaned out his window and shouted, "Will someone tell that old man to be quiet so we can get some sleep!"

That year, too, Rev. Geo. D. Watson, D.D., of Florida, well-known and popular as a preacher on holiness, would have charge after August 1. Bishop Mallalieu was expected August 3. Evangelist F. A. Morehouse would assist

---

[17] Some records indicate that Smith's first year was 1891, in which case he would have been a speaker for the last three years, not two.

throughout the meeting. Rev. E. W. Ryan, D.D., Rev. J. H. Potts, D.D., and Rev. Levi Master, D.D. would be present and preach sometime during the meeting. Mr. Geo. C. Cutler, of Ionia, an "efficient League worker," would conduct the Epworth League services.

Scriptural holiness was to be the theme of sermon, song, and prayer, and promotional material touted it as "the only Camp Meeting of its kind in Michigan, and is attended by people from other states." The Higher Life was "inculcated at every meeting," and "we have no side issues to divert attention from the one supreme purpose. An enriched experience is sought at each service."

In the first decade of its operation, four men would serve as President of the Association. James Hamilton served from 1884-1888, W. H. Thompson from 1888-1889, W. I. Cogshall from 1889 to around 1892, and Marshall M. Callen took over in 1892, a tenure that would last twenty seven years![18]

The first decade of ERC was in the history books, and it had just begun.

---

[18] Records are a bit unclear as to the end date of Cogshall's Presidency.

Spotlight on Marshall M. Callen (1849-1919)
[Tribute to Dr. Callen by D. D. Martin[19]]

In 1892, Dr. Marshall M. Callen became President of the Eaton Rapids Association. He held this position for twenty seven years until he died unexpectedly in 1919. Callen left his mark on the property physically, having donated $2,500 toward a new tabernacle as a memorial to his wife. With his own sudden passing the Sunday before camp meeting in 1919, the association moved to commemorate the tabernacle by naming it after the long-time president. Upon his death, the following tribute written by D. D. Martin was recorded in the Minutes of the Michigan Conference of the Methodist Episcopal Church:

July 20, 1919, after a Sabbath full of work and worship in which he preached with unusual power and led the congregation in singing, Dr. Callen went to the parsonage home at Marshall, Michigan, lay down to rest, and was awakened by the angel song in the morning of the Eternal Day. Since the death of Mrs. Callen, three years before, he had been lonesome. He was quite alone in the house that night. No one knows the hour of his going. He had announced to his congregation that he should leave next morning for Eaton Rapids. The people of Marshall supposing he had gone, did not notice any change at the parsonage. The friends at Eaton Rapids, supposing him detained by pastoral duties, did not inquire until later in the week when it was found that without struggle, save as one hand had been lifted as though answering a summons, he had gone to be with God.

Marshall M. Callen was born in Knox County, Tennessee, May 16, 1849. He had passed his 70th anniversary in life and his 42nd in membership in the Michigan Conference. He was of sturdy mountain stock, and his people were loyal adherents and supporters of the Methodist Episcopal Church. He received his academic training in the Methodist school at Athens, Tennessee—then known as the East Tennessee Wesleyan University. It was at this school he met Miss Helen Bosworth, a music teacher, who gave him musical training, and showed him other kindnesses, and who afterward became Mrs. Callen. For forty-three years they walked together in that devotion that made her the sharer of his success, and he the constant recipient of devoted attention and most loyal support. Their marriage occurred January 1, 1873. They continued in educational work two years, then came to Greenville, Michigan, where Brother Callen had opportunity to engage in manufacturing enterprise with a friend; but it was to the ministry he felt his life call and he entered the regular work in the Michigan Conference in 1876, and joined in full membership in 1878. At the time of his death he was the oldest in active service in the Conference save one who joined the same year.

---

[19] D. D. Martin, "Marshall M. Callen," in *Minutes of the Michigan Annual Conference of the Methodist Episcopal Church 1919*, Bishop Theodore S. Henderson, president (Lansing, MI: Michigan Annual Conference, 1919), *Google Books* (accessed December 28, 2015), 569-572.

Dr. Callen came quickly to recognition as a conference leader. He was five times elected to the General Conference, at the head or near the head of his delegation. He was five years Conference Secretary. He served five years as district superintendent of the Kalamazoo District. His pastorates were among the larger churches of the Conference. He left his place at the head of Kalamazoo District to accept appointment at First Church, Jackson, where he had given one full term in the pastorate. Other charges were: Traverse City, Saint Joseph, Portland, Lansing, Central, Hillsdale, Eaton Rapids, Ionia, Cadillac, and Marshall. In his pastorates his strong sermons and able administration were accompanied by soulful singing for which he had gifts and passion. He knew and loved the children of his parish, but was favored with none in his home. A generous giver, he always led his congregation in liberal offerings of money for the church in its local and general work. His latest large gift being $1,000.00 for the Centenary to be credited to the church at Marshall.

For twenty-eight years he had been the president of the Michigan State Holiness Camp Ground Association located at Eaton Rapids. This great meeting was on his heart. He gave it his thought and best effort. He believed in the Wesleyanic doctrine of holiness as taught there, and witnessed to the experience. The Callen Memorial Tabernacle, with seating capacity of five thousand, was made possible by his generous gift in memory of Mrs. Callen, though it will now stand as a monument to them both. Their beautiful cottage on the river front has been purchased by the association as an administration building and home for honored guests.

Dr. Callen was influential in all conference and committee meetings. He had strong convictions and could give clear utterance to them. In debate he was pungent, logical, and fearless. He commanded the attention of the General Conference, and was widely known throughout the church. He at one time received a considerable vote for the office of bishop. He had a good library, always buying the latest and best books of interest to the ministry and read them well. His papers at district meetings and elsewhere showed keen research and were listened to with great interest and profit. A brother beloved in the Conference, he will be greatly missed; possibly no one could be missed more.

The immediate relatives are: one brother, Geo. M. Callen, of Athens, Tenn., two sisters, Mrs. Mattie E. Rankin, of Athens, Tenn., and Mrs. Marguerite Giffin, of Knoxville, Tenn., with their families and the children of a deceased sister.

The funeral service was held in the church at Marshall on Friday afternoon, July 25th, and was conducted by Dr. Hugh Kennedy. D. D. Martin, W. P. Manning, A. A. Geiger, Geo. A. Brown and A. R. Johns assisted in the service, and many Conference members were present. A brief service was held in the church at Cadillac, on Monday, July 28, Dr. C. S. Wheeler of Big Rapids in charge. He was assisted by Dr. Johnston of the Presbyterian Church, and M. D. Carrel, S. W. Large, and J. W. Sheehan of the Michigan Conference. The remains rest by the side of his devoted wife in the cemetery at Cadillac. A memorial service was also held in the tabernacle at Eaton Rapids Camp Ground, Wednesday, July 30, in charge of W. P. Manning, at which P. J. Maveety, D. D.

Martin, and Evangelist Joseph H. Smith spoke. His brother and two sisters were present at this service.

Chapter 3

A New Century, 1895-1904

The second decade of Eaton Rapids Camp Meeting kicked off with camp from July 25 through August 4, 1895, with the Rev. Joseph H. Smith conducting, assisted by Rev. R. N. McKaig, D.D., of Minnesota and "a specialist of marked ability," and others. Bishop W. X. Ninde, D.D., LL.D., "lately returned from China and Japan," would preach Sunday, August 4. This was the fourth time that Smith would conduct the meeting, with many more to come. Rev. H. C. Scripps, of Detroit, would have charge of the Epworth League, and Mrs. Scripps had charge of the Junior League. 210 took dinner at Unity on Friday, August 2, 1895.

In 1895, too, the original tabernacle was enlarged with shed roofs on the east and west sides, for $115.00.

Smith would serve again in 1896, and the aforementioned *Stirling*, the ferry running between the town and campgrounds, would resume its operation, lasting through 1906.

1897 featured another enlargement to the Auditorium, and a rule not to drive faster than one can walk. Camp meeting was conducted yet again by Rev. Joseph Smith, and assisted by Rev. Isaac Naylor and "other prominent workers." Naylor was a well-known Holiness Evangelist and singer, formerly of England but who now resided in the United States. He would be present during the entire meeting, preaching and singing as "the spirit may direct." Naylor was author of many of the most popular songs in the "Songs of the Pentecost," the book that had been used for several years running, and would be used this year again.

Rev. Smith was described in camp records like this: "The eloquent and popular exponent of Scriptural Holiness, [Smith] has been engaged for the sixth year in succession to take general direction of the meeting. The meetings have steadily increased in attendance and power during his supervision and he is praying and planning for still greater things this year."

In 1898 Dr. Smith began The School of the Prophets, an evangelistic institute open to all who were attending ERC. Delbert Rose (who spoke at Eaton Rapids in 1956) writes that no one of the leaders or promoters of the National Holiness Association was more widely accepted or highly esteemed for so long a time after Methodism had sought to sluff off its holiness doctrine than was

Smith. "He had become the successor of the Palmers, Inskip, and McDonald, and S. A. Keen as *the* holiness evangelist to the General Church."[20]

Among others occupying the platform was Rev. M. C. B. Mason, D.D., of Atlanta, Georgia, one of the secretaries of the Freedman's Aid and Southern Education Society, "one of the most representative colored ministers of the south"; Mason was scheduled to preach the first Sunday of the meetings.1898 was also the year that the first bookstore was built in Tabernacle Circle.

Camp meeting the next year was conducted by the Rev. Joseph H. Smith, assisted by Rev. C. S. Nusbaum and "other prominent workers." Nusbaum, of Kansas, it was said, would assist in the meeting from beginning to close. In a letter to the President of the Association, Bishop Ninde spoke of this "Coming Evangelist" as follows: "I am glad to learn that you have secured Rev. C. S. Nusbaum of the Southwest Kansas Conference to assist in Evangelistic work at the Eaton Rapids Camp Meeting this summer. I have known Bro. Nusbaum for a number of years, having formed his acquaintance during my residence in Kansas. I have a very high regard for him both as a man and as a minister, and believe you have made no mistake in securing his services."

Bishop Ninde himself would be present to preach the first Sunday. Other speakers and assistances included President Ashley of Albion College; Rev. J. L. Berry, D.D., Chicago; Rev. William Dawe, D.D., Saginaw; Rev. W. I. Cogshall, Coldwater; Rev. W. M. Puffer, Lansing; and Rev. P. J. Maveety, Jackson. Rev. Herman C. Scripps, of Detroit, would have the direction of the Epworth League service, and Mrs. H. C. Scripps of the Junior League meetings. Miss Birdie Blodgett of Eaton Rapids would be the organist; Dr. Callen would conduct the singing.

The last page of the brochure recorded, "The Grounds are situated on the banks of the Grand River within a half-mile of the City of Eaton Rapids. Ease of Access (sic) by rail from all points in Central and Southern Michigan, 18 miles from Lansing, 24 miles from Jackson, 20 miles from Albion, and less than two hours' ride from Grand Rapids. The delightful shade of the oak trees, the charming drives, the clear water, the undulating surface, and the cool breezes from the river combine to make this an attractive Camp Ground." The brochure also included three pictures of the grounds: one of Grand Avenue, another at Point Comfort, and a third of Simpson Park—the river bank near the campfire/hotel area.

1898 was the year the bookstore was built. It had been the dream of H. R. E. Quant, who built it that year and then managed it from then until 1922, after which David Reed managed it for the next thirteen years.

In 1899 Nusbaum would assist Smith once again. Pastor of the First Methodist Episcopal Church of Ottawa, Kansas, Nusbaum could give only a limited amount of time to camp meeting work that season, but those in attendance felt fortunate in securing his services if only for a truncated duration. That year, too, "The Singing Evangelists," who had been "very successful in

---

[20] Rose, 109.

winning souls," would preach and sing the gospel during the first part of the meeting.

Rev. J. H. Potts, D.D., known and loved by all Michigan Methodists, would preach the first Sunday of the meeting and deliver the missionary address on the Monday following. Rev. J. F. Berry, D.D., editor of the *Epworth Herald*, would preach and bring inspiration and help to the work among the young people who were his charge.

Also during this time, there were plans for the enlargement of the Epworth Chapel in order to accommodate the constantly increasing attendance and interest in these League meetings. Mrs. H. C. Scripps would have charge of the Junior League meetings, and would also conduct daily conferences with and for the benefit of all who were in any way connected with Christian work among children.

Other pastors from Muskegon, Port Huron, Battle Creek, Lansing, and Albion would preach and assist in the meeting. That year, too, the "School of the Prophets" would adopt the "Two Million Souls" project, and discuss ways and means to this end. Brother Smith would have supervision of this institute, and at each session short papers would be read by prominent ministers in the state, to be followed by general discussion.

That year's brochure also made mention of the Albion District Camp Meeting joining hands with the "Work at Eaton Rapids," and both ministers and laymen from the District were expected to augment the forces at ER. Miss Ella C. Parks, of Battle Creek, served as organist that year.

The new century marked the seventeenth annual camp meeting, held from August 2 to August 12. Rev. J. H. Smith would be present, who had "pressed the battle to victory for so many years that his coming is always anticipated with pleasure." Dunham and Baker, both of Ohio, had also been engaged for service, "among the most successful evangelists now in the field, both famous singers, being members of the well-known North Ohio Conference Male Quartette." They were coming for the first time, and on the highest and most unqualified commendation by Bishops Ninde and Joyce, Dr. Bashford, and others. Bro. Baker was anticipated to have charge of the Young People's Meeting.

Rev. R. N. McKaig, D.D., of Minneapolis, MN, would spend a few days at the meeting greeting his many friends and preaching the fullness of the gospel. Rev. Manley S. Hard, D.D., Assistant Secretary of the Church Extension Society of Philadelphia, PA, and Rev. J. P. Ashley, D.D., President of Albion College, would preach Sunday, August 5. Rev. L. E. Springer, D.D., of the Detroit Conference, and others would be present and would preach as well. Mrs. Hattie Reynolds, of First M. E. Church in Jackson, would be the organist., and *Pentecostal Hymns* No. 2 would be used for congregational singing.

The meeting of the Women's Foreign and Home Missionary Societies would be held on the Camp Grounds Monday afternoon, August 6, at 2 o'clock.

The brochure for 1900 features a picture of "Point Comfort" on the ERC grounds, providing a delightful snapshot of men and women donning the quaint garb of that period. The Albion District closed its camp and joined ERC for camp meeting that year.

1901's encampment spanned the end of July into the beginning of August, and its brochure offered a bit more biography on the various workers. Smith returned, affirming his belief in Eaton Rapids Camp Meeting, and "after attending all the meetings in the United States similar to ours, ranks ours second only to the great gathering at Mountain Lake Park. Our people believe in Brother Smith, as is evidenced by the fact that his engagement this year is for the tenth consecutive year. He will reach us Monday and remain to the close of the meeting." As Mountain Lake was the place that Smith was called to evangelism and where his ministry got underway, it makes perfect sense the place would inhabit such a warm place in his heart.

Joining Smith on the platform was Rev. E. S. Dunham, D.D., of Delaware, Ohio, who "labored so successfully with us last year." He would preach at the opening service and was anticipated to be in attendance to the closing service. "Bro. Dunham is a safe teacher, an able preacher, and by his sweet spirit wins the hearts of the people."

Rev. L. H. Baker, who had been disappointed in his plans to be at Eaton Rapids the year before, was "under positive engagement to help in pushing the battle to victory from the beginning to close of the meeting. This he does by his preeminent ability in three directions, first as a preacher, second as a singer, and third as a leader in young people's meetings."

Rev. C. W. Winchester, D.D., Pastor of Sentinel M. E. Church, Buffalo, New York, a member of the National Holiness Association, and "a camp meeting preacher and worker of ability and experience, will assist in the services during the first part of the meeting." Rev. George Elliott, D.D., Pastor of Central Church, Detroit, "who has but recently come to Michigan, and who believes that the mission of Methodism is to spread scriptural Holiness, will preach once during the meeting."

Rev. C. T. Allen, D.D., Rev. D. F. Barnes, D.D., Rev. J. C. Floyd, D.D., and others from the two conferences in the state will preach. Once again, Albion District, within whose territory the Camp Ground is located and which sustains a semi-official relation to the meeting, was expected to lend material help both ministerial and lay.

Mrs. A. B. Morse, of St. Joseph, Michigan, would have charge of the work among the children, and L. H. Baker would direct the work among the young people.

Samuel Miller became president of the Board in 1901, and H. J. Milbourn was elected secretary, the same year, both residents of Eaton Rapids. The Hon. David B. Hale, another stalwart of the local Methodist Church, was elected president a few years later.

Just prior to the new century, to accommodate the ever-increasing number of faithful members in light of the inadequacy of the boarding house, plans for a hotel in a lively open section of the grounds at the bend of the river were turned over to Seth Fowler. By 1900, at a cost of $400, the building was in use, providing about 30 additional rooms—what is now the center portion of the Grace Hotel—accommodating about 120 campers. The central area of the first floor was the Dining Hall; the east (back) wing was the kitchen; and the whole central area was illuminated by the glassed-in cupola above the roofline. This greatly increased the kitchen-dining room complex, but added so few rooms that, in 1905, a 40-foot extension was added to the north end of the hotel, providing another 20 rooms at a cost of $570, with furnishings costing another $200. A year later a similar extension was built onto the south side. The two wings brought the total accommodations to 64 rooms. With 64 double beds it could now accommodate 128 adults with extra cots free for children.

The 1903 platform speakers included Joseph Smith again, lauded in the brochure like this: "This name has stood at the head of our list of workers for a dozen years, and properly, too, as for more than that length of time Brother Smith has stood in the very fore-front of Holiness teachers and evangelists. Besides, we have tried him, and know him to be a safe leader and thoroughly in sympathy with the policy of the management in pressing Scriptural Holiness according to Wesleyan standards, without unnecessary entanglements with side issues that have a tendency to divide Holiness people. He is expected to be with us during the entire campaign."

Rev. C. F. English would return as well, assisting in the meetings throughout. His work among the young people the previous year "was greatly blest in both conversions and sanctifications. His preaching, singing, and altar work were equal to anything Eaton Rapids has had for years." He would remain the whole camp meeting.

For the first time Bishop E. E. Hoss, D.D., L.L.D., of Nashville, Tennessee, would come and preach Sunday, August 2. Until his election to the Episcopacy, Hoss was the editor of the *Nashville Christian Advocate*, the "great official" of the M. E. Church, South, and was "in every sense a worthy representative of his church."

Rev. W. F. Oldham, D.D., of Chicago, had come to Eaton Rapids the year before for the first time, and was "so much pleased that he delights to come again. He would preach Sunday, July 26, and remain to deliver the missionary address on the Monday following. He hoped to bring with him two or more returned missionaries who would contribute to making missionary day the greatest in our history."

The Rev. W. G. Howson, Pastor of the M. E. church at London, Ontario, would be at camp for its first part, and he was described as "a very fine preacher" and one sometimes called the "Talmadge of Canada." Finally, Mrs. H. C. Scripps, Preceptress of Albion College, would conduct a children's service each day and also hold Junior Workers' Conferences.

Interestingly, the brochure that year also featured two advertisements. The burgeoning attendance had clearly caught the attention of local merchants, suggesting the increasing role it played in the area and the culture. J. F. Knapp, the Knapp Grocery Company, touted their grocery wares. Their ad in part read, "Grand River Camp Ground is a splendid place to spend a few weeks. Does a person good—morally, physically, and spiritually. Our business is along the physical side mostly tying up and delivering to the grounds good, wholesome, clean, and well-kept groceries...." It concludes, "We will do you good in a financial way and can wait on you in a way that will please you while you are a guest in our city. Make your headquarters at our store when down town."

The second advertisement came from Arcana Mineral Springs Bath House: "The Water from these Springs has been pronounced the finest in the world. An absolute cure for Rheumatism, Kidney and Liver Troubles, and other similar ailments. Commodious Bath House in full operation, with Hotel in connection. For full particulars call on or address, W. C. Eslow, Eaton Rapids, Mich."

At camp, attendees enjoyed thriving preaching and fellowship. L. A. Beeks, pastor of a Methodist Episcopal church in the North Indiana Conference, wrote President Callen from Bluffton, Indiana on August 25, 1903, beginning "Dear Bro. Callen":

> After several weeks removed from the Camp Meeting, I am still ready to say it was the greatest meeting I ever attended. I got a new spirit and increased power with greater measures of joy. O bless the dear Lord! Some one (sic) has been kind enough to send me [a] copy of the *Advocate* with a very good account of the meeting in it. I presume it came from you. It is postmarked Kalamazoo. I thank you very much. I have commenced the work of getting my people to go next year. What I shall be able to do I cannot say but will do all I can to get them there. I have met some of our preachers and have urged them to go. I hope we can get many to go. The spirit of true bible religion was there. It was so free from all outside disturbing things. Surely the great head of the church was greatly pleased with such a meeting in his name. He gave evidence of the same by his unmistakable presence. Bro. English was splendid. A man of God and with power. He possesses rare ability.
>
> A great meeting well managed. I hope to see you next year and it may be you can come to our conference next spring.

Keeping the camp rightly directed amid its growth and the day-to-day details of managing the endeavor was a significant concern of all involved. In or just before August of 1904, at a meeting of the Association, Rev. James Hamilton introduced the following resolution, which was unanimously adopted, with the request that the secretary (A. A. Geiger of Springport, Michigan) forward a copy to the *Michigan Christian Advocate*:

> Whereas, We have learned with joy of the appointment of a commission, on aggressive evangelism by the general conference of our church; and
>
> Whereas, The whole work of God declines where Christian perfection is not strongly and explicitly preached, therefore,
>
> Resolved, That this association, representing 20,000 Methodists in the state of Michigan, urge upon this commission the recognition of this great fact, so that in its plans for revival campaigns and in the literature

issued under its auspices, "this central idea of Christianity" may have its proper place.

1904 was an exciting year indeed! In addition to the other speakers, Rev. Henry Clay Morrison, D.D., of Louisville, Kentucky, was one of the platform evangelists. At the time Morris resided in Louisville, Kentucky. This was six years before Morrison would become President of Asbury College.[21]

The ERC brochure that year announced that that year's Revival Conference would be "held under the direction of the commission on Aggressive Evangelism recently authorized and appointed by the General Conference, of which Commission Bishop Mallalieu is President and Dr. Brushingham is Secretary. This conference will be made a very prominent feature of our meeting this year."

C. F. English would visit Eaton Rapids for the third successive year, preaching and conducting the Young People's Meetings. C. W. Winchester, President of Taylor University, would be present for a portion of Camp, and M. C. B. Mason, D.D., that "most eloquent colored minister of our church," would preach Sunday, July 31. Even if the parlance wasn't always the most racially progressive, the practice of pluralistic preaching certainly was, as befitting the universality of the Christian message.

---

[21] For the first time; Morrison held the position during two separate periods.

Spotlight on Joseph H. Smith (1855-1946)

[Biographical Sketch, Drawn from *A Theology of Christian Experience* by Delbert Rose[22]]

Joseph H. Smith lived from 1855 to 1946, one of five sons born to John and Eliza Smith. He was born on June 4 in Pennsylvania. He was very bright and finished his high school studies the same month he turned fifteen. Although raised Presbyterian, he found himself attending the Methodist Episcopal Church, mainly for social reasons. In his 1965 biography of Smith, Delbert Rose explains that after quite a bit of misbehavior in church, Smith sought God privately for eight weeks, sometimes spending much of the night in prayer. Eventually he went to the altar and prayed at ten minutes after nine in the evening, January 29, 1874. That night a friend gave him a copy of J. A. Wood's book *Perfect Love*. That book immediately put Smith on a quest for sanctification.

At that point in his life he was aspiring to become a lawyer, but he felt a call to preach. So he set aside the law books he was studying and started studying the Bible instead. He continued his quest for sanctification, studying the scriptures, reading Wesley's *Plain Account of Christian Perfection* and *Sermons*, and singing from the *Methodist Hymnal*. Two months after his conversion, he claimed to have an experience of entire sanctification. The evangelistically minded pastors in the Philadelphia area called on Smith to go from church to church for the purpose of relating the steps to and in his Christian pilgrimage. He graduated from sharing his testimony to giving sermons, and even on the first occasion of preaching, nineteen people responded with powerful effect. He would always preach with only a skeleton outline of his sermon, but without any notes in hands, a practice he maintained for over sixty years.

He gave serious thought to attending college, but decided to preach instead, feeling God's call to do so. He was sent to Georgia to minister. At this time, ten years after the Civil War, Georgia was still desperately trying to recover from its ravages. Unable to afford a horse, he walked three thousand miles on his circuit to preach his two hundred sermons and perform his other ministries, while supporting himself and his young wife on a very small salary.

He would return to pursue ordination and further preaching opportunities in Pennsylvania. He was so successful as an evangelistic pastor that he came to the attention of the leaders of the National Campmeeting Association for the Promotion of Holiness. He was elected a member of the Association and, before long, felt called by God into full-time evangelistic ministry. He would experience a bout with sickness that required him to rest for a whole year and a half, cutting off his salary, but God provided for all his family's needs.

In 1887 he felt led to attend the Mountain Lake Park Camp Meeting, in Garret County, Maryland, during that summer. Not only were the finances provided to go; he was even given the chance to preach. He preached, experienced healing, and his evangelistic ministry was underway. For the next

---

[22] Delbert R. Rose, *A Theology of Christian Experience: Interpreting the Historic Wesleyan Message* (Minneapolis, Minnesota: Bethany Fellowship, Inc., 1965).

fourteen years Smith served in camp meetings during the summer months and held revival services in various churches the rest of the year. In 1901 his conference officially appointed him conference evangelist, an office he held until he was conferred retirement status in 1923.

Rose writes, "Following his induction into full-time evangelism, at Mountain Lake Park Camp, Smith held meetings in rapid succession at Mt. Pleasant, Ohio; Jacksonville, Illinois; St. Louis, Missouri; McKeesport, Pennsylvania; New York City; Greencastle, Indiana; Philadelphia; Minneapolis, Minnesota; Des Moines, Iowa; and Carthage, Illinois."[23] He would speak ten straight times at the great Ocean Grove camp meeting, sometimes to over 10,000 people at a time. David Updegraff, a prominent Friends' minister, wrote of Smith as "our beloved brother...who is, under God, without a *superior*, in our judgment, as a preacher and a leader of the people." Updegraff was getting headlines in the largest holiness camp meetings of the period—"Pitman Grove, Mountain Lake Park, Ocean Grove, Eaton Rapids, and others," according to Rose.[24]

The largest national and state camp meeting associations early and repeatedly demanded Smith's services, including Sebring Camp and Camp Sychar in Ohio, Des Plaines and Urbana, Illinois, and Eaton Rapids, Michigan. To Smith camp meetings were schools of evangelism for himself and others who attended. "From the Scriptures, observation, and personal experience he was convinced that a successful evangelistic ministry called 'for fellowship and training' in such institutions as the camp meeting."[25] With some telling rhetorical hyperbole, he wrote, "Of a National Camp Meeting in those days, Bish. William Taylor said that 10 days spent by a young preacher amidst such influences and under such preaching was equal to a year's course in a Theological Seminary in his preparation for the work of the Lord." So Smith strived to make camp meeting a "training post" as well as a "soul-saving institution."[26] His vision was to train men as evangelists just as Sunday school teachers were appropriately trained through Chautauqua channels and through the Northfield Bible Conference by D. L. Moody. He believed that the theological seminaries were emphasizing Christian scholarship more than Christian evangelism, and he was convinced that something comparable needed to be done for evangelism—not as a *substitute for* but as a *supplement to* scholarship.

This is why Smith became so well known for the "School of the Prophets," as he conducted these itinerant educational services to equip people to minister and evangelize more effectively. The sessions combined innovative pedagogy with insightful biblical analysis. Smith conducted them in National Holiness Camp Meetings, in conventions and conferences, and in churches large and small from coast to coast. "He took his school to the people rather than ministering mainly to the people who could leave their stations in life to attend

---

[23] Ibid., 96.
[24] Ibid., 97.
[25] Ibid., 99.
[26] Ibid.

some institution in which he taught."²⁷ By 1939 Smith could write, "Now for fifty years the greater part of the summer season has been spent in camp meetings. Twenty-six at Mountain Lake, thirty-six at Eaton Rapids, twenty-five at Sebring, ten at Des Plaines, sixteen at Sychar, six at Indian Springs, and a number of others for shorter or longer ministeries (sic). A few sessions back, Brother H. C. Morrison and I figured and found that we had each spent ten solid years (night and day) of our lifetime on *camp grounds*.

"I have come to view the best of these camps not simply as products and memorials of the great National Holiness Movement; but rather as ARMY POSTS for the great Onward Movement into which this ministry is soon to advance in its recovery of *Evangelism to the churches of our day, and the spread of Sanctifying Truth in those churches whose erring philosophy as to indwelling sin has made them slow to accept it....*"²⁸

So much more could be said of the great Joseph Smith, like his tenure as the sixth president of the National Holiness Association, but suffice it to say Eaton Rapids was well served and set on the right course by this faithful minister for those thirty-six years of his ministry there. The man who skipped college and became an educator; the man whose sermons set the world aflame and never carried a shred of notes into the pulpit; the man whose prodigious and precocious gifts early made him proud, and later whose great Savior made him esteem the other better than himself. Henry Clay Morrison once wrote of Smith that he "is a great preacher of the Word. He is always forceful and clear, never excited, harsh, or dictatorial. He convinces, and draws men to the truth. He puts in the sword, not as the smiting of an angry foe, but with the careful-kindness of a determined surgeon, who will cut out the disease to save the patient...."²⁹

---

[27] Ibid, 106.
[28] Ibid.
[29] Ibid, 108.

Chapter 4

Eaton Rapids *Is*, 1905-1914

No fewer than fourteen speakers are listed for 1905, one of whom was C. J. Fowler, President of what had by then come to be called the National Holiness Association. Fowler would come to Eaton Rapids three other times as well.

This period marked quite a bit of expansion of the grounds—for the purpose of enhancing ministry and making the continued proclamation of the full gospel possible. Additions were built on to both ends of Grace Hotel in 1905. The Deaconess Cottage was built in 1906 (and named the "Sally A. Smith Memorial Cottage")—two doors west of what would be "Workers Lodge" four years later—and would house deaconesses and female missionaries. The visiting bishops, sometimes as many as five or six, were accustomed to staying with the Callens in the Rio Vista Cottage, which became known as "the Bishop's Cottage."

From *Retrospect and Prospect*: "In 1905 [or 1906; reports vary] Iva Durham Vennard had come as leader of the young people. With her winsome manner, her rich contralto voice, her guitar, but most of all her stirring, earnest message, she won their hearts for Christ. Her ministry was so exceptionally fruitful that year after year she returned. Till the end of her ministry she was on call here, returning in the later years to share her missionary insights with the whole camp and challenge the young people to service. D. Willia Caffrey, also from C.E.I. [the Chicago Evangelistic Institute], occasionally took her place.[30] There were a number of years when Dr. Frederick S. Goodrich led the youth. A professor of Bible who never read from it, he knew it entirely by heart. A number of the men who later became president of the camp served the camp as youth leaders: W. G. Nixon, H. D. Skinner, Lloyd H. Nixon, Byron Hahn, and Clarence Hutchens.

"The vigor of these years was, if anything, greater than in the beginning. The camp was still largely under the leadership of charter members, with sons and daughters nurtured in the teaching and experience of holiness growing up to

---

[30] See Dell's book for the connection between Joseph Smith and Vennard, who had been a stenographer at Smith's first Itinerant Institute. She would first found the Epworth Evangelistic Institute in St. Louis in 1902, and later the Chicago Evangelistic Institute in 1910. Smith served as a part-time instructor at the latter, and it served as his base of operations for his Midwest and Eastern evangelistic ministry. See 101.

provide a second and third generation of leadership. . . . New and great pulpit voices were heard: Buddy Robinson with his endearing lisp, W. G. Nixon, Arthur Moore, John Paul, Joseph Owen, John Church. Sprinkled among these were men whose accents or patterns of speech gave their messages added attractiveness: John Thomas of Wales, Harry Jessop from England, Scottish Canadian Peter Wiseman, and, much more recently, Irish Jimmy Gibson."

By 1907, the Forest City sported 75 cottages, and—as a mark of changing times influencing camp practice—that year electricity brought light to the ERC grounds. The electrified cottages were said to be like the Biblical city set on a hill to let its light shine. The next year, Hotel Grace was open from July 1 to September 1, 1908, new electric lights giving it "a charming effect at night."

In 1909 the "Workers' Rest," or "Workers' Lodge,"[31] was built and became ready for occupancy, taking another ten to fifteen occupants. Epworth Youth Chapel was updated and expanded, and a Barber Shop was located on the grounds.

In 1910 "The Old Story in Song #2" was the songbook used, and the following year a roof over two doors on the west side of the Tabernacle was built.

In 1912, the pressure for increased space being a constant factor as the camp grew, plans for a separate building adjacent to the hotel were drawn up. For $2,000, Seth Fowler built the two-story 30 foot by 100 foot dining hall with a one-story kitchen wing (24 x 50). Kitchen workers could now be housed in the two dormitories above the dining hall and be saved the long walk from the old dormitory. The central area of the hotel, formerly the dining room, became a lobby, as well as making possible sixteen or eighteen[32] additional sleeping rooms. The kitchen was used as a store. By 1912, too, over eighty cottages peppered the grounds.

The 1912 brochure brings clarity to an otherwise puzzling matter: when camp meeting really began. An 1887 brochure spoke of the "fourth annual" camp meeting, which would put the first in 1884. But camp meeting is said to have started in 1885, at the old Lansing Fair Grounds, and 1886 and thereafter in Eaton Rapids. The 1912 brochure helps clear this up: "In November, 1883 or 1884, the Rev. James Hamilton, then presiding elder of the Lansing District of the Methodist Episcopal Church, called a revival conference of his district for the purpose of reviving the Methodist doctrine and experience of Holiness. The meeting was held with definite blessings, and as a result an association for the promotion of scriptural holiness was organized. Under its auspices, a camp meeting was held June 13-21, 1885, on the old fair grounds of the city of Lansing, led by workers from the National Association." Owing perhaps to its early and strong relationship with the National Association, ERC was characterized from the start as a "national camp," a self-perception that arguably remained even after the local Association took on its own identity apart from the National Association.

---

[31] First called the "Evangelists' Cottage"
[32] Reports vary.

So here's the chronology: there appears to have been a "revival conference" in 1884. Then the Association developed, and the first "camp meeting" was held at the Lansing Fair Grounds in 1885. So the 1887 brochure started counting camp meetings with the revival conference in 1884, but the Association didn't actually form until after that conference. So, for present purposes, particularly since information on the 1884 revival conference is scant indeed, we will count 1885 as the first camp meeting of the Association, and 1886 as the start of camp meeting in Eaton Rapids.[33]

During those years when there was still a close connection with the Methodist Episcopal Church, bishops of that denomination were regular visitors and preachers.[34] They usually stayed in Callen's cottage by the steamboat landing (now owned by David and Kathleen Ray), which eventually came to be known as The Bishops' Cottage.[35]

Retrospect and Prospect records these paragraphs about this juncture of ERC's history:

> Many who came for the entire camp continued to rent tents and tent floors from the Association and took their meals at the hotel, or, like many of the cottagers, prepared their own. Cottages had been built, a few a year, until now there were more than 80. Some of the occupants had their own transportation, but it was much simpler to buy things on the grounds than to hitch up and make the trip into town. Thus the grocery business, two deliveries of mail daily, laundry picked up and delivered three times a week, and even a barber's cottage brought all the necessary services to the little "City on the hill." The horses, cared for in the barn adjacent to the corral at the site of the present ball park were cared for at local livery prices. Life centered in what was happening on these grounds for ten days with very little to draw one aside. To be sure, the bath houses down below the old sheep dip allowed one to change or to bathe or swim on the hot summer days, but they only made the pitcher-and-bowl baths of the hotels and cottages bearable. Neither swimming nor the use of boats was allowed when services were in session, but many evenings after the service the sounds of laughter and refreshment and their families

---

[33] The 1912 brochure also says this: "The Deaconess cottage will provide free lodging to deaconesses, lady evangelists, and returned missionaries so far as we can accommodate them. To engage rooms write to the clerk of the hotel as above."

[34] In 1906 no less than five bishops from this country and abroad were listed as speakers.

[35] The Methodist Episcopal Church was the development of the first expression of Methodism in the United States, started in 1784, with Francis Asbury and Thomas Coke as the first bishops. By the early 19th century it had become the largest Protestant denomination in the United States. In 1939 it merged with the Methodist Episcopal Church, South, and the Methodist Protestant Church to form the Methodist Church. And in 1968 it merged with the Evangelical United Brethren Church to form the United Methodist Church.

divested themselves of their starched dignity and dove from the big stone or raced each other across the river.[36]

In the beginning Eaton Rapids Camp saw itself as a part of the National Camp Meeting Association and turned to that body for its platform speakers. Before long, however, it became apparent that Eaton Rapids Camp was going to be able to provide its own momentum, draw its own crowds, be fertile ground for its own selected workers. It soon became an honor to be invited to speak from its pulpit.[37]

The opening paragraphs of a 1912 brochure, after surveying the history of ERC until that point, added these lines: "The camp meeting has always been held true to its purpose, the preaching of 'the fullness of the blessing of the gospel of Christ,' free from fanaticism and side issues. Its meetings have been wonderfully blessed with the presence of the Holy Spirit; and at its altars every year many have been saved and many have found the blessings of heart purity. Meanwhile we have steadily improved our grounds, built numerous buildings and closed [the] last few years out of debt. Although under Methodist auspices, we cordially invite to its services everyone irrespective of church affiliation."[38]

1913 also marked significant changes in camp membership, with the passing of W. W. Robinson of Detroit, MI. He had been a cottager upon these grounds every season for many years. Quiet, devout, with a gracious dignity, exemplifying in his daily walk the Wesleyan doctrine of Christian perfection, his presence was a joy and a blessing. As a member of the Board of Trustees, he for years had taken a keen interest in the success and welfare of this camp meeting. For the last three years, he had been superintendent of the Camp Meeting Sunday School.

Also in 1913 a new song book, *The Best of All*, was used. Mrs. E. E. Cuddy of Battle Creek, MI, again presided as matron to the satisfaction of patrons old

---

[36] Note the reference to the big stone there. Eventually it was decided to bury it to make upkeep of the grounds in its vicinity easier.

[37] Although this is true, Eaton Rapids maintained a good working relationship with the national body—as its congenial and long-standing relationship with Joseph Smith shows.

[38] The prior paragraph read like this: "November, 1883 or 1884, the Rev. James Hamilton, then presiding elder of the Lansing District of the Methodist Episcopal Church, called a revival conference of his district for the purpose of reviving the Methodist doctrine and experience of Holiness. The meeting was held with definite blessing, and as a result, [on November 19, 1894, The Lansing District Association for the Promotion of Holiness was formed] an association for the promotion of scriptural holiness was organized. Under its auspices, a camp meeting was held June 13-21, 1885, on the old fair grounds of the city of Lansing, led by workers from the National Association. During this meeting, a Lansing District Camp Meeting Association was organized, and arrangements made to purchase the present camp ground at Eaton Rapids. The first camp meeting was held here the following June (1886) [June 24 – July 4], and one has been held here each year since then. In 1889, the name was changed to The Michigan State Holiness Camp Meeting Association of the Methodist Episcopal Church."

and new. Rev. P. R. Norton of Vicksburg, MI, acted as clerk and financial manager during the camp meeting. Mrs. Cuddy kept the hotel open for guests from July 10 until the latter part of August.

The Association continued encouraging cottage ownership: "Why not build yourself a cottage on these restful grounds? Lots are $15 with $1 a year association tax. You have two years in which to build. The Association requests that all cottage owners name their cottages. Rates for electric light service made known on application to the secretary."[39]

An old map of the grounds dated 1913 shows that Wesley Road used to be called Crescent Avenue, and it shows the dock at the river bank just outside the gate and ticket office. It also marks where the Hitching Posts were (at the top of the map, the River at the bottom), and the location of the corral (upper right portion of the map) and the barns (above the corral). For those interested in details about the cottages peppering the grounds, all the lots are listed by number, and most of their owners are delineated; many of the names of the cottages are included as well. The cottages are divided into 20 Blocks. Names of cottages by Block were as follows:

1: Red; Unique; Crittenden; Roads Inn; Pioneer; Pleasant View
2: Come In and Rest; Ellen K; Glendale; Sleepy Hollow
3: Mizpeh[40]
4: Oakdale; Wright Cottage
6: Hope Cottage; Bangs
13: Worker's Rest; Still Waters; Deaconess Cottage
14: Rio Vista (later called the Bishop's Cottage); Bogardus; Log Cabin; The Oaks
16: Oakwood
17: Sylvan Rest; Doolittle Cottage; Shady Nook; Sweet Rose
18: Washtenong; Uneeda; Snug; Riverside; Venice; Waterborough Inn; Stirling; Sunshine
19: Bethany; Cozy
20: Unity House[41]

In February 1914, W. D. Brainerd died; also in 1914 a brochure featured H. R. E. Quant, the bookstore vendor, describing ERC:

---

[39] Mr. Seth Fowler of Eaton Rapids, MI, was the President of the Board of Trustees, and Rev. M. M. Callen, D.D., Ionia, MI, was President of the Camp Meeting Association.

[40] Spelling is hard to make out.

[41] This history of ERC won't go into much further detail about the cottages on the grounds, but this 1913 map is a good place to start for anyone interested in learning more about them. Another useful resource would be a red and black notebook in the records containing Board minutes from August 1933 to August 1962. A great many of the entries pertain to cottage sales, purchases, transfers, and the like. Specific cottages that have been discussed at least at some length in this volume are Unity House, the Bishop's Cottage, and Worker's Rest.

Sunday, August 2, saw the close of the camp meeting of 1914. Looking over the whole gathering, it can be truly said that this feast of tabernacles was the best meeting of our entire history. Isaiah 25:6 characterizes it well: "In this mountain will Jehovah of hosts make unto all peoples a feast of fat things, a feast of wines on the lees, of fat things full of marrow, of wines on the lees well refined."

The Michigan State Holiness Camp Meeting Association has been operating now for twenty-nine years. At a test made in one of this year's meetings it was found that there were present almost a hundred of those who were in the first camp of the association. While several hundred stood to being there for this their first time. This meeting stands true to name, true to nature, true to purpose. It is a meeting about which one this year said: "A camp on holiness lines that has not been spoiled."

We do not have to say of this. "Eaton Rapids was. No; Eaton Rapids is." When Bishop Oldham visited us a few years ago, he said: "It is the sanest meeting in three states." The place of this camp is an ideal spot. It comprises thirty-three acres of second growth oak and maple. The Grand River skirts the south and western sides. The grounds are fully equipped with necessary buildings, all of which, however, are all too small for the growing crowds that seek their use.

Holiness literature abounds. The book store operates a $1000 stock and sells $650 worth of it. The *Christian Witness*, *Pentecostal Herald*, and our own *Michigan Christian Advocate* have a large place in this meeting. Brother Smith this year made a glowing tribute to the *Advocate*, stating that its readers needed no substitute.

This meeting draws for its attendance on especially the ministry and laity of our two conferences, and the people of Indiana, Ohio, Illinois, and Canada. At least 3,400 people eat daily under its ministry. The work is unexcelled.

Fully 600 persons experienced a definite work of grace, some for conversion, but mostly entire sanctification. This distinctive blessing presented in the Wesleyan way, not only sends back to the home church its people more true to the teachings of Methodism, but sends its people home with a fire of holy zeal for the holy struggles of the year.

The management spares itself no expense or care to provide for the audiences the best Bible teaching that its workers, "under the direction of the Spirit," can give. Rev. Joseph H. Smith, expositor, clear in theology, definite in presentation, sweet in spirit, an interpreter of great acceptability, has been with us almost from the beginning, and almost every year. His question drawer of Friday morning developed on the plan of holiness as to the way, walk, worship, and warfare, was a masterpiece in itself. *Michigan Christian Advocate* readers will note the answers given in future issues.

Rev. Will H. Hough, of Sioux City, Iowa, is an orator, forceful, descriptive, undemonstrative, quiet. His every altar call saw scores in response. Rev. C. D. Hestwood, of Arkansas City, Kansas, the pastor evangelist, was wonderfully endowed of God in the preaching of the Word. We can never forget his "plowing among the stumps," "his kid brother preacher," "the search for Adella," and kindred illustrations wrought from his own experience. Rev. C. H. Holbrook, of Portsmouth, Virginia, was characterized at this camp as the preacher who got to the consciences. His utterances pierced the hearts of men and women like the bullets of an army.

Rev. Isaac H. Hodge, of Wichita, Kansas, the sweet singer of Israel, Southwest Kansas conference evangelist, made our camp deeply feel the blessing of full salvation applied to song. He led the people's meeting with an effectiveness unexcelled by other years. Rev. Frederic S. Goodrich, our brother beloved by Albion College students, was at the head of our young people's work. Brother Goodrich's versatility in the English Bible, experience in state Sunday School evangelism, and all round lover of young people, makes him ideal in his work. And what shall I more say, for the time will fail me if I tell of Mrs. Joseph H. Smith, Mrs. Dr. Griffith, Miss Nellie Snyder, G. W. Ridout, President M. M. Callen, George Bennard, Frank Arthur, Secretary George A. Brown, pastors and their wives, evangelists, returned missionaries, deaconesses, the chorus choir, and the large appreciative audiences, who through faith subdued kingdoms, wrought righteousness, obtained promises, worked at the altar, sang the sweet songs of Zion, and sought and obtained definite experiences...that they might obtain a better resurrection, and these all having attended the greatest meeting that this part of the country knows anything about, are now back in the battlefield of Christian services witnessing for God.

As its third decade was drawing to a close, Eaton Rapids continued to demonstrate its commitment to holiness teaching and revival; its membership was thriving, and its speaker platform was filled with ministers and evangelists dedicated to nourishing attendees with scripture rightly divided. It has persisted in this mission through today only because of the faithful souls remembered above, and the many more—unnamed and unsung—without whose commitment to and faithful completion of the work of Christ Eaton Rapids would have long since disappeared.

Spotlight on George Bennard (1873-1958)
["The Old Rugged Cross"]

George Bennard delivered one of his earliest performances of the beloved hymn "The Old Rugged Cross" in July 1912 at Eaton Rapids, with only his guitar to accompany him. He was born in Youngstown, Ohio, and when Bennard was very young, his family moved to Albia, Iowa, then Lucas, Iowa. He wanted a career in evangelism, but was forced instead to support his mother and sisters when his father died. After marrying, he and his wife worked for the Salvation Army in Illinois, and he later served as an evangelist in America and Canada. Bennard spent his last years in Michigan, where the Chamber of Commerce erected a cross near his home. The Old Rugged Cross Historical Museum in Reed City, MI, commemorates his work. Bennard's works include: *Bennard's Melodies*; *Revival Classics* (Albion, Michigan: The Bennard Music Company, circa 1935); *Divine Praise* (Chicago, Illinois: The Rodeheaver Company, 1926); and *Full Redemption Songs* (Chicago, Illinois: The Rodeheaver Company, 1933). Although he wrote the lyrics for over two dozen hymns, none was more memorable than this one:

"THE OLD RUGGED CROSS"

On a hill faraway stood an old rugged cross,
The emblem of suffering and shame;
And I love that old cross where the dearest and best
For a world of lost sinners was slain.

So I'll cherish the old rugged cross,
Till my trophies at last I lay down;
I will cling to the old rugged cross,
And exchange it some day for a crown.

Oh, the old rugged cross, so despised by the world,
Has a wondrous attraction for me;
For the dear Lamb of God left His glory above
To bear it to dark Calvary.

In the old rugged cross, stained with blood so divine,
A wondrous attraction for me;
For t'was on that old cross Jesus suffered and died
To pardon and sanctify me.

To the old rugged cross I will ever be true,
Its shame and reproach gladly bear;
Then He'll call me some day to my home far away,
Where His glory forever I'll share.

> So I'll cherish the old rugged cross,
> Till my trophies at last I lay down;
> I will cling to the old rugged cross,
> And exchange it some day for a crown.

In late 1912 Bennard sold the song for $200, as his wife was expecting and they needed the funds to support the growing family. Upon the renewal of the copyright around 28 years later, he received a final payment of $5,000. After its introduction, the hymn quickly spread throughout the region and came to the attention of the evangelist Billy Sunday, who frequently used it in his meetings.

"The Old Rugged Cross" remains one of the most popular and beloved hymns in the Christian tradition. One mark of its popularity is the number of recording artists who have produced renditions of the song—ranging from the likes of Johnny Cash to Mahalia Jackson to Willie Nelson. Stemming from the life of an itinerant evangelist, running through the history of Eaton Rapids and so many other camp meetings, with the persistent message of the power of the gospel, "The Old Rugged Cross" continues to captivate congregations across America and around the world even still today.

Part III

Between the Wars

1915-1944: America between the Wars

Intensifying imperialistic, territorial, and economic rivalries in Europe during late nineteenth century, particularly among Germany, France, Great Britain, Russia, and Austria-Hungary, led to the outbreak of World War I on July 28, 1914. America was able to remain neutral until 1917, when it entered on the Allied side, supporting Britain and France. The scale of the conflict alone, involving thirty-two countries, unsettled the nation and the world. And the devastation wrought by modern technology—such as machine guns, chemical warfare, and tanks—dampened much of the previously felt optimism about the advances human innovation could bring to civilization. Although American losses were much lower than other nations, due to its late entry in the war, the nation still mourned over 350,000 servicemen.

The 1920s, in many ways, served as a recuperation from the trauma. The country was financially prosperous, leading to the decade's nickname of "The Roaring Twenties." Advancements in civil rights were gained by way of the NAACP and the suffragette movement, with the passage of the Nineteenth Amendment giving women the right to vote. The 20s also marked a shift in social mores: women's clothing became less cumbersome and restrictive, courtship customs loosened up to allow more freedom in developing relationships without an intrusive chaperone, jazz became a popular art form that encouraged night life in American cities. Women not only voted for the first time but also became increasingly involved in education and the workforce.

Several intellectual currents from the mid to late nineteenth century became more and more influential during these early years of the twentieth and encouraged the culture's move from traditional ways of thought and life: Marxism, Darwinism, and Freudianism. Marx's work, in particular, was important for its contribution to the 1917 Russian Revolution, an event that would set the terms for American-Russian relations during the twentieth century and beyond. In America, Darwinism was brought center stage during the Scopes Trial of 1925 in which the state of Tennessee prosecuted substitute high school teacher John Scopes for teaching evolution at a state-funded school. The trial itself quickly escalated into a media circus, with both sides encouraging histrionics in and out of the courtroom. The outcome of the trial was overshadowed by the public perception that resulted: religion and science seemed very much at odds—however untrue this was historically and factually.

Sigmund Freud's psychoanalysis echoed much the same theme in a different key. Understanding the human self as centered in the unconscious, Freud argued that repressing one's desires, primarily sexual desires, leads to neuroses and that emotional well-being could be obtained only by recognizing and overcoming their inhibitions. Although Freud's seminal work was published around the turn of the century, not until leading intellectual expatriates returned from Europe equipped with his theories were they popularized in the United States. These ideas infiltrated literature in particular with writers like William Faulkner and Gertrude Stein intentionally employing Freudian elements in virtually all their work.

While these intellectual influences permeated American culture, incrementally inching it toward secularity, another—more urgent—upheaval was taking place, this time in the nation's stock market. On October 24, 1929, stocks dropped drastically, setting off a chain of events that led to bankruptcies and defaults across the nation. The shockwaves of this crash were felt for years, with the economy grinding to a standstill and people struggling to survive. At its lowest ebb, unemployment during the Great Depression reached upwards of 25%. The population of America shifted, too, as a result, with many people relocating for work. Not until World War II and the increased production required for America's entrance into it would the country bounce back financially.

Chapter 5

War Years, 1915-1924

The first tabernacle, even with the extensions, had long been inadequate. On June 2, 1916, the trustees received Dr. Callen's gift of $2,500 toward a new tabernacle as a memorial to his wife. The Reverend H. D. Skinner presented the plans. At the next recorded meeting, a committee including Seth Fowler was charged with the execution of the plans drawn up by his youngest son. On July 29, just 57 days later, Seth Fowler presented his bill for the completed structure in the amount of $3,664.23.[42] Only $822.23 was still needed. The new building was completed and in use. On Sunday afternoon, all the debt having being raised, Joseph H. Smith preached the dedicatory sermon. For the first time in many years, the seating capacity of 3,000 was nearly enough, though many families still spread blankets under the trees where babies could nap and little children move about. Henry Clay Morrison and E. Stanley Jones joined Smith on the platform.

Many more of the speakers were coming from the pastorate, men like S. H. Turbeville, Paul Reese, Lloyd Nixon, George Failing, Paul Kindschie, Dee Cobb, and Stimson Smalley. The theme, however, was unchanging with "no side issues, no fanaticism." In the prayer-saturated life of the camp, great manifestations of the Spirit of God were the rule, not the exception.

During camp meeting of 1916, on July 31, just two days after Fowler presented his completed bill, an entry, rife with grandiose claims by today's standards, was made in the aforementiomyumned W.F.M.S. Secretary Book: "The anniversary of the W.F.M.S. [Women's Foreign Missions Society] and W.H.M.S. [Women's Home Missions Society] Auxiliaries of the Camp Ground was held in the Tabernacle, Monday afternoon, July 31, Mrs. Hallenbeck presiding. After the usual opening exercises . . . by Miss Williams, Dr. Geo. Eliott was introduced as the speaker for the occasion, on Home Missions. He began by saying there are two propositions before us which hang together—namely. We never shall thoroughly save heathen lands until we more thoroughly save our Christendom, and the greatest obstacle in pagan lands is the wickedness of so-called Christian lands. He further said that we Americans have the key. We are the center of the world today. Obeying the command of Christ to begin

---

[42] One source says $3,662.23.

at God's Jerusalem and work to the edges. If America fails Him God has failed. But no! America *shall not fail*! The reason we do not take the world for Christ is because we think more of business than of the Bible, more of commerce than of Christ."

As World War I wore on, making its mark throughout American society, war prices in the cafeteria were used in 1918 as a means of breaking even. No tents were available after 1919, due to drop-off in usage. Someone could bring their own tent, and free space was available to pitch the tent. Floor boards were also available for $1.00.[43]

In 1920 the "Rio Vista" was residence for the Bishops, given to ERC by the Callens. Lots were $15.00; rent was $1.00 per year. The "Mother's Rest" was located on the front porch of Wade Memorial (New Dormitory Building), and the Youth Program was made "a special department this year," led by W. G. Nixon.

The Best of All songbooks would be used again in 1921. At camp in 1922, Lloyd Nixon from Jonesville, MI, led the choir of 100. Howard Skinner was invited to assist. Emma Perrine of Tekonsha, MI, played the piano. "One of the most promising young preachers" was working with young people and in the music ministry, namely, David E. Reed from Albion.

The invitation in the 1922 brochure is too delightful not to pass along: "To visit these charming grounds is to be enamored by the beauty. Virgin forest trees furnish cooling shade. Breezes from the waters of the flowing river, the panoramic beauty of the landscape, with the quiet, restful life combine to make this place an Ideal Retreat. Our Camp Meeting is acknowledged to be the largest and best in all the middle-west. Of all the thirty-six years of mountain-top illumination, last year stood out above them all—the high point of holy, quiet waiting with the Master, the pinnacles of saintly fellowship, the richest in sweet harmony. This year a fine corps of workers have been secured. Accommodations are ample. Auto transportation admits of a large attendance. This is Michigan, remember, super roads![44] This is the Camp Meeting to attend because it keeps the fires of Pentecostal Evangelism aglow. It is free from fanaticism. Its aim is the highest New Testament Standard or Experience and Holy Living as taught by John Wesley. Ten days spent at Eaton Rapids may work an Epoch in your spiritual experience. Certainly it will fit you for more and better service. The management hope this year will find you among the friends of this great Camp Meeting."

In 1923 Dr. William G. Nixon, who had been President of the Simpson Park Camp Meeting in Romeo, MI, since 1908, also became President of ERC and

---

[43] The Association would furnish electric current to cottagers at the following rates: For two weeks of camp meeting season, 3 lights or less, 25 cents each; additional lights, 15 cents each. By the month, 37½ cents each. Additional lights, 22½ cents each. The Camp grocery store changed from the rear of Grace Hotel to the Dorm Building, on Wesley Road, across from the Tabernacle. The front room of the Dorm Building was a room where mothers brought their tired and hungry children, to have a space and privacy to take care of the children.

[44] Well, not everything stays the same.

continued in both posts until his death in 1926. At that time Howard D. Skinner became President and continued until 1933, when Lloyd Nixon began a tenure that would last until 1952.

Simpson Park Camp is the state's oldest camp, even older than Eaton Rapids. It started in 1865 and is still going strong. It too is a holiness camp, and has had a strong relationship with Eaton Rapids through the years, sharing many participants, preachers, even—as just noted—a President! It's named in honor of the nationally respected Methodist bishop, Matthew Simpson. Simpson was a close friend and confidant of Abraham Lincoln. The president is said to have attributed his Emancipation Proclamation to Simpson's influence. Later, Simpson would lead the eulogy at Lincoln's graveside.

Another telling passage from the W.H.M.S. and W.F.M.S. notebook can be found from 1924, where it's recorded that the annual anniversary of the auxiliaries was held Monday afternoon, July 28, with Mrs. Hallenbeck, President of Home Society, presiding. "After singing a couple of songs and prayer by Mrs. Hallenbeck, Mrs. W. M. P. Jerrett of Jackson gave an interesting and inspiring address on the work of the H.M.S. among the immigrants. This was followed by an address by E. Stanley Jones of India, on his work in India. It was certainly an inspiring address and made us all feel that we wanted to do more for India. He said Jesus was not the Son of the East nor the Son of the West but the Son of Man. [He] said if we had no interest in the foreigner we would find ourselves foreigners on the other side. He went to India out of pity but stayed out of respect."

In retrospect this was a simply remarkable decade in Eaton Rapids Camp history. It featured, among many other extraordinary events, a year in which Henry Clay Morrison, Joseph Smith, and E. Stanley Jones all shared the platform, with George Bennard leading the music to boot. A remarkable confluence congregated at the river's bend of prodigious talent, consecrated servants, prayerful crowds, and divine anointing.

Spotlight on E. Stanley Jones (1884-1973)

["The Christian Answer to Suffering" by E. Stanley Jones,
Asbury College Radio Program[45]]

I'm going to talk to you this morning about the Christian answer to suffering, merited and unmerited. It's a world of suffering and getting worse. It's going to steal into many a heart and embitter it, and we have to be able to answer this question. Suffering, not answer it as a verbal thing but as a vital thing. I can understand merited suffering. It's a world of moral consequence. I am free to choose, but I am not free to choose the results of my choosing. Those results are in hands not my own. It's a world where I don't break the laws of God; I break myself on the laws of God. Action is followed by reaction, and it's according to the quality of the action that determines the quality of the reaction. I can understand that I must reap what I sow. If I do wrong, the consequences of that wrong are going to come back on me, unless of course God steps in and takes it on himself and bears it and delivers me of the consequences of my wrong through forgiveness and the new birth. I can understand merited suffering, but what about this unmerited suffering? Why should people suffer when they don't do wrong? Other people do wrong, and the consequences of that wrongdoing hit the innocent. Why should little children suffer? This war, very few people chose it, and yet here we are in a world of suffering because of the sin of not many but a few. It's at the place of unmerited suffering that the mind of man reels and sometimes rebels.

Differing systems coming to this whole question give differing answers. One answer is the Greek answer, the Stoic. He said, "My head might be bloody, but it will be unbowed under the bludgeonings of chance." He would match his inner courage against the circumstances of life. It was a noble creed. Good, but not good enough. Then there's the answer of Omar Khayyam, the great Persian poet. He said he'd like to take the steam of things entire and smash it and remake it according to the heart's desire. It's lovely poetry, but you and I can't take hold of the steam of things entire and smash it. We have to work out our destiny under things as they are in large measure. Margaret Fuller once said, "I accept the universe," and Carlyle's comment was, "Gad, she'd better." There's nothing else to be done.

The ancient Buddha had his answer. He sat under the Bodhi tree at Gaya and pondered long and deep upon the problem of suffering and came to the conclusion that existence and suffering are one. As long as you're in existence, you're in suffering. The only way to get out of suffering is to get out of existence, and the only way to get out of existence is to get out of action. The only way to get out of action is to get out of desire. At the root of desire, even for life, as we stop the weed of existence from turning round, and then you go out into that passionless, actionless state called Nirvana, the state literally of the

---

[45] E. Stanley Jones, "The Christian Answer to Suffering," originally aired May 23, 1943, *Asbury Digital Collections*, accessed December 29, 2015, https://www.asbury.edu/offices/library/archives/current-projects/digital-collections/1940s-radio-programs.

snuffed out candle. I asked a Buddhist monk once whether there was any existence in Nirvana. He laughed and asked, "How could there be? There's no suffering, and if there's no suffering, there can be no existence." In Buddha we get rid of the problems of life by getting rid of life. We would get rid of our headaches by getting rid of our heads. Too big a price.

The Hindu has his answer. He says that the thing that comes upon you from without isn't from without really. It's the result of your sins of a previous birth. They're finding you out now. Whatever is, is just. So where there is suffering, there has been antecedent sin. A Hindu said to me one day Jesus must have been a terrible sinner in a previous birth because he was such a terrible sufferer in this one. According to the strict law of karma, that's right. But I would suspect a premise that brought me to that conclusion.

The Mohammaden has his answer. He says that which comes from without is the will of God. Everything that happens is God's will; bend under it. Islam literally means submission to the will of God. But I question whether everything that happens is the will of God. If so, what kind of a God is there? His character is gone. When I turn to the Old Testament, I find several answers. One is, "No plague will come neigh your dwelling. Only with your eyes will you behold and see the reward of the wicked." In other words, the righteous will be exempt. The Old Testament prophets had difficulty in fitting that in with the facts of life. They saw that the righteous did suffer. They were puzzled.

When we come to the New Testament, a great many Christians give the Mohammaden answer: "It's the will of God, bend under it. Accept it as the will of God." Others give the answer that the righteous will be exempt. Oh, I grant you that they are exempt from a good many things that come upon other people. They know how to live better in a universe of this kind. They're not breaking their shins on the system of things all the time. They know how to live better in a universe of this kind. But they're subject to other sufferings which do not come upon the unrighteous. The world demands conformity: if you fall beneath its standards, it will punish you. If you rise above its standards, it will persecute you. It demands a grey, average conformity. But the Christian is a departure upward. His head is lifted above the multitude. Therefore, that head gets whacked. And if it doesn't get whacked, well, it's not above the multitude. "Woe unto you," said Jesus, "when all men speak well of you." You're like them. If you're different, you get hurt.

A man said in one of my roundtable conferences in India, he said, "You know I've lost my faith. I asked God for something anybody could have answered. My brother was wounded in the last war. I prayed that he might get well and might be spared. And when he wasn't spared and he died, my faith died too." A professor walked across the street in Chicago and was knocked down by a motor truck, leg broken. After many weeks in the hospital, he came back to the university chapel service and said, "I no longer believe in a personal God. Had there been a personal God, he would have whispered to me when he saw me in that danger. But he didn't whisper to me, so when my leg was broken, my faith was broken." These converge upon one idea, namely if you're only righteous, you'll be spared. And when they weren't spared, their faith crashed.

Well, let's look at it. Suppose that were true, what would happen? First of all, to religion. Well, we'd take out religion, as you'd take out a fire insurance policy. You'd say, "I want to get through the fires of suffering, and therefore, I've become religious to be exempt." And religion would be degraded to the level of a fire insurance policy—no more, no less. Besides, what would happen to the character of the universe? The universe would soon become an undependable universe. You wouldn't know what to expect. If a good man leaned over the parapet too far, the law of gravitation would be suspended. If a bad man leaned over too far, he would need an operation. You wouldn't know whether the laws of nature would be in operation or suspension because you wouldn't know the character of the person concerned. Now I know if I lean over the parapet too far, the law of gravitation isn't going to ask whether I'm good, bad, or indifferent; it's going to pull me down. So I don't lean over too far. It's a hard school, but I know the rules.

Suppose it could be proved that motor trucks would not knock you down, what would happen to the character of the righteous? Well they'd become the champion jaywalkers of the world. They'd roam around amid the traffic meditating and vegetating. And that quickness of decision which comes from a world of chance and circumstance would be taken away, and that elimination would be their exemption. Now when I walk across the road, I know if I don't belong to the quick, then I will belong to the dead. So I watch, both ways. I belong to the quick. No, that's not the answer. If that were the answer, the righteous would be the petting child of the universe, and the petting child is always the spoiled child.

What, then, is the Christian answer? It's none of these. But it's more wonderful than all of these put together. It's this. That you can take hold of suffering and sorrow and frustration and injustice and not bear it, but use it. Almost everything beautiful in the pages of the New Testament has come out of something ugly. Almost everything glorious has come out of something shameful. They don't ask to be exempt. They don't ask to be taken out of suffering. All they ask is inner soundness of spirit so they can take hold of the raw materials of human life as it comes to them—justice and injustice, pleasure and pain, compliment and criticism. And they can take it up into the purpose of their lives and transmute it and make it into something else. That is an open possibility of living—in spite of.

I know a man who went out to China on an adventure of service and love for his master, he and his family. And they came back from China a shattered, battered remnant of that campaign for Christ. The father caught an infection of the eye, which left him blind. The mother died of a painful illness, cancer— long, lingering illness. One son died of Addison's Disease; another got an abrasion upon the heel on a sports field and died from that infection. The daughter was stricken with infantile paralysis and hobbles around on crutches. The only remaining son had to give up his course at the seminary to undergo a major operation. But on an airfield in Miami, Florida, at midnight, he took me by the hand and said, "I'm proud of my family." And well he might be.

What happened to that family? The only two remaining ones at home were the father, blind, and the daughter, a cripple. Between them, they had a seeing-eye dog and a pair of crutches to come back to life with. Were they beaten? Oh, no. The father has a church where he is on the pastorate, preaches all over the country evangelistic sermons with his seeing-eye dog. And the daughter organizes the games of the church, hobbling around on crutches, and keeps house for her father, still hobbling on her crutches. Between them, they have a seeing-eye dog and a pair of crutches. Oh, no. They have an unconquerable spirit. No wonder that boy at midnight said to me, "I'm proud of my family." Well he might be. You see, they've taken hold of injustice, apparent injustice, and turned it into victory.

General Chiang Kai-shek and Madame Chiang are wonderful people. I was talking to Madame Chiang one day in China, and I said to her, "Is General Chiang a real Christian?" She said, "Yes, he is. He reads his Bible every day and prays, gets strength from God." But then she turned to me and said, "You must remember that he's only a babe in Christ." It was interesting. He was seated right there, and his wife was saying that he was only a babe in Christ. How did he become a Christian? Three influences really helped him to be a Christian. One was his mother in law. You can chalk that up in favor of the mother in laws who are so often maligned. Sometimes we should call them mothers in love. The second influence was a Negro evangelist who prayed for a child in that home where Chiang Kai-shek was, and the child was healed. . . . And the third influence was a doctor.

When Chiang Kai-shek's army swept across that country, in the early days, there was a communist left wing, and they looted a hospital belonging to a missionary left with a shell, his life work went to pieces. But he followed after the army and tended to their sick and their wounded. When Chiang Kai-shek heard about it, he said, "What makes that man follow after and tend to the sick and wounded of the very people who looted his hospital? What makes him do it?" And they said, "He's a Christian. That's why he does it." Then said Chiang Kai-shek, "If that's what it means to be a Christian, I'm going to be a Christian." Then, in the midst of an anti-Christian movement that was sweeping that country, to the astonishment of everybody, Chiang Kai-shek announced that he was a Christian. That doctor had calamity come upon him, but through that calamity, he showed his spirit. And through the revelation of that spirit, he won one of the greatest men of this age. And through him, it may win a great nation. You see, he took hold of injustice and turned it into something else. He had mastered a way to live. And it may be that through your suffering and frustration and defeat, you can show a spirit, and that spirit will do far more work than all your years of work. They'll look through that little revelation, and they'll see something eternal abiding in that moment. That's the Christian answer. The Christian answer is to take hold of everything and make it into something else. That is victory.

Chapter 6

Depression Years, 1925-1934

"The kindliest thing God ever made,/His hand of very healing laid/ Upon a fevered world, is shade./ This is God's hospitality,/ And whoso rests beneath a tree/ Hath cause to thank Him gratefully."

In 1926, five months before his death, the Rev. W. G. Nixon, President of ERC, gave a sermon entitled "The Victory Life," or "How to Keep in the Will of God," drawing from I Thessalonians 3:12-13. A full copy of the sermon is in the ERC records, and we share it in the appendix. It provides a real sense of the flavor and force, terminology and tone, of sermons from a bygone age, even while its convicting content and persuasive power is as relevant as ever as it reverberates the theme of holiness and heart cleansing.

Camp meeting 1927 used a new song book *Divine Praise*, edited by Rev. George Bennard, author of "Old Rugged Cross." Dr. W. G. Nixon had died December 18, 1926, not long after he preached that sermon, and a Memorial Service was held at the Saturday afternoon services during the 1927 ERC Camp Meeting on July 30.

This inspired greeting emblazoned on the 1927 camp meeting brochure reads:

> When the people gathered for the 1919 Camp Meeting, they were greatly shocked by the message that their President, Dr. M. M. Callen, had been called to "the church triumphant," which is before the throne of God.
>
> When we meet in 1927, we will bow our heads in submission to the Great Head of the church, because another of God's spiritual giants, our beloved President, Dr. W. G. Nixon, has been translated to the Paradise of God.
>
> "Servant of God, well done/Thy glorious warfare's past./ The battle's fought,/ the victory's won,/ And thou are crowned at last."
>
> God has wonderfully blessed the Eaton Rapids camp meeting in the salvation of thousands of precious souls. Many there have heard the call

of God to special work as missionaries, deaconesses, preachers, evangelists, and consecrated workers in every field. The holy fire has spread from these altars to scores of local churches. A great evangelist has stated that he had known as many as thirty-two revivals to occur as the outcome of a single camp meeting. When Charles, the son of Bishop Simpson, was dying a few months after he had been converted at a camp meeting, he turned to his weeping mother and said, "Mother, I shall thank God through all eternity, for the Vineland camp meeting."

In a June 1, 1930, article from *The Lansing State Journal*, the headline read, "Holiness Campmeeting Maintains Popularity." The article reported that the first day average attendance was "about normal, with 2,000 in attendance," and the "largest collection on record." Note that this was in the immediate aftermath of the Stock Market crash of 1929. Camp meeting that year was memorable, described in the article like this:

> Eaton Rapids has always had a rich program of able preachers. This year has been no exception. Rev. Paul Rees is perhaps the most able young preacher in camp meeting work today. The association has waited four years to secure him as a worker. Mr. Rees spends his winters in Detroit in a great inter-denominational work and also broadcasts every Sunday morning from 9:30 to 10:00 from station WJR, Detroit. He will be heard at the camp each day throughout the week.
>
> Rev. Joseph H. Smith has returned to the camp for the thirty-seventh year. Each morning at eight o'clock he conducts a School of the Prophets which is a most interesting feature of the camp.
>
> Rev. J. L. Brasher, D.D., until recently president of John Fletcher College, is one of the strong Bible expositors of the country who will be gladly heard at Eaton Rapids. He is preaching daily.
>
> Miss Mary Vennard, of Chicago Evangelistic Institute, is conducting a children's hour every morning at 9:00 am.
>
> Rev. Lloyd Nixon, of Grand Rapids, is leading the great congregation in songs at each service. Miss Ester Mary Atkinson, until recently, of Taylor University, is presiding at the piano.
>
> A large number of young people are in attendance with representatives of various schools, such as Asbury College, Taylor University, Chicago Evangelistic Institute, Cleveland Bible Institute, and John Fletcher College. The young people have an attractive place in which to worship in the newly redecorated Epworth Chapel. Through the generosity of Mr. Austin of Jackson, MI, the chapel has been redecorated and refurbished and remodeled into a commodious and beautiful auditorium.

The camp meeting, this year, has one of the most outstanding lady evangelists in the world. The Reverend Miss D. Willa Caffray, D.D., has preached the gospel of Jesus Christ from the Atlantic to the Pacific. She has recently returned from a two-year tour of the Orient and South America. She expects to leave soon for Africa to evangelize there.

Miss Caffray's varied traveling experiences added to her winsome youth loving personality make her a young people's worker, who is much in demand. She is broadminded, Christian, and sympathetic. Dr. Caffray is to speak to the young people at the camp every afternoon at four o'clock.

The attendance at last Sunday's meetings is reported as about the average. The collection last Sunday, regardless of the security of money, was the largest in the history of the organization for the first day. All bills have been paid and the association is in fine financial condition.

The program for next Sunday is as follows: 6 am, sunrise service; 9 am children's and adult services; 10 am and 2 pm the regular preaching service; 4 pm, young people's hour; and at 7:30 pm regular evening preaching service.

The following officers were elected at their annual business meeting for the coming year: President, Rev. H. D. Skinner, Muskegon; vice-president, Rev. L. H. Nixon, Grand Rapids, MI; second vice president, Rev. George Brown, Leslie; third vice-president, Mrs. Bertha Rush, Delton; secretary and treasurer, Miss Wheeler, Charlotte.

The year before, from a September 1929 issue of the *Michigan Christian Advocate* came these inspiring words from D. D. Martin:

As the masses gathered in the great Callen Tabernacle again this year, we were led to ask what is the magnet that draws and holds the crowd at this camp? There is natural beauty to be sure, and it never appeared at better advantage than this year. The river views were charming in their attraction, the forest of large native oak, elm, and maple was never more verdant. Many of the cottages had been painted, some rebuilt. The hotel and dining room each had an air of cleanliness, as though somebody cared. The bookstand was filled with the latest from the religious press, and eager purchasers eclipsed all previous years in the distribution of good literature. But there are other places where all these things abound, and in these days of speed and comfort of travel all could have found them.

There must be something more than these attractions of beauty and comfort which brings the crowd to Eaton Rapids with an apparent eagerness for the service and a willingness to pay the bills, so that a free will offering without pressure paid all the bills, including salary and expense of caretaker, upkeep of grounds, and all cost of talent and program. Much credit is due the conservative good sense of the management, who in quietness of brotherly love handle every phase of the encampment with precision and care that makes it attractive. Reverend M. D. Skinner is known in Michigan Methodism for having that type of wisdom that has made his ministry unbroken in its effectiveness. His presidency is a contributing element in the success of the meeting.

After all that we have mentioned we are compelled to the conclusion that it is the service from the Tabernacle platform that wins and holds the attention. This year may not be an exception to many other years, but it seems that the preaching was so divinely human and rich that souls hunger for real Gospel.[46] Commissioner Samuel Brengle, of Boston, has had a long experience in dealing with people in morals and religion; Rev. Joseph H. Smith has thought long and preached much on the deeper truths; Rev. Paul Rees, of Detroit, is a preacher of power, he will be one of the leaders next year; Rev. George Bennard wrote his name high in the esteem of all lovers of Christ, in "The Old Rugged Cross"; Rev. Raymond Browning moved the throngs with a sincere appeal; Mrs. I. D. Vennard, who knows young people, drew and held them with her messages of love and power; these all with a multitude of others gave their best to a series that will long be remembered. Rev. Lloyd Nixon grows in favor each year as a song leader and has the support of a large chorus, while Professor Howard Skinner, Jr. never disappoints at the grand piano. The two Sunday morning sermons, one by Brother Rees and the other by Brother Smith, were pronouncements well worth the entire cost of this year's camp. Other sermons and addresses measured well. The whole series was effective and closed in triumph, with a fine record of added names to the Kingdom. All will serve their best elsewhere while looking forward to another season at this hallowed camp.

H. R. E. Quant, the builder and manager of the first bookstore on the ERC campgrounds, died in 1930. Also in 1930, the year after the Stock Market Crash of 1929, the first Sunday collections were as follows: Morning: $503.07. Evening: $107.20. EV: $63.55. Total: $673.82.

In the 1930 presidential greeting, Howard D. Skinner said this: "For forty five years Eaton Rapids Camp Meeting has stood for a biblical emphasis upon the Pentecostal implication. We are ready to join hands with any and all churches that desire to celebrate this nineteenth hundredth anniversary of the day that means so much in the lives of the followers of Christ. *The Christ of*

---

[46] Here a line read, "Teaching was here gratified," which may have been a typo, or just unfortunate wording; either way it's relegated to a footnote.

Every Road, by E. Stanley Jones, presents so clearly the indisputable necessity of the Pentecostal experience for the equipment of Christian workers. 'Tarry until ye be endued.'"

Skinner then exhorted Christians to seek to be thus endued, the need for which is so evident in our churches, he wrote, noticeably in the decreased missionary offerings and in the few attending prayer meetings. He then quoted Bishop Oldham that the "only remedy is for the church to hear the voice of Jesus. Then wouldst thou see that not great buildings and mighty institutions alone, not talks of a splendid past, but having a clean heart, filled with the Holy Spirit, and a flaming zeal for the souls of men—that in these are thy strength, thy promise for a better future. Having been trusted with a great program for a world redemption, how important that pastors and people should receive this cleansing."

Skinner concluded, "Eaton Rapids campmeeting stands for this work of grace and here this year, as in other years, scores will receive this precious anointing. Then pray and plan to be present."

No brochure was printed for 1932. The Board of Directors in its minutes stated: "A mimeographed letter should take the place of the printed circular." $641.00 was still unpaid from 1931 pledges.

The legendary E. Stanley Jones made the trek to Eaton Rapids for the third time in 1933. Two of the speakers in 1934 were Paul Rees and S. H. Turbeville, each of whom wrote a greeting for the brochure anticipating camp meeting that year. Reese wrote, "To the Friends of Eaton Rapids, Lovers of the best things, all! I join with you in the earnest prayer that our 1934 gathering shall be notable and memorable for its spiritual quality and evangelistic effectiveness. May the breath of God—the living, quickening, cleansing Holy Spirit—blow fresh and strong and full upon us all and in us all. Our salvation does not lie in slogans, but some slogans are too good to let go. So I subscribe myself as, Heartily yours to 'spread Scriptural holiness' at Eaton Rapids and everywhere."

Turbeville's kindred and resonant message went like this: "The fame of Eaton Rapids Camp Meeting is worldwide. To the lovers of full salvation it has been and is easily one of the great Camps of the Whole Country. Its merit has been established by devout and wise. . . control holding tenaciously in its preachment to scriptural holiness."

In its fourth decade, Eaton Rapids continued to prove its staying power, weathering one of the most difficult periods economically in the history of the United States. While it's true that accommodations had to be made, such as reducing printing and other costs, and financial challenges like unpaid pledges accounted for, the camp's steadfast commitment to the holiness message and to fostering a community of believers for edification of the saints both enabled and fortified the ministry on the grounds, no matter the challenges faced.

Spotlight on Henry Clay Morrison (1857-1942)
[Biographical Sketch]

Henry Clay Morrison was born in 1857, and died in 1942 (a century after a Tennessee Methodist bishop from Tennessee also named Henry Clay Morrison was born). In 1904 he was 47 and one of the ablest holiness teachers, a "most eloquent preacher" scheduled to be at Eaton Rapids a few days and to preach each day while in attendance.

By his ministry's end, Morrison would be a Methodist evangelist, a writer, an editor, college president, founder of Asbury Theological Seminary, and a staple of camp meetings across the nation. Reared in Kentucky by his paternal grandfather, Morrison was converted at the age of 11 in a Methodist revival at the Boyd's Creek Meetinghouse near Glasgow, Kentucky. After experiencing a call to the ministry, he was licensed to preach at the age of 19 and began his work as circuit rider and station pastor.

In 1890 Morrison moved into evangelism. He also began editing a religious publication called *The Old Methodist*, which later became the widely read *Pentecostal Herald*. Morrison's reputation as a Methodist evangelist grew rapidly from his home state of Kentucky to most other states and many foreign countries. The camp meeting became one of his favorite evangelistic venues, and throughout the rest of his life he gave much time and effective leadership to this religious movement.

Morrison was Dennis Kinlaw's father's favorite evangelist at the Indian Springs camp meeting in Georgia. It is reported that William Jennings Bryan regarded Morrison to be "the greatest pulpit orator on the American continent." Like Dennis Kinlaw more recently, Morrison would serve one tenure as Asbury College president, leave the position, and be asked to assume the presidency for a second term later. Morrison served fifteen years in his first term, and seven more years in his second; in 1923 he was also instrumental in founding Asbury Theological Seminary, which became a separate institution (from Asbury College) in 1940. Morrison also published 25 books, all directed toward laymen.

John L. Brasher, the noted preacher, later in life once told Dennis Kinlaw, when Kinlaw was just a student at Asbury, a story about Morrison. Brasher told the young Kinlaw of a time at a camp meeting when he and Morrison were both preaching. Brasher preached on a beautiful Sunday morning, and described it as one of those special occasions when he preached, to a full tabernacle, better than he was capable of preaching. That night Morrison preached on Moses giving the law at Sinai. Morrison was a truly great preacher, whose sermons were masterpieces, but on this occasion Morrison seemed to push a bit too hard—almost as if he was trying to match what had happened earlier in the day. Brasher then told Kinlaw what happened after the service was over. It was dark and quiet, and Brasher was in his cot in his tent, but hadn't fallen asleep, when he sensed someone fumbling with the flap of his tent coming in. The man entered, stumbled around until he found the foot of Brasher's bed, knelt at his feet with his head buried under the covers, and wept like his heart was breaking. It was Morrison. Neither spoke a word, but it was as if spirit spoke to spirit.

Brasher repeated the lesson of the story to a young Kinlaw who never forgot it: "Henry Clay Morrison was a great man."

Chapter 7

The Golden Jubilee and War Again, 1935-1944

Camp meeting 1935 was wonderful. The *Christian Witness* recorded this from Secretary Ray A. Birdsall concerning that memorable year:

> The golden jubilee camp meeting held on the camp ground of the Michigan State Holiness Camp Meeting Association at Eaton Rapids was the best meeting in years.
>
> Newly painted association buildings and privately owned cottages greeted the visitor. The first few days were given to young people especially. Rev. Byron A. Hahn of Jackson had charge of this work, and had such helpers as Rev. Hugh Townley of Croswell, Mildred Smith, Cecelia Learn, Harrison Wilcox, and Dora Chadwick, as well as a message by Rev. J. L. Brasher and Rev. Lloyd H. Nixon, the president. Throughout the whole camp the help of the young people and the inspiration of their bright faces kept everybody rejoicing. When a young person gets a clean heart, who knows where he may go for God?
>
> Preaching by Rev. Joseph H. Smith, Rev. Paul Rees, Rev. John L. Brasher, Rev. George G. Valentyne, and President Nixon was of the highest order. Prof. and Mrs. Howard M. Skinner of Pontiac furnished the music. The historical service, at which time Rev. H. D. Skinner, former president, and Rev. Joseph H. Smith became reminiscent, was one of the great meetings. A set of chimes, the gift of Mr. and Mrs. Edward C. Barr of Lansing was dedicated. Miss Anna McHie spoke at the missionary service, and a good offering for her work was the result.
>
> Miss Leah Brown of White Pigeon, Michigan, did a splendid work with the children and presented them for the annual demonstration.
>
> Financial returns were better than for years, and the camp promises a great future.

The Lloyd H. Nixon Chimes were dedicated by the musician Prof. Howard Skinner, the son of the former president. The camp grocery store was run by the Prosser family, and songbooks were changed from the previous *Divine Praise* to *Full Redemption Songs*.[47]

President Nixon's greeting the following year of 1936 emphasized the role of the camp grounds in preparing attendees for God's work in their lives, how the remove from one's daily habits opens up a sacred space for spiritual renewal:

> It is my high privilege to anticipate, with a multitude of Christian friends, the 1936 encampment of our Camp Meeting Association. Physically, the grounds are calling us. We can vision the winding river, the lofty, verdant trees, the grass carpeted banks, and the fragrance of the countryside can be well imagined as we write. Away from the noisome city streets, away from the details of our highly overlapping life, away from the spiritual dearth of the world that surrounds us, we will come to familiar scenes and inviting spaces.
>
> The fellowship and fervor generated about altars sanctified by the tears and dedications of age and youth alike, throw their spell about us and our hearts are hungry. We would renew friendships and strengthen the holy bonds that bind us. Shall we not so plan, that for a little time we may come apart to pray and to hear what the Lord would say unto us.
>
> We greet you with the printed word and hope ere long to grasp the hand and return your greeting. In the name of Him who is able to save unto the uttermost, we greet you. In anticipation of outpoured blessings and expanded lives we greet you. Do not miss the feast of good things to be spread in the camp of 1936.

Gladys Watson, daughter of Dr. W. H. Watson of Detroit—Superintendent of the Detroit District of the Evangelical Church—was one of the musicians that year. Also, a sacred Choral Concert was presented Sunday afternoon at 4:15 by the Acapella Choir of the First Methodist Church of Battle Creek, Michigan, Harlan W. Cleveland directing. This organization of 42 mature voices was promised to thrill and inspire.

It was around this time that something interesting indeed took shape, evidence of what can happen at camp meeting in a young person's life. John Oswalt shares the following poignant story: "In the late 1930's the pastor of the Methodist Church in Dansville, MI, convinced a young mother that she and her son should come with her (the pastor) to Eaton Rapids Holiness Campmeeting. They did and fell in love with it. Because they were very poor, there were

---

[47] 1934 or 1935 was also the time when it was decreed that all outdoor toilets must be demolished.

summers when Mrs. Young could not come, but her son Jim would work in his Uncle's general store to get enough money to buy crackers and cheese and bus fare, and would come and pitch a pup tent in Tabernacle Circle for the 10 days. He later went to Asbury College and went on to earn a doctorate. Dr. Jim Young was my major professor at Taylor University and one of the two most influential people in my life."

This decade also marked the remembrance of John Wesley's Aldersgate conversion. 1938 was exactly 200 years after Wesley attended a meeting of the Moravians in Aldersgate Street in Greater London, where he underwent a profound religious experience, describing it in his journal: "In the evening I went unwillingly to a society in Aldersgate Street, where one was reading Luther's preface to the Epistle to the Romans. About a quarter to nine, while he was describing the change which God works in the heart through faith in Christ, I felt my heart strangely warmed. I felt I did trust in Christ, Christ alone for salvation, and an assurance was given me that he had taken away my sins, even mine and saved me from the law of sin and death."

To commemorate this defining moment in Wesley's life and the Methodist movement, ERC issued this challenge in 1938: "This is Aldersgate Year and the emphasis on the need for the warmed heart is shared by all communions. Especially, we who hold to the Wesleyan Doctrine of Christian Holiness, ought to welcome the renewed interest in vital experience and encourage that type of evangelism that will produce the needed result. It was a strong contention of John Wesley that young converts ought early to be urged on unto perfection. Bring your heart hungers to Eaton Rapids and find in service and fellowship the answer to your deepest yearning."

Also in 1938, according to Elaine Webster, Ruth and Earl Champlin first attended camp meeting where they accepted Christ as their savior. Feeling the call into ministry, Earl accepted his first church in 1941. The following year they rented a cottage and began taking youth to camp from their church. This was back before the present day youth program. Then they had a youth service in the morning and the youth were required to attend the evening service. About the third year, there was no money to rent a cottage, but one day Ruth was walking down the street in Vassar, Michigan, when she found a twenty dollar bill. She picked it up, took it to the local police station where they held it to see if anyone would claim it. The following week, they contacted her saying that no one had claimed the money and to come in and get it. That twenty dollars was just the amount that was needed to rent a cottage.

After attending and taking youth for several years, Ruth and Earl, along with Fred and Sarah Briggs, managed to get enough money to purchase Unity Home, which had earlier served as the hotel. During this time, there were always youth staying there, some years more than others. They could come by paying $10 for the ten days and if possible send some food along. After several years, Fred and Sarah, growing older, decided to purchase their own cottage, leaving the ownership and management up to the Champlins. It was during this time that Milton and Mary Ten Have, Mary a foster daughter of the Champlins, began staying there and shortly thereafter purchased their own cottage.

Ruth and Earl operated Unity Home up until about 1976 when, Earl having passed away, Ruth decided that it was getting to be too much and so returned the cottage back to the Association. This time witnessed three generations of Champlin/Websters attending camp. Today you will find four or five generations staying in the camping and cottage areas. The cottage is now called Unity House and is used to house the post-teen group.

Elaine Webster also shared a most charming story of something that happened while her family was renting one of the cottages by the river during the time Lloyd Nixon was serving as president. Back behind the cottage was the path used to walk from the tabernacle to the hotel and dining hall. Her brother, Don, was probably about five or six years old at the time, and he had built a dirt wall across the path with the intention of charging people to go across. Elaine didn't remember how much he charged, but probably somewhere between a penny and a nickel, she thought. Well, as it happened, the first person to come down the path was the Rev. Lloyd Nixon himself. He paid the toll but then explained to Don that he had to do away with the wall and couldn't charge people to go down the path.

The following passage comes from a 1939 brochure:

For fifty five years spiritually minded people have been looking forward annually to the session of the now historic Eaton Rapids Camp Meeting. Mindful of the insistent hunger of contemporary Christians for reality in religious experience, for truth at once understandable and livable, for fellowship both elevating and inspiring, the Planning Committee presents a strong and vigorous program for the helping of the multitudes who will make our camp a spiritual oasis in the desert of modern life.

The physical grandeur of the bending shoreline of old Grand River, of the towering oaks and spreading maples, and the grassy stretches of sodded slopes, is only surpassed by the moral and spiritual grandeur of the mighty presence of the infinite Spirit made regnant in redeemed lives. Here is declared in confidence a gospel that offers a Savior who is able "To save unto the uttermost." Challenged by its call, youth and age alike find altars of prayer places of satisfying visitation. Here the Wesleyan interpretation of Scriptural Holiness is faithfully proclaimed, not as an end but as a means, not as the Omega of experience and fruitfulness but as the Alpha.

In the 1940 brochure President Nixon wrote about W. W. Robinson of Detroit for whom the Robinson Memorial Bell is named. "He had been a cottager upon these grounds every season for many years. Quiet, devout, with a gracious dignity, exemplifying in his daily walk the Wesleyan doctrine of Christian perfection, his presence among us was a joy and a blessing. As a member of our board of trustees, he for years had taken a keen interest in the success and welfare of this camp meeting. For the last three years, he was superintendent of our Camp Meeting Sunday School."[48]

1940 saw this appeal issued by ERC: "When the Robinson Memorial Bell rings on the old camp grounds, it reminds one of worship, of things of the Spirit, of rest, and spiritual refreshment. Let all who it hear know a feast of good things is in store for them: soul-stirring music, preaching that instructs and inspires, altars filled with needy souls making quest for God. Here the atmosphere encourages that quest, the truth declared gives immediacy to it, and victorious testimonies make its pursuance seem imperative. Hear the call and join us for a season of waiting on God."

In 1941 there was another exceptionally strong platform team with Henry Clay Morrison, John R. Church, and Warren McIntyre preaching, and Miss Lela McConnell as the missionary. Each of these was a powerful speaker in his or her own right.

In 1941, 1944, and 1945 the number of brochures and their size was limited because of wartime paper rationing. The 1943 one-page brochure described the grounds in detail, from its winding river to its bushy maples, its tall oaks to grassy slopes, offering "the welcome quiet of a place apart from noise and bustle of city street and factory," "the ideal spot for a vacation capable of providing restoration for body and spirit." "Most certainly the camp will be held in spite of all the obstacles that appear to be in our way."

The brochure continued, "The War of Nerves holds the nations while multitudes live in fear and the tensions of our accelerated life are such as to call for some calm retreat where the souls of men may have a chance. We present a gospel intended to meet the deepest need of man and our altars are places of spiritual revival and renewal. Ministers that present truth whole and do not equivocate in the portrayal of sin, and that proffer salvation to all on scriptural terms, bring life and truth into focus that earnest hearts may seek and find."

In a similar vein, while the Second World War still raged, the next year's brochure spoke of the daily tension of life in a "warring world" that are "great enough to require a place of respit (sic) and refurnishing for the soul that would not succumb to the destructive forces which prey on human personality. Here, where devoted Christians pray together, where great assemblies sing the songs of Zion, where ministers of word preach truth in its attractive fullness; here is a 'Place of sure retreat,' a Bethel for the responsive spirit."

---

[48] In a document called "Gleanings from the History of Eaton Rapids Campmeeting," prepared for the July, 2010 125th Anniversary Celebration by President Oswalt with the assistance of ERC historian Joelee Bateman, we find this passage written about this juncture of the history: "It is appropriate to observe that over the years some of the world's finest missionary speakers have spoken from this platform and the one that preceded it. Included in that list are: E. Stanley Jones of India; Bishop J. Waskom Pickett of India; Miss Lela McConnell of the mountains of eastern Kentucky; Bishop W. X. Ninde of India; Melvin Trotter of the City Mission; Dr. Willa Caffray of South America, India, China, and Africa; Dr. Iva D. Vennard of Chicago; Dr. Marjorie Burt of the mounts of eastern Kentucky; Dr. Bill Gillam from Columbia, SA; Dr. Paul Rees of World Vision; and Dr. Sam Kamaleson of India and World Vision."

Again the aesthetic appeal of the grounds continued to be accorded pride of place: "The natural beauty of these historic grounds contributed toward that restful poise which is experienced by multitudes who come this way. The winding river skirting the rolling banks of the shoreline mirrors the sun and reflects the deep shade of the flanking trees alternately. Tall oaks and symmetrical maples make home and shelter for birds that sing and squirrels that flit from bough to bough. The dew of the morning gives the freshness to the day that the morning prayer gives to life. Here, where the God of nature speaks through living things and where the beauty of his world speaks of his love for man: let the God of life minister to the spirit and let the beauty of holiness be characterized in our worship and fellowship."

Eaton Rapids was first known for its curative mineral water; now ERC had become a place for rivers of living water to quench the deepest thirst of its participants—a place where truth, goodness, and beauty could clasp their hands and dance.

Spotlight on Lloyd H. Nixon (1893-1952)
[Tribute and Presidential Address]

Lloyd H. Nixon served as president of Eaton Rapids Camp Meeting from 1933 to 1952. He also served as Chairman of the Board of Trustees for the Chicago Evangelistic Institute. John Lakin Brasher writes of Nixon that he was "full of humor, full of play, firm as a rock, a preacher of marvelous versatility and range." Over the course of his ministry, Nixon pastored several large churches of the Detroit, Michigan, conference. Brasher calls him "a great comrade" who "held aloft noble and Biblical standards":[49]

> Outstanding among the many great sermons I heard him preach was one on the eighth chapter of Romans, and one on the tenth chapter of Hebrews. In these messages he reached a grasp of both books that I have never heard equaled by any in exposition. He and his father were my close friends, and their fellowship was blessed. Brother Nixon and his cultured Christian wife paid us a visit not so long before his death. They took noon dinner with us and left a blessing upon us. He preached on a Sunday morning, then, after dinner, rested a while, and "was not, for God took him."

Nixon brought this same noble spirit to his work at Eaton Rapids. His presidential address of 1935 ran as follows:

Fifty years of inspiration, of devoted loyalty, of soul saving ministry, and of consecrated living and giving environ us as we face the Camp of 1935. On these sacred grounds, hallowed by heaven's blessing and gracious fellowship, the multitudes have sought, found, worshipped. Joy tides have often run high while conviction has simultaneously held men to claims of eternal truth.

Many saints will not celebrate with us here. Their jubilee is perpetual. I wonder, will they look over battlements of Glory with strange awareness as we gird ourselves in holy dedication for the years ahead. We do know Jesus is "Expecting until his enemies become his foot-stool." Ours is a rich heritage: we have something to live up to.

The verdant forest, the bending river, associations of the years, the splendid program of 1935, the Spirit of worship and of God, these all combine to call us to holy convocation and needful preparation in a day when man's soul is not only severely tried, but also greatly in need of God.

We greet you in the name of Him who is able to save unto the uttermost, all them that come unto God by Him. We urge you to attend this significant and historic session of the camp. We exhort you to pray for outpoured blessings that the session may be more than a celebration. WE NEED YOU that this work of Scriptural Holiness may prosper.

---

[49] "Lloyd Hinman Nixon," http://collerkin.com/772.html, accessed December 30, 2015.

Interlude

Fourteenth Decade Underway

Five Dangerous Prayers (Psalm 139:23-24)
Sermon by David Gallimore

Sunday evening's service was memorable! Using Psalm 139:23-24, Gallimore spoke on 5 Dangerous Prayers: (1) Search me, and know my heart, giving God permission to examine us through and through. David exhorted us to be willing to get on God's operating table. (2) Break me. Ask God is there any offensive way in us. (3) Stretch me. Get me out of my comfort zone; find out my anxious thoughts. (4) Lead me: in the way everlasting. God has plans for each of us. (5) Use me. Aim for a life that counts for the kingdom's sake. Has my life been spent for His glory? Even when we're not good, God still is.

    A remarkable feature of this service was the masterful use of stories by David to illustrate the points. Telling anecdotes of key junctures in his own life, told with transparency, was by turns inspiring, challenging, hilarious, and deeply moving. The Holy Spirit seemed to show up in a palpable and powerful way, inspiring many to go to the altar afterwards, willing to pray these five dangerous prayers.

    David's ministry is one of "encouragement, equipping, and evangelism." David's greatest gift is his ability to encourage local pastors and congregations. His relational skills and powerful ability to communicate strengthen any church or organization. Mentored by John Maxwell and Stan Toler, David is able to reach and resource local churches and boards in the areas of leadership and stewardship. And in terms of evangelism, he has a "fire in his bones" to go into all the world and passionately preach the life-changing Word of God. Dennis Kinlaw has stated that in today's culture "the Evangelist is God's neglected gift to the church."

    David bridges the gap between the revival days of old and the modern day multi-sensory worship era. He is a Tenured Evangelist in the Church of the Nazarene and has conducted hundreds of evangelistic meetings in America, as well as conducting missionary Outreach in Africa, Russia, Ukraine, Romania, and the Islands of the Caribbean.

    Following the evening service was the Prayer Walk, led by Davenport, canvassing the Nursery, the Campers, Peace Chapel, the Youth Program, the grounds keeper and his wife, the Children's Ministry, the Hotel, the Cafeteria, and more.

A Conquering and Convincing Ministry (2 Corinthians 2:12—3)

Bible Study by Bruce Moyer

Monday morning's Bible study with Moyer continued in 2 Cor., this time 2:12-17 and the whole of chapter 3. The first lesson of the day was about "Conquering Ministry." A conquering ministry has the following salient features:

First, it discerns God's direction. The apostle Paul demonstrated that he would take full advantage of obvious God-given opportunities. Note that this is consistent with opposition by many. Paul was sure God was in control of the steps he was taking. Great opportunities are one place to look for confirmation. God wants us to know His will—unlike those who think He relishes concealing it.

Second, a conquering ministry is defined by victory. Paul suggested we're part of a perpetual victory parade. A "Roman Triumph" featured a conquering Roman general returning from battle in a huge parade. Before the General would be priests spreading incense, and following the General would be captives taken in war, usually being ushered to their executions. Does Paul see us as the conquering General or the captives to Christ? Moyer admits this is a bit of a vexed question among biblical scholars. But what's clear is that we are always being led in triumphant procession. But this requires a long view, for we won't always find ourselves in triumphant circumstances.

Third, such a ministry infuses the scent or aroma of Christ, the fragrance of the knowledge of Him. His triumph can be not just seen and heard, but smelled—just like the Roman Triumph! Everywhere we go we are influencing the world's attitude about Jesus. As we emit that fragrance, some will be attracted, others turned off. To some we're the smell of death. This was the case with Jesus and Paul! Grace doesn't cease to be grace even if it's rejected. If everyone hates us, there's probably a love, grace, or mercy deficiency; if everyone loves us, there's probably a truth deficiency. We are *to God* the aroma of Christ.

In verse 16, it's noted that if some will reject and some will accept, who is equal to such a task? This leads to the next point:

Fourth, a conquering ministry is marked by a delight to please God, not people. We have to be willing to offend some with the message we share. Paul doesn't "peddle" a message—which always carries with it the idea of trickery. To sell or hawk usually by misrepresenting. Instead, he speaks as if a man sent by God. The world wants to see the power of a transformed life. We should strive for a sincere life that delights in pleasing God.

The second lesson of the Bible study that day drew from Chapter 3: "A Convincing Ministry." First, a convincing ministry produces changed lives.

Letters of recommendation were used in Paul's time. What did Paul appeal to in order to convince others that he's of God? Paul told the Corinthians that *they* were his letter. A convincing ministry is always producing changed lives. In Philippians 3 Paul mentions his credentials, but then says they're nothing compared to the surpassing greatness of following Jesus. Paul's one major concern was transformed lives. The people of Corinth had wasted lives, and they were now pillars of the church.

Second, a convincing ministry prefers Christ over self. Any confidence we have should be in Christ. Jesus changes lives; we don't.

Third, a convincing ministry promotes liberty over legalism. Where the Spirit of the Lord is, there is freedom. We must not fall into the trap of following rules of do(s) and don't(s). In contrast, live by the Spirit—the surpassing glory of the Spirit. It's a ministry of righteousness rather than one of condemnation, of liberty over legalism. Competition, too, is precluded if we're living in the Spirit; competition is to live in the flesh. Only the Spirit can transform us into living epistles. God's law is good, but was never meant to lead to salvation.

Fourth, a convincing ministry practices what it preaches. Not just others are being transformed; we ourselves are being changed into His likeness. The change here is a metamorphosis, no less dramatic than a caterpillar turning into a butterfly. Far more so, in fact.

Expect Big Things (Mark 11:12-25)
Sermon by David Gallimore

In Monday morning's 10:30 service, Gallimore reminded us that we prayed big prayers the night before—for God to search us, know us, use us, and the like. Now he exhorted us to *expect* big things. To a large degree, he said, what we're expecting to receive will shape how we live, how much we put into something. What's the greatest burden you have? The impossibility in your life?

The context of the passage is the arrival of Jesus in Jerusalem, welcomed with the waving of palms. Later that afternoon Jesus was hungry, and, seeing a fig tree in the distance, went to eat some figs. Expecting to see figs, he saw there were none. A few verses later, he would go into the temple, expecting to see worship, and finding the moneychangers, which he then drove out. Plenty of expositors connect these themes, but David wanted to take it in a different direction from usual.

He asked, what's withered and died in our lives—like the fig tree after he cursed it for being unproductive, despite that it wasn't the season for figs? What in our lives is unfair? We're inclined to ask God if He's going to fix it.

The answer comes in 22-24: *Have faith in God*. If anyone says to this mountain, be removed, it'll happen. So get your eyes off the problem and onto the hills from whence comes our help. We should tell the mountain, without doubt in our hearts, to be removed, trusting God with the results or the precise manner of answering.

Jesus is taking life's circumstances as they are and telling us to learn to expect fruit that's even *out* of season. To learn to expect the unexpected. Faith is the assurance of what's hoped for, the evidence of things not seen—a message that's been abused by some. Still, the Bible is clear: without faith it's impossible to please God. So let's stretch our expectations. Whatever we ask for, believe that we've received it, and it will be ours. Let's learn to expect fruit out of season, because we've got fruit that's out of this world.

What does it mean to expect such fruit? When the doctor says there's nothing more that can be done. When the situation looks dire and bleak and hopeless. Of course there are simply times to leave matters in God's hands—but that's the best place to leave things. Either when grieving a death or believing in a miraculous healing or help with finances or whatever, let's learn to leave it in God's hands. Pray in faith for the mountain to move, one way or another.

After lunch the Association Meeting was held. A new directory made its appearance (thanks to the energetic efforts by Tracy Lively), requisite elections were held, but, perhaps most importantly of all, Dr. Oswalt gave his final President's Report, which in pithy and prophetic fashion summarized his tenure and looked to the future.

Kathleen Ray came up after the meeting and directed those interested to pick up a biographical sketch of Oswalt at the back of the tabernacle, and then spent several minutes highlighting some of his more personal attributes: his sense of humor, his being a "softie," and his sweet tooth. She gave him a framed plaque expressing the Association's deep appreciation of Oswalt, invited people to give toward a contribution to the Francis Asbury Society in his honor, and, lastly, conferred on him a huge framed cookie to satiate his sweet tooth. The Association then gave him a second standing ovation.

ERC has had a rare talent and great man at the helm since 2006, and he is owed our most robust and heartfelt thanks for his selfless and distinguished service and friendship. He has left an indelible mark and distinctive signature on the place, and we are all better for it. He will be missed.

In that evening's 7:30 service, French spoke again, this time on 2 Samuel 11. He prefaced his sermon by saying that ours is a culture awash in technology and smart phones and the like, meticulously preoccupied with being attuned to everything—except God's voice!

Hear God's Voice (2 Samuel 11)
Sermon by Jack French

Does God speak to us? Yes, French said, in all sorts of ways.

Yet this passage tells us of a man with the heart of God, who wrote a great deal of scriptures by the inspiration of the Holy Spirit, who stays home, looks out his window, and sees a beautiful woman taking a bath. Ignoring God's voice not to do it, he sends for her, sleeps with her, and then tries to cover his tracks. His efforts are aimed to hide his misdeed; he further ignores God's voice and arranges for the husband to be killed in combat, all to save his reputation and to look good.

We may not have done what David did, but French said there were still likely people here to whom God was speaking, people who weren't listening to God's voice.

Nathan the prophet tells David of a rich man who stole his poor neighbor's one lamb for a feast rather than sacrificing one of his own. David was purple with anger and indignation—angry at another's sin, while being guilty of his own. David said the man should die, but Nathan famously responded, "Thou art the man." How did he know? God had spoken to him.

David was told what he did disgraced the name of God, despised the word of the Lord, and that the sword, as a result, would never depart from his family.

When we ignore the voice of God, God's work suffers and our family pays the price.

French then spoke of his own moral failure in the past that had led to a time away from ministry—all because he refused to heed the voice of God, and it cost his family and ministry a great deal. God restored him eventually, but only when he began to listen again to God.

Cherishing the voice of God provides the seeds from which great revivals come.

Tuesday morning was crisp and cool, at least comparatively. After several inordinately hot and muggy days, relief finally came. I didn't make it to the Prayer Meeting at 7 a.m., and have missed a few mornings. I was attending Bedside Baptist, or was it Pillow Pentecostal, or Mattress Methodist? Couch Congregational? At any rate, camp meeting offers lots to do, quite a full program, something for everyone, including prayer meetings every afternoon at different points on the campus. It's virtually impossible to take it all in. But camp meeting can be enjoyed without feeling the need to be legalistic about attending each and every function. As I type this on Tuesday afternoon, there's a "Meet the Speakers" gathering scheduled to start in ten minutes. I'd really enjoy that, but the duty of keeping up with this daily record calls. Nor will I attend the Women's Auxiliary this afternoon at 3:15 in the Picnic Pavilion—though their contribution to camp meeting since its start thirteen decades ago has been remarkable.

A Consistent and Compelling Ministry (2 Corinthians 4-5)

Bible Study by Bruce Moyer

The 9 a.m. Bible study continued examining the question, "What can we learn from Paul about life and ministry?" The first text covered on this picturesque morning was 2 Cor. 4:1-16, a pericope bookended by the admonition not to lose heart, and which speaks of a "Consistent Life." To lose heart is to grow faint, to become spiritless, to lose joy and vigor in our work. Paul says this should not happen, even if we see others succeed by using improper means. What keeps Paul going? Moyer spoke here of several secrets, six keys, of a consistent life, while reminding us that the enemy tries to make us give up.

1. *A consistent ministry is a gift of God.* Note Paul doesn't take credit for it. We must not think we deserve it, or that the ministry is ours. It isn't. (verse 1)
2. *The truth always prevails over gimmicks.* We are not to use deception, to be duplicitous. We are to renounce secret and shameful ways—that which is disgraceful and dishonest. Refuse to wear masks and play games; there's to be no dishonest manipulation. Truth prevails over gimmicks. We are to have integrity—in private, public, and in how we handle the Word of God. Paul didn't give up in part because he didn't use gimmicks. Truth is the most exciting thing in this world. If we can count on God's Word to transform lives, then there's no need for gimmicks. Anything less than the truth will fail, and so will we. Love people and preach the truth; sounds simple, but that's the ticket. (verses 2-4)
3. *Understanding the Lordship of Christ and the servanthood of the minister.* Paul didn't preach about himself. We are servants in this ministry. Don't aim to impress others, but to serve others. Be willing to be an armor bearer—a servant; don't look for servants of you. (verses 5-6)
4. *Understanding we're clay pots.* Why would God commit such a precious treasure to such fragile, breakable vessels? To show the power is of God. Verses 8 and 9: troubled on every side, but not distressed; perplexed, but not in despair; bearing in the body the dying of the Lord Jesus, but so the life of Jesus might be made manifest in our body. Paul was a hardheaded realist. A groggy fighter reeling from near lethal blows, almost surprised he's still standing. We'll throw in the towel if we're not realistic enough to know there will be troubles. Like a good pot, our job is to remain clean and available for service. (verses 7-12)
5. *Faith is essential to consistency.* Believing leads to Paul's speaking. What he believed shaped his words and ministry. We know the end of the story! Knowing the outcome keeps us consistent. Do we really believe victory is ours and God will get the praise? (verses 13-15)
6. *Daily renewal is essential to long-term success.* There's no replacement for time alone with Jesus. (verse 16)

The second part of the Bible study that day got underway by examining 2 Cor. 5: An Effective Life is a "Compelling Life." Christ's love is what compels us. To be compelled in this way is to be claimed and governed by Christ and his love. What holds our life together is Christ's love. Here are five (or at least for now the first two) things that compel Paul and hold his life together:

First, effective ministry is compelled by *permanence*. Paul contrasts the temporary with the eternal; what's light with what's weighty; troubles versus glory. Keep as your end that which is permanent.

Second, effective ministry is compelled by *perspective*. We walk by faith, not by sight. Four times Paul refers to what's seen and unseen. In this context the body is characterized as a tent, something about which Paul knows a great deal—including, no doubt, their tenuousness and susceptibility to damage and the like. Moyer would continue this lesson next Bible study.

That morning's 10:30 service featured Jack French once again, this time preaching on Philippians 1:20-21. What must we believe to live through times of injustice and trouble and oppression? To live is Christ, and to die is gain. Christ isn't to be part of our life, or merely a ticket to heaven; He is to be our life! Here are key parts of the passage:

Expectation: a marvelous thing. "According to my earnest expectation and my hope...." Our expectations shape our lives, as we saw in an earlier message.

Determination: determine not to cause shame, or do anything shameful, or be put to shame by preaching the most glorious truth. We won't be perfect, but people want to see something genuine.

Declaration: With all boldness, share the Good News. If only perfect people could proclaim the message, nobody would. Boldness is not brashness. It's a willingness to overcome our natural fears and, despite feeling in the flesh disqualified, being true to one's calling. We can magnify Christ—not Christ himself, of course, but people's perceptions of Christ.

Evaluation: Christ is to be magnified in both our life and death. How would we evaluate our lives? Are we boldly declaring the gospel? Are we filled with hope and expectation in Jesus? Are we determined not to do anything shameful or be ashamed of proclaiming truth? To follow Christ come what may, and let go of any anger or bitterness about those times of difficulty we'll encounter?

The Wages of Sin (Hebrews 12:1 and 12:15)
Sermon by David Gallimore

Tuesday evening came, and it was time for the evening service. David Gallimore spoke on the theme that some things aren't what they seem to be, using Hebrews 12:1 and 12:15 as his text. The passage tells us to set aside anything that would weigh us down as we run with patience the race set before us. And we are to look diligently lest any man fail of the grace of God, lest any root of bitterness springing up trouble us, and many others. David drew several lessons from these two verses.

First, poison grows up in the dark. Just because it's out of sight doesn't mean it isn't there, and in fact it'll grow all the more. Sometimes for some sin long since forgiven, God might lay it on our hearts to do restitution, to make something right. If we know to do right and don't do it, it's sin. If there's something in our life to deal with, it's an obedience test whether we do or not.

Second, the damage attaches to us quickly. A bitter root will grow up. We need to ask if there's something untoward or ungodly filed away deep down within us.

Third, this always causes great trouble. Bad attitudes and unforgiving spirits will, in time, generate problems. David exhorted us to bring our burdens to God and leave them with Him. What would happen, he asked, if we allowed God to reveal the junk in us, the stuff beneath the surface, and we would repent?

Fourth, this is highly contagious, defiling many. Sin is progressive, and, if unchecked, can become like a spiritual Ebola virus, wreaking horrible havoc and destruction and death.

David's a great preacher, and this was another wonderful message, shared in his inimitable style that's so disarming and charming at the same time. But my mind couldn't help but ponder a case rather messier. What about someone who is doing horribly unjust, unfair, and hurtful things to us right now? And this person is unrepentant, despite perhaps paying lip service to repentance and confession—even while the despicable behavior persists? It's not simply about forgiving the person for some wrong in the past, but for what the person is *continuing to do*. It makes sense that harboring bitterness against the person is not the way to go, but what does forgiveness look like?[50]

Perhaps the rest of the context can help. Hebrews 12:3, a verse in the same chapter as the two verses considered in the sermon but not discussed, says, "Consider him who endured such opposition from sinful men, so that you will not grow weary and lose heart." Jesus was the supreme example of one who suffered at the hands of the unjust and unrepentant, yet He still chose to pray for their forgiveness and for God to have mercy.

And elsewhere in that chapter we're told to let the suffering that will invariably come in this life to serve a purpose, irrespective of its source. God's in the business of redeeming suffering, and, if we allow it, He will use it to discipline us, which is evidence God is treating us as His children. If we aren't disciplined, then we're illegitimate children and not true sons. God disciplines us for our good, so that we may be made holy—for those who have been trained by it. David, my wife, and I would have occasion a few days later to discuss this harder case when we drove him to the airport Saturday morning.

---

[50] The Bible seems to indicate that, on occasion, if a person persists in wrongdoing, something is called for—some sort of accountability, some call for repentance, some break in fellowship if need be, a confrontation or intervention. (An abused wife certainly shouldn't continue allowing herself to be abused, for example.) If the wrongdoer repents and accepts the forgiveness, that's one thing—and a sermon from a few days before made clear that, in such a case, time for reconciliation would be at hand. But what of the obstinately unrepentant? What of the person who refuses the forgiveness offered? Who continues metaphorically stabbing you? What does "leaving it at the altar" look like in such a case as this?

Missionary Day
Seth Porter, Papua, New Guinea

On Wednesday morning at 9 a.m., Seth Porter, who was serving with his wife in Papua, New Guinea, gave the morning address. From Pennsylvania and a self-described country boy, he admitted to the worries he had about learning a new language; but within six months, after arduous effort and a lot of practice, he learned the language and was able to preach using it.

Seth spoke of the way God placed a passion in his heart for the people. God called him to be their servant. In the last service before coming back on furlough, he washed the feet of another in a church service to demonstrate his sense of calling. Numerous times he's been called to operate outside his comfort zone, yielding remarkable results. Through our weaknesses God is made strong.

Most of the people there in New Guinea, including ministers, have very little chance for education. Pastors often have nothing beyond a second or third grade education, and yet they're leading a flock. Seth wanted to do more to help with this, and to start up some vocational training as well.

In general, he said, it's not the programs, but time with the people building relationships, that has had the biggest impact.

God, he said, had used them in ways they didn't realize they could be used, and Seth challenged us to ask ourselves if we're allowing God to use us as He wants to, to let God use us in ways we feel weak so His strength can shine through. Or are we staying inside our comfort zone? Likewise, are our churches reaching those God intends? Seth characterized his first term of service as simply coming to God in obedience.

After his talk came a variety of questions, which he fielded well. For example, it's a very oral culture he's ministering in, so telling stories plays a big part in his preaching. Regarding the natives' attitudes toward ministers, there's a lot of respect for missionaries. Most people there already believe in God; in fact, they believe in a number of deities and they fear mistreating missionaries would be dangerous to them, which keeps them from doing that.

Responding to another question, he spoke of the way Papua is filled with quite a bit of tribal warfare, which even divides Christians. So, much of his ministry is devoted to encouraging Christians not to hurt each other. Dr. Oswalt mentioned at this juncture that Rwanda features a similar dynamic; millions of Christians—Tutsi versus Hutu and even Hutus pitted against other Hutus—killing one another with machetes. The apostle Paul, remember, would use all sorts of images—family, body, temple—everything at his disposal to keep Jews and Gentiles from killing each other.

The 10:30 service was the second missionary service of the day. It began with music both traditional and contemporary. Leadership at the Camp has discussed music quite a bit, finally settling on a program that includes both forms of music in order to maximize appeal to a spectrum of people, young and old alike.

Missionary Day
James Kigumwa, One Mission Society

James Kigumwa, from OMS (One Mission Society), originally from Kenya, spoke, sharing a bit of his background. Born again at 20, growing up in Nairobi, eventually earning his doctorate, he ended up, in what he characterized as the first half of his ministry, starting a Church Literacy Ministry. He spoke on Psalm 90, the whole chapter, but mainly verse 12: "Teach us to number our days, that we might apply our hearts to wisdom." As we begin to understand that our days are few, we gain a heart of wisdom.

With so very much to do and such little time to do it, it's important we be about the business we're called to do. We must pursue the call God places in our hearts. Time passes, and soon life is over. In the meantime, life has its seasons, and we should be mindful of where we're at and what we're doing.

It was appropriate, I think, that such a sermon be given at camp meeting. The rustic setting and closeness to nature reminds participants of the seasons, of the natural rhythms of life and passage of time. It lends itself to reflection, too, as it forces everyone to slow down and think about the important matters of life, rather than being swept up in the continual barrage and incessant tyranny of the urgent. Like Holden Caulfied's visits to the Museum of Natural History in *Catcher in the Rye*, the camp seems largely unchanged from one year or even decade to the next, save for a new building project or other, but each time we go there we know we're not the same. Life has moved on, we enter into new seasons of life ourselves. Caulfield lamented the loss of the past, though, and the need to leave childhood behind. Those at camp meeting should be striving toward a goal, embracing change as needed, recognizing the onset of new chapters in life, and pressing forward.

What motivated James' literacy initiative was the functional illiteracy of a billion people in the world. One in five adults can't read. Biblical translation the world over is far ahead of literacy, which creates, among other things, a discipleship challenge. Acts 17:11: "These were more noble than those in Thessalonica, in that they received the word with all readiness of mind, and searched the scriptures daily." He challenged us to think about the plight of those who can't read, and to help if we can.

On that afternoon, Missions in Action met in the Hart-Topliff Pavilion to assemble backpacks for the Salvation Army Down River Corps in Detroit, which would be distributed to schoolchildren that fall.

In the evening was the last missionary service, in which all offerings went toward missions. Oswalt challenged Eaton Rapids by pointing to the Indian Springs camp in Georgia discussed earlier in the book—which this year gave over $100,000 toward missions!

The speaker for the evening was Hubert Herriman, president of WGM (World Gospel Mission) for the past thirteen years, on the verge of stepping down. Before that, for 26 years, he was a pastor in Indiana, and before that a missionary to Argentina. WGM started 105 years ago in a camp meeting!

Guided by the Spirit (Luke 1:1-4 and Acts 1:1-8)
Sermon by Hubert Herriman

Herriman's passages for the night were the first four verses in Luke and first eight verses in Acts. Luke was the author of both books. In the Acts passage, we are promised to receive power when the Holy Spirit comes on us, resulting in Mission Active Christians, the call on us all. Luke moves directly to the promise of the Spirit at the end of Luke into the Holy Spirit's coming at the beginning of Acts. Herriman likened it to a mighty river into which a new river flows, the way he once traveled with his brother in Bolivia from smaller waterways eventually into the Amazon. Luke saw a river in a river, running from the Old Testament to the New, culminating in the coming of the Spirit at the start of the church.

The Holy Spirit came to accomplish God's work, and is not to be neglected. We can't accomplish what God calls us to do without the Holy Spirit.

Luke, under the guidance of that Spirit, used his gift of writing to get the truth out. God's given us all a mind that we are to use. With our minds under the Spirit's direction can come great ingenuity and innovation and creativity. With the Spirit of God man can do wonders.

Journalists get the story no matter what; Christians should tell the story no matter what, come what may, whatever the cost. There's a world that needs to hear the gospel; we need people who know the Holy Spirit and spread the good news.

Luke captures the stories of people whose lives were transformed by the Spirit, and Luke was passionate about the outcasts—the women, the children, the Samaritans, the prisoners. The message was for all.

But Luke didn't just share words, he got involved; he didn't just communicate with his head, but with his heart, and, most importantly, with his hands. Research indicates words alone account for just 7% of communication; vocal tone for 38%. But body language for 55%! God Himself got bodily involved in the story by the Incarnation; the Word of God became flesh and dwelt among us.

Luke didn't just share words. He got involved in the story. Christianity is at its best here. In the Roman Empire, among the most important reasons for the growth of Christianity—so argues Rodney Stark in *The Rise of Christianity: How the Obscure, Marginal Jesus Movement Became the Dominant Religious Force in the Western World in a Few Centuries*—was the way Christians would remain after the conquering Roman armies would leave an area and take care of the sick and wounded, the untended corpses and unwanted babies.

Luke starts using the word "we" in the course of the narrative because he was a Mission Active Christian. God wants every one of us to be one. The greatest danger of truth is that it be reduced to words alone. Closing our hearts to those in need is something we must not do; we must love in truth and in deed. When God gets ahold of an individual, creative and great things will happen.

A Compelling and Commended Ministry
(2 Corinthians 4:17—6:13)
Bible Study by Bruce Moyer

Since Wednesday had no Bible study due to Missionary Day, Dr. Moyer opened Thursday's 9 a.m. message by reviewing the previous days' coverage, after which he picked back up from Tuesday's discussion of 2 Corinthians 4:17-5:21 about what can *Compel* an effective ministry. His third point centered on how an effective ministry is compelled by pleasure—that is, what pleases *God*. The various translations of 5:9 illustrate that our motivation in ministry should be pleasing God rather than others or ourselves: this should be our goal (NIV), our ambition (NASB), our aim (NKJV). For, as verse 10 explains, these motivations will be revealed at the judgment seat of Christ; in this instance, Paul uses the word *bema*, which refers to the platform in Greek towns where orations, public decisions, and awards were delivered. It was a place, as the judgment seat of Christ will be, where hidden things were made public. Therefore, we should live in such a way now so that, when all secrets are revealed (Matthew 8:17), it is clear that we were motivated by pleasing God, a task that requires study of His Word to know what it is that pleases Him.

Continuing on, Dr. Moyer explained that an effective ministry is compelled by passion, i.e. Christ's love (2 Corinthians 5:11-17). *Compel*, Dr. Moyer reminded us, refers to "control" (NASB), "rule" (Good News), the "spring of our actions" (Phillips), and what "move[s] one." Christ's love transforms our life in at least three ways outlined in verses 15-17: we no longer live for ourselves but for Christ (15), we have a new perspective of others (16), and we view Christians differently (17). We ourselves, and fellow Christians, are new creations at salvation, a work only Christ's love can enact within us.

Finally, drawing on 2 Corinthians 5:18-21, Dr. Moyer showed us that an effective ministry is compelled by partnership with God. We are vessels through which God speaks, his representatives (Message translation), a means by which God appeals to others (Phillips translation). King James uses the term "ambassador" to describe our function. As an ambassador, we can speak with authority because of the one we represent, but we also are accountable to the message we've been given and must deliver that and only that.

After wrapping up this final point about what compels an effective ministry, Dr. Moyer moved on to 6:1-13 to consider how an effective ministry is *Commended* (6:4). Translations of this term include "laud," "praise," "extol," and "applaud." The first mark of commendation on Paul's ministry is the *partnerships* it has formed—with God primarily, and also with others (6:1-2). In this partnership, we cooperate (Phillips) and work together with God (Good News). We are his partners (NLT) and companions (Message).

Additionally, an effective ministry is commended by the *purpose* for which it exists (6:3). Moyer then addressed what he characterized as a prevailing spirit in today's church—that people must accept us as we come. But Paul recognizes here that often someone's conduct can be a stumbling block to others accepting his ministry and that we must be on guard to remove such obstacles.

In laying out his next few points, Moyer said that Paul records three lists of nine items each: nine kinds of circumstances, nine traits of character, and nine sets of contrasts. What some of this list shows us, unexpectedly, is that an effective ministry is commended by the *problems* it victoriously endures (6:4-5). These problems include *tough circumstances* (troubles, hardships, distresses), *tough opposition* (brought about by others—beatings, imprisonment, riots), and *tough commitments* (hard work, sleepless nights, hunger—specifically fasting). He wrapped up this section by challenging us to consider how our lives stand up to Paul's.

Ministry of Reconciliation (Genesis 32—33)
Sermon by David Gallimore

Thursday's 10:30 service was another occasion for David Gallimore to preach—not so much, he said, *from* a text as *to* a text. The text was Genesis 32 and 33, the story of Jacob. The topic of the sermon was something Gallimore thinks keeps us from revival and, often, from prayers getting answered, namely broken relationships, and he wanted to use Jacob's story to make two main points about healing them.

As far as Jacob's story, he came out of the womb grabbing the heel of Esau, his twin. Later Jacob wanted Esau's birthright, and got Esau to sign it away. Likewise Jacob manipulated circumstances to get his father's blessing that, again, belonged to Esau. He got what he wanted, but it resulted in a broken relationship. Then he had to flee, and he worked for Laban for seven years to get Rachel's hand in marriage, but he was tricked and given Leah. There's irony in hearing Jacob complaining about the trickery. Then he worked more years—twenty in total—before marrying Rachel. When the time came to leave, he took the best livestock for himself, again straining his relationships, this time with his in-laws.

Then Jacob hears Esau is coming after him. Jacob tries to bribe his way out of trouble, but it doesn't work. So he goes to meet Esau, and here Gallimore makes two main points:

First, *pursue reconciliation regardless of your expectation*. Be active, not passive; take a step, rather than playing the waiting game. We've been called to a ministry of reconciliation. And here's a good reason to seek reconciliation: On Jacob's way to meet his brother, Jacob meets God, wrestling with him until break of day, until the blessing came. And then Jacob had to give his name: Jacob—which literally meant trickster, deceiver. But God changed his name, and by implication his character. His new name was Israel.

Second, *pursue reconciliation for the sake of the next generation*. Children play a prominent role in the narrative, and they saw Jacob and Esau reconciled. Joseph was among the children, and he would one day forgive his own brothers—perhaps in part because he remembered the reconciliation of his father and uncle.

To forgive and let go of bitterness, remember to clarify the goal of reconciliation: it's not to agree with the other person, but to accept them. Use Jesus as a guide: even as the greatest indignities and injustices were perpetrated on Him, He prayed, "Father, forgive them, for they know not what they do."

Thursday afternoon at 2 p.m. the Rev. Jim Lively conducted a book review of *Midnight Rider*—a fictionalized account of the life of Francis Asbury—in the Ice Cream Shop porch. That day also featured in the cafeteria baked oatmeal and eggs for breakfast, chicken tenders or roast beef for lunch, and dinner was pasta night.

Thursday evening brought Jack French back to the platform after a mini-concert by a group from Kentucky Mountain Bible College, a three-member singing group. That holiness and ministry-training college is the tenth least expensive college in America; part of what holds tuition so low is that all of the faculty live on faith, taking no salary. These three young men seemed to have a genuine heart for God, ministry, and missions, and from a very young age indeed. They also sported quite a bit of singing talent.

Spiritual Healing (Psalm 51)
Sermon by Jack French

French picked up his theme of the dangers of ignoring the voice of God. In David's case it meant the sword would never leave his family. After Nathan confronted David, Psalm 51 was David's prayer. This is one of the few places in the Old Testament where God looks at the inside of a person; usually the focus is on wrong actions that undoubtedly spring from inner sources, but the focus is usually on the outward fruits. But not here.

We can ignore the voice of God in a variety of ways. We can quench the Spirit; we can assume we don't have to listen now that our relationship with God is secure; we can count on delayed judgment; we engage in selective hearing; we can presume God will forgive us; we can let God stir our emotions, but not move our will.

But when we realize that we are "the man," the one who needs to repent and listen to God, and we do, what happens? First, there comes a time when we're willing to listen. David got to such a point, developing a taste for God—and nothing else would do. Sometimes people don't need counseling; they need spiritual healing and they need Jesus.

Second, they move beyond confession. They stop negotiating and really start listening to God.

Third, they discern that God is the offended party. Why is it that we can be in wrong relation to God and we only care when another person finds out? We should most care about what God thinks.

Fourth, David is saying that he not only wants forgiveness, but a new heart. Change me, he prayed. But this requires that we get serious with God; kingdom fullness and the fullness of joy are no small matters.

Because of David's sin, there were some things he couldn't fix. If God tells us to do something, we must do it, must not wait too long to lose the chance that will last only so long; but we can know that He'll do it with us. We'll never be so free as when we do what God directs us to do.

After the evening service came the Galilean Service, a smaller service usually led by a youth minister down by the cross at the river's edge. Sitting on permanent wooden benches facing the river on its bank, we sang worship songs and sensed God's presence in nature. This particular feature of camp meeting began in the 1950s here at Eaton Rapids, and it's been a regular fixture since. My mother loved the service, and would often regale me afterwards with vivid descriptions of how lovely it was. Lit candles, as dusk settles in, come into view, gently floating on the river. They seem to defy both gravity and the water below as, in the dark, they practically seem to hover and glide along, hundreds of them. Something unmistakably elegant and simple and beautiful marks the service. Under a canopy of trees and a star-filled sky and prominent moon, sitting at the riverbank and watching this floating constellation of lights illumine the darkness, we get swept up in the spirit of the service. It's easy, sitting there, to think that truth, goodness, and beauty all really do ultimately cohere. Some suggest that large urban cities contributed to atheism, as they alienate people from nature; the Galilean service is a rather nice corrective, as nature is all around us—dynamic and organic. Streams of abundance flowed, as we sang songs led by a single guitarist, reminding me of that day decades ago when young George Bennard, with only his guitar to accompany him, performed "The Old Rugged Cross" on these very grounds.

Salt and Light (Matthew 5)
Galilean Service

The message came from Matthew 5, as the youth had been studying from the Sermon on the Mount all week at camp. The passage emphasized that we're to be salt and light. Life's journey on a highway is easy and fast; off road it's much more difficult and slow going. Our culture seems to be moving more and more away from Christian thought, and the days ahead might become more metaphorically off road, more of a challenge and struggle. But our mandate to be salt and light remains.

Salt is not just for flavor; it's a preservative. The speaker told a story of Dennis Kinlaw, who, as a child, performed his chore of rubbing salt on pork too quickly, and the pork was soon ruined. Ours can be a preserving ministry in a morally degraded society. Like the candles on the river, we too are to be sprinkled throughout our country and culture. Perhaps days ahead will be like those of Jeremiah, who didn't perform miracles, or preach sermons that were heeded, or win any popularity contests; quite to the contrary. Yet he did God's work, so much so that some thought Jesus was Jeremiah returned; at this point my mind went back a year to Dr. Stone's teaching about Jeremiah.

And what of light? The darker it gets, the greater the opportunity to shine as lights in the darkness—a point Dr. Martin Luther King, Jr. never tired making. We have a battle ahead, but we're not to forget who our real enemy is— principalities and powers, spiritual forces of darkness and wickedness—and that the battle, ultimately, is not ours, but God's. The fight to come may not be the one we would have chosen, but we'll be judged by how we conduct it nonetheless. We have the chance, by God's strength, to shine as the stars shine above.

I happened to attend this service without my wife, and being there without her reminded me of all the times my mom attended the Galilean service without a family member to accompany her. It made me mildly wistful as I regretted not having gone with her more to this service she loved so much. Leaving the service, encouraged but nostalgic, I walked past the point on the grounds where the idea of writing this History first occurred to me three years before, as my mom was in the hospital freshly diagnosed with cancer. I walked past the cottage of an old friend who never makes it to camp anymore. I walked to the cottage that had been my mom's, simple, unadorned, but, to her, precious. And I drove off the grounds, passing the bathhouse my dad used more than twenty years before. And then I drove past the camper site, where, as a kid, I remember seeing it filled to overflowing; now the numbers could no longer compare, though this year seemed more encouraging than the last few.

One image replaced the next, each stirring memories and evoking emotions; it was a night of nostalgia, a time to reflect on the rich history of these grounds, and the prospects for its future. I found myself hoping that its greatest days were still ahead, and not behind; that nostalgia turns out to be more about the future than the past; that Eaton Rapids once more can be known as a place to go for water that heals and cleanses—and quenches our deepest thirsts.

Part IV

Post World War II

1945-1984

Cold War America

At the close of World War II, America was installed as the world's superpower. While World War I was to be the "war to end all wars," WWII quickly surpassed the overall devastation wrought by that earlier global contest. The death toll of WWII is estimated between fifty and eighty million, a figure difficult to calculate, never mind fathom, because of the number of civilians targeted, not to mention the sheer brutality that defies analysis. As in WWI, America was spared much of the direct onslaught, being geographically well positioned and entering the contest years after it had begun.

Ideologically as well as militarily, America emerged victorious. The atrocities committed by Germany and Japan, in the minds of many (though not all), justified America achieving victory through atomic warfare, a technological coup that catapulted the United States to global leadership. This position the U.S. held unrivaled, at least for a few years until the USSR recovered economically and developed their own nuclear technology. The USSR's increasing technological capabilities led to the infamous Cold War between the superpowers that lasted from the 50s through the 80s. The two nations sparred over ideology, competed to outstrip the other with weaponry advancement and space exploration, and fought proxy wars in Korea, Cuba, and Vietnam.

At home, factories that had fired up for the war effort transitioned to manufacture consumer goods, catering to GIs and their families who sought stability and security after decades of upheaval that began with the Depression. A baby boom followed, with the number of live births during the 1940s increasing by half over those of the 30s. Suburbs grew up, with Levittown, New York, as the model. Interstates soon appeared, and by 1958 there were more than sixty-seven million automobiles in America, more than one for each household.

1949 marked the famous Los Angeles Crusade of Billy Graham, the first great evangelistic campaign for the most important evangelist of the twentieth century. Scheduled for three weeks, it was extended to eight, during which time Graham spoke to 350,000 people by its culmination. Some would later describe it as the greatest revival since the time of Billy Sunday.

Television was another novelty of the 50s that soon became an American staple. By 1950 over four million households had a TV set, with those numbers ever increasing—at the rate of 20,000 a day being purchased by 1956.

Television itself served in many ways to homogenize culture, promoting mass-produced goods to all corners of the country and distributing to all the same news stories and entertainment. As such it was a powerful tool for the newly emerging Civil Rights Movement because people around the nation witnessed visual depictions of the struggles of black people fighting for civic equality.

Throughout the 60s, figures like Martin Luther King, Jr. and Malcolm X sought to awaken the national consciousness to the existence and negative effects of segregation and Jim Crow laws in southern states. Although the movement faced internal divisions over purposes and methods, it sparked lasting positive social change, notably in passage of the Civil Rights Act of 1964 and the Voting Rights Act of 1965. Interestingly enough, King drew on camp meeting imagery to help his audience envision this fulfillment of justice: "So in Montgomery, Alabama, we can walk and never grow weary, because we know that there will be a great camp meeting in the promised land of freedom and justice."[51]

The 1960s marked many other remarkable social changes. 1968, in particular, was a tumultuous year in which infamous sparks flew when William F. Buckley and Gore Vidal locked horns in several acerbic nationally televised events. A decade of revolution, it ushered in the Vietnam War and its concomitant protests; it saw the nation's first Catholic president elected and embraced the youthful optimism he embodied; it experienced a renewed feminist movement that encouraged women's equality in the workplace and the legality of oral contraception. The courts sided with those who supported unencumbered access to birth control, with Griswold v. Connecticut ensuring a Constitutional "right to privacy" in 1965 and extending that ruling to cover abortion with Roe v. Wade in 1973.

In the face of these cultural shifts, the Moral Majority was formed in 1979. The leading voice of the movement, Jerry Falwell, effectively mobilized conservative Christians to political action. Their platform supported the traditional family; strove for reintroducing Christian traditions and values in the public square, including the educational system; and, most significantly, outlaw abortion. Although the group had some measure of success—garnering name recognition, helping ensure the election of Ronald Reagan in 1980 and again in 1984, and establishing the Religious Right as a power player in the Republican Party—it was eventually dismantled in 1989. It also provided a cautionary tale to conservatives about forming too close an alliance with a particular political party.

---

[51] James M. Washington, ed., *A Testament of Hope: The Essential Writings and Speeches of Martin Luther King, Jr.* (San Francisco: HarperCollins, 1991), 88; cf. p 141, 461.

Chapter 8

Scene by the River, 1945-1954

As technology claimed more territory in cultural media, so, too, did it influence the camp meeting practice. The first public address system was installed in the Tabernacle in 1945. It was in that same year that Wallace Haines came from the Chicago Evangelistic Institute to be the youth speaker. Wartime rationing was in effect for copies of the 1945 brochure, and records are a bit thin for a few years. Between 1946 and 1949, Paul Rees would return as a speaker, a favorite through the years. Board minutes throughout this period registered a number of cottage transfers and concerns over various logistical matters like electric lines, lighting during camp, and road repairs. As mentioned, Wallace Haines would work with the youth, and he would later become one of the most distinguished Presidents in the history of the Association.

A new songbook called *King's Highway* began to be used in 1949, a delightful book of one hundred camp meeting songs bound with a modern plastic cover and of pocket size and published by Haldour Lillenas. It would be used for several years, and attendees were encouraged to bring their own copies.

In 1950 Marjorie Louise Snell wrote the following poem entitled "Scene by the River":

> 'Mid towering oaks our cottage stands
> Upon a wooded knoll.
> And from the spacious porch we view
> The Grand's majestic roll.
> When winter's bound the river in
> And ground is bleak with snow,
> It makes me sad to see this place
> Where in the summer's glow
> The hills are thick with woodland flowers
> And birds' song fill the air.
> Where sky is blue and hearts are light.
> And joy is everywhere.
> When winter's cold has left the land,
> A call the breezes bring;
> I leave the city far behind

> And go to meet the spring.
> I stand among the scented pines,
> My heart so gay and bold,
> I watch the awe inspiring sight
> When buds first light behold.
> I want to cry, or laugh and sing,
> And throw my arms around
> The whole of the enthralling scene
> The beautiful camp ground!
> I love it so, for one can be
> So close to nature there;
> My heart is filled with peace and calm,
> I lift to God a prayer.
> The Father up above us all
> With His all-powerful hand,
> Has given me eyes with which to see
> The wonders of His land!

That same year, on May 31, the Rev. J. C. McPheeters, editor of *Pentecostal Herald*, and one of the true luminaries who would speak at ERC (four years later), wrote "Camp Meeting Time." The article shares his hope that camp meeting, once again, would be used of God as a spiritual correction to America's decadence:

> It has now been 150 years since the first camp meeting was held in Logan County. The camp meetings are now a time-tested and proven instrument of God in the spread of the kingdom over the earth. They have resulted in a vast harvest of souls, including many thousands saved and sanctified, and other thousands called to the Christian ministry and the mission fields of the world. The camp meetings formed an important part of the spearhead of the great revival of 1800, which broke the shackles of lawlessness and immorality which held a death grip on wide areas of the young republic. Conditions were so changed under the influence of the revival that the general assembly of the Presbyterian Church in the year 1800 declared: "The state and prospects of vital religion in our country are both more favorable and encouraging than at any period within the last forty years."
>
> The periods of apostasy and spiritual decline within our nation during the past two decades have been quite similar to the period of lawlessness and immorality that held sway during the period that preceded the revival of 1800. Again the revival fires are burning over the nation in a manner to give encouragement to the people of God. It is the earnest prayer of multitudes that we may now be in the beginning of another revival period, similar to the great revival of 1800, in which the camp meetings played so conspicuous a part. The camp meeting still has a large and

important place in this mid-century period. We should plan and expect large things of God during the camp meeting season of 1950. The revival tides are coming in and every camp should help to swell these tides to new heights that have not hitherto been reached.

There are yet higher heights to be attained and deeper depths to be reached. We need to go deeper yet in the undergirding of our camps with more prayer. Some camps are finding it tremendously helpful to have one or two all-night prayer meetings during the camp. The whole world is skirting on the brink of destruction. The only saving power that remains for mankind is the power of the living God. All other remedies have proven to be as futile as scented rose water for the treatment of cancer.

Only the mighty miracle-working power of God in the hearts of men can change the threatened destiny of destruction through hydrogen bombs and other unspeakable weapons of death. The most solemn task and responsibility that now rests upon the people of God is to give themselves wholeheartedly and without reserve to the task of bringing about a mighty spiritual awakening that will save civilization from a course of self-destruction. Everyone who can possibly do so should attend an old fashioned camp meeting during the summer. May the power of God rest mightily upon us in the camp meeting days that are immediately ahead!

McPheeters served as President of Asbury Theological Seminary from 1942-1962, and also wrote a short piece called "Undergirding the Camp Meeting with Prayer" that reads as follows:

Prayer is the lifeline of the camp meeting. The camp meeting movement in America was born out of much prayer. The announcement of the camp meeting should be the announcement to a call for prayer. The physical environment of the camp meeting is in line with the pattern set by Jesus when He withdrew from the multitudes and went aside for a time of prayer and meditation. A major purpose of the camp meeting is to call people aside from the busy affairs of life to spend extra time in prayer and meditation. The camp meeting flourishes in an atmosphere of much prayer. It depreciates in an atmosphere of little or no prayer.

There are many and varied prayer patterns which God uses in the camp meeting, one of which is community prayer. The camp meeting is a community where people live apart from the world for a period of a week, ten days, or two weeks. Community prayer involves praying one for another, and praying unitedly for specific requests. To obtain this goal the entire camp should be organized into prayer circles on three age levels: adult, youth, and children. Each circle should have from five to seven members and should pray daily for each by name, and for certain unsaved persons whose names have been submitted by members of the circle.

There are a number of methods by which groups may be divided into small prayer circles: (1) To have an alternating count up to five, with those who have the same number getting together in groups of five; (2) Captains may be appointed to select members for their prayer groups; (3) A committee may make assignments to the prayer groups.

An appointed time, including not less than ten minutes daily, should be arranged in the camp schedule for the meeting of the prayer circles. A bell should ring for the opening and closing of the prayer circle period. Some camps make the prayer circle period a part of the daily morning program, immediately preceding the morning preaching service.

The whole camp should stand at attention during a daily three-minute prayer period, announced by the ringing of a bell, with light taps of the bell continued throughout the entire period.

An early morning prayer service before breakfast and an evening prayer service preceding the evening preaching service has been a long-established custom in many camps, with far-reaching results. Some camps observe the evening hour of prayer, with cottage services held in the cottages of the campers.

The camp meeting affords an opportunity for observing nights of prayer and for keeping chains of prayer. The unbroken chain of prayer is made possible by a sufficient number of people observing one hour or a half-hour period of prayer in relays, so that the chain is unbroken for a specific period of time—such as twenty-four hours or throughout the whole of a night. Some camps observe two or three nights of prayer during the camp session, and there are even some who maintain an unbroken chain of prayer every night of the camp session.

Another opportunity in prayer for the camp meeting is prayer for the healing of the sick. A number of camps hold one service for this specific purpose. The healing touch of God for the body as well as the soul has been graciously manifested in these services.

The rich experience of prayer on the camp ground should be made continuing experiences as the people return to their local churches. The camp meeting should be specifically remembered in prayer throughout the year. With such a background in prayer, the people will return to each camp session with high anticipation for mighty manifestations of the Holy Spirit.

1951 featured Rev. Wm. Cox and his wife Ruth Cox in charge of the youth, evangelist Rev. L. S. Hoover, and the Rev. Morton Dorsey as platform speakers, and Rev. Clay Milby as Song Leader and soloist. The Flint Citadel Band of the Salvation Army played at the afternoon service July 29 and for a special sacred concert at 4:30—"one of the best organizations of its character in the country."

Dorsey's daughter, Patricia Perrelli, gives the following account of her father's salvation and ministry experience:

Rev. Morton Dorsey was born January 10, 1923, in Winchester, Ohio. He was saved at age 13 during a revival in Winchester. He soon felt the call to preach and preached his first sermon on March 14, 1937 at Bainbridge, Ohio. With his older brother John and sisters Joy and Anna Lou, they formed the Dorsey Four quartet in the summer of 1937 and traveled extensively singing and the boys preaching. Morton attended and graduated from Chicago Evangelistic Institute (CEI) in Chicago, Illinois (later changed to Vennard College and moved to University Park, Iowa). He met his wife, Sarah Cooper from Findlay, Ohio at college and they were married in June of 1948. They traveled together as Morton held evangelistic meetings across the country.

Perrelli also recalls fond memories of her family's summer treks from one camp meeting to the next:

During the years when Daddy was in traveling evangelism, most of the summers were filled with camp meetings around the country. After school would let out, the family got to travel with him so that is how we spent our summers – traveling from camp to camp. We drove in an old station wagon with no air conditioning and four girls, all who frequently got carsick. Daddy would entertain us with songs, stories, and quoting poems that he had learned from his mother. I can remember the excitement of driving into a new Camp Meeting. We would wonder what the accommodations were going to be, would the kids be friendly, would we find boyfriends, etc. And I can remember the pride of seeing Daddy in the pulpit as he expounded on the word of God. He was an eloquent and captivating preacher. His sermon illustrations would evoke powerful images. I can still quote many of the lines he used. People would flock to the altar calls. Daddy was very dignified and proper as a preacher. No matter how hot a service would get, I never saw him remove his suit jacket until when he would come down from the pulpit. I can remember going up to him when he would be kneeling with seekers. His jacket would be slung over his shoulder and he would be warm but still would welcome me and put his arm around me as I stood close to him.

In the late 1950s, the old dormitories above the dining hall, having fallen into disuse, were cleared, and Clarence Hutchens—Dean of Youth—purchased new double-deckers from MSU. In the same general movement, the outside stairways were reconstructed inside. The old east porch entrance to the dining hall gave way to first floor restrooms, and the present entrance was added. Recent renovations of the lobby of the hotel, as well as the dining room porch area have been made possible through faithful gifts of ERC members.

In the 1940s, frequent reference was made in trustee minutes to the condition of the rotting timbers and the leaking roof of Epworth Chapel. In 1953, the Epworth Tabernacle was torn down and Peace Chapel replaced it. Peace Chapel was dedicated August 1, 1954, to the memory of Lloyd H. Nixon (who passed away October 27, 1952) and his father, W. G. Nixon, who together had given so many years of service to Eaton Rapids Camp Meeting.

1953 marked the passing of H. D. Skinner, and in that year, too, the first official Memorial Service was held on opening night of camp meeting, Thursday, July 23. That camp meeting, too, was the first candlelight (Galilean) service led at the riverbank by Dr. Hahn.

Camp meeting of 1954 featured Dr. McPheeters and, also from Asbury, the Harvard-trained Dr. Harold Kuhn; the invitation to publicize the camp that year went like this: "Here in BEAUTIFUL SURROUNDINGS, on the banks of the Grand River, amid the tall oaks and maples, where grassy slopes invite to rest and meditation, one may find a PRICELESS FELLOWSHIP on the full-salvation level that will delight and enrich the souls of all who will give themselves fully to Christ."

Seventy years removed from the opening camp meetings at Eaton Rapids, the invitation remained consistent—calling folks to set themselves apart to focus their time and attention on the life-giving work of the Holy Spirit, ministered to by church leaders and laypeople alike, with many opportunities to participate in that ministry themselves.

Spotlight on J. C. McPheeters (1886-1983)
[Article on Camp Meetings by J. C. McPheeters]

Francis Asbury once called Camp Meeting a battle-ax and weapon of war to counter corruption and sin. Thinking much in this vein, J. C. McPheeters, published the following article in a *Camp Meeting Manual* prepared by the National Holiness Association:

While the camp meeting is a distinctly American institution, outdoor preaching reaches back to the time of Nehemiah. John Wesley in England, Francis Asbury and his circuit riders in America, and George Whitefield in both England and America, spoke before thousands in the open. On the American frontier great crowds gathered in weekend sacramental services.

It was in Logan County, Kentucky, in 1799, that the first camp meeting broke out. James McGready, a Presbyterian minister, had migrated to Logan County in 1796, coming from North Carolina. The three churches of his circuit were located on Gasper River, Muddy River, and Red River. Religious and moral conditions on the frontier were at a low ebb. The great move westward brought adventurous spirits of varying description. Low manners and morals were the result of a transplanted society. At McGready's Red River circuit "Rogue's Harbor" was known as a hangout for highwaymen, horse thieves, murderers, and thugs. McGready had early in his three-point circuit organized a prayer band. During the third year he held a weekend sacramental meeting. Two brothers, John McGee, a Methodist, and William McGee, a Presbyterian, on their way from West Tennessee to Ohio, stopped over for the meeting. A great visitation from God accompanied their preaching and conviction swept the audience until wicked men fell to the ground. They arose to witness to the power of a changed heart.

In July, 1800, the first planned camp meeting was held on the banks of the Red River. Tents, wagons, and brush were used for shelter. The preacher's stand was located in the center of a square, around which the people sat on log seats.

On August 6, 1801, in Cane Ridge, Kentucky, it is estimated that from ten thousand to twenty-five thousand gathered at one time in this great "general camp meeting." Peter Cartwright, converted soon after 1800 in a Logan County camp meeting, became the most famous of the early camp meeting preachers for over half a century.

The camp meeting spread across the American frontier and to the Atlantic seaboard. By 1820 nearly one thousand camp meetings were in existence in America. "Combining this new mass revivalism outdoor plan with the circuit system, the class meeting, the love feast, and the weekly prayer meeting, Methodism largely built a new denomination from 1800 to 1840."

By 1840 the frontier and "old fashioned" camp meetings had declined. Some reasons for it were: financial prosperity, the slavery issue, westward migration, and ranting fanaticism at the camps.

By 1830 and 1840 permanent camp sites were gradually acquired in the east. The "old fashioned" brush arbor camp of frontier fame was slowly replaced by the "socialized" permanent camp ground. Although the preaching of the experience of holiness had been encouraged by Bishop Asbury and his preachers, there had arisen a lukewarm clergy. Within the ranks of the "new fashioned" camp meeting there was found a mixed multitude. However, in the midst of this spiritual decline a number of leaders, mostly Methodist, boldly declared the doctrine and experience of entire sanctification.[52]

Of great influence in promoting the cause of full salvation was the "Tuesday meeting for the Promotion of Holiness" organized by Mrs. Sarah Lankford in 1835. Two Methodist churches in New York City combined the ladies' prayer meetings, of which Mrs. Phoebe Palmer, wife of Dr. Walter C. Palmer and sister of Sarah Lankford, became the foremost leader. Four years later the meeting was opened to men and continued for sixty years as a dynamic spiritual force.

The meetings were quiet: the Bible was the textbook; and holiness of heart was the main emphasis. The first distinctly holiness periodical, *The Guide to Holiness*, first known as *The Guide to Christian Perfection*, was purchased by the Palmers in 1865. It had a circulation of 40,000 copies, and reached around the world in its influence for full salvation. Dr. and Mrs. Palmer, for many summers, visited camp meetings in both Canada and America where they saw a great harvest of people saved and sanctified.

In the period following the Civil War there was great moral and spiritual regression. A growing concern among the more deeply spiritual called "loudly for a revival of primitive simplicity and power of Christianity." The time was ripe for a special technique to promote the doctrine of entire sanctification.

In August, 1866, Reverend John A. Wood suggested that a camp meeting be held whose main emphasis would be the promotion of holiness. On the morning of June 13, 1867, a called meeting took action to hold a holiness camp meeting at Vineland, New Jersey, July 17-26. Names prominent in this planning committee were: George C. M. Roberts, R. V. Lawrence, William B. Osborne, Alfred Cookman, George Hughes, A. Longacre, J. S. Inskip, Anthony Atwood, J. A. Wood, John Thompson, and R. J. Andrews. The name given the new enterprise was "The National Camp Meeting for the Promotion of Christian Holiness." John S. Inskip became the first president. For many years the Association did not have a constitution or bylaws. The second National Camp Meeting was held in Manheim, Pennsylvania in July of 1868. In 1869, Round Lake, New York was the scene of the camp. At least twenty thousand people

---

[52] William James, the great American pragmatist philosopher and psychologist, was legendary for assigning primacy to religious experience. In his classic *Varieties of Religious Experience*, he quotes Wesley at one point where Wesley expresses his conviction that entire sanctification, full salvation, commonly, if not always, is an "instantaneous work." James then wrote, "For Methodism . . . unless there have been a crisis of this sort, salvation is only offered, not effectively received, and Christ's sacrifice in so far forth is incomplete. Methodism surely here follows, if not the healthier-minded, yet on the whole the profounder spiritual instinct. The individual models which it has set up as typical and worthy of imitation are not only the more interesting dramatically, but psychologically they have been the more complete." See his *Varieties* (NY: The Modern Library, 1994), 251.

and one hundred fifty ministers were present on the Lord's Day. In 1870, in response to many pressing invitations, three National Camp Meetings were held.

Because of the quickened interest in the doctrine of sanctification, many additional holiness services were held in churches, campgrounds, and in tent meetings.

From 1867 to 1883 fifty-two National Camp Meetings had been held. John Inskip, President of the Association, presided at forty-eight of these. The National Committee had arranged for only the first two. By invitation, the Methodist Episcopal Church arranged for the other fifty.

The holiness camp meeting promoted a deep spiritual unity among all denominations that espoused it. In the early seventies the "National Publishing Association for the Promotion of Holiness" had been formed. *The Advocate of Christian Holiness*, later known as *The Christian Witness*, was first published in July of 1870. This periodical served to promote, educate, and instruct on holiness, and encouraged and fed those who had received spiritual experiences at the camp meetings. Dr. Henry Clay Morrison published the first issue of *The Herald* (proclaiming Methodism's historic message) on December 14, 1888, under the name "The Old Methodist." After changing the name two different times, the paper was published for many years under the title "The Pentecostal Herald." In 1888 the Reverend Martin Wells Knapp began the publication of *The Revivalist* (God's Revivalist). These periodicals gave strong support to the holiness camp meetings.

The National Camp Meetings spread until in 1894 eighty-four had been held in twenty-two states of the Union, one in a territory, and one in Canada.

At the death of John Inskip, William McDonald became the president of the National Association. He was followed by C. J. Fowler, 1894-1919.

Many new denominations came into existence among the holiness groups in the period between 1893 and 1907. These new bodies initiated camp meetings on a denominational as well as interdenominational basis. Because of the growing number of camps among the holiness denominations, it seemed less needful for the National Association to hold such meetings. The Association now holds an annual convention and actively seeks to promote the doctrine and experience of entire sanctification. At these meetings seminars are held on missions, camp meetings, publishing interests, literature, colleges, and youth.

A history of the camp meeting would not be complete without mentioning the great camp meeting movement in India and in Africa. In November, 1923 a small group of missionaries met in the heart of a large jungle in Nizam's Dominion in India. As a result of a mighty outpouring of God's Spirit, a rebirth came to whole conferences of Methodism. A young missionary, Alexander Reid, read of the camp meetings of India and was inspired to initiate camp meetings in the Congo. These camp meetings are believed to be a major contributing factor in the mighty revival of the Belgian Congo.

The camp meeting continues to be used as a special technique for promoting holiness by both interdenominational and denominational groups. To quote Charles L. Blanchard in his thesis, "A Study of the Modern Camp Meeting":

This modern revivalistic center exists for the church. Some of its objectives are: the salvation of the sinner; the sanctification of the believer; the espousal of a deeper spiritual life under rugged gospel preaching, particularly a holy life; the conservation of the local church; the enlistment of students for holiness schools, the ministry, the mission field, the professions, and business; the promotion of a broader fellowship among spiritual people; the inauguration of a supernatural revival among the churches; and, finally, the preparation in life's workshop for eternal habitations and eternal service. The soul-satisfying experiences of conversion and entire sanctification, attested by the witness of the Holy Spirit, gloriously meet the needs of the human heart. Such experiences provide for growth in grace and maturity in holy character. To this end the modern camp meeting exists.

Chapter 9

Camp Ground, 1955-1964

On Monday, August 1, 1955, the Board of Trustees recommended to the Association that they accept the offer of Mr. Dickson to build a bookstore on the grounds under their direction. At the next meeting, two days later, W. Brown moved that they proceed with tearing down the current bookstore and erecting the new one in time for the next camp, and his move was supported and carried. They also recommended the Caretaker be placed on Social Security, and on August 6 it was moved a letter of thanks be sent to the Hatter family for the piano donated to the camp; then it was supported and carried.

The ERC Executive Committee on October 10, 1956, was unanimous in their desire to secure the services of Billy Graham for one Sunday for any camp in the future when he could be obtained. The men suggested that President Hahn write Paul Rees because he had worked so closely with Graham and ask him how they might obtain his service for a Sunday. Rees replied, "Billy Graham, as you can well imagine, is a hard man to 'get' these days. His invitations are just about innumerable. But there's nothing like trying!"

He then offered a word of advice about the letter that Hahn would write to him. We have a copy of that letter in the records, dated October 19, 1956: "Dear Brother Graham: The Executive Committee of the Eaton Rapids Camp Meeting Association strongly desires to obtain your service for the first Sunday of our encampment, at your earliest possible date." The letter then listed dates ranging from 1957 through 1967, and asked, if any of those were available, for Graham to indicate which it was. Records don't contain a reply by Graham, and he never ended up speaking at Eaton Rapids.

1958 marked the death of the Rev. George Bennard, whose heavenly music had bathed ERC for decades. Fitting that that was one of many years "The Singing Shepperds" performed their music on the grounds.

The late 1950s also marked the time that Alice Camber reports that her funny bone was always tickled by comments that if it was too wet in the cafeteria (hosted by the Rev. and Mrs. Luella Showers) you could walk over to Grace Hotel (hosted by the Dryers).

A. Boyd Chamberlin composed this poetic celebration of ERC in 1959:

CAMP GROUND

I'm back again on the old Camp Ground
That lies on the river's bend
Back on the old grounds where I found my Lord
To be such a real true friend.

Back where so many have yielded all
And started their life anew,
To labour now in his harvest fields
Where laborers are so few.

Surrendered all to his blessed will
To walk in the way He planned,
Tho it take them away from friends and home
Perhaps to a foreign land.

Or stay at home if that be His will
By grace that he will supply,
To walk the path that he has marked for them
And never once asking why.

I thought of the life that I have lived
And asked, "Has the path I've trod
Helped some lost soul to surrender all
To the blessed will of God?"

Have I walked with Him, tried to do His will
Or selfishly done my own,
Forgetting the path He has marked for me
And foolishly walked alone.

In 1960 the Revs. Clarence Hutchens and Paul Conklin were vice presidents. A 1960 pamphlet contained this summation: "Many great evangelists have declared the unsearchable riches of Christ from the camp pulpits. Among these was the highly beloved conference evangelist of the Philadelphia Area of the Methodist Church, the Rev. Joseph H. Smith. Brother Smith served the camp for thirty three years." The overview continues by offering the following history:

> The original incorporated name of the organization was involved, but it gave a clue to the denominational connection which has been maintained, officially or unofficially, across the years. It was known as the MICHIGAN STATE HOLINESS CAMP MEETING ASSOCIATION OF THE MICHIGAN AND DETROIT CONFERENCES OF THE METHODIST EPISCOPAL CHURCH. While the leadership has been largely Methodist, there has been a fine fellowship with a great many

members and ministers of other denominations. Two of the evangelists for this anniversary year are other than Methodist.

This great camp has grown across the years under the leadership of many devoted ministers beginning with C. E. Holbrook. The list includes W. I. Cogswall, James Hamilton, Samuel Miller, David Hale, Marshall M. Callen, William Nixon, Wallace Manning, Howard Skinner, Lloyd H. Nixon, Byron A. Hahn, and the present president, Warren E. Brown.

If the trees and the water and the leaf-strewn paths could speak, they would surely tell of the high spiritual moments in the lives of hundreds who have fought spiritual battles and have overcome in the name of the Lord. It is our solemn charge and challenge to carry on this great ministry in the years to come.[53]

A newspaper article from 1960 called "Camp Meeting 75 Years Old" was written just prior to Sunday, July 31, as "the faithful gather on the Camp grounds to observe the 75th anniversary" of ERC. The article says they need not, however, like their predecessors, be burdened with tasks like bedding down horses or pitching and securing tents. The article reiterates relevant facts of ERC's history as recorded in W. Scott Munn's *The Only Eaton Rapids on Earth*, including how Salvation Army's Captain George Bennard composed his famous hymn and sang for services in Eaton Rapids in years gone by—a song featured by Billy Sunday and recorded, played, and sung the world over.

Included in the diamond anniversary program the upcoming Sunday, "Anniversary Day," would be the Salvation Army band from the Citadel Corps in Lansing at the special 3 p.m. afternoon service and the choir of the First Methodist Church at the 7:30 evening service. The Spring 1960 issue of *Echoes* announced a few changes in the itinerary. Dr. Paul Rees had been planning to attend camp, but was called into a world tour for World Vision for the summer. Dr. Harry Denman, too, was called to South America by the General Board of Evangelism of the Methodist Church.

---

[53] The brochure also listed Camp Officers as follows: Warren E. Brown, Pastor, Pres. Mt. Hope Methodist, Lansing. G. Russell Nachtrieb, Pastor, 1st VP, Aldersgate Methodist, Detroit. Clarence Hutchens, Pastor, 2nd VP, Wesley Pk. Methodist, Grand Rapids. Mr. Paul Conklin, 3rd VP, "Bible Nook", Lansing. Milford E. Bowen Sr., Pastor. Treas. Methodist Church, Bellevue. H. James Birdsall, Pastor. Sec'y. Lakeside Methodist, Muskegon. Mr. Harry Walker, Mem. Ex. Comm. Wausoon, Ohio. Mr. Clarence McNeil, Program Comm. Lansing, Michigan. Members of the Historical Committee were listed as Miss Leah Brown, Mrs. Russell Burrows, Mrs. Earl Prosser, the Rev. Mr. Dorr Garrett, and Mrs. Nellie Hahn. Camp workers for 1960 were Dr. Stimson R. Smalley, Minister Gresham Methodist, Chicago; Dr. C. I. Armstrong, Evangelist, the Wesleyan Methodist Church; Dr. Paul F. Elliott, President Owosso Bible College; Dr. Glen Johnson, Dir. of Music, Methodist Church, Dallas, Tex.; Mrs. Joseph Edwards (Children), Lansing, Mr. Hope Church. Youth workers listed were John Bullock, M. E. Bowen, C. W. Hutchens, D. Garrett, Lawrence Maxson (and others).

Excellent replacements saved the day. Speakers slated were Dr. Paul F. Elliot, acting president of Owosso Bible College; Dr. Stimson R. Smalley, pastor of Gresham Methodist Church of Chicago; Dr. C. I. Armstrong, evangelist and vice-chairman of the Board of Directors of World Gospel Mission; and R. Glen Johnson, minister of music in the Lover's Lane Methodist Church of Dallas, Texas. Leah Brown and Mrs. James Birdsall again accompanied on the organ and piano. Mrs. Joseph Edwards worked with children that year. That year's camp brochure was emblazoned with a picture of a diamond, and its catchwords for that year, prominently displayed on the first page, were "wholesome," "Wesleyan," and "worshipful."

Prior to camp was scheduled a "paint up" "fix up." "Seventy five years is a long time! Few of our buildings have spanned all these years. Some are getting old enough, however, to require plenty of repair and 'fixin'." The men's auxiliary was exhorted to spearhead a workday to this end.

Echoes also reported that at the close of camp meeting 1959, income had been sufficient to pay all of the current bills and get them started on the budget for 1960, a portion of which was already earmarked for a "floor fund" and another for the "new store" fund. Contributions were solicited. Additionally, it mentioned that some churches were contemplating putting Eaton Rapids Camp Meeting in their budgets, "a step that will assure a continuing program that can undergird the work of local churches and help to assure the continuance of a camp that has been a benediction to thousands." Above all readers were exhorted to pray for the upcoming camp meeting daily.

A *State Journal* article dated September 21, 1961, written by William Duchaine, captures an image: a Mr. and Mrs. Dewey Weiss of Imlay City busily getting a summer cottage ready before the annual session of camp meeting. "We're fixing up the place for our son, Rev. James Weiss, who bought it recently as a summer home," said Mrs. Weiss. "I believe more young men are inspired to enter the ministry at these camp meetings than anywhere else," she said, going on to explain that she and her husband began taking their son to the Romeo camp meeting when he was ten. In 1961, the son was now thirty-six and pastor of the Methodist Church at Berkley, near Detroit.

As it happens, one of my best high school friends at the Dearborn Free Methodist Church during high school was John Weiss—one of three children of Rev. and Mrs. James Weiss. Not only were John and I friends at church; we would come to discover the Eaton Rapids connection as well, because his parents had kept that cottage all through the years, making it possible for Eaton Rapids to comprise an important part of John's heritage, too. In fact, John's sister and brother-in-law eventually received the Weiss cottage from her parents, keeping it in the family. John and his wife and daughter along with his sister's family remain active at Eaton Rapids to the present time. Indeed, his sister Mary's husband, Scott Crecilius—music minister at Bridge Community Church (and Director of Bands at Larson Middle School) in Troy, Michigan—has served as a song leader at ERC for several years more recently. John's daughter and his sister's children are, of course, third-generation descendants of Mr. and Mrs. Dewey Weiss who, in that timeless snapshot of 1961, are still cleaning out the cottage and readying it for camp meeting and their still youthful minister son.

After camp in 1962 the old camp store, which had stocked groceries and supplies for the campers, was torn down and a new concrete slab and foundations were poured. Most of the lumber from the old building was used in the new one. One of the speakers in 1962 was H. B. (Jim) Jones, from North Carolina; he flew his own plane to get there!

Warren E. Brown died March 5, 1963, the year that also marked the first of a half dozen appearances by Philip Hinerman on the camp meeting platform.

A July 16, 1964 local paper article was called "79th Eaton Rapids Camp Meeting Begins Today," subtitled "Ex-Congressman Judd Key Speaker." The article began, "Reaching toward four score years of service as one of the oldest and most inspiring church camps in the Midwest, the 79th Annual Eaton Rapids Camp Meeting began today at the 33-acre site on the eastern bank of the Grand River in Eaton Rapids."

A few paragraphs down, it continued, "One of this year's outstanding speakers will be former Congressman Dr. Walter H. Judd of Minneapolis, Minn., who also spent nearly a decade in China as a medical missionary. Dr. Judd served 10 terms in Congress and gained recognition as a national authority on U. S. foreign policy. He was a member of the Foreign Affairs Committee for 16 years and played an important role in establishing U. S. relieve, recovery, re-armament, and economic development programs abroad."

Judd had served as a medical missionary in China from 1925 through 1931, sent to assist Edward Bliss; from 1931 to 1934 he worked at the Mayo Clinic in Rochester, Minnesota. In 1934 he returned to China as a missionary physician until 1938, when he returned to Minnesota. He was elected to the U.S. Congress from Minnesota in 1942. He served for twenty years from 1943 until 1963 in ten consecutive congresses. He was known for his eloquent oratory and expertise in U.S. foreign policy, and outspoken in his criticism of communism and efforts at rapprochement with China at Taiwan's expense.

Judd had given the keynote address at the 1960 Republican National Convention, which met in Chicago to nominate the Nixon-Lodge ticket. In 1962, Judd was defeated for reelection by liberal Democrat Donald M. Fraser. The District had been redrawn after the 1960 census, making it heavily Democratic. Judd was the last person to attempt to run for president on a major party ticket to have been born in the 19th century, though he did not make it past the primaries. In 1964, Judd's name was placed in nomination at the Republican National Convention for President and he received a smattering of votes.[54] There was

---

[54] In 1981 he received the Presidential Medal of Freedom, the nation's highest civilian award; throughout the 1970s and 1980s, he was actively involved in the Council against Communist Aggression in Washington, DC. The Fund for American Studies, an educational and internship program that works in partnership with Georgetown University, annually presents The Walter Judd Freedom Award in cooperation with the Center for International Relations to recognize individuals who have advanced the cause of freedom in the United States and abroad. Past recipients have included former United

speculation—by Wallace Haines, who had visited with Judd in his Washington home in September 1963 (at the time Haines was Associate Secretary General of the International Council for Christian Leadership)—that, if Judd got the vice presidential nod at the Republican Convention in 1964, that would probably preclude his ability to speak at Eaton Rapids that year.

Other speakers that year were Minneapolis pastor Dr. C. Phillip Hinerman and Dr. J. Sutherland Logan, president of Vennard College.[55] Clarence Hutchens became President of the Association in 1964 and would serve until 1971.

States President Ronald Reagan, Jack Kemp, and Jeane Kirkpatrick. Judd died in Mitchellville, Maryland on February 13, 1994.

[55] Vennard College was a non-denominational Christian college located in University Park, Iowa. It was announced on November 12, 2008 that the college would close at the end of the 2008 fall semester because of a decline in enrollment and financial difficulties. At the time of its closing, Bruce Moyer was at the helm, who has spoken at Eaton Rapids numerous times, and whose wife's family has deep roots at ERC. Vennard had begun as the Chicago Evangelistic Institute in 1910 with the stated goal of sending Spirit-filled people into the ministry and to promote Scriptural holiness. In the early years of ERC, a very close connection obtained between Eaton Rapids and CEI. In 1951 it moved to Iowa and was renamed Vennard College after the 1910 founder Dr. Iva Durham Vennard. Three other Christian colleges had formerly occupied the Iowa campus: Central Holiness University, John Fletcher College, and Kletzing College.

Spotlight on Clarence Hutchens (1914-1998)
[Newspaper Articles]

Clarence Hutchens served in several roles at Eaton Rapids Camp Meeting throughout the middle of the twentieth century. He was Dean of Youth during the 1950s, co-Vice President—along with Paul Conklin—in the early 1960s, and President of the Association from 1964 through 1971. A *Clinton County News* article about Hutchens' participation in a series of Lenten services in the St. Johns area during 1968 gives the following overview of his life and ministry:[56]

> Rev. Mr. Hutchens has served pastorates at Vernon, Ind. and the Michigan communities of Montague, Sparta, Wyoming, Ithaca, and Lansing. He is currently president of the Eaton Rapids Camp Meeting, has served 12 years in the district youth camp as counselor, registrar, and for three years as dean. He's been on the Michigan Conference Board of Evangelism both as chairman and executive secretary and recently served on the board of Wesley Foundation at Central Michigan University. Five years ago Rev. and Mrs. Hutchens participated in a preaching mission in Ciudad Quesada, Costa Rica. He is a graduate of Asbury College in 1942 and Asbury Theological Seminary in 1945. He and his wife have three children, including two daughters at Asbury College and a son at Dwight Rich Junior High in Lansing.

Hutchens, himself, in a November 1969 *Eaton Rapids Echoes*, wrote that "the great services of song and praise, the opening of the word of God by our evangelists, the enthusiasm of our youthful members, the prayer, fellowships, the mingling and visiting together as we met at the cafeteria, the contemplation of God in nature, all of these things and more helped us to get closer to God and to meet the question 'who am I' and 'what does God want to do with my life'? While we are not together enjoying the inspiration of the prayer and gospel messages prevalent on the grounds, we can be enjoying the abiding presence of God and sharing the Good News with our family, friends, and acquaintances as the Lord gives opportunity. Thus, in a sense, Camp Meeting goes on the year around. In fact, the true value of a Camp Meeting may be judged by how much it is taken out of the gates and into the world."

In an article published on December 13, 1951, *The Sentinel-Leader*, the newspaper of Sparta, Michigan, covered Hutchens' recent speaking engagement at the local Rotary Club:[57]

---

[56] "Lansing Pastor next Lenten speaker here," *Clinton County News*, March 21, 1968, accessed December 29, 2015, http://www.clinton-county.org/Portals/0/newspaper/1968/1968-03-21.pdf.

[57] "Rotary News," *The Sentinel-Leader*, December 13, 1951, accessed December 29, 2015, http://spartahistory.org/newspaper_splits/The%20Sentinel%20Leader/1951/The%20Sentinel%20Leader%20-%2012_1951%20-%20Page%206%20.pdf.

"Before I begin to talk, I want to say something" got a big laugh from club members and guests as the Rev. Clarence Hutchens, pastor of the Sparta Methodist Church, was introduced by president Bromley as the guest speaker. Rev. Hutchens used as his topic "The Relation between Religion and Rotary." "Rotary," he said, "was not a substitute for religion. If a choice had to be made, the church would win. To be a true Rotarian, one must be a Christian. What we are is more important than what we do," he declared. "If it's to be good at all, it must be done for God."

Chapter 10

Who among These Sturdy Oaks?
1965-1974

The date of camp was changed from the traditional last Thursday of July/first week of August to the last two Sundays in July, starting with the 1965 Camp Meeting.

On March 24, 1965, President Hutchens addressed the Eaton Rapids Rotary Club about ERC. He related that his first contact with camp there was about thirty-five years before, when Howard Skinner was president. He shared his first reactions as President, which had been twofold: to maintain its interdenominational flavor, but make the program more Methodist-oriented; and to strengthen the program by bringing men who communicate to our "space age day." He spoke of how they had added variety to the program without compromising, and of the need for our "Tiltin' Hilton" to be updated.

The real estate appraiser Charles R. Green issued a smartly bound "property study" to Hutchens on March 25, 1965. It is worth quoting the cover letter in full because it concisely reveals several of the needs of the property that, over the next decade or so, would be addressed.

> Pursuant to your request, I have made a study of the above property and submit herewith a brief report and analysis for your consideration.
>
> The property understudy includes a total land area of approximately 17 acres located along the northerly bank of the Grand River in the village of Eaton Rapids, Michigan. The property is located in a heavy wooden section with an abundance of mature shade in an area which is quiet and serene. The property was dedicated as a non-profit ecclesiastical association approximately 80 years ago. The improvements which were constructed about 1890 include a tabernacle, hotel, cafeteria building, and various other buildings in the compound. The total area of land has been platted [sic], streets have been dedicated and approximately 70 lots have been improved with cottages.

The buildings were constructed during an era when horse and buggy were the principal mode of travel and the use of the camp was designed for operation during short periods of the summer months. The buildings are in a deplorable condition. Little, if any, maintenance has taken place over the past 40 years and, as a result, the depreciation which has resulted places the buildings near the end of their economical life.

The recommendations which I make to you in this report entails [sic] an expenditure in excess of $100,000 and although this may seem somewhat ambitious, it is a prerequisite if the buildings are to be preserved for future use. The program which I recommend for your consideration employs a two stage development and maintenance program. First, a crash program must be instituted which will rehabilitate the existing facilities and to [sic] bring them up to, or near, the existing codes. The second stage will require a long range program which will in all probability take several years and a very intense effort if the program is to be successful.

In this report, you will find recommendations and estimates of cost for both the crash program and the long range program of rehabilitation. The crash program includes the upgrading of the cafeteria building through a remodeling program which when completed, will convert the second floor to a dormitory with bath facilities and the first floor of the cafeteria to a kitchen, dining hall, and fellowship building that will be usable during not only the summer months but during other periods of the year.

In addition, I have made a brief analysis of the leasing program to the cottage owners with recommendations for your consideration.

Camp meeting 1965 had several remarkable features. It was the first time Dennis Kinlaw spoke. Also, Senator Frank Carlson, listed the year before by *Time Magazine* as one of the six most influential U.S. Senators, gave two messages on July 22; his greatest desire was "to bear a clear and undaunted witness for Jesus Christ." And Mrs. W. C. Briggs, if she was going to be in attendance at camp that year, would have extended her span of camp meeting attendance to eighty years, beginning from the first camp in 1885.

A Board of Directors meeting on November 30, 1968 featured several ideas, pertaining to prayer and music, greater publicity and public attire. A couple points for present purposes stand out in particular: "Need to press for a greater publicity. Have ground designated historically. Then could be put on entrance to city 'Home of Eaton Rapids Camp,' thereby putting on city and state maps. Historical Society should be contacted about marker. People in Eaton Rapids are not aware of camp. Need for more publicity of history. We should be proud of our history. Old folders, steam boat, tickets, etc. could be on display at Anniversary."

That same month an issue of the Camp Meeting *Echoes* was sent out, including a section called "How to cancel out a campmeeting"—a take-off from C. S. Lewis's famous *Screwtape Letters*. This idea had been used at a Faith at Work Conference, and Rev. Hutchens read an alleged transcript of a conversation between Screwtape and Wormwood, the two devils imagined by Lewis. The exchange went like this:

Screwtape: So it came off. Another cursed E.R. Camp Meeting! Laymen honestly sharing their needs and problems and what our enemy, Christ, has done for them...openness and humor and gaiety instead of stuffy little sermonettes. . .

Wormwood: How can we cancel out the damage to our cause?

Screwtape: Here is what we must do:

Capitalize on the weariness of all who have been involved. See that irritations are thrown in their way. They are up on cloud nine. Make them concentrate on how they feel. Then when the normal let-down comes you can suggest that they have just been fooled by their imagination and that this thing is not real.
Get those who were involved to feel superior—to look down their noses at those who were not involved, and develop a critical spirit.
Many people have been made hungry for this New Life the Enemy gives. Channel this hunger into talk instead of action. The more talk the better. If you let this hunger express itself in action we are in trouble!!
See that the wives who came to the conference without their husbands go home and try to convert their husbands. Make them try real hard. But NEVER let them go home and accept their husbands and love them unconditionally. This would be tragic!
Keep those who have given their lives over to the Enemy from sharing their faith with others. We know to our sorrow that the more they give it away, the more they have themselves. Do not let them form the habit of meeting in honest open fellowship with other pilgrims along the way...
Those who served on the team are a real threat to us. They have tasted the thrill which comes when they find that the Enemy can use them to channel His love to other people. The best approach is to make them proud of this, instead of grateful. Suggest that they are now experts. Get them to switch from sharing to "Preaching." Get them to "evaluate" each other's performance, preferably in the absence of the one who is being "evaluated." If we can get them to be critical of each other we can undermine the Fellowship.

Although the date of this composition is unclear, Mrs. E. E. Williams-Childs from Lansing was inspired by ERC to write this lovely poem sometime around this period:

Years ago I came to Jesus, bowing low at his dear feet,
And the work of my forgiveness then and there was made complete;
Then I longed to be made holy, and God granted that desire.
And most blessedly baptized me with the Holy Ghost and fire!
But I quickly learned a lesson—'twas that all along the road,
There must needs be fresh revealings of the mighty power of God;
So, one happy day in summer, as I paused awhile to rest,
At the camp at Eaton Rapids, I was most supremely blest!

I have often tried to fancy what the sight of heaven must be.
With its gates of pearl and jasper, and its tranquil, glassy sea;
With its house of many mansions, where the saints are all at home,
And its streets with golden pavement, where their happy feet may roam;
But my fancy always faltered at the glory of the sight,
And my eyes grew dim with straining toward the city fair and bright;
Till, one happy day in summer, giving joy a glad new birth,
At the camp at Eaton Rapids, I found heaven here on earth!

I have often paused to listen for the music of the skies
As I've watched the night-stars glisten, or the silvery moon arise;
I have wondered just what anthem they were singing over there,
Or what precious holy symphony was sounded on the air.
But my ears—earth-clogged—were heavy, and I could not catch the strain
Though the ransomed saints in glory sang it o'er and o'er again;
Till, one happy day in summer, clear, melodious, full and free,
At the camp at Eaton Rapids, heaven's own music came to me!

I have often vaguely wondered what the fellowship of heaven
Would reveal to saved immortals, unto whose freed souls 'twas given;
And I've longed to reach the city, that I too, at last might know,
That companionship so blessed, born of love's great overflow;
But, praise God, I have discovered that the blood-washed need not wait
To enjoy this sweet communion, till they passed the pearly gate;
For, one happy day in summer, waiting there before the throne,
At the camp at Eaton Rapids, this great joy became my own!

Praise the Lord, whose hand has led me all along life's rugged way,
Till my eyes beheld the sunrise of that wondrous, joyful day!
When, with his saints assembled, where they yearly love to meet,
Hand clasped hand across the altar, in love's fellowship so sweet;
Oh, I ever shall remember (though just now I do not know
What the coming hours may bring me of human weal or woe).
That one happy day in summer, when my feet first pressed the sod
Of that camp at Eaton Rapids—holy meeting place with God!

Minutes from a May 1969 Board Meeting span a range of topics—from a report of the spring prayer retreat (which one evaluation described as "the best weekend of my life") to the filling of the position of an auditor to the death of Mrs. Byron Hahn to camp meeting song books and prospective camp meeting preachers—and also included plans for prayer. Mrs. Hayden Carruth spoke to the possibility of having in every block on the Camp Grounds one home available for prayer at the various assigned hours. It was planned that a Call to Prayer be included in the forthcoming letters to the entire constituency, to pray for the fulfillment of the camp's aims, and to undergird its financial needs with prayer.

In the fall of 1969 a letter from Carruth to the ER Finance Committee outlined the urgent need for a new Children's Center. Children's work was "no longer an adjunct to the Eaton Rapids program, but it represents an essential contribution to our central mission." Tents of various sizes and shapes had proven inadequate and unsatisfactory. She proposed a new children's tabernacle be erected on the promontory southeast of the Briggs cottage, sufficiently removed from other activity centers so that one will not impose on the other, and accessible by foot and vehicle. Outside dimensions were suggested to be 30' x 60' to accommodate 60-100 children, with a concrete slab floor, side walls opening out like the big tabernacle, with one end of the structure permanent and able to be used for storage, and the other end mostly glass so that the children, during periods of worship, can draw inspiration from the camp's greatest physical asset: the out-of-doors. She wanted to make every effort to ensure the roof was in place by 1970.

Her summary ran like this: "As Eaton Rapids is planning to make important investments, none is more imperative or more urgent than our children. It has become a truism in campground conversations that the future of Eaton Rapids is in the hands of our youth and our children. Although the children's work deserves perhaps the highest priority among the many important competing interests at ER, I am convinced that the establishment of this necessary facility can be accomplished without infringing upon other activities. Authorization is requested to start now."

Around July and August of 1969 Earl I. Prosser wrote at least five articles for the *Eaton Rapids Journal* about ERC because "so many area residents are unaware of the activity carried on at the Michigan State Holiness campground here, particularly during the summer." Prosser, a long-time resident there, had written for the *Grand Rapids Press* for four years, and was a retired Methodist minister after forty-three years of service. He had attended his first camp meeting in 1912 and had owned a cottage on the campground since 1944. His "Campground Comments" chronicled how the Christian "boom town" inside Eaton Rapids city limits had burst into full operation that summer. He described cottage renovations, old-timers traversing great distances to attend camp meeting, and such highlights of camp as the Murk Family Musicale Saturday evening, when "nearly all the 1,800 seats in the main tabernacle were occupied."

In that same issue were such Eaton Rapids recollections as these: "Old Father Clancy sings 'Just beyond the Eastern Gate'. . . . Howard Skinner is at the grand piano in knickers as Lloyd Nixon led an hour-long song service between rest time and the afternoon service on Sunday. . . . People spreading their blankets out on the grass west of the Tabernacle because the Tabernacle was full. . . . John L. Brasher soaring in heights of eloquence as he preached about seeing the Savior 'that bright day', . . . The feasts after evening service at the Bartlett cottage. . . . The smell of the new mown marsh hay on the Tabernacle floor. . . . Picking berries where the tents were. . . . Going to the lean-to shed at Miller's farm where Mrs. Miller handpacked the delicious custard ice cream in the tall round carton. . . ."

New songbooks with a short history of ERC excerpts within (*Retrospect and Prospect*, by Beth Carruth) were commissioned. Here are the final paragraphs from that publication:

> "The old order changeth giving place to new." The delightful old excursion boat has long since ceased to make its run. Gate admission has been discontinued. The corral fell into disuse as the river banks began to fill with cars. Bath houses decayed and were not replaced as the river grew more murky and swimming less attractive. New young families have come, developed interest, and begun to lift. The English Nursery cottage has been adapted and furnished for care of their children. Young people light up the night with their campfire services at the Hahn Cross. The riverside candlelight service has become a lovely part of the camp's life. The Nixon Chimes carry the melodies of the old songs across the grounds. The Brown Sittin' Fund has given relief to aching backs with the new well-shaped benches. Gone is the lovely fragrance of the marsh hay—and the dust—replaced by the concrete tabernacle floors. Rickety old Epworth Chapel and the dormitory-store have yielded to the wrecking ball; Peace Chapel and the Snack Bar have taken their place. Generous gifts have made possible major design change and winterizing of the hotel lobby and the kitchen-dining-hall, opening the Retreat Center for year-round use.
>
> We could speak of what Eaton Rapids Camp is worth in terms of dollars or investment in buildings, the escalating value of its land, and what it is costing to maintain it. The more important dimension, that for which the camp was founded, is clearly immeasurable. Thousands all over the world have found Christ because of this camp. Preachers have been true to the apostolic message and have preached with contagious winsomeness and power because they found the Holy Spirit real at these altars. Laymen have been freed to be what God intended and have gone back to carry a new creative spirit into all their relationships in church and community.

These intangibles, difficult as they are to assess, are what Eaton Rapids is all about. In this day when the charismatic movement of the Holy Spirit is breaking out in unlikely places all over the world, we thank God for any way we have been used in seeding this New Life. We stand on tiptoe at the opening of a new decade awaiting what God will do among us.

Also in 1970, Beth Carruth began to work with the children, eventually graduating with them to work in the youth program. On July 11, 1971, Hayden Carruth, Sr. wrote the Chairman of the Grounds Committee, Fred Briggs, and admitted that he lacked knowledge and perspective of the necessary projects to the buildings and grounds. Knowing that what he was asking for would be a miserable task, he nevertheless felt it necessary to ask for a comprehensive list of buildings and grounds needs as Fred saw them. He asked Fred to indicate the items that had already been authorized by the Board, but not yet implemented; projects that have been started but not completed; the next projects that should come before the Board for consideration; and a sense, in all of this, of priorities, along with, for each item, an estimation of time and money involved.

Prior to the 1971 encampment, Mrs. Hayden Carruth, with regret, announced the cancellation of the children's craft program that year. With some exasperation she related how, for a half dozen years, efforts had been made to upgrade the quality of contact with the children, but the efforts weren't very successful. "Enough is enough. We began last fall getting *serious* about appropriate housing for the children's work by 1971. Sketches, measurements, plans were shared with the Board of Directors. Authority to consult with builders was given. The more hopeful avenues of exploration proved to be *dead ends*. By April it was clear that we could not have a facility, or any stage of a facility, ready for this camp session." She then expressed, with a measure of renewed hope, that in the last meeting of the Board action was taken to open a fund for a new Children's Center, which would be ready by 1972.[58]

A Board of Directors and Committees meeting on September 6, 1971, featured a few interesting aspects. The Youth Committee, of which Ed Richmond was Chairman, asked that the youth have a full-time youth minister, allowing for a longer morning youth service. With the expected new Children's Building, the youth would have the opportunity to change the inside of Peace

---

[58] During Advent 1971, Mrs. Carruth had written a heartfelt letter to the families of ERC, beginning the letter, "Greetings in the name of the Christ Child! May the season bring you renewed joy as your family gathers round and together you honor the Savior whose birth season we celebrate." Then she wrote, "At Eaton Rapids Camp the tender lives God puts in our hands for a few days each year are our deepest concern. Those days can, and often do, determine the direction of a lifetime. This is a tremendous responsibility for us, one we take very seriously, one we cannot bear alone. Prayerfully we make our plans, select our people, and in prayer we think of you and your family, of those children whom you will entrust to us." She then shared in detail the need for a new Children's Center and the financial costs it would incur, adding that the "gift you give is a seed you plant, a seed to be miraculously multiplied in harvest in young lives. We know you'll be proud to be a part of the next fifty years of work with children at Eaton Rapids."

Chapel to a more functional and suitable meeting place. The youth also preferred to have buses leased for transportation to their recreation. They also requested use of the recreational facilities of the nearby Junior High School. A youth day during camp was also suggested so they could give their testimonials in the service of the tabernacle.

It was also requested that an ad hoc committee be appointed to spearhead the funding and building of the Children's Center. Clarence Hutchens made the suggestion that, in the placing of a new building, a Camp Architect might be helpful in the overall development of any camp construction. Bill Elzerman suggested that Michigan State University be contacted for their help in the design and placement of buildings, through their department of architectural design.

In other news, *Echoes* would be edited by Milton Ten Have. The possibility of an article in the *Michigan Christian Advocate* on the story of camp meetings in general, and Eaton Rapids camp in particular, was suggested as a promotion of the program, as was the hope to "sell the camp" to ministers as relevant in these times.

The Retreat Center promotion and a plan for reservations were discussed. A small brochure—both sides of an 8½ x 11 sheet, printed with pictures, 2000 copies, at a cost of $75.00—was to be sent to churches in adjoining counties. The mailing list of Evangelical Fellowship to the Detroit Conference was available.

The next day, on September 7, Pat and Gladys Downing stepped down as caretakers of the grounds, no longer able to do the heavy work of building preparation. They were willing to stay on through April and do all the other duties of caretaking until then.

An undated document around this time circulated among the leadership started with a reference to Hebrews 6:18: "Laying hold on the hope set before us so that we...might grasp the hope that He holds out to us," and then this paragraph: "Every hope for Eaton Rapids Camp is one with the hope that Jesus Christ might be known, loved, and obeyed in all His saving purpose and full salvation provision for all people of all ages. Believing that so high a hope is worthy of the finest possible administration of our responsibility we share together the following possible ways of achieving our maximum efficiency." There followed various plans to be implemented by the Program Committee, the Finance Committee, the Facilities Committee, and the Publicity and Public Relations Committee.

Mrs. Edson Vane died on August 9, 1971, at eighty-eight years old. A few months later, in a letter to Paul Conklin, Chairman of the ER Membership Committee, on November 3, 1971, Dr. Carruth wrote the following:

> When you and Louise Cookingham and some others did that wonderful job recently of compiling and publishing the Eaton Rapids membership list, there was a discovery that was most surprising, to me, at least: most Association members don't know most other Association members. All of us seriously, honestly wish to expand the circle of involvement in

service to God and Eaton Rapids Camp to the fullest extent, but we don't know people well enough—interests, talents, etc.—to do this very effectively. I wonder if the Membership Committee might wish to engage this problem? If so, you probably will need first of all to enlarge your committee for this purpose. And so, you run headlong into the basic problem: Who would like to work on something like this? Who would do a good job? Difficult as it may be, I think we must do something about this.

We might attack this issue at two levels:

What can we do to stimulate know-each-other-relationships among people who are now members? Wayne Sparks and Bette Futrell, representing the Auxiliaries, were exploring the establishment, last Labor Day weekend, of a recognition Dinner or an Awards Banquet, or some such, to honor Fred and Mory and Hutch and Lee (and probably others) on the occasion of their leaving their well-established posts on the Board of Directors. Nothing came of this because nobody could be found to serve a meal on the date which was under consideration. (Many thanks to Wayne and Bette for their efforts anyway!) But I'm still wondering whether some such function, if it ever becomes practical, might be arranged in a way so that acquaintanceships might be broadened and enriched. Incidentally, Labor Day 1971 was remarkably well attended: 99? It occurred to me when it was too late that we might have discovered some friends then. Afterthoughts are great!

What can we do as we admit new members to assure their full integration into the Campground community? At the annual meeting when new members are received, Hutch has always been so gracious that [it] takes on a special meaning for all who are involved. I guess I'm looking for additional ways of extending Christian hospitality and for creating near-neighbors among our people.... Will you and your committee give attention to these questions, and plan to give us guidance?

In a letter to Wayne Sparks on February 15, 1972, Carruth confirmed the speakers at that year's meeting: Rev. Herbert Bowdoin, Dr. Kenneth Kinghorn, and Rev. Tommy Tyson. "Let me add that Wayne Pede . . . will be song leader, and Barbara will preside at the Steinway. The full time youth worker will be Steven J. Harper. . . . I'll ask the Pedes and Harper to send public information materials directly to you. Leah Brown will continue at the organ. Also, we are announcing that Mrs. Dorothy Kell and Mrs. Jane Harshe will be the children's workers again. (In this connection, perhaps I should indicate that ground will be broken for construction to be in full operation during Campmeeting. Thus, a well-rounded program will be available for children, including both religious instruction and varied craft activities.)"

Bowdoin was a United Methodist pastor and evangelist, originator of the idea of *The Story*, the first color religious television series in America. He served as its President eleven years. In 1970 Bowdoin began his own series of radio programs, "Methodist Hour," which had been on 130 stations nationwide by 1972. Bowdoin had worked on nearly 300 revival crusades, many of them with Dr. Ford Philpot, of whom he wrote the biography *It Took a Miracle*.

At that time, in 1972, Harper, the full time youth worker, was still an M. Div. student at Asbury Theological Seminary, readying for his senior year. He was serving, too, as student body president. Prior to Asbury, he graduated high school in Texas in 1966 as salutatorian, entering McMurry College in Abilene, Texas, and graduating Summa Cum Laude in 1970 with a B.A. in Religion and Sociology. He had preached from the age of fifteen, and in the nine years of his ministry he had already preached nearly 1500 times and been engaged in various ministries. Harper was committed to an in-depth program and concept of evangelism. In addition to the regular preaching ministry in his meetings, he would conduct discipleship seminars with committed Christians to aid them in witnessing for Christ. His philosophy of evangelism closely paralleled that of Robert Coleman and James Kennedy, committed to a ministry in evangelism that is Christ-centered, in-depth, and relevant to our age. At this time in Harper's life, despite that he had been pastoring two churches in Kentucky, he felt a leading back into evangelism and would devote his last year in seminary to that work rather than his pastoral ministry.

Harper would return to minister at Eaton Rapids in subsequent years, finish his doctorate at Duke, and spend his career teaching spiritual formation and Wesleyan studies at Asbury Theological Seminary. He would write nearly thirty books and, in 1997, be tapped to lead as founding Vice President and Dean of the second Asbury campus, in Orlando, Florida, capacities in which he served faithfully until retiring in 2012. Dr. Timothy C. Tennent, President of Asbury Seminary, said this concerning Harper at his retirement: "Nearly a decade ago Steve wrote, 'We are never nearer the purpose of our existence than when we embrace the idea of life lived for others.' Steve has lived out his purpose every day in extraordinary ways, and Asbury Seminary is richer for it."

In recent correspondence with me, on the fourth of July 2015, Harper reflected, "Jeannie and I treasure our visits and memories of ministry at ERC, beginning in 1972 with youth ministry and then moving to the tabernacle as Bible teacher and Evangelist in subsequent visits. Our children, John and Katrina, were also blessed by their years at ERC making lasting friendships and having significant experiences with God."

In April of 1972 a Board of Directors meeting was held that covered an array of topics. One of them pertained to the work that had begun on Peace Chapel, making it a Youth Center. The pews had been removed. Some cement work was needed at the front of the building, and the hope was that the cement could be poured at the time of the pouring of the floor for the Children's Building. A fireplace would be set in the center of the room. Eventually, the platform at one end was discarded; new concrete was poured in the platform area; and the entire floor covered with carpeting. The young people developed a habit of removing their shoes at the door, and as the program grew, valuable space was spent for shoes. A long dreamed rear entry with rack space for 200 pairs of shoes and a special registration area was built, bringing the building into excellent shape.

Another item on the agenda was whether to allow the Free Methodists to use their property again, largely under the same terms from the previous year. It was agreed to charge them $2,750.00. Another agenda item involved plans for a new brochure to come out June 1, and, concerning other publicity items, it was suggested that, in the future, there might be some short television spots publicizing the camp and its program. Pastors in the area could be invited for a day to be guests of the Camp, perhaps on a Sunday. The possibility of a Minister's Recognition Day was floated, as was the prospect to invite the Detroit Conference Evangelical ministers to hold their spring retreat at ER the next year, and to bring in a similar group of men from the Michigan Conference.

Also in April of 1972, on the fourth, in the late afternoon of that Tuesday, in a bitter wind, the corner stakes for the new Children's Center were driven. That evening the committee met in the Cookingham cottage and pored over the blueprints for this "dream come true." Beth Carruth reported on the state of the finances for the building as follows: 30 pledges and gifts from the July appeal, paid in before the December mailing: $3,200. Due, and being paid on pledges: $1,000. Results from mailing (970 letters, 45 new responses): $1,800. Total: $6,000. Amount of final bid: $12,400. Needed for lumber for cupboards and tables and additional chairs: $600. A letter was authorized to be mailed the next week, confirming and describing progress on the building and suggesting the distribution of the needed pledges. After a lengthy discussion of memorials, book-of-gifts registry, and other possibilities, it was the consensus that they should not offer such options.

On Monday, April 10, ground was broken. The following Monday, Gerald Topliff began clearing the site. He was paid for his labor by the wood he removed. The large chunks of white oak remaining were to be used by Kenneth Wanty in the landscaping of the site, which is his contribution. Work moved steadily forward from this point with the expectation that by April 24 or thereabouts the slab floor would be complete. Plans for a service of dedication as an adjunct of the first service of camp were formulated.

During the summer of 1972 one of the new youth initiatives was made clear: during camp, each youth camper was to be assigned to a small group with a counselor, who would function as a discussion and prayer leader to reinforce what happened during the morning hour with Harper. The welcoming message to that year's camp meeting went like this: "Welcome to Eaton Rapids, 1972. Founded in 1885, this is the 87th year of service to the Kingdom of God in this beautiful place. The lives that have been redeemed here cannot be counted, and the value of those lives certainly can never be calculated. Nor is there any way for us to count the young men and women who have dedicated their lives here to Christian service in all the jobs and professions and callings there are. These 87 years have accumulated for us an incredibly rich heritage. And to that heritage we'll be true. And I have faith, I confidently believe that the best is yet to be.

We thank God for the promise that is Eaton Rapids 1972, and all the years after."

As a part of the opening service of that camp meeting, Thursday July 20, Hayden Carruth introduced each member of the Board. And in that connection, he had earlier inquired if some of them would be willing to entertain at supper in their cottages on that Thursday evening members of the city government of Eaton Rapids. After supper, it was Carruth's hope that the officials would accompany them to the evening service so the Board members could present them to the camp meeting. From time to time they had discussed this sort of camp-town contact, and Carruth thought it was perhaps the right time to act on it.

In a September 3, 1972 meeting of the Board of Directors, in the opening of the business session at 7 a.m., Carruth told of an experience during World War II when, following a staff meeting at the Eisenhower headquarters in London, he went to Westminster Abbey. There, near the Tomb of the Unknown Soldier, he found an order of worship for a service that contained the words of the familiar "There's a Wideness in God's Mercy," which he read for the Board's inspiration. The English version contains several verses not contained in America's well-known hymn.

A 1972 newspaper article in *The State Journal* chronicled some of the effects of modernization at the camp ground—pavement of former sawdust trails, a sounding board reinforced with a public address system covering the whole camp—but said the "vitality of the message at the camp meeting is as vigorous now as ever. Its purpose remains steadfast—to preach the Gospel of Christ to others." As the 87th annual meeting got underway, the Rev. Clarence W. Hutchens, former President of the Association and pastor of Grace United Methodist Church in Lansing, reflected on the changes that had taken place.

After mentioning the founding of the camp, he continued, "However, if one of those original pioneers of Eaton Rapids Camp Meeting could return, he wouldn't believe his eyes. Only the wooded area and the river are the same." Hutchens noted, for instance, that in place of their rugged Yankee ingenuity to "make-do" with whatever simple comforts they had, now there's an array of cottages, in varying degrees of permanency, as well as a wide variety of camping equipment—from tents to campers and trailers to motor homes. "What a far cry from that occasional piece of canvas stretched between trees as a partial protection from the sudden summer rainstorms," Hutchens added.

Back in the day there was a corral for horses, now long dismantled, and the old oil torches sold at auction a few years before. Originally the only construction on the ground was a platform from which the speakers could be seen and heard. The only roof over the heads of the people as they listened was the branches of the stately oaks and elms. There had been a succession of tabernacles, each eclipsing the previous one, and progress from rugged benches to new seating.

"Some of the great spiritual orators of past generations have brought the glories of heaven down to where men could reach and respond, and respond they did—in great numbers," Hutchens said. "And it was real! Lives were changed.

Young men and women were challenged to preach the gospel at home and in countries around the world."

"While the occasional 'amen' expressed in a service today is no comparison to the chorus of 'amens' that spontaneously rose from the congregation to a point of mutual agreement in former days, yet there is more of a personal relationship between speakers and listeners today, an identity that elicits more of a 'one-to-one' response."

Hutchens said the speakers at camp meeting at the turn of the century arrived by train and were either ferried across the river by boat or brought to the grounds by livery. He said they wouldn't understand how present-day speakers can book engagements back-to-back states apart. Speakers, the article went on to say, are encouraged to bring their families and become part of the total program that has as its prime purpose "a family vacation with a purpose." The youth, by this time, no longer swam in the river, but had an organized recreational program concentrated around the Youth Center. In 1972, for the first time, the younger set had its own Children Center, a commodious building for both teaching and crafts.

After camp, at this time, more of a developing community was taking shape on the grounds—with a caretaker and a few permanent residents along with visitors at times other than during camp. Other church groups used the grounds for their activities. The cafeteria doubled as a winterized "Retreat Center" available for groups numbering up to eighty persons.

"So while there has been quite a transformation in the outward appearance of the grounds and a different accent from the platform, the purpose is still the same," said Hutchens. "It is to help people to know Jesus Christ as Lord and Master of their lives and to encourage Christian people to grow in their personal loyalty and dedication to the One with Whom they walk."

Earl Champlin died on April 3, 1972, having finished his earthly walk. Also in 1972 an unknown author, "out of love for Eaton Rapids Camp," wrote the following poem, entitled "Who among These Sturdy Oaks?"

>Who among these sturdy oaks
>By this steadily moving river
>Were touched by
>Amazing Grace and Perfect Love?
>
>Who, where sunsets
>Kiss the reflecting water
>And the shorelines provide witness
>To that beauteous wedding
>Of stream and light,
>Lifted psalm and hymn
>And spiritual song
>In confidence that
>Pentecostal Fire Is Falling?

Who among these sturdy oaks
By this steadily moving river
Prayed into being an on-going movement
Of heart purity,
A movement whose sanctifying currents
Were to cleanse and refine
From uttermost to uttermost?

Who, within acres
Of the same number as the
Years of our Lord,
Were to combine gifts of love
And of faith to build here
A Place for His Presence?

Who among these sturdy oaks
By this steadily moving river
Gave mind and heart to the hearing
Of that host of spiritual skylarks,
They who to this day stand among
The "preaching greats" of all time?

Heralds of the holy life
Men of amazing gifts
Of tongue and of trust,
Men of the mighty inner strengthening
Of the Holy Spirit,
Eloquent ambassadors to the world
For which Christ died,
Morrison and Carradine,
Ruth and Rees,
Such men of mission
As Bishop Walden of Africa,
Bishop Oldham, Bishop Warne,
And E. Stanley Jones who long since
Has carried a whole world in his heart.

Who among these sturdy oaks
By this steadily moving river
Are there now?
Many there are now who know they can
Never expect too much
From the Lord of Lords
And be disappointed;
Who know now
How vividly close to Life they are,

> How pure His love,
> How evangelic His power,
> How deep and indelible His reachout.
>
> Many there are
> Who know now
> That in every receiving heart
> Pentecostal Fire Is Falling,
> Falling, sanctifying, empowering,
> Here among these sturdy oaks
> By this steadily moving river.

On November 27, 1972, Mrs. Carruth wrote another letter to raise funds for the now completed Children's Center. She reported that in the first round of contributions $6800 was given. In the second round at the 1972 camp meeting, $2,700 was pledged, most of which had already been paid. The Ad Hoc Committee on the Children's Center formally accepted the structure in September, and the builder was paid in full. In order to do this, it was necessary to borrow $4,500. To save interest, she noted that they would like to pay this off within the next several weeks, if this was possible. She then asked for financial help to do so.

She concluded the letter like this: "If you were able to visit the new building last summer, I'm sure you will agree that this project was the best possible investment of dollars committed to the Lord's work at this time. Standing or sitting in the building, looking out past the cross through the glass into the trees and the sky, as the children do during their worship, is an inspiration never to be forgotten."

In 1973, the Extensions '73 from Vennard College, located in University Park, Iowa, presented a concert at ERC on Thursday evening at 7:30. The musical group was made up of nine students who aimed to bring a new dimension to sacred music. They sang and told of their own experiences, making their enthusiasm palpable. Coming from six states and four denominations, they represented well the students of Vennard. They were, at this time, on a ten-week tour of various sections of the country. A July 18, 1973, article in the *Eaton Rapids Journal* described the group's contemporary style that had proven enjoyable for young and old alike, and invited readers to hear this group of "nine happy, enthusiastic young people as they share their joy of living with the people of the Campmeeting."

The same year, Dennis Kinlaw was a featured speaker on the platform. I was likely in attendance that year as a young boy, but I don't recall much from those earliest days, save some of those fleeting images indelibly etched into my mind's eye. I would come to know Kinlaw later on, hearing him preach at Eaton Rapids, on more than one occasion, at a friend's graduation from Gordon Conwell Seminary in Massachusetts, and many times in Wilmore, Kentucky, both at camp meeting there and in the college chapel. He was president of Asbury College when I attended the seminary across the street between 1989 and 1992. I still vividly recall his saying this in a sermon at Eaton Rapids: "Jesus wasn't worried there was something in the leper that could hurt Him; He knew there was something in Himself that could heal the leper."

Kinlaw is a great preacher and a remarkable man, and my wife and I were privileged to go visit with him in 2013, since we were blessed to become friends with his daughter and son-in-law (Katy and Stan Key, now president of the Francis Asbury Society) during that year's trip to Eaton Rapids. Stan was the early-morning Bible teacher—but more about him later.[59]

Kinlaw was at the helm of Asbury College (now University) during the famous 1970 revival; in light of which, along with the fact that he spoke at Eaton Rapids on numerous occasions, we wanted to go meet with him and pick his brain a bit about revivals and camp meetings. Below we'll share a few portions of that remarkable time spent with him, but first we'd like to share his words in an article he wrote entitled "My Camp Meeting Experience." Camp meeting, for Kinlaw, wasn't merely a place he preached; it was a place where he was mightily touched and called by God. When thinking of what camp meeting can do in a person's life, think of him. An amazing scholar, and an even more amazing man—because of what Christ did in and through him. Here's Kinlaw's article in its entirety—which can offer the reader a flavor of the sort of way Kinlaw talked and preached:

> It was in the depths of the Depression, in 1933, that my father unexpectedly found himself in Georgia in Indian Springs Holiness Camp Meeting. One of the preachers—he was my father's favorite—was Henry Clay Morrison, the president of Asbury College and Asbury Theological Seminary. My father died before I was able to hear from his own lips what that experience was like, but it evidently influenced him significantly. When he returned to his home and family in North Carolina, he said to my mother, "Sally, we have to take the family."
>
> The next summer he took my mother and my older sister with him and they went to Indian Springs. It was in that session that Christ found my sister and she was converted. I was only twelve, but it was obvious to me that she was changed and, from my perspective, it was for the better. The next year she went to Asbury College as a student, met the one who was to become her husband, and they spent their life together in ministry in the Methodist Church in Michigan.
>
> A new pattern was established that year in our family. The camp meeting at Indian Springs became the anchor point around which our family arranged its schedule. Our family bank had failed and we never afterwards had the money for a family vacation, but my father found the

---

[59] Dennis Kinlaw, as of 2015, is now in his nineties, but his mind seems as sharp as ever. We were thrilled when he was willing to write the foreword to this book.

finances to take us all to camp meeting for the ten days that it met in August.

It was in 1935, when I was thirteen, that I found myself headed, not too happily, to an event that meant five religious sessions for me every day for ten days. My attitude during the trip home was completely different from my attitude on the way down. I was not only in a different mood. I was in a different world. I had met One that actually changed my life. And his name was JESUS!

I had heard about him before, but now I had actually met Him. And the center of my existence had radically changed. Instead of being centered in myself, He was now not only with me. He had captured the central spot in my inner being. Instead of a deep and rather terrifying existential dread at the thought of ever actually confronting God, I found myself in an intense and joyous love affair with Him and his Father and even the Holy Spirit. And for the first time that I could remember, I felt clean—real clean—inside.

I was in a different world.

One's world is pretty small and fragile when you are only thirteen and you alone, in loneliness, reign in the center of your own little kingdom. What a difference when you find yourself filled with the Presence of that One who is larger than the whole world of which you are a part. At thirteen, you may not know much about the extent of that kingdom, but somehow your borders are gone and you sense something that later you will call infinite and eternal. And, inexplicable as it all is, you know that this is where you belong and you are suddenly willing to give your life and even yourself so that others may find such as their own, too.

It was not that I had never heard about Christ before. The third pew from the front on the left in our Methodist Church was the Kinlaw pew and nobody else ever sat there. Everyone in the church knew that it belonged to the Kinlaw clan. And I knew as I grew up that after Sunday School in the morning and Epworth League in the evening, I was to be with the rest of my family in that pew. But it was all in the third person. It was about Another whom I had never really met. But now that world had changed, too. I knew not only *what* it was all about, I knew *who* it was all about. And He was not only real to me now, He was a permanent part of my inner person, the central part, the friend of all friends, the *key* to everything. I wanted to share the glory of it all, so I told my pastor. I was sure he would rejoice with me and tell me how glad he was that I had finally caught on to what it was all about. I was caught off guard when I sensed that he was a bit apprehensive about this thirteen year old. His comment was, "Well, Dennis, you don't think that this has to happen to everybody, do you?"

Years later, in a moment of mutuality, I shared all this with a Jesuit friend. He responded, "Dennis, that is beautiful, but, you know, we don't think that such is for everybody." In both cases, my thoughts took me back to Indian Springs, for it was there that I came to know that God loved His world so much that He gave His one eternal Son on Calvary so that the emptiness of a thirteen year old's heart could be filled with the very life that His Son sacrificed on that cross outside the city of Jerusalem. Somehow, I knew it had to be for everyone.

During those high school years, it was almost impossible to find anyone who understood what had happened to me in my world. Years later, at Princeton in a course with the philosophy professor, Dr. Emile Cailliet, in which he asked us to tell the story of our spiritual journey, I shared. His response was simply, "Beautiful! Now can you intellectualize this?"

During those next lonely years in high school I certainly would not have been able to intellectualize it. There were some things, though, that I knew. The One who had found me was the One who made the whole world. He loves the whole world. His offer of Himself *has* to be for the whole world. That love precludes any other possibility. He, being who He is and loving with the love with which He loves, is not in the exclusion business. And now because He was in my heart that same universal love was flowing there. I did not know the promise in Rev. 21:25 about the Holy City, the eternal Bride of Christ, that its gates will never be shut, nor Frederick Weatherly's conclusion that the gates of that city are never shut so "that all who would might enter and no one was denied."

A thirteen year old has a massive amount yet to be experienced and learned, but I suspect a thirteen year old may be as *smart* as he is ever going to be. A decade later, for three years following my seminary education and before I was ordained, I travelled from church to church in evangelistic meetings around the country offering the Good News that I had discovered in Christ to any who would listen. The force that drove me during those years was the same as that which I found stirring in my heart on that trip home from my first year at Indian Springs.

There was a wisdom in Henry Clay Morrison and those who were leaders in the camp meeting movement that I have understood better and appreciated more with the passing of the years. I had no comprehension of it then. It was never mentioned by them. It seems that they just assumed it as if it were to be taken for granted. They seemed to feel that a certain fullness of grace is as available for a thirteen year old as for a veteran saint. The sermon that was preached by Morrison for the most determinative evening of my life was on what he called entire sanctification, or "the baptism of the Holy Spirit." All of the theological terminology was new to me, but that did not keep a profound message from coming through to me. I was a three-day-old Christian. My sense of the forgiveness of my sins, His acceptance of me, and the fact of His presence with me was all very real. But the word that came through to me that night was that He now wanted me to tell Him He could have all that I knew of my heart. But beyond that He also wanted me to give Him the key to my heart so that He could claim for Himself even that which I did not yet know about myself. I was told that if I gave Him the key, He would take me, possess me for Himself, and then fill me to the full with His Spirit. Somehow I knew, unwittingly I think, that it was not so much me giving myself to Him as my permitting Him to take, to possess, me fully for Himself.

It was only later that I realized that this put me in the Wesleyan tradition. It was only later that I would understand that time and human discipline are not necessary additions to the sacrifice on Calvary and for the realization of the promise that is implicit in Pentecost. It is that filling that will enable one to learn much more about Him and His ways and a whole lot more about oneself. Those around may not perceive what is on occasion happening in the thirteen year old in a good camp meeting but, apparently, heaven does and likes it. I do, too.

As mentioned, in 2013 my wife and I were able to visit with Dr. Kinlaw in his Wilmore, Kentucky, home. It was a thrilling time; it felt a little like going to meet Yoda. We wanted to ask him questions about the Bible and philosophy, about his tenure as college president, about the Asbury revival, and we were able to, sitting in rapt attention at his profound insights and infectious laughter. Finally, for the purpose of this project, we asked him about camp meetings, specifically, what it is, to his thinking, about camp meetings that lends them their power, their ability to make such an impact, just as Indian Springs had done in his own life.

Interestingly, Kinlaw answered the question with an illustration—a painting, to be precise, that was hanging in another room of the house. He asked Stan to go and retrieve it, and Kinlaw, with veritable giddiness, held it before us. The painting is, as it happens, a well-known one called *The Presence*, by A. E. Borthwick, painted in 1910; and it has an intriguing story. The scene is the Cathedral itself (he painted it in St. Mary's Cathedral in Edinburgh), where communion is being distributed to the faithful in the distance at the High Altar. In the foreground, though, a kneeling penitent, a woman, is comforted by the presence of Christ behind her, washed in light.

The painting visibly moves and touches Kinlaw, for a number of reasons, but mainly because of the immediacy about the relationship with Christ visually depicted. I suspect the picture reminds him of when he was thirteen all over again, his own night of fire. The church can tend to take a mediating position, denying this immediacy of Jesus, he said, but he thinks this a mistake. Not that the church doesn't have an important role to play, for it surely does, he hastened to add; note, he pointed out, that the scene is *in* a church. But the relationship doesn't come about through the ordinary processes of the church, but through the closeness of Jesus with the woman in the painting.

"It can be hard to get that in the church," Kinlaw said. "But camp meeting isn't church, but it's *inside* the church. Camp meeting is in the back corner here," pointing to the penitent's place. Camp meeting, Kinlaw is convinced, as much now as ever, is powerfully, perhaps uniquely, able to introduce people to Jesus. The historically ecumenical flavor of camp meeting illustrates that it's not mainly about making folks Methodists or Baptists or some other denominational adherent; that doesn't have primacy. It's rather about becoming a follower and lover of Christ—coming to know Him, being in Christ, standing in the very presence of God, whose Spirit is not just sprinkled or poured *over* us, but liberally poured *inside* of us.

Kinlaw also spoke of the great Salvation Army preacher Samuel Logan Brengle, who, in 1885—the same year Eaton Rapids camp began—had a dramatic sanctification experience. Brengle spoke at Eaton Rapids in 1929. Kinlaw recalled the way a professor of his at Princeton had shared a portion of Clark Hall's biography of Brengle, and, after sharing it, said, "This can happen to you." Brengle described his experience as a full immersion in the love of God. He would later write of the experience: "I walked out over Boston Common before breakfast, weeping for joy and praising God. Oh, how I loved! In that hour I knew Jesus, and I loved Him till it seemed my heart would break with love. I was filled with love for all His creatures. I heard the little sparrows chattering; I loved them. I saw a little worm wriggling across my path; I stepped over it; I didn't want to hurt any living thing. I loved the dogs, I loved the horses, I loved the little urchins on the street, I loved the strangers who hurried past me, I loved the heathen, I loved the whole world." This experience would become his life's focus as he taught and admonished believers to seek "the blessing."[60]

Kinlaw of course had had his own Aldersgate, at camp meeting. After having accepted Christ as Savior just days before, he sat under Henry Clay Morrison and heard God's call to give all of himself to God. So he did, going forward to the altar, and God showed up. Kinlaw described the way he felt "clean" on the inside after his experience with Christ there at the altar, and he said he felt like he was "in" Christ, that if he punched out he'd touch him. Only later did Kinlaw discover that in John 13-17 "in" occurs 66 times, and that Paul, in Romans 8, says there's no condemnation for those *in* Christ Jesus. Kinlaw would go on to study at Princeton and be a college president, but the anchor point of his life was what happened at camp meeting when he was thirteen years old.

---

[60] Here are the only known two remaining recordings of Brengle's voice: https://www.youtube.com/watch?v=KK5dF6a1Dhk&app=deskto

Eaton Rapids leadership often had to schedule speakers well in advance. In a letter dated August 13, 1973, Carruth invited Dennis Kinlaw back as a speaker, leaving it to Kinlaw which date would work best, anytime between 1976 and 1981. Carruth wrote, "Your impact in 1973 in instruction, in insight, and in inspiration is truly memorable. Your return is of greatest importance to the enhancement of the Kingdom in this part of the country, and, consequently, to us." Kinlaw couldn't return until 1980, lamenting that it "seems too bad that it has to be that far away but at least it gives us something to look forward to," and adding, "Let me thank you for the aggressive leadership that you are giving to Eaton Rapids. Keep it up." Kinlaw spoke at Eaton Rapids on numerous occasions, first in 1965 and in 1997 for the last time.

Another interesting feature of the 1973 letter to Kinlaw from Carruth came from these words: "Of special interest in our future planning at Eaton Rapids Camp is your suggestion that campmeetings across the country capitalize on the nation's bicentennial. Highlighting the role of the campmeeting in the history of America, and vivifying the prospective contribution of the campmeeting to the country today is a theme that can be really exciting. I'll talk with Eaton Rapids colleagues about this on Labor Day."

On March 3, 1973, in a meeting of the Board of Directors, comment was made that the Free Methodist Conference had expressed hope that a three year term, at the least, might be arranged. They were without a campground of their own to use for their annual church camp, and wanted to lease the grounds at Eaton Rapids. They were looking for a new property to purchase and develop for their use, but it would be three years before a new facility would be chosen.[61]

A humorous note can be found in the minutes to that meeting in which, discussing the prohibitive costs of an ambitious building project, Jim Weiss (the finance chair) suggested that since the Association wasn't at the time able on its own to consider such a project, the Free Methodists could be appealed to on the basis of their missionary zeal to "make us one of their missionary projects." This wasn't the only example of Weiss's humor. In a letter to Carruth later that year (September 29), Weiss concluded, "Until all our debts have been repaid, I would strongly oppose any approval of major capital improvements for next year," and then he added this postscript: "Does that not sound like a typical finance chairman?"

The leasing of the grounds by the Free Methodists actually proved a boon to growth because, on their own dime and labor, the Free Methodists would propose several improvements to the grounds for carrying out their summer program. Among the proposals were more showers and restroom facilities, recreational facilities like a volleyball and basketball court, provision for more electrical power, an upgrading of the public address system with more horns and a mike in the office for paging, and a shelter of some sort for rainy day recreation.

---

[61] On a personal note, this was the window when the Baggett family, as part of the southern Michigan Free Methodists, first came to Eaton Rapids and became familiar with it, later attending the ER camp and purchasing a cottage on the grounds.

On the aesthetics front, also discussed were the 140 trees that had been marked for cutting chiefly in the pie-shaped area beginning with the secondary trailer area and fanning out across Outer Drive to the fence (between Antioch and Canaan Streets and their extensions). The criteria governing trees selected for cutting were size, nearness to the time when death of a major portion or all of the tree will have occurred, dead limbs in the top, or excessive leaning.

Commenting on the asset to the Camp Grounds of its trees, Charles Cookingham shared the comments of a landscape engineer writing for the *Flower and Gardening* magazine on the erosion, sound control, pollution diminishing value of trees as well as their psychological and aesthetic value. The belief that the Camp Ground trees represented an ever increasingly important value to the Camp was shared by the entire Grounds Committee and Board. It was clear to all that only such trees as needed to be cut for the sake of the existing trees and in keeping with the total beauty and usefulness of the grounds would be felled and removed.

Carruth issued a document entitled "Where Do We Go from Here?" in 1973, delineating a number of needed and ongoing projects on the grounds. Twenty one items were listed: continued improvement of the public bath house; remove tired trees; develop additional camping areas north of Outer Drive; create plans and specifications for a garage-workshop; an overhaul of Workers' Rest; needed work on Wade Cottage; renovation of the hotel; improve existing camping areas; consider a new bath house in the camping area; picnic tables for camping area and river bank; improve and maintain streets; improve Asbury Trail (from bookstore to cafeteria); some gutter building; leaf collection; tabernacle painting; door-trimming at Tabernacle and plans for better latching; increased lighting in the Tabernacle; landscaping around the Children's Center; additional seating in the Children's Center; more double-deckers with good mattresses in the Retreat Center; renovation of cottage donated by Rev. Mullen; a number of windows and screens; grass planting for the purposes of brightening the place, cooling the climate, controlling erosion, and in anticipation of overflow crowds in the Tabernacle.

The next month, April of 1973, a list was drafted outlining the duties of the caretaker of the grounds. The general headings of the list included Gate Closing, Grounds Care, Maintenance and Repairs, Meter Reading, Mail, but not repairs to private cottages, and additional duties might arise if given him and requested by the Committee on Grounds. In terms of the Retreat Center, its operation would require cleaning of only those facilities requested, arranged based on a special supplementary fee. The following January, Carruth took steps to arrange a Board meeting to hire a caretaker, and to decide on the application to the position submitted by Jack Futrell.

On May 14, 1974, Carruth responded to Rev. James Birdsall's request to become a candidate again for a position on the ER Board of Directors for the following three years. He accepted with "deepest appreciation, and with some genuine reservation," writing the following:

I think your Nomination Committee needs to be dead-sure that Hayden Carruth is the man for this time. I sometimes feel that a new voice, a new style, a new energy is needed to keep Eaton Rapids moving. We praise God for the things that He has achieved through our people in recent times: in physical improvements, in financial stability, and most of all in commitment to Jesus Christ. But I fear a let-down, just when our opportunities are ready to come to fruit. One of these days—soon—the Holy Spirit will come down on us with real power, and Eaton Rapids will never be the same again. The whole leadership, including the presidency, must be committed to this expectancy. Your Committee is looking and praying for this.

Whatever the upcoming election brings, I must say that it has been a great privilege for me to be President of Eaton Rapids during the past three years. If you will forgive me, I mean this in a really selfish sense. Jim, I wonder if you remember the moment in the closing of the last service last year. We had been lifted to the heights in singing together Malotte's "The Lord's Prayer," and we were saying goodnights to dear friends, and you said to me, "You know, Hayden, you have grown in the job of president." I didn't have the wit or the grace to deal with this remark, so turned it aside. As I have thought about your comment, I have come to realize how correct you were. God has been very, very good to me, particularly in the last year or two or three, to our family, and to the enterprises which we serve, and I am grateful. I have a vast distance to go, but I know the way.

On May 20, 1974, Carruth wrote Dr. Roy Putnam, trying to arrange for Putnam to come to ERC a few years later. In the course of the letter, Carruth wrote that "Eaton Rapids is being blessed in a variety of ways. A couple of years ago, a new children's center was built and the youth center was renovated, all paid for. The big tabernacle and other central buildings are freshly painted, and new facilities building is now underway. Attendance has doubled in two years. Most important, it's a long time since the power of God was more evident. Lives are being turned around. The Holy Spirit is really moving. This is truly a wonderful time to be alive!"

June 1974 brought news of the death of Mr. V. E. ("Monty") Ward, of White Pigeon, who had been in charge of facilities at ERC, and who, together with his wife, were stalwart prayer supporters of the ministry. He was commemorated with these words:

Whenever I walk the grounds at the Camp again, I shall feel that the experience there holds an added dimension for me: the realization that Vern has joined the goodly company of those who have served so wholeheartedly and prayed so earnestly to make the witness of the Camp one that is being blessed forever. Vern was a Christian gentleman of the highest order; his transparent sincerity and his capacity to help us all to be at our best spoke of the depths of life and love to which his devotion to Christ reached. Many have walked the grounds at Eaton Rapids and poured their best into its ongoing, but none have loved the Camp more purely, gave themselves to its work more unreservedly, and exemplified its aims more accurately.[62]

---

[62] On September 28, 1974, the Board of Directors of ERC met at the Carruth cottage at 7:30. The meeting was devoted to a consideration of prospective expenditures during the period 28 September to 1 July, 1975. Estimated income for the period was $9,000, and normal expenditures estimated to be $5,600. Special projects authorized for completion and funding before July 1, 1975 included re-roofing the kitchen, insulating the caretaker's apartment, constructing a workshop, removing trees, some electric work, repairing the water system, improving the women's side of the public bathhouse, and building an addition to the nursery.

Spotlight on Hayden Carruth (1911-1998)
[1992 Biography of Hayden Carruth]

Life in America was tough in those days—growing up in Mississippi during the depression is only a faint memory of hard times. In those days, families from various states migrated to the village of Wilmore so that the children could study at Bethel Academy, later named Asbury Academy.

Dr. Hayden K. Carruth said goodbye to the "magnolia state" and soon made Wilmore, Kentucky his home and Asbury his college. In retrospect, a career as speechmaker and educator was firmly set in place early while a student at Asbury Academy. It was in 1931 that he won the Kentucky high school state championship in dramatic interpretation while completing his high school studies.

Campus achievements once in college included editorship of *The Collegian*, described that year as the student weekly for "students and Asburians around the globe." Debate was Dr. Carruth's love. Suitcase and research material in hand, he debated teammates and traveled through the mid-west as a leader for Asbury's varsity debate team. Some classmates were certain his forensic skills had predestined this graduate to become one of America's foremost evangelists. God had other plans however. First, romance turned his attention toward Michigan, where his college sweetheart was now a teacher.

Fifty-five years are now history since this English major ventured from the Bluegrass. Accolades in higher education give testimony of this man's achievements:

> Executive Secretary and later president of the Michigan Speech Teachers' Association.
>
> A member of the executive board for the United Speech Association.
>
> Honored twice with the "best teacher award" at the University of Michigan as a faculty member in speech.
>
> For nine years he served that university as Associate Dean for the College of Literature, Science, and Arts with more than 2000 senior and junior faculty under his guidance.

At his retirement in 1978, this great university honored this man as Dean Emeritus and Professor Emeritus of Speech in the College of Arts and Sciences. When we turned to his colleagues to find out what this man was really like, Dr. Frank Rhodes, now president of Cornell University, said Dr. Hayden K. Carruth was a man of integrity and discretion—total dedication to undergraduate education—a man full of grace and courtesy in the midst of university pressure and chaos.

Dr. Bill Frye, now vice president for academic affairs and provost at Emory University in 1992, tagged Dr. Carruth as the "chief operating officer" for the

College of Arts and Sciences at Michigan. Dr. Frye, at that time, witnessed "the gentle wit, warm smile, and unselfish service" Dr. Carruth demonstrated to student and faculty alike.[63]

In a letter to Rev. Leslie Woodson dated June 18, 1973, Carruth wrote a bit about his dual commitments: "Yes, I'm a deantype at Michigan. Specifically, my administrative parish is the 900 professors and 1200 teaching assistants who give instruction to our 12,000 undergraduates and 4,000 graduate students. That's the College of Literature, Science, and the Arts where I am the Associate Dean. Although working for the Campmeeting is something of a busman's holiday, the College and the Camp each offers its own satisfaction. I must say that Eaton Rapids holds a promise and a potential that is really thrilling. The Lord is so good to us, and we praise His name."

---

[63] Hayden Carruth, Jr. recently told me his dad was also Kentucky state champion in ping pong! And a patient teacher of it to Hayden, Jr.

Chapter 11

Dappled with Sun and Shade, 1975-1984

On March 12, 1975, Carruth wrote a letter of invitation to James Buskirk, professor of evangelism at the Candler School of Theology at Emory University in Atlanta, to serve as one of three evangelists in the 1977 encampment. The penultimate paragraph of the invitation is worth reiterating: "We believe you will enjoy your days in Michigan. We expect that you will find refreshment in our 31 acres stretching along the bank of the Grand River, with a cathedral of great oaks overhead, and good fellowship running rampant throughout the campus. Really, God has been awfully good to us. Three years ago we built and paid for a new children's center for a children's program that is truly outstanding. At the same time, we renovated the youth center as a revitalized setting for a remarkably effective youth program. Last year we built and paid for a new utilities building. Most public buildings have been brightened by fresh paint. Right now we are doubling the size of our nursery, and we are doubling our camping areas. Attendance has increased at a substantial rate. Most important are the evidences of the power of prayers as our people anticipate Campmeeting each year. Under the Holy Spirit, lives are really turned around. We believe that you will add an important dimension to our ministry to the people of this area."

The next year, June 21 of 1975, Carruth wrote the Members of the Board of Directors of ERC, asking for reports to be sent to Louise Cookingham by July 7 to facilitate the compilation of "another impressive Annual Report." Then Carruth added a request about the closing of the last service of the upcoming encampment. "If the Lord leads us, as He has in the recent past, to sing Malotte's The Lord's Prayer as a benediction, I would very much appreciate it if all Board Members and their families would join the circle of prayer by coming to the platform, after the sermon and the closing song, and before the singing of the benediction. As I say, if the Lord leads this way, it surely will be a blessed moment for us all."

A few months before, Carruth had attended to a number of more provincial and logistical chores associated with the camp, sending to the Camp Committee a letter on March 10 about details from a meeting two days before with Howard Coil, Gordon Vandemark, Duane Tanner, and Phil Haines. Discussed were trenches to be dug, installation of sewer lines, water line materials, funding for some camping facilities, sinkhole business, and the design of new campfire circles for after-service fellowship. His last point is worth repeating: "It was decided that no Czar of camping would be needed, but that Gordon Vandemark's leaflet on Good Citizenship and Christian Love would make police power unnecessary. It was also agreed that, if a complication should occur, Chief Howard Coil would call a pow-wow of his braves and settle it."

On February 25, 1976, Hayden Carruth wrote Mr. Norman Storteboom, petitioning for the privilege of being placed on the list of those who are approved as prospective cottage purchasers. This request broached the topic of whether the Association should permit one person, or one couple, to own more than one cottage on the grounds.

At any rate, the immediate reason for Carruth's request was the "serious problem which we face in housing our professional staff this summer. The Kamaleson family is coming, and we are overjoyed that they are. The Victor Hamilton family are coming, and we are delighted. Dr. Roy Puttnam is being accompanied by his wife, Flada. Our music director, Gordon Vandemark, has asked for housing for his family; this is an entirely appropriate request. Adapting and up-grading Workers Rest might help some, but the replacement of primitive plumbing will take a pile of money. The Futrells have permitted us to use their cottage during two summers past, and we are hoping that Jack and Bette will allow one of the 1976 worker families to live there. But, the best that we can do is inadequate, particularly in providing family cottages. Let me stress the importance of our having workers' families. This adds a dimension to our community that is beyond calculation. Some of our famous visitors will come only on condition that they be accompanied by their families. The other side of this is the happy fact that Eaton Rapids is known nationally, not only because of our outstanding program, but also simply because it is a delightful, happy place.

"The Association is categorically unable to meet this need at this time. If Beth and I are able to finance the thing, we'd like to try to bridge the gap. When worker housing is no longer the chief focus, we need housing for friends and relatives whom we wish to introduce to Eaton Rapids, and who are likely to become established constituents. Beyond this, our children, most of whom are visibly and powerfully committed to ER, will require future consideration."

He concluded the letter by saying the whole issue of purchasing a cottage might prove moot, as he didn't have much by way of a cash reserve. But he was soon intending to trade homes in Ann Arbor, and if his home sold favorably he hoped to have a bit of money to apply (under Board authorization) toward some urgent need at the Camp. He hoped for a good financial turn as he was contemplating the possibility of requesting the privilege of early retirement from the University of Michigan.

On the first of May, the Board turned to plans for the Work Days, Saturday and Monday, May 29 and 31. The Campground Store was to be the base of operations. Workers would report to the store at 9:00 a.m. before starting the day's activity. On Saturday and Monday, each family was to provide their own brown bag lunches. On Sunday was planned a 2:00 potluck dinner at the Cafeteria for all those on the grounds who wished to share this fellowship. The following projects were approved, along with the leaderships for each and the financial support for each: Concrete walls poured in each of the ladies' showers, to lay the shower curtain against, and to keep the outer territory dry. (A lady's voice was heard to say, "We might as well dam the man, too!" So this added four more showers to the project.) Chairs and tables in the store were to be repainted, and certain windows there would be hinged and otherwise adapted for opening, closing, and locking. Seeding, ramps, sticks and stones, and a fence to extend the Nursery play yard rounded out the projects planned.

Nine days later, on May 10, 1976, Ruth Champlain offered the Unity Home as a gift to the Association. This is the letter in full:

Dear Hayden,

I drove over to DeWitt and talked to Ed Richmond about Unity Home. There seems to be very little hope of anyone wanting a place of that size. Ed did mention that you were looking for a place to fix up for apartments for the workers, so that they could bring their families.

Could you use Unity Home if I made you a gift of it? As far as I know the building is structurally sound. It may need some new roof boards when a new roof is put on, but I don't know of anything else. We have flush toilets and showers on both floors. I put in a gas furnace about three years ago so there is heat. If they get the water connected, I'd pay for that and the summer taxes and you can have it at the end of camp.

I really think it could be fixed up into something special. I understand it was the first hotel and this would keep it through the years and insure its continued use through the years to come. Its location is ideal. It is quiet and peaceful and there is no place on the camp grounds (to me no place in all of Michigan) that has as beautiful a view as from our front porch.

I hope you will at least consider it if you are not already committed to a place.

In Christian love,

Ruth

A July 1976 printing of the Constitution and By-Laws of the Michigan State Holiness Camp Meeting Association won't be reproduced here in full, but Article II—the Object of the Association—is worth reiterating: "The object of this Association shall be the conversion of sinners and the promotion of Scriptural Holiness. In doing so, the Association shall encourage and provide inspiration and opportunity for the experience of a personal commitment to the Lord Jesus Christ, and support the closest possible cooperation among all the friends of Scriptural Holiness.

"The Association shall also provide the best possible physical facilities dedicated for the use of a Christian community. To accomplish this objective, the Association shall hold at least one Camp Meeting each year on the Camp Grounds, located in Eaton Rapids, Michigan; to be known as the Annual Camp Meeting; and may permit other religious, temperance, and educational groups to use the facilities of the Camp Ground which are in accord with the object of this Association."

On July 4, 1976, a consortium of Eaton Rapids area churches co-sponsored a day of worship and celebration. People were invited to share in a potluck dinner on the grounds at 2 o'clock, followed by a worship service at 3:30. The service included an address by featured speaker Hon. Donald E. Holbrook, Judge in the Court of Appeals of Clare, Michigan, who was widely known throughout the state for his Christian leadership in church and in political activities. The service also featured a presentation of traditional folk and Christian music sung by an interdenominational choir, directed by Mrs. Helen Hovis of Eaton Rapids.

Camp that year started eleven days later, in anticipation of which Carruth extended this invitation: "As a Christian community, it seems appropriate that we use this special Campmeeting as a time to praise God for His goodness in America. Thanks to Him we are well fed and prosperous, even in hard times. The Lord has protected us and blessed us as He has few other nations on earth, and this in spite of our shortcomings.

"In response to His love, let us direct our attention to praising and glorifying Him, while we honor our nation's 200th birthday with special music and the spoken Word. May a spirit of peace and thanksgiving be shared by us all this Campmeeting season."

Music had long been a central part of ERC. With few exceptions, the music team from 1976 to 1987 was Gordon Vandemark leading, Ruth Tennant on the piano, and Leah Brown on the organ.

Earl Prosser died on September 12, 1976, at eighty-eight years old. Two months later, in a Board of Directors meeting on November 6, Howard Deardorff spoke of his concern for Eaton Rapids Camp for the next 100 years and the environment and stewardship of it. The trees in and around the campgrounds and the planting of them were a major concern, along with the boundary and development around the campgrounds, health and safety issues, protection of the grounds and the river, erosion, and the like. What was to be done about all of these matters? The minutes read as follows: "Establish our priorities and then take action. We need a map, a topographic one. Check with the City Clerk, the Fire Dept., the Board of Education and from our own Board and their knowledge of the grounds and put all the pieces together."

In a letter to Carruth on December 1, 1976, Samuel Kamaleson wrote, among other things, the following moving and prophetic paragraph: "Time, experiences of life, and death are all our servants because we belong to Christ and Christ belongs to God! The biblical emphasis is that we are programmed to 'live' and not programed to 'die.' The 'clock of aging,' which is within our bodies, cannot tamper with the eternal quality of this existence in Christ Jesus. Everything becomes our servant because everything moves us ever forward toward that 'summum bonum' which is to resemble Jesus Christ in every way (Romans 8:28-29). Praise God for this!"

In 1977, Mary Conklin died at 70 years old; Maurice Glasgow died on August 25, at just 43 years old. He had directed the youth program and was the Associate Secretary. Nellie Bartlett died on October 11, at 102 years old; she first attended ERC in 1901.

That same year, in a document dated January 13, 1977, with the word "confidential" handwritten on red at the top (so of course we're telling everybody!), is a list of prospective speakers in upcoming encampments. A few brief notes from this document are worthy of repeating for their delightfulness.

First, John Oswalt was slated to speak this year, and the document says this about him: "[W]hen we invited him, he was to have been our new unknown; now rapidly achieving national eminence; respected and warmly received by major congregations." Oswalt, indeed, would later become President of ERC, and, in 1983, the thirteenth President of Asbury College. A telling line from his Presidential Charge to the Class of 1983 at Asbury went like this: ". . . the greatest experience of your life may be that moment when you hit the bottom of your resources and discover the bottomlessness of His resources."

Oswalt was born John Newell Oswalt in Mansfield, Ohio, on June 21, 1940. He came to the Lord at age 5, and at 13 felt a call to ministry. By the age of 15, he was rebelling against this call. He studied law at Taylor University in Upland, Indiana, hoping for a career as a lawyer. He would call this time at Taylor a "critical point in my life," for it was there, during his sophomore year, he completely surrendered himself to God. After hearing former Asbury president Dennis Kinlaw speak at a Spiritual Emphasis Week at Taylor, Oswalt gave his all to God. He then knew he must pursue the pastoral ministry. While at Taylor, he met Karen Kennedy, whom he married in 1962. They have three children: Elizabeth, Andrew, and Peter.

Oswalt went to Asbury Seminary and became interested in a career in missions. Later, he received a definite call into teaching, particularly teaching at a Christian institution. He hoped it might be Taylor, but he secured his first teaching position at Barrington College in Barrington, Rhode Island. In 1970, he was offered a position at Asbury Seminary and returned to Wilmore. After twelve years as a successful and popular professor, he was asked to assume the reins of the college at the age of 42.

Second, "Dr. J. Edwin Orr was the Staley Lecturer at Asbury College in 1975. Dennis Kinlaw says that Orr is the world's expert on revival, both in inspired scholarship and in remarkable preaching. Some faculty and some students in Wilmore say that Edwin Orr is the only speaker who can compete with Kinlaw in non-flambouyant [sic], incisive, powerful preaching. He has written more than a dozen books, mostly all on Revival. . . . Speaks on Wesleyan holiness, repentance, demands of revival, and such. I called him in California recently and learned that I cannot nominate him for 1978. He is the kingpin in an international seminar on Revival at Oxford University the last week of July each year. Church leaders from around the globe enroll. He wishes, however, to pass leadership of the Oxford activity to someone else soon."

Carruth hoped Orr might come in 1980 or 1981, but the records indicate that it didn't happen.

On March 31, 1977, Carruth reported in a letter that the Board had authorized a number of projects at the Camp, and he extended an invitation for help on some of them. "Surely the most important part of this kind of enterprise is the fellowship which is created. Necessary as these physical projects are, the most valuable dividend, I think, is the sense of community which Christian workers communicate of each other."

Projects included picnic tables, the roof on the bookstore, structural repair of the cafeteria-dormitory roof, removal of trees that were rotting roofs, new windows in the Emmaus House, grass planting near the tabernacle, and fire escapes for the second floors of public buildings. In addition, "The log cabin has been given to the Association for an Eaton Rapids Campmeeting Museum. Plans for the rehabilitation of this structure will be in the hands of a special committee. In due course, this committee will need volunteer help in developing this very appropriate facility."

On April 19, 1977, Carruth, having been asked to do so, reflected on the future of ERC. Here is the document in full:

To Anyone Who Might Be Interested:

Clarence Hutchens asked me some time ago to comment on the future of Eaton Rapids Camp. This is the beginning of a response. You will observe that this is something of a personal statement—one with which there will be some agreement and some disagreement. Each of us has his own dreams and his own priorities for Eaton Rapids Camp.

And so, much of what I am about to say relates to what might be called the "programs" of ERC. Frankly, I am not titillated by leaks in roofs, peeling paint, or the ubiquitous leaf problem. It is true that shabby facilities depress the spirit, while lovely grounds and well-kept buildings help to create an environment for praise and worship. And the physical labor that we do together establishes a Christian camaraderie far beyond what can be measured in mere physical accomplishment. I must confess, however, that I am more concerned with the way the Spirit can work on the campground than with the campground itself.

Before abandoning physical reality, however, I must say two things: 1) In 1973, we published a document, "Where Do We Go From Here?"—three pages, single space, elite type. Of the 21 improvements proposed on those pages, most have been done, or nearly done. 2) One major undertaking of this character remains: the hotel must be upgraded. Some existing walls should be removed and the lumber used for additional benches (pews) in the big tabernacle. We need 83 additional pews. Partitions need to be reorganized along the lines proposed by Mary

Conklin. Insulation, paneling, etc., etc. can bring the hotel up to standard, and this should be done in early seasons.

I am, and always will be grateful to God for the way He is moving and guiding our people; and for the generous dedication of the whole campmeeting community. We have been blessed beyond my highest expectations. If we continue to grow under the direction of the Holy Spirit, future Boards will need to make some new decisions. Our hotel nowadays tends to be filled to capacity. Most cottages, too, during campmeeting. Beds in the dorms are usually taken, and most camping sites are used. The big tabernacle is fairly well filled for about ½ of the services. Additional drive-ins at night and on weekends will begin to create parking problems. Cafeteria service may reach its limit. At some point, a future Board may have to say, "We're full. We can't handle any more." Major expansion of public facilities is out of the question. Building costs are prohibitive. It may become necessary, therefore, to have more than one campmeeting in the summer. If we had two, then the 100-150 workers who make the campmeeting possible would need to be doubled.

A variation might be developed in the form of one-day, two-day, or three-day special events at various times during the open season. Our Program Committee might consider offering a Retreat for Lovers—the Married Kind (marriage enrichment). Or an Upper Room with Maxie Dunnam, world editor of the Upper Room. (A most engaging speaker!) Or a musical event. Probably NOT Ichthus II, tho[ugh] more kids attending in Wilmore each year are from Michigan than any other state. More likely something like Mark and Diane Yashuhara, of concert hall quality and tabernacle spirit. Or a religious drama. If Dave Wilkerson will attack the drug culture, as he did so effectively at one time, perhaps we should turn him loose in our area. Or get Oral Roberts for a day or so. The cardinal considerations are the *quality* of the presentation, the appropriateness to our setting, and evidence of need among our people. *And* our ability to stage such events. This involves womanpower and manpower (this place abounds in leadership opportunities), and probably *money*. Though some activities may pay for themselves, the Board should be prepared to underwrite some ministries simply because they are part of our mission. This kind of pinch can be painful. If general funds money is to be poured into revising buildings and machinery, as a practical matter it can't be invested in revising the spirits of the people. WE MUST PRAY MIGHTILY FOR THE GUIDANCE OF THE SPIRIT.

A week later, on April 26, 1977, in his invitation letter to Paul Mickey (a Harvard and Princeton-trained Cleveland United Methodist pastor) to speak the following year at ERC, Carruth reflected a bit about Eaton Rapids Camp and its constituency: "The Campmeeting was founded in 1885 by Methodists of the Lansing (Michigan) District. It soon became clear that the purposes of this enterprise were not adequately served by the parent organization. . . , so the Campmeeting separated from the church, and has been independent ever since. Our people—at least this is my perception—range all the way from rigid second-blessing holiness ('If you didn't get it a certain way, you ain't got it.') to beautiful fuzzy-headed charismatics who really love the Lord, but don't know why. There are more Methodists than others (mostly stalwarts in 150-200 churches), with representations from various denominations—including two or three Catholic families."

On May 17, 1977, Carruth responded to Mr. Winfred V. Amstutz regarding the question of appropriate dress in worship areas at Eaton Rapids Camp Meeting. Carruth admitted this issue was one of continuing concern, and had been over the years—and not only with reference to the worship areas. The issue was complicated, he said, by the differences among areas where differing modes of dress might be in place. Indeed, he added, other complications grew out of the changing styles of dress that were generally accepted by the Christian community. Small wonder, he said, that it's a topic that should still arise from time to time.

Then he wrote these wise, measured, and felicitous words: "I'll be seeking counsel from the official leadership of the Camp regarding this topic to see if some new initiative is in order at this time. It is entirely possible that I, as one person, would agree with you regarding what our practices should be. But in a major Christian activity like the camp meeting, sensitive matters cannot be governed by one person. I am quite sure about one thing, though. And that is the absolute necessity that we, all of us, view this issue through the eyes of love and compassion. If I become censorious, my hostility probably would drive away the very people who need most the ministry which we strive to offer. So, we shall continue to pray for Jesus' love and Christian understanding to guide us in this and all other matters."

Just before camp meeting, on July 25, 1977, Carruth wrote this letter to the Members of the Association:

> At the end of two terms as president of the Association, I must pause for a moment to give thanks for the privilege of working in this part of God's Kingdom. This affiliation with the Campmeeting has yielded an incredible array of blessings and satisfactions. My own life has been immeasurably enriched and my commitment to Jesus Christ has been greatly deepened by association with this community of God's people.
>
> Specifically, I want to thank the members of the Board of Directors with whom I have worked closely during these six years. These men and women have served with heart-warming devotion, logging considerable mileage to attend frequent meetings of the Board, carrying out their chosen responsibilities with initiative and unfailing good will, and participating in meetings with a constructive spirit and a practical

wisdom that is truly inspiring. I have said many times that I look forward to Eaton Rapids Board meetings because they are sure to be a great blessing.

Also, I am indebted to all the members and friends of the Association. These dedicated people, under the guidance of the Holy Spirit, have set high standards for operation of the Campmeeting, and these lofty expectations have been a challenge that has beckoned all of your servants in the organization to vivid commitment and rigorous endeavor. It is miraculous the way in which God has met the needs of Eaton Rapids Camp through the generosity of our members and friends. It is the gifts both of money and of time and talent that are, in practical matters, the life blood of this place. It is this generosity, and the prayers of our people, that assures the continued growth and improvement of Eaton Rapids Campmeeting in program, in physical facilities, and in relationships.

It is my fervent hope that each of you is sharing fully in the abundant blessings which are mine.

During camp meeting 1977, on July 28, this announcement was made about the tabernacle roof: "Did you ever stop, here on these beautiful grounds, to count up the heritage that is ours? Almost a mile of riverfront, the great trees, this cathedral of ancient timbers—given us, free of charge. But one element of this heritage needs attention, now. The tabernacle must have a new roof. The roof up there has been there for about 34 years, and it leaks. Not great pouring leaks, but subtle, insidious soaking. After rains, as the snow melts, large areas are wet. The moisture slides down, and the lower roof boards are rotten. We didn't really realize what was going on until recently. The rotting will spread, it will get into major timbers, and that is 100% catastrophe. I am informed that $10,000 is needed to meet this need—and I believe the need is urgent."

After this the collection was taken to address this need. We have a record of the invitation to give: "Using the yellow piece of paper which you have, we are hoping that we can meet this need in the next few moments. We are talking about a contribution for a single, one-shot purpose—once in 25 years. How many of us might give $500—once in 25 years; if there were 20, that would do it. How many can give $200—once in 25 years; 50 would do it! A member of our community said there certainly are 50 who will give 200! A hundred who give $100 each will do it. Any, all contributions will be gratefully received. The fact is, $10,000 is needed now to save this sacred place. We could recount the souls saved here, the lives to be enriched here in the next quarter of a century—all of the things that take place here that are beyond any dollar price. The reality is that dollars are needed to preserve this worship center.

"Dear Father, give us the long look as we consider this giving to your work. Give us the sense that we are investing in tomorrow and tomorrow, and tomorrow. Thank you for your guidance in this crucial moment. Thank you Father. Amen."

After camp meeting that year, on August 4, Phil Hinerman, one of the platform speakers and Senior Pastor of Park Avenue United Methodist Church in Minneapolis, penned the Carruths this warm note:

Dear Hayden and Beth,

Just this little note to tell you what a great Camp Meeting it was! I just thought this was one of the better encampments.

As usual you two human beings did such a marvelous job. I can't imagine a president and wife team that do a better job. I came home and told Adora that your leadership is just the finest I've ever seen on a Camp Meeting platform.

You all handle the pressures, the problems, and the people so beautifully. Please know that I have nothing but words of affirmation and a great sense of being deeply impressed with all that is happening at Eaton Rapids. We just praise God and say that it's a miracle, a lot of hard work plus a miracle! That's what I say about Park Avenue and that's what I say about the miracle of Eaton Rapids resurrection.

May all blessing be yours in days to come.

In personal correspondence dated September 2, 1977, Clarence Hutchens wrote Hayden Carruth, telling him of a recent trip to Europe. "We had a great experience this summer in the British Isles, one that is indelibly imprinted in our memories. I hope I can share parts of it with you and others according to your interest. They do not seem to have the equivalent of Camp Meetings in England, although they have something similar on a college campus. There is also an equivalent to the Good News Movement there as well. When in Wales we ran into an Evangelical Youth Camp where their feeling was rather hopeless of reviving the church. This was more Baptist and Presbyterian, however."

That year the *Michigan Christian Advocate* reported that Dr. Kenneth Kinghorn, a nationally known biblical scholar and theologian, conducted three "Days of Discovery" at the Eaton Rapids First United Methodist Church in November. Kinghorn spoke on the platform at ERC about five times throughout his ministry.

Also in 1977, on September 30, the Board wrote Mr. and Mrs. Lute Hartenburg, each member of the Board personally signing the small note, which read as follows: "We want to thank you for your effective leadership in the preparation and planting of Tabernacle Circle on the campground. Your interest and your labors have created a delightful beauty spot on the grounds. Your dedicated spirit and your professional know-how have wrought something of a miracle. This achievement of yours will enhance the quality of worship in this sacred place for years to come."

A kernel of a letter from Carruth to Mrs. Virginia Kelly on November 21, 1977, is instructive concerning the general theological orientation of ERC: "Philosophically, theologically (though I certainly don't qualify here) the Camp is ecumenical in flavor, with a Wesleyan bias—and a very definite evangelical thrust! For example, altar calls are made in some services, but not necessarily, depending upon the guidance of the Spirit and the preference of the speaker. Worship services tend to be flexible and comfortable."

In a letter to Keith Granger on March 16, 1978, Carruth offered his profuse thanks for Keith's insistence that the roof of the cafeteria-dorm be structurally strengthened before snow time. A number of buildings in the community had recently collapsed under the weight of the heavy snow, but the building in question on the grounds withstood the storm because Keith's advice had been heeded. Carruth wrote, "Beth says of you, 'That man is a prophet!' Recent history appears to prove this."

An article by Thelma Harnett in *The State Journal* Saturday, July 22, 1978, read as follows:

From preacher to hotel manager to dining hall manager.

Planning menus, ordering food and supervising the preparation of 5,000 meals during an 11-day period can be a monumental task, but Rev. and Mrs. Gordon Showers of St. Johns seem to have the system down pat.[64]

The retired United Methodist minister and his wife have been in charge of the cafeteria each summer for 11 years, during the Eaton Rapids Camp Meeting. Earlier they managed the Grace Hotel on the grounds for 12 years. Their son and daughter-in-law, Rev. and Mrs. David Showers of the Crestwood United Methodist Church, now manage the hotel.

Operating the cafeteria might well be called a family affair as the crew of 20 also includes a niece, Miss Kathy Johnson of Saginaw, and two grandsons, Douglas and Randy Vandemark of St. Johns who help wait on tables, and Mrs. Showers' sister, Mrs. Alger Johnson of Saginaw, who does the cashiering and bookkeeping for the cafeteria.

There are three cooks and each one has an assistant, and youths attending the camp meeting work to partially earn their room and meals.

The Showers' son-in-law, Gordon Vandemark of St. Johns, directs the music at the camp meeting, which opened Thursday and will continue through July 30.

---

[64] ERC records include a 1986 article from the *Michigan Christian Advocate* announcing the 50th wedding anniversary of Gordon and Luella Showers. Gordon had been a longtime pastor in the West Michigan Conference of the UMC.

About $8,000 is spent each summer to feed the large crowds on the camp grounds, said Mrs. Showers, noting that about 800 to 900 pounds of meat are purchased.

Managing the cafeteria is a real challenge, she said, as the cooks never know how many people will be there for a meal.

Breakfast is served at 7:30 a.m., necessitating the Showers and others of the crew to start work by 6 a.m. Working 12 hours a day, with sometimes an hour off in the afternoon, they finish up about 7 p.m.

"It's a lot of hard work, but it is a real contribution," said Showers, who retired in 1975 from the active ministry after 36 years of service.

Mrs. Showers said that her family has been attending the Eaton Rapids Camp Meeting for about 25 years. She admitted that managing the cafeteria does cut into their time for attending meetings, but that they are able to see people they have known through the years and make a lot of new friends.

"The camp meeting has been a good influence on members of our family as they were growing up," said Mrs. Showers. "I'm glad to see our grandchildren enjoy it as much as our children," she added.

Upwards of 1,000 persons were expected to attend the evening services, beginning at 7:30 p.m. in the open air tabernacle, and featuring some of the top Holiness preachers. Services also are being held at 10:30 a.m. each day.

Among the speakers are Dr. Paul Rees, past president of World Vision International; and Dr. Paul Mickey, national chairman of Good News in the United Methodist Church, and associate professor of Pastoral Theology at Duke University, Durham, North Carolina.

Highlights will include Missionary Day next Wednesday and the annual Galilean Candlelight Service next Thursday night on the banks of the Grand River.

"The Lord has been extraordinarily good to Eaton Rapids Camp," said Dr. Hayden Carruth of Ann Arbor, who is beginning his eighth year as president of the camp.

Carruth is the 12th president of the Eaton Rapids Camp and the first layman to hold that position in its 93-year history.

Recently placed on an emeritus status by the University of Michigan, after being a member of the faculty for 31 years, Dr. Carruth was a professor of speech and associate dean of the College of Literature, Science, and the Arts.

Eaton Rapids Camp first served as a Lansing district camp for the ... Methodist Church, presenting the teachings of John Wesley, founder of Methodism. While the program is now geared to all denominations, the teachings of John Wesley continue.

There are 70 cottages on the grounds, two youth dormitories, and Grace Hotel, all of which are filled to near capacity each year. There are also 150 camping sites in the wooded area.

"Worship in a natural setting brings people to a closer relationship with God," said Carruth.

It is not the facilities, the acreage, or the oak trees that are important, however, Carruth said, but rather, what really happens in the lives of people.

Mrs. Carruth said their 10-month-old grandson, Benjamin, of Wilmore, KY, will be the fifth generation of her family to attend the Eaton Rapids Camp Meeting.

Recalling her childhood days at camp, she said she remembered people registering at the gate house at a charge of 50 cents for the entire camp meeting or 10 cents a day. Today the camping fee is $35 for the entire period, or $4.50 a night.

"I used to feel when I passed through the gate as a child a cool breeze, like the Spirit of God is described in the Old Testament—a breeze, a breath, or a wind."

Mrs. Carruth has been in charge of children's work at the camp for 18 years and also is in charge of the youth program. She and Dr. Carruth recalled how before the construction of the Children's Center in 1972, she tried to teach the youngsters in a tent, and later in two camper tents put together, and how often she had to wade water when it rained.

The Children's Center now houses an effective arts and crafts center, and a worship area in which the children look out of a large glass wall on to nature's setting.

Mrs. Carruth selected the site for the Children's Center and designed it.

Referring to the youth program, Mrs. Carruth said that in addition to thorough instruction received throughout the life of the camp, the skills of group dynamics are being used in small groups to enhance and to strengthen the impact of the Christian message.

The article above mentioned Paul Rees. As a young man, his was such a special ministry at ERC that he had a standing invitation to preach there, which he did as often as possible—close to a dozen times through the years. The brochure from 1978 said of him, "As the author of 14 books, radio preacher for 18 years, and frequent speaker at Bible conferences, youth conventions, and college preaching missions, Dr. Rees's name is known world-wide. We joyfully welcome him back to Eaton Rapids."

A Board meeting held on July 24, 1978, featured two people stepping down from their positions. Rose Belcher resigned from her post as secretary, and then Vice President Ronald Houk took charge of the meeting to receive the resignation of President Hayden Carruth, Sr. to take effect as of July 23, 1979. The motion was made and supported "to accept the resignation with many thanks for his service to the camp and our Lord."

A few months later Carruth wrote Dr. Paul Mickey with gratitude for his service: "For years to come, our people will be remembering and thanking you for your ministry in the Campmeeting. In the delightful and privileged life of the Camp, Paul, you are special. Your impact is unique, refreshing, and permanent. We will continue to be very much in your debt!"

In 1979 the Eaton Rapids Camp Scholarship Fund was established, having as its focus helping those young people of long association with the camp who have been called to specific Christian service. For some time there had been a growing sense that the ERC community should be acknowledging, in a special way, the needs of those young people whose vocational direction had been particularly affected by the message and ministry of the camp. Moneys received throughout the year and during camp meeting would be divided among the young people chosen annually by the Scholarship Committee, chaired by Marjorie Garnaat.

On February 12, 1979, Ronald A. Houk, pastor of First United Methodist Church in Ann Arbor, Michigan, wrote Dr. Hayden K. Carruth, Sr. then president of camp meeting. Houk told Carruth how impressed he was with Lt. Colonel Bramwell Tillsley, the Provincial Commander of the Salvation Army for Newfoundland, Canada. "During the Ministers Conference at Asbury Theological Seminary, I had a chance to chat with him after one of the services and inquired whether he was available for speaking engagements and whether he had ever participated in camp meetings. I really think that he has the perspective and balance that would warrant our offering an invitation to him for a future camp meeting date." Tillsley told Houk that he was booked up for a couple years and that he would need plenty of time for including ERC in his schedule. Houk included a tape of one of Tillsley's messages and concluded, "I cannot speak too highly of this young man." Tillsley did eventually become a platform speaker at Eaton Rapids, but not until three years later in 1982.

Sharing the platform in 1982 was H. Eddie Fox, who had been a speaker in the 70s. Originally scheduled to come back a few different times before 1982, Fox, part of the United Methodist Church's Board of Discipleship, had to defer his return because of other commitments. He couldn't come back in 1981 as originally planned, for example, because he was a member of the World Methodist Council and had been appointed Regional Secretary for North America for the World Evangelism meeting during the 1981 camp meeting.

A 1979 ERC brochure extended this invitation: "Come, take part in Campmeeting activities, and enjoy the special fellowship of Christian campers—around the campfire, in the pathways, along the river, and most especially, with our Lord. More than 100 large lots are available—dappled with sun and shade, interspersed with campfire pits and picnic tables, and close to restroom facilities with showers; play areas, Nursery care, the Tabernacle, and other central Camp activities...."

1980 marked the third year that Miss Leah Brown (organist) and Mrs. Ruth Tennant (pianist) teamed up to do music. Brown had a special affection and concern for ERC since, in her words, she was "literally brought up on these Campgrounds." At that point, since 1910 Brown had attended all but four camp meetings.

Prior to camp meeting that year, a large tree was blown down in Tabernacle Circle the day before the meetings were to start. Volunteers went to work and removed all traces of it so the services could begin with no delay.

Joining Dennis Kinlaw on the platform that year was Dr. Kamaleson, once again, and Dr. Merne Harris. In 1968 he became President of Vennard College (former CEI), and his ministries included pastorates, evangelism, youth work, camp meeting preaching, ministerial conferences, Christian education, and contributions to Christian publications.

From June 26 until July 4, 1981, the city celebrated the 100th Anniversary of the signing of the City Charter of Eaton Rapids, Michigan. Clara Squires and Jean Kline put together a booklet, an "Official Souvenir Treasury of Memories." It wasn't meant to replace *The Only Eaton Rapids on Earth* or *Island City, A Pictorial History*, but rather focus on what was more recently happening in the "beautiful city on the Grand." The booklet noted that many changes had been made in the previous century, changes with "purposeful direction and with meaning. They were years of toil and triumph and now we come to a point in time when we recount for succeeding generations the great things that have taken place and what is happening in 1981." The book then chronicled the changes that had taken place: changes in homes, in industry, on Main Street, in financial institutions, educational facilities, in churches, in services, in health care, in communications, in transportation, in agriculture.

The booklet also contained notes from an 1881 "Home Town Paper," five years before the first encampment in Eaton Rapids. Stephen Mills had erected a new "uptight" saw mill a couple miles north of Eaton Rapids, a new dancing and deportment academy had just opened at the Anderson House, teaching "all the latest Eastern steps to gents and their ladies," the local grocer was selling can corn at three pounds for 13 cents, and J. E. Walker advertised "Let me be your undertaker."

To celebrate the Anniversary, the city also re-lived the days of the *Stirling* paddlewheel passenger craft that carried passengers to the campground in years gone by from the livery by the (then) Majik Market. Captain John Chamberlain arrived on July 2 with his 60-passenger "Princess" and remained three days to transport passengers from the same docking place to the same campground destination, bringing the same sense of excitement and thrill to a whole new generation. The booklet reported, "The boat is all a-twinkle at night with over 2000 lights. An awning covers the top deck and entertainment is provided including a player piano."

The booklet also contained a precious portion of a two-column editorial in the local paper from a hundred years before: "A person who has never visited Eaton Rapids has a link missing in his chain of happiness. Here are beautiful drives, shady walks, delicious water, magnificent invalids [these were women of means who flocked to Eaton Rapids from Boston and points east to 'take the waters'—the aforementioned mineral waters thought to possess curative properties] in gorgeous profusion. We have dams by mill-sites and mills by dam-sites, noise, hum, and bustle. Also all kinds of crafts, now excepting witchcraft and you will be bewitched with frantic haste to make inquiry as to what will happen next!"

The 97th year of camp meeting, 1981, featured, as was the custom, Wednesday as Missionary Day. That year the missionaries were Dr. Thomas H. Hermiz, President of World Gospel Mission; Roger and Mary Lou Skinner, missionaries in Ecuador under OMS International; and Elwyn and Cynthia Hulett, having served in Liberia, West Africa, and Sierra Leone. The President of ERC, Mr. Coil, issued this invitation for the upcoming encampment:

> In John 17:20-23 Jesus gives us a corollary to His great commission—that we be so willing to lay down our lives in practical ways for our brothers and sisters in the Christian communities in which we function, that the world will be drawn to Him by these unique expressions of His love.
>
> Join with me, will you, as you come to Campmeeting, praying that personally and corporately we will let His Holy Spirit make the Eaton Rapids Camp community even more attractive to each life it touches during these ten days—"that the world may know Him."

The 1982 Camp brochure, edited by Miss Alice Camber, had for its prominent verse emblazoned on its cover page I Peter 1:15: "As he who hath called you is holy, so be ye holy in all manner of life." It contained information about that year's speakers, some new, some old. Dr. John Bergland and Eddie Fox were two of the speakers, the former for the first time. Colonel Bramwell Tillsley, Principal at the International Training College in London, England, was another, the speaker who had so impressed Houk in Wilmore.

1982 marked the departure of Howard Coil from his post as President, and his last Message to the Camp ran as follows: "Never has the example of Jesus Christ shown us in Hebrews 12 been more appropriate. The tenor of the times we live in continues to be one of personal and corporate challenge—spiritually, physically, politically, and socially. We encounter mountain tops and valleys in every area of our lives: family, vocation, and finances."

"Join with me, will you, as we come together determined to better know His intent for each of our lives as He speaks to us, especially in vs. 11-15. May we know more fully the implication of 'striving for peace with all men, and for the holiness without which no one shall see the Lord.'"

The incoming President-elect, Wallace Haines, shared this message:

When Alice called me to London, I was praying for Eaton Rapids, going from cottage to cottage mentioning the occupants and going around the last board meeting seeing faces. Revival always begins among God's best people. Prayer is where the action is. The American who preaches at historic Westminster Chapel, London, said two sins hinder revival: unbelief and self-defense (hard hearts)—Hebrews 3:12-15.

We should launch "Project Future 50 Years" for spiritual renewal, regional evangelism, and camp property restoration, I think, for our children's children.

1983 can be an important year for preparation—preparation for the 100th Anniversary in 1985. Much can be done by prayer and the paint brush.

The Old Testament speaks of revival as God "doing a new thing." Whereas prayer is always fundamental to spiritual awakening, the evidence and manifestation is unpredictable. God wants to do a new thing for us, His people. Let us not be afraid for He works in goodness and mercy. A visitation of the Holy Spirit on our camp in 1983, as has happened many times in the past, will increase our attendance, our giving, and our outreach ministry.

Will you come for the 1983 camp to pray and lend your support for what God wants to continue to do with this historic, holy place? Will you be preparing even now for the great celebration envisioned for 1985?

1983 marked the second and last time that Dr. William Baggett Coker was a platform speaker.[65] 1974 had been the first. Coker taught at Asbury Theological Seminary for two years, then at Asbury College for seventeen years (with a two-year break to work at OMS International in Indianapolis). At Asbury he was also appointed for a season by Kinlaw to be Vice-President and Dean of Academic Affairs. From Asbury he went to World Gospel Church, where he pastored for

---

[65] No relation to the author of which we are aware.

19 years. After retirement, he helped out at Hulman Street Wesleyan Church and filled in for pastors of other churches when they needed a substitute. In 2015 he was one of a handful of Golden Graduates invited to Wilmore to commemorate the fiftieth anniversary of their graduation from Asbury Seminary (a group that also included Dr. David Thompson, who's also spoken at Eaton Rapids, and another former professor of mine).

Before camp meeting, 1984, an initiative was afoot for an ambitious project of completely outfitting the Tabernacle with comfortable benches. The total cost would be $9,720 for 120 more benches, which would fill the Tabernacle. This came out to $81 per bench. Each Association member or family was encouraged to buy a bench for $81 apiece, in order to retire this debt before camp meeting.

The 1984 camp brochure carried this announcement:

> Throughout 1984 churches with a common heritage were celebrating the Bicentennial of Methodism. The Michigan State Holiness Camp Meeting Association joined this celebration. Although the Association enjoyed participation by members of a variety of church affiliations and had no formal organizational ties with the United Methodist Church or other churches of the Methodist tradition, Eaton Rapids Camp had its beginnings in 1884 when James Hamilton, the Presiding Elder of the Lansing District of the Methodist Episcopal Church, put out a call for a revival conference. The present 33-acre campground was purchased in 1885 and the first encampment was held there the following summer. It is thus fitting and timely during the 1984 encampment to contemplate our heritage in the Holiness Campmeeting movement in preparation for the celebration of our own Centennial in 1985. We thank God for the consecration and dedication of men who, like John and Charles Wesley and Francis Asbury, through the years have been faithful in spreading the truth of the Gospel.
>
> We welcome all who can join us beginning Thursday evening, July 19, through Sunday evening, July 29, at Eaton Rapids Camp to celebrate our life in Jesus Christ and grow in Him. If you are unable to attend for the entire encampment, feel free to commute, joining us for a service, a day, or a weekend. No reservations are necessary for participation.

President Haines issued this Message concerning the imminent Centennial celebration: "The Centennial Committee has appealed to you to help in the preparation for our 1985 Celebration. Committee suggestions have been circulated to all the membership. A united effort, everyone doing something, will mean a united spirit. Psalm 119 speaks five times of doing a thing 'with my whole heart.' Ability and success are not required. God asks for 'a whole heart' in prayer and all efforts in His work. Surely He wants a camp renewal, better appearance, and larger attendance, with revival at all levels in all departments."

The President continued: "'Thy judgments are a great deep.' Psalm 36:6. God has a pattern, a plan for each life. If we believe this on a New Testament basis (see Romans 8:28), we may be able to discern God's way with us. Joseph is outstanding because of his reactions to great injustices. He did not become bitter or refuse what God allowed. If he had, it would have destroyed God's plan for him and the Hebrew race. With animosity and sin all about him, he let God hold him steadfast in love and forgiveness. May the preaching of 1984 help us to forgive and determine to stand steadfast in the midst of temptations."

Among that year's speakers were Drs. Steve Harper, Lawrence Lacour, and O. Dean Martin. Lacour was impressed at an early age that speaking for God was "more important than being the President, a corporation executive, a movie star, or a sports hero."

Mrs. Champlin died in May of 1984.[66] As early as January 1984, President Haines and Vice President Ronald A. Houk sent a letter to friends of the ERC about the special upcoming Centennial celebration. It made mention of the Centennial program committee that had been formed by the Board to begin making plans for the 1985 celebration, and the letter tried to elicit areas of interest in which people would be willing to serve. The list of potential events, emphases, and projects wasn't meant to be exhaustive, but this was an early attempt to be intentional about responsibilities to plan for the 100-year celebration. Among the proposals and projects described were Gateway Reconstruction, Tabernacle Banners, Homecoming Day, Guest Choirs, a Centennial Song Book, a Centennial Walk Way, an Expanded and Updated History of the Camp Meeting ("To authorize a revision and expansion of the Eaton Rapids Camp Meeting Association history and printing for distribution. Needed are artifacts, photographs, printed materials, and anecdotes"), Historic Site Registration, a Centennial Garden, a "Paint Up & Fix Up Impetus," and a Major Fund Drive for a Retreat Center.

---

[66] Less dramatically, I graduated high school in 1984. Nothing particularly Orwellian about it.

Spotlight on Wallace Haines (1910-2007)
[Biographical Sketch and Tribute]

In 1983 Haines began a six-year tenure as President of the Association. His international ministry meant that there was an unusual variety of speakers during that time period. He took particular joy in preparing for and leading the Centennial Celebration in 1985. Unknown to most in the Association, Haines also quietly and sacrificially donated out of his pocket quite a bit of money to update the electrical system on the grounds. Upon his passing, his son Stephen Wallace Haines wrote a eulogy that gave insight into his ministry:

> Haines was born on the Fourth of July, 1910, in Wichita, Kansas. He was educated at the University of Missouri, receiving his B.A. in History in 1934 and his M.A. in History in 1937 with a thesis on Hugh of Dié. He taught at The Chicago Evangelistic Institute (now Vennard College) for several years, where he met his wife and wrote his own textbook on Speech. While attending The University of Chicago and teaching, he also worked at Marshall Fields and was known as their best clothing salesman. Although he never completed his Ph.D. at The University of Chicago, he was awarded the honorary degree of Doctorate of Laws by Milligan College in 1977.

For many years, in the 1940s, he was booked across the country as an Evangelist. His son reflects, "He was indeed a great preacher. I remember his sermons, whether at Eaton Rapids or Keswick, England, never written in advance but always emotional, challenging, even thrilling, plumbing his travels throughout the world, his conversations with great missionaries, an Anglican priest in Africa, a penitent in India, or the head of an orphanage in Vietnam."

In his thirties, Haines came to know a great Norwegian immigrant named Abraham Vereide, who finally prevailed on him to "pioneer" in Europe the strange new idea of a "Prayer Breakfast," a gathering of lay and episcopal leaders of all Christian denominations to pray together and discuss Christ in their practical lives. This very ecumenical movement led him to contact the retired Queen Wilhelmina of The Netherlands and begin adapting this idea to European culture.

His son adds, "He was involved in many of the political developments of Europe following the Second World War, a friend of government officials throughout the continent before, during, and after they were in office. He brought Edmond Michelet together with the struggling Prime Minister of France, Pierre Pflimlin, in May of 1958, using their common devotion to Jesus as a bridge toward reconciliation. The fact that Edmond Michelet convinced Pflimlin to resign in favor of de Gaulle was a political result of the intervention of prayer."

Douglas E. Coe wrote the following letter to Wallace Haines' family after Haines' passing, which gives a personal angle on Haines' work of reconciliation and how he carried that out.[67]

Dear Family of Wallace E. Haines,

It was a privilege to walk with Wallace in the relationship we shared in Jesus. Wallace was a man of long experience, deep convictions, and wide relationships.

In preparation for going to Europe, Dr. Abraham Vereide gave Wallace a direct and simple charge—Go to a city, see what God is doing there, relate yourself to what He is doing. Then repeat the same approach in another city, and in time relate the persons involved in each place to one another. By this process, a web of relationships developed around Jesus throughout Europe, both on the continent and in the United Kingdom.

There is no way to adequately express the long-term impact of Wallace on people worldwide and on our personal lives and family. Wallace was 100% single-minded. He saw opportunity for God's Kingdom work in every situation. He wrote voluminous letters filled with the details of God's Spirit leading him, and the vision he saw of the growth of the family of faith at home and abroad.

In the many times we traveled together, it was fascinating to hear Wallace's grasp of history, particularly that of Europe. I had so many questions and Wallace never tired of answering clearly and expanding on the questions with increased background and knowledge.

We flew together in a small plane to Vereide, Norway, and prayed together by the cross carved out of live stone beside the fjord. The point at which Abram Vereide had departed Norway so many years before.

It has been a privilege to serve the Lord with Wallace in our generations. We commit ourselves to his family and wide circle of friends to continue on the path which Wallace has helped to blaze and to map for us all.

May God comfort, strengthen, and sustain us all in this process.

Your friend,

Douglas E. Coe

---

[67] Douglas E. Coe, Letter, *In Memory of Wallace Haines*, accessed December 29, 2015, http://www.wallacehaines.com/inmemoryof.htm.

In recent personal correspondence, Alice Camber wrote that Haines was in her hometown in May, 1948, holding evangelistic meetings. "My mother and I almost died at the time of my birth. My mother always told me that both of us lived because of God's intervention and the prayers of the Rev. Wallace Haines."

Eaton Rapids History, Picture Record

The town of Eaton Rapids

Deaconesses

GRAND AVENUE—EATON RAPIDS CAMP GROUND.

1897

1897

1900

POINT COMFORT, EATON RAPIDS CAMP GROUND.

1900

1902, Deaconesses

BISHOP TAYLOR AS HE APPEARED WHEN THE EDITOR VISITED HIM IN
FEBRUARY. 1902)

1902

WHEN IN...
EATON RAPIDS
DO NOT FAIL
TO VISIT THE

ARCANA MINERAL SPRINGS BATH HOUSE.

The Water from these Springs has been pronounced the finest in the world.

An absolute cure for Rheumatism, Kidney and Liver Troubles and other similar ailments.

Commodious Bath House in full operation, with Hotel in connection.

For full particulars call on or address,

W. C. ESLOW,
EATON RAPIDS, MICH.

1903

NEW HOTEL.

1903

1905

Miss Nellie Snider

W. H. M. S.

With a great deal of delight we announce that Miss Nellie Snider, the National Organizer of the W. H. M. S., will give the address for that society again this year. Miss Snider has appeared on our platform twice before, and stirred all hearts with her eloquence.

You will want to hear her on Monday, July 30, 1906.

1907

1907

1908

1908

DR. JOSEPH SMITH

DR. C. J. FOWLER

DR. E. F. WALKER

MRS. IVA D. VENNARD

1908

Cottages, Camp Ground, Eaton Rapids, Mich.

1911, front row, second from left, George Bennard;
Henry Clay Morrison; Joseph Smith

MICHIGAN STATE HOLINESS CAMP MEETING
27th Annual Meeting, July 25th to August 3rd, 1912, at Eaton Rapids, Michigan

1912

1912

1913

No. 3162. Tabernacle Camp Ground, Eaton Rapids, Mich.

Callen Memorial Auditorium

1919

A Quiet Street in Our Forest City

1921

1922

Rev. Jacob Plancy, Albion's "Grand Old Man," the Hero of a thousand Battles, a lover of Eaton Rapids, "sighted the Golden Gates" April 22, 1922.

Converted at eight years of age, experienced and lived the sanctified life.

Seventy years a preacher and through his children has contributed 242 years of definite Christian service.

He lived among us ninety-one years. He lives with Christ forever.

1925

DR. W. G. NIXON

A Memorial Service for our beloved Dr. Nixon will be held on Saturday afternoon, July 30, at the 2:30 hour.

1927

Rev. H. D. Skinner, President, Muskegon, Mich.

Rev. H. D. Skinner, of Muskegon, Michigan, our beloved President is one of the Charter Members and has for more than forty years been an ardent supporter. It will bring him great joy to welcome you to this meeting.

1928

Rev. Lloyd H. Nixon, Grand Rapids, Mich.

1928

Welcome to our Forest City

1929

By its Borders, like a thread of silver, flows the River "Grand"

1929

1929

1929

1929

Hotel, Comfortable and Commodious—Come and Rest Awhile

1929

Epworth Chapel

Dr. Brasher outside his Alabama home

1932, Joseph and John Owen and Lloyd Nixon

1935, Paul Rees

1935, Lloyd Nixon Family

Miss Leah A. Brown

1936

1940

1940

Rev. Byron A. Hahn

1942

Gasoline rationing was but a distant threat, something that had happened to the East, when this picture of Main street, looking north, was made.

1942

WALLACE HAINES
Youth Leader

1945

1947

*Mystic Candle Lights
Moving steadily with soft
But gallant gleams, adown
This gently flowing River -*

*Where do you take our heartfelt
Prayers and commitment on
This quiet summer night?
In Our Hearts We Know!*

Galilean Service

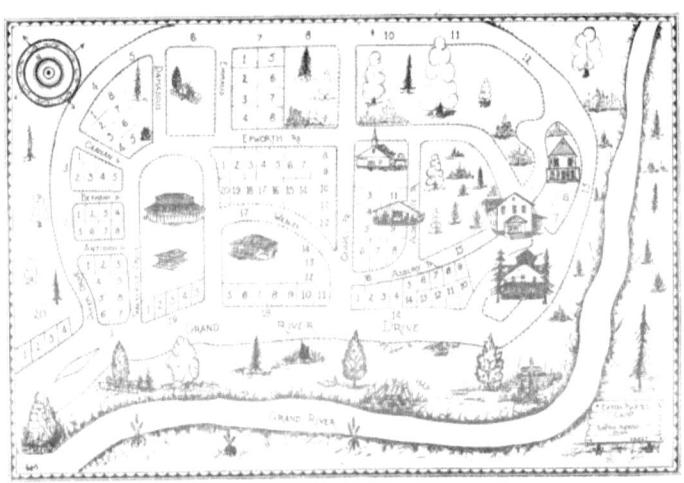

1976, Samuel Kamaleson

1976, Victor Hamilton

President Hayden K. Carruth

1976

Beth and Hayden Carruth

1981

John Oswalt

Part V

Contemporary America

1985-2015

America in the Information Age

Ronald Reagan's presidency dominated American culture of the 1980s. Reagan's conservative fiscal policies, tough line on communism, and bold leadership, conjoined with his optimistic faith in the American spirit, encouraged economic growth and technological innovation. By the end of the decade and in response to Reagan's foreign policy, the Berlin Wall was brought down, a move that signaled the dissolution of the Soviet Union, which was formalized in 1991.

Although the Cold War had officially ended, America faced a new threat with the rise of Islamic terrorism. The most memorable of these attacks came on September 11, 2001, with the coordinated hijackings of four airplanes that were used to bring down the World Trade Center buildings and to cripple the Pentagon. But there were many precursors, including the bombing of Flight 103 over Lockerbie, Scotland, all born out of retaliation for western involvement in Middle Eastern affairs, particularly America's support of Israel in the Six Day War of 1967 and beyond.

American involvement in the Middle East continued through the end of the twentieth century and into the twenty-first, with operations in Kuwait after Iraq's invasion in 1990, in Israeli-Palestinian peace talks, in both Iraq and Afghanistan after September 11, and, more recently, in Yemen and Libya. The volatility of the region and the vexed geopolitical questions raised by its instability ensure that the Middle East will remain at the top of America's foreign-policy agenda for some time to come.

Another cultural shift occurred at the end of the twentieth century, with personal computing becoming more affordable and widely available by the late 1980s. Price wars and competition to make products more user friendly followed, and by 2002 more than 500 million personal computers were in use worldwide. The Internet was opened to the public in 1995, increasing the demand for PCs and encouraging more innovation by tech firms. This shift changed the face of American culture, moving much commerce online, offering massive amounts of information at the click of a button, and—with the advent of social media—providing a platform for connecting with and influencing others in a grassroots mode.

The networking capabilities made possible by the World Wide Web, in many ways, decentralized information and challenged, in new ways, prevailing authority figures and institutions. Arguably, social media was a primary catalyst of the early twenty-first century sea change on American attitudes toward same-sex marriage. What had been a minority position in 2001—when well over half of the population opposed such unions—became the majority position in 2015, only fourteen years later, the same year in which the Supreme Court deemed marriage a fundamental right and guaranteed that right for same-sex couples.

The United Methodist Church, owing to the predominance of liberal leadership and its bending to the influence of the culture, is likely, at its next General Conference in 2016, to alter its official policy on homosexual relationships. Traditionalists tend to see such a trend as cultural capitulation rather than a biblically informed decision.

Chapter 12
The Centennial Celebration, 1985-1994

On May 11, 1985, Hayden Carruth wrote a letter to the friends of ERC to discuss the list of ongoing activities planned for the Centennial celebration. Owing to financial constraints, nothing left over could be spent on the celebration. So, he wrote, "in a statement of the self-evident, and after wide consultation among our membership, I told the Board of Directors on January 12, 1985 (1) that the Centennial would spend no General Funds money at all, but would use only monies offered as special gifts to the Centennial, and (2) that only three of the projects would survive the financial crisis in the Association: HOMECOMING DAY; the design, construction, and display of BANNERS in the big tabernacle; and CENTENNIAL WALKWAY—story plaques identifying 8, 10, or 12 places on the grounds of particular historical or popular interest. In short, special gifts are paying for the materials required for these three projects, and the work involved will be done by competent, loving hands."

A sheet of paper contained "A Woodland Walk," delineating points along a walking tour on the grounds, read as follows:

Let us embark together on a walk into our past and into our future.

Walk first along the river road away from the gate, toward the end of the grounds which is farthest from the entrance. You will eventually pass the large white Grace Hotel, the rust-brown Deaconness Cottage, and Workers' Rest Cottage. Climb the hill to the ball field, which was rebuilt by Jerry Topliff and Ralph Hart and friends a few years ago. Continuing to walk parallel to the river, cross the ball field and approach the woods.

Here our adventure begins.

At the point where you are standing, the border between Campground property and "Miller's Woods," nearest the river, many will remember there was for many years a wire fence, and a STILE over that fence. It was, in the day when the fence was built, the "style" for a small staircase to be built over a fence so that the people could get out but the animals could not. Miller's Dairy cows, however, being the exceptional animals that they were, did not know this. Many times they strayed from the field where they were supposed to be grazing into the woods. And because it was dark when they did this (don't ask why dairy cows were outside of the barn at night), they wandered around in the woods, bumping into trees. In fact, they bumped into the trees so hard that they could be heard, bumping and moo-ing, on the campgrounds and disturbed the campers! Finally a further fence was built, and the cows stayed put. (PLEASE FOLLOW THE PATH INTO THE WOODS, CLEARED JUST FOR YOU.)

Now take the right-hand fork in the path, which leads you downward toward the river. The red marker designates the point at which, out in the water, there is a deeper, clearer area known as the "Ol' Swimmin' Hole." Ask any one of the parents of college-to-high-school-age youth about this place, and watch for the fond, wistful smile. (RETRACE YOUR STEPS BACK UP TO THE MAIN PATHWAY, AND TURN RIGHT TO CONTINUE YOUR WALK.)

Soon you will arrive at another marker which designates the former location of the picnic pavilion and hitching bar. Imagine a quieter, more leisurely time of long, organza dresses, parasols, and wide-brimmed hats. A day's entertainment might consist of packing a picnic hamper, saddling horses, and taking a gentle ride to this spot in the woods near the river. There was an open-air building, really just a roof with supports and a floor, in case of rain, and a large clearing for sport, picking wildflowers, or just sitting on the grass and talking.

"X MARKS THE SPOT" where a retreat center might someday be built. This location is favored because of the completely wooded area, and the fact that this is the highest spot above the river. With some thinning of the trees directly beside the water and in the riverbank area, a magnificent view can be revealed, which would help to make weekend occasions at the Eaton Rapids Retreat Center memorable.

The President's Message for 1985, the Centennial of ERC, began with John 16:24: "Hitherto you have asked nothing in my name; ask, and you shall receive, that your joy may be full." Then Dr. Haines continued, "This 1985 season can be the beginning of a new era on these beautiful dedicated grounds at Eaton Rapids, where 100 years of preaching and praying have brought victory. As we praise Him for what He has done, we can expect Him to do even more in the future. Certain questions face us during the Centennial Celebration. Are we obedient to His commandments? Do we accept and rejoice in the growing perspective He gives? Do we readily perform that to which He puts our hands and heart? We are urged to 'ask and receive.' We attempt the seemingly impossible tasks He places before us, confident that, in His strength and power, they will be accomplished because He has promised, 'Greater things shall you do because I go to the Father.' John 14:12."

The delightful and endearing Walter E. Eschtruth wrote this poem to commemorate the 100th anniversary of the Eaton Rapids Camp Meeting and campground:

I'M A LITTLE BIT OF PARADISE

Nestled in the gentle curve,
Of the river Grand
I'm a little bit of paradise,
Created by God's own loving hand.

I was acquired by you Methodists,
In Eighteen Eighty Five.
I received my second blessing,
Became vibrant and alive.

You came by horse and buggy,
By river boat, and rail.
To reach my paradise of peace,
You walked the river trail.

You worked together, with loving care,
Built a tabernacle on my hill,
A place to meet, to hear His word,
To sing His praise, to seek His will.

I have watched a hundred years unfold.
You were young at heart or searching youth
In my little bit of paradise,
You learned to know the Truth.

Walter actually dedicated a collection of his poems in 1985 to Wallace Haines, writing that "his encouragement inspired me to record these words as received at the Eaton Rapids Campground 100th Anniversary Year 1985." "I'm a Little Bit of Paradise" was just one poem in this collection, which also included "Seeds of Faith," "Thanks Giving," "Forgiving Father," "Accept His Forgiveness," and "God's Child." But the one additional poem we will share here is "Eaton Rapids Camp":

I'm just a bit of virgin land,
Wooded hills along the Grand.
In 1885, through my creator's grace,
The Methodists came and bought my place.

Faithful people come each year,
Best ministers in the land to hear.

Preaching God's love by the riverside,
How forgiveness will halt evil's surging tide.

They built a tabernacle on the hill,
For comfort as they seek His will.
Singing His praises every day
With desire to learn the Christian way.

Telling of an experience of one great soul,
His heart was warmed, he reached his goal.
How he accepted the way of the cross,
Where the Son of my Creator paid a tremendous cost.

Now, I don't have a heart to warm,
I'm subject to many a blustery storm.
I gratefully accept the sun's bright rays,
For the snow and rain my God I praise.

I must admit, I cannot understand,
Why God's way is so difficult for man.
Like many who at the benches knelt,
I too have the second blessing felt.

Here beneath God's clear blue skies
Many saints my paths have trod.
Lovingly waiting at every turn,
Was the beauty of my God.

Look about you, my God seeking friends,
See here the peace He sent.
Look about you and learn,
Learn to be content.

Take an early walk along my river,
On its banks of dewy grass.
Look about my wooded hills,
View the maple, oak, and sassafras.

I have watched 100 years unfold,
You came as searching youth,
Finding freedom, peace, and joy untold,
You learned to know the truth.

> Come, come to seek His will,
> Learn of His love, His prevenient grace.
> Accept the joy that's meant to fill,
> To overflowing, the unfilled space between your heart and God.

On July 27 of that year (1985), the Hayden Kenna Carruth, Sr. and Beth Nixon Carruth Endowment Fund was established for the glory of God and in support of certain programs of the Michigan State Holiness Campmeeting Association. The Fund would be established to enhance two specific areas of camp meeting life: the tabernacle platform, and the programs for youth and children—to make possible certain new and different features that enhance the designated programs and enrich the camp meeting for everyone. Innovative proposals would be invited from the Board of Directors, members, and any and all friends of the camp meeting.

A 1985 pamphlet marking the camp's centennial asked, "Why a Centennial Celebration? What would be its purpose? What would be its focus? What would God have us do?" It then quotes Verne Summers: "Kindle—Rekindle an awareness of the tradition out of which we have grown in such a way as to hold us to it." The pamphlet then, for each day of that year's encampment, designated a decade since the camp meeting's inception. Friday, July 19, 1985, remembered the Decade 1886-1895, punctuated with I Corinthians 3:5-7. Saturday remembered 1896-1905, and the biblical passage for the day was Ephesians 2:19-22. Sunday, July 21, involved remembering the Decade 1906-1915 and the corresponding text: I Thessalonians 3:12-13. July 22 remembered 1916-1925 and cited Genesis 41:38-39. July 23 celebrated 1926-1935 with Matthew 14:21. July 24: 1936-1945 (Matthew 28:19-20); July 25: 1946-1955 (John 1:5); July 26: 1956-1965 (Psalm 98:4-6); July 27: 1966-1975 (Psalm 33:4,18, 20-22). And Closing Sunday, July 28, 1985; Remembering the Decade 1976-1985, commemorated with Psalm 42:4: "These things will I remember, as I pour out my soul: how I went with the throng in procession to the house of God, with glad shouts and songs of thanksgiving, a multitude keeping festival."

The pamphlet also contained, for each day of the encampment, the Centennial Walkway, a series of markers on the grounds, a gold lectern with a red edge, mounted on a brown pole, easily visible as one moved about the grounds. The text thereon contained interesting facts about a building or area. Marker (Centennial Walkway) 1 was "Point Comfort," just inside the gate, to one's left. Centennial Walkway 2: The Tabernacles (in front of the bell pedestal); 3: English Memorial Nursery (across from campgrounds, Damascus Road); 4: Dormitory – Snack Shop (across the road back of the tabernacle); 5: The Ticket House (then the well house on Wesley Circle); 6: Epworth Chapel (at the far upper end of Chapel Road); 7: Children's Center (on one's right, going up Chapel Road); 8: Boat Landing (at the foot of Chapel Road); 9: Bishops' Cottage (proceed along Grand River to Rio Vista); and, finally, 10: Centennial Walkway Hotel and Dining Hall (at the north end of the hotel). Forgive any redundancy here, but what follows is the background on each of these stops on the tour:

Point Comfort: One of the first considerations of the new Association was the housing of its guests. Joseph Morgan, who owned one of the fine mineral spa hotels downtown, contracted to build a small "boarding house" with 14 rooms, 4 to a room, and a large central dining room. Board was $5 per week; board and lodging $1 per day; 25 cents for board and supper; 35 cents for dinner. At the end of the first season it was recorded: Resolved that we as trustees of the Association to place the hotel privileges beyond our control. The meeting moved to the Morgan Hotel downtown where on November 23, 1886, they agreed to purchase everything from paint to pillows for $372. James Hamilton and David B. Hale gave their notes to cover the cost and the camp was in the hotel business, leasing it to members of the Association for management for a number of years.

After the move southward with the new hotel and dining hall, the building was used less and less as lodging. In 1934 Ruth Champlain had become very interested in renting it from the Association, but the cost was $20, an amount she could not even imagine. But walking down the street past the drug store she saw a $20 bill on the sidewalk. What a struggle of conscience! For a week the druggist held it for her in case someone should claim it. That became her first year's rent and down payment. She and her pastor husband Earl brought a succession of families and parish children to camp. They were joined in the effort by Fred and Sarah Briggs. During this period it became known as *Unity Home*.

When Mrs. Champlain became unable to carry the load any longer she gave it to the Association, after a number of attempts to interest a succession of younger couples in continuing her work. It no longer could pass health inspection of plumbing, heating, etc. Too costly to repair and too important as a landmark to tear down, it still stands waiting for the right combination of people, ideas, and funds to put it to work again.

The Tabernacles: In the fall of 1885 work was begun on the first tabernacle on the south side of Tabernacle Drive with its enclosed pulpit end toward the river. In a very short time the 55' x 100' structure became too small and 12 feet were added on each side at a cost of $115. At a trustee meeting on June 2, 1916, the Rev. H. D. Skinner presented the plan for a new tabernacle for which Dr. Callen, President, had made an initial gift of $2500 as a memorial to his wife. At the next recorded meeting a committee including Seth B. Fowler was charged with the execution of the plans drawn up by his youngest son. By July 29, 57 days later, the new building was completed and in use. Of the cost of $3,662.23, only $822.23 was still needed. Sunday afternoon Joseph H. Smith preached and conducted a dedicatory service, all the debt being raised. For the first time in many years the seating capacity of 3,000 was nearly enough, though many families still spread blankets under the trees where babies could nap and little children move about.

In 1919 when Dr. Callen's sudden death the Sunday before Camp shocked and grieved the community so deeply, it was moved to commemorate the tabernacle by a wrought iron sign: CALLEN MEMORIAL TABERNACLE, thus making it a memorial also for the founder and quarter-century President.

The sign, standing about a foot high along the roof line, withstood the weather for thirty seasons until it was brought down by a heavy storm, weakened and twisted beyond repair.

Lights and fans have been installed. The clever design of the clerestory windows has created a natural updraft to ventilate and relieve the heat. Many series of seats and benches have come and gone, but the beautiful rugged beauty of inspired design still holds our deep affection.

English Memorial Nursery: An empty dilapidated cottage with a broken down porch stood here unused for more than two decades. Then a man with ideas and energy began to think about it. First, off came the old porch. For a couple of years in the mid 60's the old daybed was covered by a clean bedspread and a basket of blocks plus mothers' contributions of snacks and time kept a little nursery going. The interior was dark and dirty, not well planned for use as a nursery, but with a gleam in his eye Fred Briggs (who redesigned the hotel lobby) showed Beth Carruth, then in charge of work with the children, how a stairway could be turned against a wall and open up a whole big room, even making space for a bathroom.

The construction was begun and another couple, Fred and Gertrude English, began to identify with it. At home they started the quest for cast-off toys, painted bright little chairs and tables, collected cribs; Sarah English and Gertrude made fluffy curtains, and within a year a bright inviting nursery was opened to care for pre-school children during tabernacle services. Within a couple years a large play area was fenced in. Not long after, it was doubled. Someone gave money for swing sets, the youth built and painted huge sand-boxes, and the children continued to come. The upstairs was carpeted a soft blue and filled with cribs for babies with a special attendant in charge. A wing was added by Cal Tompkins to double the downstairs space. Between forty and fifty children were cared for during each service. One year 74 child-hours were recorded as this very serviceable unit drew young families to our grounds.

Dormitory—Snack Shop: The Unity Home with only 14 rooms didn't go far in accommodating evangelists and other guests. In 1887 on the knoll across from the back of the tabernacle, a dormitory was built with separate rooms downstairs and two separate large chambers upstairs for housing of the cooks and kitchen helpers. At one time a screened porch was added onto the north side facing the tabernacles to accommodate mothers with tiny babies. When the grocery needs of the camp were no longer being met by the huxter carts and a grocery in a wing of the hotel, the lower floor south of the dormitory was converted to a more centrally located grocery and ice-cream parlor.

Finally, in the early 1960s, the upstairs having long been unoccupied, the condition of the building did not warrant further repair. A crew of men on the buildings and grounds committee had a great day tearing it down. Footings and a concrete floor were put down and the present snack shop was constructed. No longer really needed as a grocery store since it was so easy to shop in town, it became a gathering place for the young people and for evening food seekers. It also offered office space after the small secretary's building near the bookstore was demolished.

Ticket House: The earliest pictures of the gateway show a small structure beside the gate. It proved much too small and later was replaced by a larger building of better design with door-windows that opened up and shelves that extended to provide writing space. For nearly forty years the entrance to the camp provided an opportunity to register one's presence (10 cents per person daily; 50 cents for the entire encampment), pay for one's vehicle (10 cents a day or 50 cents for ten days) or horse (5 cents for a single horse; 10 cents for a team), make a deposit for hay for one's horses (purchased, incidentally, from Dennis Miller, who made the ice cream), and take possession of the wooden ticket which one would keep until one's departure. In the beginning business wagons, butcher, baker, grocer, and iceman were allowed in for free. Later they were required to pay a $5 fee. In 1921, when it was decided to open the gate and depend only on offerings for the support of the camp, the building was closed. When the wells were electrified in the late 40's, the ticket house was moved to protect the Number One well and its workings.

Epworth Chapel: By 1890 the many functions of auxiliary groups for children and youth required a place of their own. Seth Fowler designed a handsome building with an elevated floor, a closed north end for a platform, windows, porches, and steps surrounding the other three sides. It was handsome and functional for a time, but early pictures show that it necessitated groups carrying their chairs outdoors to have enough room. Soon after Grace Hotel was built in 1900, it was decided to rip out the floor, porch, steps, and windows, and redesign the building along the lines of the main tabernacle with raised doors, increasing the capacity to 150. Some of the windows were reinstalled in the four upper peaks of the roof structure for light.

In 1953 the Epworth Tabernacle was torn down, due to its rotting timbers and leaking roof (first noticed in the 40s), and Peace Chapel replaced it. Dedicated in 1954 to the memory of Lloyd H. Nixon and his father, W. G. Nixon, who together had given so many years of service, it still somewhat failed of its purpose. Immovable seats had been installed which made the building difficult to use, almost impossible for small children.

The year that the new Children's Center was built, this building also underwent radical change. The seats were removed, the platform at one end discarded, new concrete poured in the platform area, and the whole covered with good padding and colorful multi-hue shag carpet. The young people developed the habit of removing their shoes at the door, and as the program grew valuable space was spent for shoes! A long dreamed-of new entry with rack space for 200 pairs of shoes and a special registration area was built, bringing the building into excellent shape. The young people, returning year after year through high school and college, are the foundation for the future.

Children's Center: A common vision of a new Children's Center was shared by Maurice Glasgow and Beth Carruth. Over a period of five years sketches were drawn, enlarged, corrected. Working drawings were contributed in 1969 by an architectural student and taken to the Board for approval. Consent was finally given to begin a fund for the building. The last night of Camp in 1971, $4,600 was pledged and another $4,000 was raised by mail during the following year. The finished cost was a little over $14,000. The remainder was covered by private funds. Designed to serve 100 children, 50 then being the largest occasional attendance, it seemed enormous. Enrollment in the Children's Program immediately increased and frequently exceeded the building's maximum. The personnel who came with the change of place—Gay Sommerfield and Kay Starks, Alice Camber and Helen Arnold—bear much of the responsibility for this growth.

The movements of small feet and little chairs over the cement floor of the worship area was so distracting that carpet was laid in that section of the building within a couple of years. When Jack Futrell retired, he donated all of the counter-height cabinets from his store, thus greatly increasing the needed storage capacity. The little ash and oak chairs were furnished from the earnings of the children's workers themselves.

Boat Landing: Because of the supposedly healing mineral waters available at springs in several of the large resort hotels in Eaton Rapids, an atmosphere approaching the carnival prevailed in town, especially during the summer months. There had been for several years a large side-wheeler river boat, the *Stirling*, that offered the town's patrons a river trip as far as the camp area. The river was too shallow to permit it to go much farther, so at the foot of the present Chapel Road, earlier called Epworth, was the steam-boat dock.

After many years of fine service to the camp, eliminating many miles of travel since the State Street Bridge did not yet exist, the owner had a bright idea. He provided himself with a scow which he could tow. This increased the capacity per trip by 30 people. One day when many were waiting, he added an extra eight or ten passengers. Fortunately it was in fairly shallow water within sight of the campground that the scow succumbed, dragging the *Stirling* under with her. It happened in front of the George V. Meseroll boat livery located on the east end of Broad Street. The row boats were manned quickly and rushed to the craft in distress and very soon all of the passengers were rescued, albeit with drenched luggage. No one was hurt and everyone was quickly rescued, albeit with wet luggage. But the *Stirling* never again applied for a dock permit!

The Bishop's Cottage: The official registered name of this cottage, built for Marshall M. Callen by Seth Fowler in 1890, has always been *Rio Vista*. In its early glory it was surrounded by a wide porch across the front and partway down each side. An upper deck of equal size was available by upstairs doors and railed with a fancy "carpenter gothic" railing. The lower porch was always plentifully provided with hospitable rocking chairs. Dr. Callen, one of the Camp founders and prominent in Michigan Conference affairs, had occasion to know many of the Methodist Bishops, since they moved from conference to conference each year. As he would extend an urgent invitation to these men to come and speak at Eaton Rapids Camp, there was also proffered the invitation to lodge with him and his wife. As many as six were known to have accepted at one time. Little wonder it came to be called "The Bishop's Cottage."

Grace Hotel and Dining Hall: In the spring of 1900 plans for a new hotel in a lively open section of the grounds at the bend of the river were turned over to Seth Fowler. By that season's camp, at a cost of $400, the building was in use providing about 30 additional rooms. The central area of the first floor was the dining hall, the east (back) wing was the kitchen, and the whole central area was illuminated by the glassed-in cupola above the roof line. This greatly increased the kitchen-dining room complex but added so few rooms that in 1905 a forty foot extension was added to the north end, providing another 20 rooms at a cost of $570, with furnishings costing another $200. A year later a similar extension was built on the south side.

Five years later, the pressure for increased space being a constant factor as the Camp grew, plans for a separate building adjacent to the hotel were drawn. For $2,000 Seth Fowler built the two-story 30' x 100' dining hall with a one-story kitchen wing 24' x 50'. Kitchen workers could now be housed in the two dormitories above the dining hall and be saved the long walk from the old dormitory. The central area of the hotel (formerly the dining room) became a lobby, as well as accruing 18 additional sleeping rooms. The kitchen was used as a store. In the late 50s the old dormitories above the dining hall, having fallen into disuse, were cleared. Clarence Hutchens, Dean of Youth, purchased new double-deckers from Michigan State. In the same general movement, the outside stairways were reconstructed inside. The old east porch entrance to the dining hall gave way to 1st floor restrooms, and the present entrance was added. A bequest made possible the complete renovation of the lobby and provided new furniture.

The all-star lineup of speakers for the Centennial encampment included Drs. Maurice Boyd, Donald English, and, once again, back by unanimous demand, Dennis Kinlaw. The Chaplain of the U.S. Senate, visiting the Camp, mused with these words: "One hundred years of praying and preaching. One feels it."[68]

The president's message from Dr. Haines read like this: "One hundred-and-one years of Camp Meeting at Eaton Rapids! And what we have learned from our impressive past is, truly, that 'Great is Thy faithfulness!' God's mark has been powerfully and unmistakably on this Camp through war years, through Depression years, through boom years, though years of plenty. The continuum of God's leadership in this Camp, and the people's response in service to Him, is unbroken. Let us look forward, then, to Eaton Rapids Camp Meeting 1986, as the beginning of a new century in service and praise to Him, knowing that God is *absolutely* faithful to His people!"

In addition to featuring Drs. John Oswalt, William Ellington, and Harold McElvany as speakers the next year, the Camp featured for its opening message

---

[68] Around this time Beth Carruth wrote this letter to the Eaton Rapids Camp community regarding its history: "You may recall that you and I were looking forward to my writing and publishing the history of the Camp Meeting this year. An episode last September, however, has made it impossible for me to do any work on this delightful task. I was eagerly and happily looking forward last autumn to the challenge and the satisfaction of completing this writing. But an event of major proportions interposed, the product of forces beyond my control or influence, and I have simply been unable to advance this activity. Because of your interest in the History, I wanted you to know of the present status of this project, and of my own personal disappointment. Thank you for sharing my enthusiasm for Eaton Rapids history."

Bishop Judith Craig, who, in 1984, had been elected only the third woman bishop in the United Methodist Church. She arrived at that position through outstanding achievement at every level of church life: as director of Christian education, in the pastoral ministry, and then as the appointed Director for the Council of Ministries of the East Ohio Conference. Clara Hutchens died September 6, 1986, at 95.

The Tabernacle needed work in 1987, so a special workday and picnic was held on July 4. Leading up to camp meeting 1987, President Haines' Message began with these immortal lines from Horatio G. Spatford: "When peace, like a river, attendeth my way, when sorrows like sea billows roll – whatever my lot, Thou has taught me to say, It is well, it is well with my soul," then added this:

> In thinking about the 1987 Campmeeting, these familiar words come to mind. For more than a century, women and men of faith and commitment have worked to understand and articulate this Truth from our platform. No one view has been favored and no special interest served—only Christ.
>
> Eaton Rapids Campmeeting has been and is headed in only one direction: to provide people with a pure and soul-satisfying Gospel, interpreted by the finest Christian minds of the day.
>
> We have withstood the "sea billows" of changing time and values. We continue to seek God's clear message. We can truly say in unity of spirit: "It is well with my soul."

The brochure for that meeting said this concerning the musicians: "Eaton Rapids Campmeeting has been truly blessed in countless ways! One of the most visible, and perhaps least publicly mentioned, is our Music Department. As individuals, they are recognized soloists and musical leaders, with solid training, experience, and God-given talent. As an ensemble, they cooperate and blend so perfectly that the depth and delight they add to each service strongly support and enhance our worship experience. Thank you, Gordon Vandemark, Leah Brown, and Ruth Tennant, for your devotion to Eaton Rapids and to God!"

Around that time it was Rev. Wesley Smith who painted the entire Tabernacle in one day (ten hours) with an airless sprayer and the help of three other people. Bob Watson, who was the caretaker at the time, ran the tractor with a bucket on the front so as to carry Wes along within reach of the heights. Mr. "Bud" Bemis and Phyllis Smith also worked at sweeping down the cobwebs and dirt from the large doors. From the roof he was able to reach the windows which had been painted over several years prior to this time as it was determined that too much sunlight was bothering people's eyesight. However, a couple of years later it was decided that the paint needed to be removed so as to let in more light. Then it was Rev. Robert Betts who carefully removed the windows, taking them down to his workbench where he could remove all of the paint from them. It's not a certainty when this was done, but it may have been 1988 when

Wesley did the painting. It did not need to be painted again for another twelve years, or thereabouts, as the airless sprayer penetrated the paint deep into the wood. It was the Christian Carpenters who later came and painted it then, along with Wayne Spalding, manager at the time.

1988 also marked the conclusion of Dr. Wallace Haines' six years of service as President. The camp meeting family recognized his maintaining of the excellence of the platform speakers, also noting that "We have very much appreciated his tireless work in updating and refreshing many of the campground facilities. We are grateful for what he has done!" The President-Elect was Dr. William Shapton. With a doctoral degree in Mechanical Engineering, Dr. Shapton had pioneered the field of vibration analysis, one of America's areas of technological prominence. As the world's leading scientist in this field, Dr. Shapton had served as consultant to a number of major manufacturing companies around the globe. As a young man, he had helped figure out how best to float the candles for the Galilean Service—that engineering prowess came in handy!

Shapton grew up at Eaton Rapids Camp, having been brought as a child by his parents Lee and Ruth in 1945, leaders in the Association. On the Campgrounds, he was known as relaxed, quiet, and witty. At his home church, he was Vice Chairman of the Administrative Board, Chairman of the Pastor/Parish Relations Committee, and teacher of an adult Sunday School class. At Michigan Technological University, he was Professor of Mechanical Engineering in the largest department of its kind in the state. Although he was well known among fellow engineers and the recipient of many awards, he considered his witness for Christ among faculty and students to be his most worthwhile endeavor.

In the spring of 1989, a remarkable opportunity came to the Camp. Land adjoining the campground along the Grand River had been available for some time. But in January, the Board of Directors learned that the land was to be auctioned in parcels in early spring. The Board undertook an analysis of the Camp for expansion, and an assessment of our ability to fund such a purchase. At a special Board meeting on March 18, 1989, the Board decided to purchase the entire tract of 77 acres at a price of $210,000. This action was completed in May.

Areas of growth for Eaton Rapids Camp had been germinating in the minds of Camp leadership for a number of years. This land purchase would provide space for expansion in any of several programs. One plan that was being considered was construction of a year-round retreat center overlooking the river. The center would serve as a hotel during camp, leaving Grace Hotel for use by an expanded youth program. The center would be used by various church and college groups during the year, bringing visibility to the camp and its program.

It was hoped that this additional facility and program would have a synergistic effect, increasing participation in all aspects of the camp meeting while allowing better stewardship of the grounds by making use of them year-round. The actual use of the land would be studied during the upcoming year and a long-range plan developed.

At that time, it was the intent of the Eaton Rapids Public Schools to purchase about 26 of those acres from the camp for the price of $100,000. Due, however, to limited funding, the school district withdrew their offer and left Eaton Rapids Camp Meeting with the task of raising the money to cover the shortfall. With God's help and the generosity of Association members, that goal was reached.

Several members of the camp had been involved in an advanced giving program to underwrite this acquisition, certainly the largest project to be undertaken in many years. At that point they'd obtained pledges for nearly $125,000, with $80,000 already paid. With those initial gifts as a start, the Association was seeking additional help. The Board had moved boldly to capture this opportunity; if they hadn't moved expeditiously, the opportunity would have been lost. So the leadership of ERC issued this exhortation to its supporters: "In prayer, in counsel, in giving, and in all aspects of the development of this new frontier at the Camp Meeting, and with no departure from our historic beliefs and traditions, we urge you to join with us and become actively involved in supporting this venture."

The 1989 camp had its detractors. Clyde Leigh wrote President Shapton a letter on September 4, 1989, expressing two major concerns. He wrote that there were many things he saw during Camp that he appreciated and was thankful for, but that there were two negative trends. First, he criticized the youth program for putting an inordinate emphasis on entertainment, its "game atmosphere." "The youth program used to be the catalyst—no, not the catalyst, but the spark—for much of the response at the altars at ERC. The response now is pitiful." He was also concerned that the youth were withdrawing more and more from the main services of Camp.

Second, he was concerned that there was a sustained, gradual move away from holiness preaching from the platform, a preponderance of sermons meant to encourage and build people up, "tickle and titillate," but without providing nourishment on the words of the faith.

> The absence of holiness of preaching from the pulpit of ERC has continued long enough so that I cannot consider it an anomaly of our direction in preaching. It is a tendency fast becoming the new orientation of the Campmeeting. It is not a direction I find supported in the Constitution of the Campmeeting. I fear that it is being chosen, consciously or unconsciously, as a result of following what is fashionable in Christianity right now. This ignores our Campmeeting heritage, Wesleyan theology, and general good common sense.
>
> I know that the partiality of people is to the less demanding call of emasculated Christianity; I see it in the popularity of certain speakers and sermons as I fill tape orders. But there has also been a group of people who select sermons that try and test them and call them to even closer walks with Jesus in Holy living. These people have been finding fewer sermons to choose from in the last several years. An encouraging area

this year was Missionary Day. Although overall tape orders were down, requests for tapes from Missionary Day were up!

If Scriptural Holiness is not taught from the platform, how will people attending learn of the doctrine? If prospective members learn of us through our preaching, and the preaching is that of feeling good, rather than that of discipleship, how soon will it be until the last vestiges of holiness are purged from the Campmeeting as archaic hold overs of ignorant nineteenth century preachers? This seems extreme, but I see how quickly and easily organizations change. How many members received this last year or two really understand what ERC stands for? I wonder if those who have begun to attend in the last three years could express it even vaguely.

For the record, Leigh mentioned that speakers like Steve Harper and John Oswalt, in his estimation, continued in the classical tradition of holiness preaching, and were thus exceptions to the trend he discerned and lamented.

Five days after Leigh's letter there was a Board Meeting, on September 9, 1989. Both of Leigh's concerns were broached and discussed. Shapton mentioned to the program committee—consisting of Clarence Hutchens, Wallace Haines, Will Shapton, Sue Haines, and Bill Doubblestein —the issues raised by Ken Rietz and Clyde Leigh. He questioned if there had been a change in holiness emphasis in the speakers, but then said there had been no intentional change and the same committee had been in effect for the past six years (Sue Haines and Bill Doubblestein were new that year, but they wouldn't have an effect on the selection of speakers until 1992).

Will Clegg read letters from Ken Rietz, Will Clegg, and some of the 1989 counselors, stating their concerns about the youth program. Alene Harter, Brent Walter, and Noelle Dryden, 1989 counselors, were visitors at the meeting; A. Dryden and Gay Summerfield, youth committee members, were also in attendance. Questions raised were the relations with the kitchen staff, the need to reintegrate the youth into the complete camp meeting, the need for youth and adults to rub elbows, and the youth being off campus for one whole day.

Will Clegg felt that part of the problem with unruliness was due to the fact that the youth were not allowed to collect in the cafeteria for discussions and fraternization, such as piano playing and singing. He also affirmed that he stood firmly behind the current schedule and there had to be an attitudinal change on everyone's part to make this a success. After lengthy discussion and brainstorming, the Board gave a vote of confidence to Will Clegg and commended him for his work. Diane Hazle moved, Jerry Hippensteel seconded, that Will Clegg be offered the opportunity to take some continuing education as youth director, to be paid for by the Association. Will Shapton suggested that a member of the Youth be chosen to be on the Board.

Long-time musician, children's worker, and camp meeting member Leah Brown died at 85 on January 19, 1990, the daughter of George Brown and the sister of Warren Brown, leaders in their own right.

President Shapton's message for the 1990 camp meeting began with this familiar refrain: "Surely the presence of the Lord is in this place; I can feel His mighty power and His grace." Then he continued thusly: "The Eaton Rapids Campgrounds have been a holy place for many years, visitor after visitor has commented on feeling His presence while they walked these grounds. During the last year we have acquired adjoining land along the Grand River, a parcel twice the size of the existing Camp. This year we will dedicate this land and begin, along with the Board of Directors, to develop a vision for the future of the Camp, so that generations to follow will continue to sense the presence of the Lord in this place."

Platform speakers that year were Steve Harper, once again, along with the Reverends A. Bradford Dinsmore, Jr. and Dr. Alvern L. Vom Steeg. That year's youth evangelist was Rev. Matt Kreh, Assistant Pastor at Trinity United Methodist Church in Lansing. Mike and Debra Long, members of the camp family, led the youth music program, and the music program was led by Scott McPherson, Gerard Faber, and Ruth Tennant-McLean.

There was a Dedication Service of the new property on July 27, 1990. Mrs. Hayden Carruth was one of the speakers. Here's a bit of what she said: "It occurred to me this morning as I was praying about this service and going over the things I'd been thinking about, that though I doubt that I am the oldest person here, I think it's quite possible that I am the person who has had the longest contact with this camp. . . . This is my seventy-fifth season since my parents brought me as a baby, three months old, to Eaton Rapids Camp. In my lifetime. . . I have had twenty-eight total changes of residence. . . . Eaton Rapids has been for me the place of permanence, the place I could count on being the same in essential ways. It is by all odds my spiritual home. Steve spoke in one of his first messages about Eaton Rapids being a benchmark place in his life. I thought the use of that term was significant: a *bench*. And you know what those benches have meant in your lives. There is a little bench that stands about so high up in the Children's Center, where at eight years of age, I gave my heart to the Lord. Like the Israelites, I had a lot of wandering after that, but that basic first commitment never was abrogated; it has only been deepened over the years."

1990's brochure, under "Our Aim," reprinted this section from the Article of Incorporation, Michigan State Holiness Association, 1885: "To promote the closest possible cooperation among all the friends of Scriptural Holiness; for the promotion of the doctrine and experience of entire Sanctification as a definite work of grace wrought in the heart by faith subsequent to the experience of regeneration and to secure the conversion of sinners to the Lord Jesus Christ."

1991 featured Dr. John Oswalt returning as a featured speaker. That year's brochure introduced him as one of the translators of the Old Testament for the New International Version of the Bible and a very popular evangelical speaker. "Possibly this is because he manages to successfully 'translate' God's truth as he finds it in the ancient Hebrew writings he loves, into the problems and questions we face in everyday life." With a Ph.D. from Brandeis University and scholarly writings appearing in Bible encyclopedias and other publications, Oswalt had been Professor of Biblical Languages and Literature at Asbury Theological Seminary for several years, and past president of Asbury College. But "Oswalt's presentation is far from dry and didactic. In fact, he is alternately vivacious, humorous, and never fails to touch his hearers' deepest need."

Joining Oswalt on the podium that year were Dr. Leonard Sweet, who had first spoken at ERC in 1988, and was a prolific author and scholar of church and American history, and at the time President of United (Methodist) Theological Seminary in Dayton, Ohio. As of 2015, he was the E. Stanley Jones Professor of Evangelism at Drew University, and a noted expert in semiotics and theology. The Reverend Barbara Brokhoff, who also first visited ER in 1988, had served as pastor and evangelist in the Missouri and Georgia conferences. She was a well-respected author and preacher, and her sermons were said to sparkle with wit and originality.

In a protracted letter on January 15, 1991, Youth Workers Ron and Nancy Kuhlman wrote President Shapton about various innovations planned in the upcoming encampment's youth ministry, particularly to address the dwindling numbers of youth involved at camp meeting. Much of the focus would direct attention to training counselors on matters of prayer and seeking the will of God. An intention was to focus and build on the historical and unique nature of ERC, namely, of enhancing personal holiness, as opposed to keying on evangelistic efforts. This approach was based on the belief that the opportunity for evangelism would present itself as youth campers excited about their growth and positive experiences at ERC would bring their friends to camp. In an effort to facilitate prayerful, supportive relationships between the counselors and other ERC leaders, it was hoped that a counselor retreat could be held in June of 1991.

Greg Wood, the youth evangelist, led services in Peace Chapel in July of 1991, calling Christian youth into a common commitment to serve others for the sake of the gospel—a reminder from Paul to Timothy that being young does not discredit a Christian from becoming a leader of others by patterning their life after the model of Jesus. The names of the nine sermons were as follows: "Not Too Young to Lead," "You Have to Train," "Do Not Neglect Your Gifts," "Don't Hold Back," "Watch Your Life," "R-E-S-P-E-C-T," "Don't Play Favorites," "Charity Belongs at Home," and "Watch What You Say."

In 1992, on January 6, President Shapton wrote a letter to the Board apprising them of an offer from the Eaton Rapids School District for about thirty acres of the new land ERC had purchased. The District wanted to purchase the northern strip along their present land for about $100,000. This would leave ERC with everything that is south of the then-current line, simply extending the border along the camping areas straight across the new land. ERC would keep all of the riverfront and part of the open field. At the time they owed about $60,000 on the land, so accepting the offer would allow them to pay off the land and have about $40,000 left. The decision would have to be made at the upcoming Board meeting, which took place on February 29, 1992 at 9:30 at the Eaton Rapids United Methodist Church. The deal was tentatively agreed to at a Board meeting on January 25, but assurance was needed the District wouldn't resell the land for housing. Members of the camp meeting were invited to attend this meeting or let a Board member know their recommendations before the meeting. Shapton, in a letter to the friends of ERC, wrote, "We are all reluctant to sell any part of the land, but this appears to be an excellent opportunity to sell a portion for which we had no real plan, and at the same time, allow us to pay off our remaining debt on the land."

On February 29, the Board decided to sell the land, but Mike Long moved that a proposal be made to the school to amend the selling agreement to include a first opportunity to purchase the land if the school board should ever decide to sell it. The proposal passed on a vote with no opposition. The question of reaffirming intent to sell the land to the school board was then put to a vote and passed with no opposition, but in the end the deal fell through.

In the winter of 1993, a new newsletter for the camp was initiated called "Riverside Reflections." Over the years, ERC had circulated several newsletters designed to keep the Camp family in touch during the months between encampments. This new effort was made possible through the cooperative help and encouragement of the Board of Directors. The contact and spearheader of this initiative was none other than Hayden Carruth, Jr. who resided in Adrian.

The newsletter shared some highlights from the January 16 Board meeting—the new land had been refinanced at 7.5%; the new organ and piano were paid off; speakers for the 1993 camp; Buildings & Grounds Chairman Ed Richmond reported that three or four cottages were available for purchase to qualified buyers—and noted that a new Camp Video was available. For $20 anyone who wanted one could purchase the ERC Promotional Video. This five-minute presentation had been professionally filmed and produced, providing an excellent way to tell others about camp meeting. With the video would also come a list of suggestions for ways one could use this convenient presentation, along with an informational handout that could be photocopied and distributed to those who watch.

Vice President William Doubblestein wrote the following paragraphs for the newsletter:

I *am* thrilled to see this newsletter come out. For a group that only sees one another once a year, it is very important for us to be tied by the news of what is happening among us and with the camp.

I am looking forward to this year's encampment with a great deal of excitement. The speakers promise to be again both inspiring and challenging. We are just beginning to finalize the Missions Day platform. I am always looking for missionary speakers for that day, especially those who can deliver for us a challenging message. In these days of expanded opportunity for evangelization and missionary outreach, it is important for us to issue the call to as many hearts as God has prepared to go and preach and teach and make disciples. These are exciting days to be a Christian, and they are challenging days to be part of the Holiness movement. Once again I believe we are being raised up afresh as a people called of God, "... *to reform the nation and to spread scriptural holiness across the land.*"

These are days which are calling out for a moral revival in our nation and it will take a people who have seen the holiness of God and have consecrated themselves to be a holy people to once again turn our hearts back to God. I look forward to that work, and I hope you are also.

Our first challenge, however, is to continue rebuilding the vigor and spirit of our campmeeting. Let me challenge you to help by inviting and bringing one new family to camp this year. And, if you haven't been to camp for a while, let me invite you back this year. If we are to meet the challenging days ahead, we must be equipped as Eaton Rapids Camp and her teaching of holiness has prepared saints and servants for generations. With the standard of holiness raised, join me in bringing this message to those who are perishing without Christ.

The Campers' Corner section of the newsletter accorded accolades to Earl Carpenter and Diane Hazle for serving as Bell Ringer and Registrar, respectively, and announced that the restroom/showerhouse had been remodeled and painted, with eight new benches, thanking Jack and Grace Jurmo for that work; also, a new barrier-free unit available for those with special needs was now available.

Cottage Owners' News announced their new Auxiliary President, Phyllis Smith, and, among other announcements, welcomed new cottage owners David and Charlene Minger and (my parents) Leonard and Evelyn Baggett.

Nursery and Youth updates, along with Membership Information, rounded out the newsletter, save for Bill Doubblestein's "Book Nook," his short reflection followed by a book suggestion. His reflection went like this:

"Be diligent to present yourself approved to God, a worker who does not need to be ashamed, rightly dividing the Word of God." (2 Tim. 2:15, NKJV) At least one translation suggests that the word *diligent* here means to study, or become knowledgeable. If you have been in Camp these past few years you already know my passion for a holiness people who read and study and clearly understand what we are talking about when we talk about Holiness of heart. It's been my experience that even in Camp Meeting settings there are many who have little idea of what the Bible means by Holiness. And that's dangerous to a generation that has grown up without the message clearly being taught in our churches and seminaries. I've been asked to write a book review with each newsletter. I appreciate the opportunity to suggest a few of the classics in the Holiness tradition. While I will suggest other reading for a Wesleyan Evangelical readership (I hope you will forgive my zeal for a tradition I belong to not out of choice but from a firm conviction of its Biblical faithfulness), I will focus on those books that will help us better understand Wesley and the Holiness tradition that has grown out of his understanding of the Biblical witness.

Doubblestein then chose for that newsletter's book A. W. Tozer's *The Knowledge of the Holy*, choosing this passage to share: "What comes to mind when we think about God is the most important thing about us. The history of mankind will probably show that no people has ever risen above its religion, and man's spiritual history will positively demonstrate that no religion has ever been greater than its idea of God."

The Summer 1993 *Riverside Reflections* reported on the matter of reforestation: "Eaton Rapids Camp has applied for and been accepted as a participant in the state administered Forest Stewardship Program. This program shared the costs of reforesting and improving our property. The government pays 75% of the cost and we pay the balance. A management plan has been developed with the help of Dr. John Hart, a state-certified forester from Michigan State University. Plans include the placement of 24 nesting boxes, preparation of the soil for planting, and planting a combination of deciduous and evergreen seedlings. Some work will be done this summer and planting will take place in the spring of 1994. More information will be available during camp."

A July 23, 1993 article by Sheila Schimpf in the *Lansing State Journal* called "Refreshing the Spirit" discussed camp that year:

Inside the tabernacle, it still feels a little like 1885.

The second-story windows are held open by ropes. The sides are propped by two-by-fours. Fans on the big barnlike ceiling run silently. And the trees and the bushes outside are the same ones that stood witness generations ago on the banks of the Grand River near Eaton Rapids.

Like religious truths, campmeetings are timeless.

The faithful troop in, dressed casually, happy to see each other. They take their seats on park benches, Bibles or hymn books in hand.

Up on the platform, Gerard Faber plays the new organ, clear and true. The sound system carries the music out over the summer air, bringing comfort.

"Music is ministry," Faber says later. "It sparks a spiritual language and ministers to the spirit."

Stepping under the banner that reads "Be Ye Holy," Bill Goold, a professor at Asbury Theological Seminary in Kentucky, starts the morning with Psalm 95: "Come let us sing for joy to the Lord."

Then the mid-morning audience, almost 300 on this workday, rises to sing the first hymn, "Higher Ground."

"It's a wonderful balance between hanging onto the past and looking to the future," Goold says later. "Some campmeetings are dying. They haven't been able to keep a sense of where we are today or where we've been."

The Eaton Rapids Campmeeting was started in 1885 by the Methodist District superintendent.

It is now interdenominational, run by the Michigan State Holiness Campmeeting Association, open to all who support "the conversion of souls and the promotion of holiness." Most of its participants follow the Wesleyan tradition, says the Rev. Clarence Hutchens, a retired United Methodist minister who lives at the campground.

Campmeeting runs only 10 days a year, but 70 turn-of-the-century cottages on the Grand River site just south of Eaton Rapids are owned by families who come and go all summer. They provide a sense of continuity and rootedness.

Campers—many are regulars who return year after year—fill RV sites, and others stay in the Grace Hotel, a 1906 boarding hotel with 58 rooms and nominal fees.

About 600 or 800 people comfortably fill the Tabernacle, which seats 1,000, for the evening services.

Many of those people take a week's vacation for campmeeting. Many others are retirees.

"You come and what you find is so warm and inviting and good, you want to come back," says Alice Camber, who runs the craft sessions for children. She has been coming for 21 years.

"Our families have been coming here for years," said Will Shapton, Michigan Technological University mechanical engineering professor and president of the association. "It's a chance to get 10 days away from the usual pressures, a chance to be with the family. It's a good place to get values."

The camp's youth and children's programs are intense.

Younger children memorize Bible verses and older children remove their shoes before entering Peace Chapel.

'It's tradition," Ron Kuhlman, youth director, says. Kuhlman, associate dean of students at Ohio Northern University, is in his third year at Eaton Rapids. "We are walking on Holy Ground, and we are respectful of that. It's very strictly adhered to."

The theme for his program is "On a Mission from God."

"It helps them see how special and unique they are in God's plan," Kuhlman said. "Young people may be the people who catch the ear of the sleeping giant. Our kids come here to be serious about that."

Kuhlman says the camp is not a recreation camp.

About 50 kids in the youth program go to three worship services a day. They have a special youth service at 9 a.m. and they attend the regular adult service at 10:30 a.m. Then they have an afternoon service, which includes small group discussions of the morning's guest speaker.

"Youth camps are always intense," said Jason Werner, 20, a University of Missouri senior. "Kids do everything in fifth gear. The benefit here is you get to hear all the preaching. It's a unique opportunity."

Jennifer Shepard, 21, has been coming for nine years and talks about spiritual growth.

"It's the peace you feel when you come on the campgrounds," Shepard said. "When you leave you feel refreshed with the spirit of God that comes within you."

The regular adult services are held three times a day. A core of professional guest speakers—lined up several years in advance—rotate. For example, the Rev. Douglas Crossman, a Welshman who has recently moved to Massachusetts, might speak one morning, the next evening, and the afternoon the third day.

On that morning, Crossman had preached about I Chronicles. "God so often takes up the unwanted," he thundered from the platform into the huge tabernacle, "the illegitimate. We are not responsible for our backgrounds."

That kind of deep thought is what brings the Rev. Clyde Leigh, a Nazarene pastor from Faribault, Minn, back year after year. "The ministry I receive here has a depth I don't find anyplace else," he said. "This is where my spiritual roots are."

As Eaton Rapids launched its second century, hoping it would be as storied and sacred as its first, voices from the past joined with those of new generations to proclaim anew the imperative to hear and heed God's call to holiness.

Spotlight on Samuel Kamaleson (1930-)
[Biographical Sketch]

Samuel Kamaleson would speak at Eaton Rapids no less than six times throughout his ministry. Well known for his books, record albums, radio, and preaching ministries, he participated in preaching missions all over the world. When he was 44, he began a new position, working closely with church leaders throughout the world to determine how World Vision can best serve their needs. The evangelical humanitarian agency was aiming to expand its worldwide ministry of Christian leadership training through seminars and pastor conferences. Kamaleson's service began with street ministry in Madras (now known as Chennai), India. After completing his degree in veterinary medicine, Kamaleson came to the attention of an American administrator for the Methodist Church working in India, J. T. Seamands (brother of David Seamands, author of, among other well-known books, *Healing for Damaged Emotions*, and a platform speaker at ERC in 1971).[69] J. T. Seamands mentored the young Kamaleson and helped him enroll at Asbury Theological Seminary, where he first studied sacred music. He earned a master of divinity and, later, a master of theology.

After ordination, Kamaleson, in partnership with his wife, Adela, served parishes in India and in Texas. After earning a doctorate of sacred theology from Emory University and working as a district superintendent for the Methodist Church of Southern Asia, Kamaleson was tapped in 1974 to become vice president for World Vision International, where he served in various roles until his retirement in 1996.

Some claim that Kamaleson has spoken to more church leaders than anyone in the history of the church. While that can't be verified, it still suggests the breadth of his influence. Having appropriated a lesson from an early mentor of his own, he aimed to make people feel important and to meet their hunger. "Including myself, I have seen hundreds of young pastors and church leaders who have made a deeper commitment to serving Christ and his people as a direct result of Kamaleson's teaching and preaching," said Martin Alphonse, professor of intercultural studies at Multnomah University in Portland, Oregon.

Kamaleson wrote Hayden Carruth a letter on August 27, 1976, which included these lines: "I often sit down and reminisce over the blessed times we as a family had at Eaton Rapids. God was very, very close to us. And through your love He blessed our minds and hearts. Truly, we all were blessed by His presence during those days."

---

[69] I was working in the kitchen the night Asbury Seminary hosted David Seamands' retirement dinner. At the end of the night, Seamands spoke a few words, and I remember hearing him say this, "I wanted to put a sign in front of our house that said 'The house that damaged emotions built,' but my wife wouldn't let me."

Chapter 13

A Third Century, 1995-2004

1995 featured several Asburians, including Drs. Lawson Stone and David Thompson on the platform. Goold again led the music, and Charles D. Killian performed in a special John Wesley and Francis Asbury presentation.

Around 1996 residents of Eaton Rapids, including those who lived on the campground, endured a siege by leaf-eating caterpillars that turned into gypsy moths. The campground was one of the hot spots of infestation in a statewide plague of the moths. The Eaton Rapids Garden Club conducted a public meeting on the nuisance March 12, 1997, at City Hall, as the community braced itself for another attack.

Rev. Clarence Hutchens, former president of ERC whose home is in the camp, said at the time the city should pay for whatever tree spraying is necessary—including the campground. In 1996 the campgroup and a few nearby homeowners paid $1,500 to aerial applicator Gene Robinson of Olivet to spray the trees, sweeping clean the camp in time for camp meeting. In a March 1, 1997 article in the *Lansing State Journal*, Becky Bullock, Hutchens' daughter, whose house was one of seven year-round houses on the campgrounds, said that, at the least, city officials should coordinate any caterpillar fighting it does with the timing of an upcoming camp ground spraying.

Asbury was again well represented in 1996 and 1997. In 1996 Harper returned, along with Dr. Robert Mulholland, a noted New Testament Bible scholar who also served a long stint as Provost of Asbury Seminary. The next year Kinlaw returned, along with Dr. Elsworth Kalas, who served for a time as President of Asbury Theological Seminary.

In 1998, just as camp was beginning, the water in the camp well was declared unfit for drinking. The problem was cleared up in a few days, but it sparked serious discussion about connecting with the city water system. Later, during the presidency of Clyde Leigh, this connection was made after lengthy negotiations.

In that same year, 1999, Hayden Carruth, Sr. and his wife Beth Nixon Carruth died, and the next year, two other stalwarts were lost: Grandpa Lee Shapton (October 6, 89 years old), and Paul Conklin (December 21, 88 years old). With those four deaths the third generation of camp leaders was coming to an end.

Walter Eschtruth's testimonial, rife with poignant recognition of the rich history of ERC, read in an evening worship around 1999, is a delightful gem:

> This is our sixteenth summer as a resident here on the Campground. Previous to now I have been able to avoid standing behind this pulpit. It's not that I object to being here but I just feel more comfortable sitting in the pews where you are tonight. I do consider it a privilege to share this time of worship with you tonight. My personal feeling is that worship or prayer time is most importantly a time of glorifying God and giving thanks. So as I mention briefly some of the many things I am thankful for, perhaps you will be reminded of a similar experience that occurred in your life. For instance, we have all experienced our first time entering the gates of this Campground. My wife, Dorris, and I are thankful we first came as guests of our minister Harold Jacobs and his wife Winifred in 1961. Since that time there has been a sort of magnetic attraction that has kept us coming back. I am sure we returned at least once a year for a camp meeting, a weekend with our church youth, a day session for church planting, or just to drive through this "Little Bit of Paradise." We are also thankful that most of you have brought a friend or family member to this place of worship. This has always been the best way to bring others to Christ and to build our community of faith.
>
> After retiring in 1983 we had decided to spend our winters in Arizona and were considering spending our summers in our travel trailer here in Michigan. Once again our thoughts turned to Eaton Rapids Camp and we came for a two week stay. How thankful we were as we experienced our first full-time Camp Meeting. How thankful we were that a cottage was available to re-model for a simple summer home. Later when we needed a downstairs bedroom, we were asked if we would remodel the cottage next door. We were very thankful as we planned and remodeled to fit our need. By this time, looking back, it became very obvious that a plan far greater than our own personal needs had been working in our lives since our first introduction to Eaton Rapids Camp. We are so thankful that we not only have been able to help maintain these grounds but have had the joy of working with so many of you. We worked together to build water lines, install drainage tile, rebuild roads, and re-paint the buildings that those who came before us provided for our comfort and enjoyment. We are thankful that each generation before us, with faith and the labor of love, have worked to improve this sacred ground and its facilities. I am thankful for the faith that this Campground will continue to serve the needs of God's faithful people as it has for the past 115 years. That faith becomes even stronger when, each year, I see the future leaders that are gathered here in the front rows each night for the worship service. If we will provide the best possible program for our youth, they in turn will fulfill our future need for leadership.

I am sure that everyone here continues to come to this place of worship year after year, not out of habit but because we experience spiritual fulfillment, spiritual renewal, and form lasting friendships with others who share a common faith. We are members of a community of faith seeking to more clearly understand the lessons that Jesus taught and to glorify God.

July 2004 was an important time for elections. On July 19, John Werner was elected as Secretary of the Association by the Executive Committee. On July 24, Kathleen Ray was officially elected Vice President of the Association and Dr. John Oswalt President, the end of whose tenure corresponds with the end of this History. Dale Nuoffer, at the July Association meeting, reported how the hard work over the past 11 years had begun to mature in developing a reforestation program for the acreage nearly sold to the Public Schools and planting hundreds of seedlings.

After that sale of property to the Eaton Rapids Public Schools in 1989 fell through, the Eaton Rapids Schools once again found themselves in a situation where they needed to expand their administration building and their transportation department. They entered negotiations for a piece of property that was proving to be both expensive to develop and not located adjacent to their current campus. In mid-November of 2004, they again approached the Board of Directors about the possibility of purchasing some of ERC's property. The Superintendent of Schools and another representative from the district attended the November 20 Board of Directors meeting with a proposal to purchase from ERC approximately 18 acres of camp property, which is adjacent to school property and is located on the northern boundary of the original Miller Farm. Unfortunately, the school board was facing deadlines and needed an answer from the Camp's Board of Directors that day as to whether the Board would consider their proposal.

After much discussion and soul searching, the Eaton Rapids Camp Meeting Board of Directors voted to go ahead with negotiations to sell this property to the school with the stipulation that any money that would result from the sale would be placed in a separate account, to be held until the Board of Directors, with input from Association members, can determine and prioritize how the money is to be spent.

Within two weeks the school district and Board of directors were in negotiations, and an agreement was reached. Some of the details of this sale included: The school district would purchase approximately 18 acres at the price of $25,000 per acre, resulting in over $400,000 for the camp. The district would relocate as many of the trees as had been planted as was possible, to create a green belt between the school and camp property. The district would install a security fence along the shared property line and would also install a fence along the east boundary of the ERC property, helping to secure the camp. The district also agreed to halt construction during the 10 days of camp so as not to disrupt worship or the camp meeting experience.

In this decade of 1995 to 2004, Alice Camber, Beverly Sloothak, and Helen Arnold worked every year with the children—and plenty of years before and after. Each is a paradigmatic example of those wonderful, quiet, faithful, often unsung servants of God who's sure to be one of the great ones in heaven. More recently Alice is ministering abroad, and her presence at Eaton Rapids is missed; it's always a delight to hear updates of her ministry, someone who will always be such a significant part of Eaton Rapids Camp Meeting, someone who's exerted such an untold impact on the lives of countless children with the beauty and truth of Jesus. Only heaven knows what Dennis Kinlaw or Joseph Smith or Samuel Kamaleson she and Beverly and Helen (and the other youth workers through the years these represent) may have taught and sparked and mentored through the years.

Alice Camber recently reflected about ERC in a letter:

The children's program grew, quite dramatically, Helen Arnold joined me, planning for and supervising the 1st, 2nd, and 3rd graders as I concentrated on craft programming for the 4th, 5th, and 6th graders. The first year the children's program started with 18-24 children. There was one day, probably in the 1980's, that there were 120 children present for crafts! We were bursting at the seams! Over the years, many people volunteered to help with the craft sessions and the music, teaching, Bible verse memory work under the direction of Gayle Sommerfeld and later, Beverly Sloothaak. Several years, your mother volunteered to help Helen with the younger children.

ERC has been such an important part of my spritual growth. It seems there is a special value in setting aside 10 days to leave behind ordinary routines, and coming away to a place where I am reminded constantly of God's presence in my life. It is as though, for 10 days, God has my attention and can work in my heart in a deeper way. Being surrounded by God's Word, God's family, constant prayers, God-directed conversations, in combination with a heart that is seeking God's will creates an atmosphere in which He can accomplish amazing things in our lives! The most significant periods of spiritual growth in my life have happened during Eaton Rapids Campmeeting. I am ever grateful for the privilege of being a part of ERC.

Spotlight on Dennis Kinlaw (1922-)

[Essay on Indian Springs Camp Meeting, by Dennis Kinlaw]

Sin is not just an act. It is a disposition. When man sinned in the beginning, he turned away from his friend and Maker and reoriented his life around himself and his desires rather than around God, his will and purposes. Luther said that he became "curved in upon himself." Thus the "I" reigned within, not God, and the "I" was hostile to God. Wesley called this "our bent to sinning." Richard Taylor has a descriptive word for this: "a hard core of idolatrous self-love planted deep in the self." That self love permeates our being and corrupts every act. Thus our sins are the inevitable result of the sin that dwells within us (Romans 8:17). We know better but can't live according to the highest that we know. This means that a person needs more than forgiveness. He needs to have the disposition changed.

The consciousness of our sins comes first. So as we seek forgiveness, Christ begins to walk with us. Then we begin to find how deeply that sin permeates and determines our being. Even our good deeds, done for Christ and in his strength, we find can be tinged with self-centered self-interest. This raises the question of a clean heart and of an undivided heart full of the love of God. Can God really cleanse a believer's heart and unite it so that his offering in God is clean and pure? The true believer's heart, as he walks with Christ, longs for just that. The Scriptures clearly promise that God can purify and unite our hearts to where we love him with all of our being. Peter says that this is what happened to him, the other disciples, and many others on the day of Pentecost when the Holy Spirit filled them (Acts 15:9). So, like the disciples, many of us have to walk with Christ for a while before we see how our self-centeredness and self-interest has permeated the depths of our psyches and defiles even our best. That is why the experience of a clean heart and of a perfect love for God is often described as "a second work of grace." The identification of this need in the believer's life and the provision in Christ for a pure heart is the special mission of the camp meeting.

Chapter 14

Walking with God, 2005-2014

2005 saw the return of Kamaleson, Kinghorn, and Oswalt as teachers and preachers. Then, on April 11, 2006, President pro tem John Oswalt wrote Clyde Leigh informing him that the Board, at its meeting on March 11, 2006, regretfully accepted his resignation from the office of President. The Board asked John to express its appreciation for Clyde's faithful service since 1999. "Many things have been accomplished during these years, perhaps most prominently the new water system. You have also worked hard to get new and workable policies in place. You did not shirk difficult tasks, but shouldered them courageously. You have also brought onto the Board persons such as Larry Holley, Carol Johnson, and Carol Bergman who have helped the Association move forward. For these and many other accomplishments all of us give you sincere thanks."

Oswalt shared a message to the Association in the Spring 2006 *Eaton Rapids Ripples*: "I step into this position of leadership with very mixed emotions. It is not something I do in fulfillment of any ambition to be President of Eaton Rapids Campmeeting. Neither is it something I do because of a need to fill otherwise empty days. I do have a 'day job' teaching at Wesley Biblical Seminary. So why have I accepted the responsibility? I have done so because of my deep belief in Eaton Rapids Campmeeting and its mission. Our founders, nearly 120 years ago, believed that American Christians needed a place where they could be challenged with the wonderful possibilities of the Spirit-filled, holy life, and where non-Christians could hear the great good news that Christ died for *them*. Much has changed in the last 120 years. Those changes sometimes require us to rethink some of our methods and ways of doing things. But the needs have not changed at all. In fact, they are even more pressing today than they were then. Almost daily we hear of Christians whose 'walk'—their manner of living—is indistinguishable from the 'walk' of the lost around them. We know of numbers of churches where the proclamation of the Word of God is nearly lifeless at best and heretical at worst. Is there a need for a place where the revealed Word is effectively and dynamically preached, where children and youth who have been immersed in a God-denying culture can have their eyes lifted to something better? Oh, yes! I am willing to use whatever gifts and energies I have in a cause like that. Will you join me?"

Around 2007 local resident and author Diane Vogel and her husband were canoeing on the Grand River, unaware of the existence of ERC. It happened to be the first Saturday of camp meeting, and as they got closer to the camp, she said they heard music that made her think of angels. Fortunately there was someone close enough to the shore to satisfy their curiosity and defuse their befuddlement. That was the day they became aware of the grounds and of camp meeting, which they have attended ever since—rather religiously.

A 2007 *Eaton Rapids Community News* article entitled "Camp Meeting Strengthens Faith" characterized ERC as still having "all the spiritual trappings of an 1800s tent revival." "The main purpose of the camp is to keep alive the goal of holy living," Larry Holley is reported to have said, a Board member of ERC and building and grounds manager at the facility. Holley said the reason to hold a 10-day camp meeting is to get people to set aside worldly concerns and "bring us back to what's really important in our lives."

The article describes the tabernacle nestled among the shade trees with the simple message "Be Ye Holy" boldly proclaimed on a sign suspended between the pulpit and a large white cross.

"People plan their vacations around the meetings and come here from all over the country," Holley said. This year, there were campers from Florida, Virginia, Kentucky, and other states besides. Holley said they draw heavily from Michigan itself, with large numbers coming from the Detroit, Flint, and Muskegon areas as well as from the Upper Peninsula.

"We go because we are Christians and we serve a risen Lord," Chuck Hazle of St. Johns said when asked why he and his wife Diane come to the camp. The Hazles have been regulars at the camp meetings since the 1970s. "It's just part of our lives. It's a way to recharge our batteries."

Rather than driving the 50 miles from St. Johns to Eaton Rapids each day, they bring their camper and spend the 10 days on site. "You get a lot out of the fellowship with others," said Hazle, who has developed long-term friendships with others from as far away as Oregon, desiring to spend their time in an intense ten days of worship. "It's the love that God shows to us, and then we show that love to others."

Over the years Hazle has seen families who brought their children and are now bringing their grandchildren to the camp. "They still like to come back; it's very much a part of their lives." Holley said the camp strives to provide a good program for youth, providing them with religious classes and services, and offering time for play as well. Youth activities this year included swimming, canoeing, and bowling. They also went to the city park to spread wood chips and clean up the grounds.

Holley, who's been a regular at the camp meeting for about fifty years, said the numbers fell off during the 1970s, but they are seeing an increase over the past several years. "It's spread by word of mouth by people who come here and then tell others," he said. "Overall, it was fantastic," said Chris Austin, facilities manager for the campgrounds. "There were definitely more people here than we've had in the past few years."

Dallas McFarland, pastor of the Church of Nazarene in Eaton Rapids, has been going to the camp meetings since he came to the community about six years before. He said he has seen the numbers of worshipers increase over the past two years, when Dr. John Oswalt took over as the director. "It's a great camp, our people just love it," he said, while also noting that the Church of the Nazarene is part of the same holiness movement that is preached at the camp.

While at the meetings, McFarland sees many church members of his congregation. "I've always been open to these camp meetings, and there's a lot of heritage in this one." Like the generations of worshipers who come year after year, the camp was also looking to the future, with plans underway to mark the 125th anniversary of 2010.

A Fall 2007 issue of *The Ripples* featured several people giving their thoughts on camp meeting 2007, where God made them to Lie Down in Green Pastures. Comments came from a variety of folks: campers, cottage owners, hotel residents, "old timers," and "new timers." Ruth and David Green, from Clinton, Michigan, wrote this: "This was our first time at Campmeeting and what a memorable time. We loved the open-air tabernacle and the ringing bell. Every speaker was outstanding as was the music. We appreciated the reverence for God and the goal of excellence in all that was done. The meals were delicious and it was great camping under the oak trees with full hookup. Thank you to all who made Campmeeting so special."[70]

Ken and Karen Wambsugh offered this testimonial: "We thought that this year's Campmeeting was outstanding. What a blessing to be able to focus on the Lord for 10 days with such powerful and Biblically based preaching and teaching. We are truly blessed to have such an organization in existence to help us draw closer and go deeper into our relationship with our Lord and Savior."

Kevin Rudolph added this perspective: "My impression of Camp this year was of growth. An exploration of new ground; a seeking of ways to meet unmet needs. Discipleship was at the core of much of ERC '07—excitement for what is to come, progress. God is definitely moving at ERC."

And Paul and Elaine Webster shared these heartfelt impressions: "To us Eaton Rapids Camp is like going home. You know the Spirit of the Lord permeates the ground and the depth of the messages from the speakers is something not always found in our home churches. If you are lucky enough to be able to spend the entire 10 days there, you can't help but receive blessing. We've watched our children grow in the Lord in this special place and now our grandchildren. I don't understand why anyone would want to spend these last days of July any other place."

Matriarch Helen Arnold passed away in May 2008, after, the year before, Wallace Haines passed, one of the greatest Presidents ERC ever knew. Funeral services were conducted for him both in Eaton Rapids and in Washington, D.C.

---

[70] Ruth lost her first husband years before in a tragic accident. In the aftermath of his loss, she wrote *Instantly a Widow* (under the name Ruth Sissom). She's since written a few other books as well. She would later marry Dave Green who, by coincidence, had gone to the same Free Methodist Church as my family did in the late sixties and seventies in Dearborn, Michigan.

For many years, the Board of Directors had dreamed of having a place on the campgrounds that could serve as a museum honoring its 125+ year history, a library, with a collection of quality Christian Books, and a hospitality house, where individuals visiting the grounds for the day can relax. In 2010, the Association was given ownership of the former DeYoung Cottage, located at 709 Tabernacle Circle. The Board designated this cottage to fulfill those purposes. Further, in honor of Larry Holley, his dedication to the camp, and his love of history, the Museum/Hospitality House was officially named The Holley Memorial Cottage. The exterior of this cottage has been repaired and refurbished, and the cottage has been appropriately furnished. Since it is to serve as a museum, library, and hospitality house, the goal is to supply the cottage with quality books and furniture and household items (that can be used for hospitality) from the last century.

On June 9, 2009, President Oswalt wrote a letter to the Rev. Stephen Skinner, informing him that the Board of Directors had met June 6 and voted to offer him the position of Facilities Manager for the camp meeting grounds. "Thanks for making yourself available for this significant role in the Campmeeting family. For most of the people in the Eaton Rapids area you will be the face of the Association. I am confident that you will perform this task and all your others faithfully and well."

Four days later Skinner replied to Oswalt with enthusiasm, noting that the camp meeting had been an important part of his and his wife Charlene's childhood. "We have fond memories of the various youth activities, especially the time of singing around the campfire down by the river."

Dr. David Bauer, who had been my teacher at Asbury Seminary, taught on Galatians during the Bible study that year, using the following outline of the book and his usual careful, methodical exegesis of the text:

Introduction (1:1-5)
Experiential/doctrinal theology (1:6—4)
Statement of Problem (1:6-9)
His own experience (1:10—2:21)
Galatians' experience (3:1—4:31)
Move to practical, how lived out (5—6)
Consequent commands, apart from legal ones (5:1—6:10)
Conclusion (6:11-18)

Bauer, a brilliant biblical scholar, emphasized over and over again the apostle Paul's recurring pedagogy of moving from indicatives to imperatives: from the truth of the gospel and what God has done for us to what we should do in response and obedience to God. Good theology should entail faithful practice.

Summer 2010 solidified plans and ideas for the historical museum. Making it presentable, displaying artifacts of the 125 years of history, and starting a reading library were priorities. Long-term goals included having a museum housing all historical materials from ERC. "Pictures hung; items displayed; tapes and CDs of past speakers available; past brochures on display; newspaper articles and publications about ERC; banners and decorations of the past (signs)." Planned, too, were tours of the campground and materials housed in the museum conducted by senior members of the Association.

The Spring 2010 *Ripples* reported on what was new at ERC. The Grace Hotel had undergone updates that year. All new vinyl siding and windows had been installed, which made the hotel more attractive and much more maintenance-free while preserving its rustic appearance. A new steel roof was to be installed soon.

A second youth dorm had also been constructed adjacent to the bathhouse and dorm that was built the year before. The plan was to have sidewalks constructed between the dorms and the bathhouse prior to camp meeting. A new septic drain field was planned at the recreation field next to the Facilities Manager's house. This new field would service the Grace Hotel, the cafeteria, Deaconess Cottage, Worker's Rest, the blue McDonald cottage, and the Facilities Manager's house. This new field would eliminate all of the septic problems experienced the past two camp meetings. Improvements had also been effected to the Young Adult program at Unity House. The garage was to be converted that year to be able to house the young men involved in the program. Updates were also completed inside Unity House to make it more comfortable for the ladies.

On February 14 of 2011 Larry Holley was called home to the Lord. He had been the Chairman of the Buildings and Grounds Committee at Eaton Rapids Camp Meeting for many years. He was well known to the Eaton Rapids community as a former mayor. His contacts with the city had gone a long way in improving the relationship of ERC with the city. He was born July 28, 1941, and was 69 years old at the time of his passing. He was survived by his wife Judy and three children. "Larry's dedication and contributions to Eaton Rapids Campmeeting will always be remembered. Larry was truly a man of God." In the March Board meeting, it was proposed that new trees be planted in the big boy camping area as a memorial to him.

In 2011, on July 22, a service of dedication was held for the Holley Memorial Cottage. It began like this: "We are gathered here to thank God for the life of Larry Holley, long time member of the Michigan State Holiness Camp Meeting Association, and of the Association Board of Directors, and to dedicate this cottage in his memory. The Association and the Campmeeting have benefitted from Larry's selfless service in a host of ways. We are blessed that God permitted him to come our way. In view of Larry's service the Board of Directors voted to name this cottage the Holley Memorial Cottage. This naming is doubly appropriate since Larry had a special interest in history, and one of the functions of this building is to be a historical center."

Psalm 1 was then read, and then this litany of dedication:

Leader: We give thanks for the memory of Larry Holley.

Congregation: We thank you for his faithfulness, his energy, and his creativity, all given over to service of you and your people.

We give thanks for the DeYoungs, who owned this cottage for many years.

We give particular thanks for Don DeYoung and his interest in the holiness theology which has been central to the camp's existence.

Thanking you for these memories, we dedicate this cottage to you for your purposes among us.

We dedicate it to be a place where blessed memories of your working in the past can be preserved.

We dedicate it to be a place where you can work among us through rest, relaxation, and friendship in the present.

We dedicate it to be a place in which past, present, and future can be brought together for the sanctification of your people.

This prayer was then offered: "Our Father, you are the Holy One whose grace makes it possible for us your people to share your holiness. In your goodness you brought this camp meeting into existence 126 years ago. We do not know the future, nor how you wish to use these grounds and facilities in the future. But we rededicate ourselves and them to your service to make known the good news of free salvation for all people and full salvation from all sin. In particular, we pray your blessing on this cottage for the fulfillment of your sacred purpose. We pray all these things in the name of Jesus, your Son our Savior. Amen."

The service closed with a singing of "Great is Thy Faithfulness."

A spring 2012 newsletter announced that construction had begun on the new restrooms at the Grace Hotel. Renovations were on schedule, and would be completed prior to the start of camp. Each floor of the hotel would have six new private bathrooms; four of these would have showers, the other two just a sink and toilet. All of these bathrooms on the main floor would be handicap-accessible, and one would contain a handicap shower stall. Each of the bathrooms would be spacious, with plenty of changing room—attractive and functional new bathrooms "without detracting from [the hotel's] historic ambiance."

Leading up to camp meeting 2013, John Oswalt wrote this message: "Many of us visit a physician once a year for a physical checkup. We may have been feeling a little below par or we may be feeling fine, but we just want to be sure that everything is functioning as it should and that nothing beginning to take shape is going to cause problems down the road. In Psalm 139 the writer invites God to perform a spiritual checkup on him: 'Search me, O God, and look into my heart. Put me to the test and discover my anxieties. See if there is anything dangerous in the way I am living, and put me on the path that leads to eternal life.' In many ways that is exactly what camp meeting is about: an annual checkup. Don't miss your appointment with the Great Physician this year. Join us by the river and let him remove anything stopping the flow of the River of Life in us."

Camp meeting 2013 featured, among others, Stan Key as the Bible teacher. Unknown at the time was that he would be appointed President of The Francis Asbury Society (FAS) on March 1, 2014. Stan and Katy Key came to FAS after ten years of missionary service in Paris, France, and eighteen years of pastoral leadership at Loudonville Community Church in Albany, New York. Joining the FAS team in January of 2013, Stan contributed to the ministry of the Society through preaching, teaching, writing, and serving as Director of Operations. He also served as Spiritual Dean with the Pan African Academy of Christian Surgeons (PAACS) and served on the Board of One Mission Society. He travels and speaks in churches, retreats, conferences, and camps both here and abroad. Katy also serves in many capacities at his side, and they serve at FAS as a team. Katy is the daughter of the founder of FAS, Dennis Kinlaw. Stan and Katy have three grown daughters and four grandchildren.[71]

In accepting the new appointment, Stan spoke about the identity and purpose of the Francis Asbury Society:

> God raised up FAS to proclaim the one Name given under heaven by which we must be saved (Acts 4:12). Our calling is first and foremost to promote the name of Jesus, not to propagate a doctrine, perpetuate a tradition, or promote a personality. However, as the name of our society reminds us, we are to do this in a specific context. Francis Asbury devoted his life to spreading Scriptural holiness over the land. The blood of Calvary and the Spirit of Pentecost make possible a life where victory over sin is a reality and one is enabled to obey the Great Commandment to love the Lord with all our heart and our neighbor as ourselves. In accepting this call to leadership I want to live according to the watchword of Nicolas Von Zinzendorf who said, "Preach the Gospel, die, be forgotten."

Key's Bible teaching at camp meeting involved "preaching the map" and was entitled "The Geography of Salvation." It is an eleven-part series that he wrote up in the form of a pamphlet for the FAS, and it describes the richness of salvation using the metaphor of a journey. Sometimes the biblical message is explained with the image of a courtroom, sometimes as a father and children metaphor, and at other times as a marriage. Key likes to talk about the *journey*, using biblical images of God as Lord and King, Jesus as a Guide and Fellow Traveler along the way, believers as pilgrims, our need as that of being lost and

---

[71] As of this writing, in January 2016, Katy is fighting to recover from a recent stroke and is in our hearts and prayers.

homesick, the solution of turning around, repenting, and following Jesus, then being led by the Spirit and walking worthy of the vocation to which we've been called. Key emphasized that many writers, both Christian and secular, around the world and throughout history, have used the metaphor of a journey as the framework for presenting their vision of the meaning of life. Homer's *Odyssey*, Baum's *Wizard of Oz*, Tolkien's *Lord of the Rings*, Lewis's *Voyage of the Dawn Treader*, Twain's *Adventures of Huckleberry Finn*, and Bunyan's *Pilgrim's Progress* are salient examples.[72]

The bulk of Key's series used the exodus of the people of Israel out of Egypt to highlight aspects of God's deliverance. Through the Red Sea, the desert, to Mount Sinai, the people are on their way to the Promised Land, even as Christians are on their way to a victorious life. From Kibroth-Hattaavah to Kadesh Barnea, through the Plains of Moab and the Jordan River into Canaan—each stop on the journey rife with spiritual significance. Many holiness preachers through the centuries have used Jericho not, as Bunyan did, as an image of heaven, but of the sanctified life here in the earth. Denis Applebee's *When I Tread the Verge of Jordan* comes to mind. Likewise did Key emphasize this—but in a way that doesn't come across at all as denominationally provincial. He's taught this to good effect in holiness, Baptist, and Pentecostal settings, and more besides.

Even in Canaan, Key taught, the land is occupied by giants who live in fortified cities. Once in the Land of Promise, the people still need to learn realities about the abundant life—such as the need for total dependence on and trust in God to live victoriously. Receiving the promised inheritance isn't the end of the journey; there is much that must be possessed. Though they have entered their rest, they immediately discover there is much work to do.

In a 2013 issue of *The High Calling*, the publication of the Francis Asbury Society, Beth Luce Reed wrote an article about her experience at camp meeting. It's shared below, but first a word about the origins and convictions of the Francis Asbury Society. After stepping down from the presidency of Asbury College, Kinlaw started the Society. The Society's *Statement of Purpose* reads as follows: "The purpose of this society shall be to spread the message of Scriptural holiness to the ends of the earth in accordance with the Great Commission. Jesus said that His disciples were to be the salt of the earth. They were, through His grace within them, to be the counterforce to the corruption that is perpetually at work in our fallen world. The Church is never stronger, no man is ever happier, and no society ever healthier than they are holy. God in Christ is in the business of drawing to Himself a people whom He, through His Spirit, can renew in His own holy image. The members of this Society, committed to the inerrancy of the Scriptures of the Old and New Testaments and the power of the Spirit of God, through Christ, to regenerate and sanctify wholly the human heart, give themselves to do what they can that all come to know Christ, be confirmed in Christian discipleship that produces character and

---

[72] Incidentally, speaking of *Huckleberry Finn*, Chapter 20 contains a colorful characterization of a camp meeting by Mark Twain. This was definitely one of the more famous literary depictions of this important cultural phenomenon.

integrity, and enjoy the freedom and power that comes to those who are fully sanctified by His cleansing Spirit. To this we commit ourselves."

The camp meeting that most changed Reed's life, just as Kinlaw's, was our sister camp Indian Springs. We include her article here as another example of how God uses camp meetings to transform lives:

> Camp meeting seems to be in my blood. I've been going as long as I can remember. At the tender age of four months, my parents took me, along with my two older brothers, to Indian Springs Holiness Camp Meeting. In my 55 years, I've only missed two or three times. I love camp meeting.
>
> I have a long family history at Indian Springs: my great-grandfather was one of the four founders of the camp in 1890. My grandfather served on the board for many years, my father was president for ten years, and my brother is the current president. I love the multigenerational impact of camp meetings. Many families have shared the tradition this way. When I started teaching in the elementary school age program at Indian Springs, I was teaching the children of my childhood camp friends. What a joy to lead some of them to the Lord and others into an understanding of fully surrendering their lives to His will for them! The daughter of one of my childhood camp friends wrote me a note in her sweet, eight-year-old handwriting:
>
> Dear Miss Beth,
>
> *Until now*, I never really understand all about Jesus. Now I do.
>
> Camp meeting is like a small town that comes to life for ten days each year. Family cottages are often shared by multiple generations. The quarters can be quite cramped at times, but that doesn't seem to bother folks much. Family togetherness brings grandparents together with grandchildren and even with great-grandchildren, passing on a spiritual heritage in a relaxed atmosphere where time seems to stand still. Rocking chairs abound, inviting us to slow down, reflect, and engage with those around us.
>
> For children, camp is one of the safest places on earth. Where else can children walk alone from home to a meeting place to the cafeteria? In the children's tabernacle, there are Bible stories, lively singing, snacks, crafts, and missionary stories. Missionaries visit and tell stories of their exciting adventures with Jesus in other countries. They challenge the children to go overseas if the Lord calls them. An offering is usually taken to support a project overseas. Children do chores or sell lemonade to make money to help needy children their age. Some children also enjoy watermelon seed spitting contests, swinging on porch swings,

eating homemade ice cream, catching frogs around the main tabernacle, and meeting new friends while spending time with old friends. The double blessing of all these things is that they happen in the context of putting down deeper spiritual roots and understanding God's Word.

One of the greatest impacts of camp is studying and memorizing scripture. As a preteen one year, I memorized Ephesians 6:1-18 on the armor of God. There was friendly competition among my friends to memorize all the verses and win a prize. The real prize is that those verses are locked in my heart and memory because of learning them at a young age. In high school, I studied the entire book of Exodus and the book of Mark in the ten days of camp, taught by seminary professors. How many high school students can say that? Those studies created in me a love for the Word and a hunger to study more on my own.

Another strong emphasis at camp meeting is missionary outreach around the world. Sharing times around a meal and hearing stories of the needs overseas challenges me to get involved through prayer and support. There are fresh stories of how God is currently working in many places that I may never visit personally. My world is expanded as I hear of God's faithfulness to these missionaries. I'm challenged to be a missionary right where God has placed me to serve Him.

Lifetime relationships are formed at camp meeting. I look forward each year to reconnecting with friends who have shared the same depth of Biblical teaching as I have. We connect on that deeper spiritual level and encourage one another in our faith journeys. Continuity of community with a shared history is a rare gift these days in our highly mobile world. Camp meeting gives us a place to return to a simpler life for ten days. In the midst of the incredible busyness of our lives, it gives us time to focus on what is most important in life.

The deep Bible teaching and instruction prepares us to serve better in our local churches and small groups. I enjoy conversations that stem from our teaching times and the messages of each speaker. God allows us to put our spiritual roots deeper and deeper at camp. We come away feeling like "a well-watered garden" as Isaiah 58:11 puts it:

The LORD will guide you continually, giving you water when you are dry and restoring your strength. You will be like a well-watered garden, like an ever-flowing spring.

Camp meeting provides a time for spiritual refreshment. It is a place of restoration, a place to gather strength. It is a place to come when you are thirsty for more of God, more of His will, more of His glory. He calls us to come away, to set ourselves apart in order to be quiet so we can hear

His still, small voice. One of my Dad's favorite camp meeting hymns was "Ho! Everyone that is Thirsty" by Lucy J. Meyer (1849-1922):

Ho! Every one that is thirsty in spirit,
Ho! Every one that is weary and sad;
Come to the fountain, there's fullness in Jesus,
All that you're longing for; come and be glad!

I will pour water on him that is thirsty,
I will pour floods upon the dry ground;
Open your hearts for the gifts I am bringing;
While ye are seeking Me, I will be found.

Camp meeting provides a haven of rich spiritual refreshment when we are weary and thirsty from living in a spiritually dry and barren land. It brings health to our hearts and life to our souls. What a rich heritage! I'm so thankful that camp meeting is in my blood.

In the Spring 2014 issue of *The Ripples at Eaton Rapids Camp Meeting*, President-Elect LaVerne Davenport wrote the following message:

Eaton Rapids Campmeeting is a very special and important part of my life. I began attending in 1981, when I began dating the wonderful woman I married. Our children are now the 5th generation in our family (on Mary Jane's side) to attend. Over the years I've sung in the choir, camped in the campground, lived in a cottage, attended Bible study and worship, prayer groups and special programs. I've volunteered with children, youth, and young adults during our annual campmeetings as well as joining work days and a prayer retreat at other times. While serving on the Board, I focused much of my attention on developing a place Young Adults could call home, a place they could afford to stay, a place where they could continue friendships and make the transition to life as adults in our great association. I still serve as the Director of the Young Adult Program, working together with a wonderful team.

My Christian faith began early, when I learned much from my mother, my grandmother, and some faithful mentors in the faith. One of my greatest joys was when my father accepted Jesus as Lord and Savior, and we could really worship as a family. God has richly blessed me, and I love living as His servant. Trained as a choral music teacher, I enjoy a wide variety of musical styles. Called by God to serve as a pastor, I had dual concentrations in Biblical Studies and Pastoral Care during my seminary education. As a pastor, my greatest passions are preaching and teaching God's Word, and sharing love with people near and far. In the churches I have served I have urged strong mission involvement, not only knowing God but reaching out in God's name with love and grace.

Over the years a task I have been called to again and again is working with my denomination's Committee on Ministry. This committee is tasked with working for the health of the relationship between pastors and churches. This work includes helping churches and pastors live through stressful situations, to refocus ministry direction, to help congregations choose staff with the right gifts and skills for their needs and location. In one region I served as chair of the 36 member committee for several years, and the skills God gave and developed in me proved of great value. I continue to use those skills in the local church and region where I live and serve.

With great humility and after much prayer and consultation with those I respect and trust, I accept this nomination. It is a joy to be able to serve God here at ERC. Please pray with me that God will continue to use all of us to help His ministries thrive. To God be the glory!

There were also messages by the Treasurer Mark Sandford Shapton, and from new or returning Board Members David Minger, Mary Crecelius, Nathan Sparks, Sylvia Davenport, and David Price. In the same issue of *The Ripples* was an announcement about how the New English Memorial Nursery was under construction. "Because we never want to forget our debt of gratitude to the past—or the generosity of those who have given—the Board has decided that the new nursery building will continue to be known as the English Memorial Nursery." To help remember the generous gift of the original nursery building, photos of the original structure will be proudly displayed inside the new nursery building.

The name of this newsletter—*The Ripples*—is explained by the definition of ripple cited and explained on its first page: *to flow or move in tiny, gentle waves*. "In this manner the Holy Spirit moves in and through each of us." The newsletter also identified the 2014 camp meeting speakers as Rev. Todd Eckhardt, Dr. Eldred Kelly, and, once again, Dr. Lawson Stone, a Yale-trained Old Testament scholar who teaches at Asbury Theological Seminary. Stone's Bible study was on Jeremiah that year, and received the highest marks on the assessment forms circulated.

The newsletter also mentioned the new play equipment for use during camp meeting: the new Octa-Ball court, the new Frisbee Golf Course, and the recent donation and construction of some new play equipment for younger children near the Hart-Topliff Pavilion in the camping area.

About a month after that issue of *The Ripples* was distributed, another newsletter for the upcoming camp meeting came out. President Oswalt offered this message on the front page: "Each year the Israelites went up to Jerusalem to celebrate with one another and with God. Ideally the men would go three times, but typically the families would go once a year. Their choices were Passover and Unleavened Bread, about the end of March, Pentecost, about June 1, and Tabernacles and Yom Kippur (The Day of Atonement), at the end of harvest, about October 1. During this latter celebration, people lived out in the open air in lean-to's of brush, remembering how their ancestors had lived in temporary shelters in the desert. In this country, camp meetings began in what were called sacramental meetings. After the wheat harvest was complete, families would come together for a week or more, living in tents and 'brush arbors,' in a great celebration of communion (which many could not take very often throughout the year because of a lack of ordained ministers), of inspired singing, and great preaching. It was a time to give thanks for the year past and to prepare for the year ahead. For most of us, completion of harvest has lost its significance. But we still need a time to come together, to hear one another's stories of battles fought and victories won, to weep together over losses, and laugh together over gains made, to celebrate God's goodness, and allow the Holy Spirit to shore up the weak places. Believers have been doing this for at least 3000 years. Don't miss out on the party that will be held again this year!"

The month before camp meeting a two-day prayer retreat called "Conversations with God: Living Prayerful Lives," was held on June 6 and 7, led by the Rev. LaVerne Davenport. It was designed as a prayerful adventure planned to impact prayer life leading to camp 2014 and beyond.

On a beautiful Friday evening, July 18, the 2014 encampment got underway. Welcomes, greetings, and robust songs reverberated in the air. After the song "How Great is Our God" Dr. Oswalt's prayer focused on the way God's greatness is most clearly demonstrated in His grace, His Spirit, and His ability to touch the heart's deepest chords. The Reverend Todd Eckhardt, a longtime laborer for World Gospel Mission, delivered the first sermon. He began by talking about his love for church camp. Having grown up attending it every year, he admitted that it was the site of many spiritual milestones in his life, including his call to ministry. He made reference to a Wilfred Fisher for being powerfully instrumental in his life.

What makes the time and place of camp meeting so special, Eckhardt contended, are the people in whose hearts Christ dwells and the transforming presence of God. He went on to preach about the refuge believers have in Christ and the freedom available in Christ, freedom that we need to learn what to do with. He challenged those in attendance to consider that they too, like Mary's cousin Elizabeth, may be called, even this week at camp, to be a refuge for one struggling with freedom in Christ. He exhorted those assembled to find an asylum in nothing less than the presence of God.

Immediately following the service was the dedication of the new English Nursery. President Oswalt began the service, held outside the new structure, with these words:

> Jesus said, "Let the little children come unto me." In recognition of that invitation, many years ago the English family gave their cottage to the Eaton Rapids Holiness Camp Meeting for use as a nursery. The building served God and the Camp Meeting well for many years, but recently it became clear that the building was no longer adequate for the needs and number of children who were being cared for there. A survey of the

facility made it clear that it was beyond reasonable repair, and that it needed to be replaced. That has been done and this new facility is the result. We come with gratitude this evening to dedicate it to God.

Hear this word from the Scripture: "Unless the Lord builds the house, they labor in vain who build it; Unless the Lord guards the city, the watchman stays awake in vain. . . . Behold, children are a heritage from the Lord, the fruit of the womb as a reward. Like arrows in the hand of a warrior, so are the children of one's youth. Happy is the man whose quiver is full of them; they shall not be ashamed. . . ." And this: "Surely, I say to you, unless you are converted and come as little children, you will by no means enter the kingdom of heaven. Therefore, whoever humbles himself as this little child is the greatest in the kingdom of heaven. Whoever receives one little child like this in my name receives me."

Oswalt then led a responsive litany of dedication:

Our Father, we thank you for children, which we recognize as a gift from your hand. They represent to us your ever-recurring promise of life and hope. In their lack of self-consciousness, their receptivity, their laughter, and their joy they remind us again of the conditions of heaven. Thank you for them. *Amen*

Our Father, by taking upon yourself the title of Father, you remind us of the importance of the task of parenting, of providing for the basic needs of those who cannot care for themselves, of giving security, love, and kindness. To these tasks we rededicate ourselves. *Amen*

Our Father, you have given us the gifts of time and money, and you have moved us to use these gifts to create this nursery facility. May our temporal generosity be a constant reminder of your unending generosity. *Amen*

So, in the light of who you are and what you have done for us in Jesus Christ, we here dedicate this building to you for your good purposes in it. May this be a place of care, of patience, of security, of love, and of laughter. May the tears of childhood find relief here in the arms of those who will care for them unselfishly for Christ's sake. *Amen*

After a prayer of dedication the doxology was sung.

A few days later, after the morning service in the Tabernacle on July 20, I was introduced to an elderly gentleman with recollections about ERC. The man was a soft-spoken, silver-haired geriatric named John Bullock, and I spent several minutes conversing with him, asking him to share with me his memories of the place. Although John was advanced in years, what he had to share came from his perspective as a youth. John's parents both attended Asbury College, and likely met there, later becoming active at ERC. His dad ran the store on the grounds for several years. John was a teenager in the 1940s and, with his family, an active participant at Eaton Rapids. Quite the coincidental twist to the interview was discovering that the first cottage he and his family stayed at in the 1940s was the very cottage that would one day become my own.

He remembered a diversity of people from those days, hailing from various states, including Ohio, Indiana, Kentucky, and of course Michigan, together making up enthusiastic congregations enjoying good musicians—piano players and singers. He recalled quality programs for kids, who, he told me, considered it a treat when conferred permission to take off across the field to make a trek to the Miller Dairy Farm.

Harkening back yet further, he recalled hearing stories from the 1880s and 1890s when Native Americans would canoe up the river and sell goods to the campers. Speaking of the river, when John's brother died and his body cremated, the ashes were spread in the Grand at Eaton Rapids.

John grew up learning about the holiness tradition at ERC, at least unofficially tied to Methodism—which he laments has, in many of its contemporary corners, gone in rather liberal directions. He recalled, even in his advanced years, the large numbers of folks of a holiness persuasion he met at ERC, and he shared his ongoing appreciation of the tradition. John thought that one of the old preachers he heard was named Ironside. He recalled as well having heard about such holiness luminaries as Henry Clay Morrison and Z. T. Johnson. He remembered Lloyd Nixon from his youth, and especially what a commanding presence Nixon was in the pulpit, even telling a story of Nixon putting a stop to a couple kids, of whom John was one, making play with a water pump. Seeing their behavior at a fair distance, Nixon forcefully indicated his wishes while behind the pulpit. John assured me they put a stop to their mischief immediately.

Spotlight on John Oswalt (1940-)

[Presidential Report 2015, by John Oswalt]

In this my final report to you, I want to express my deep gratitude to God, to you members of the Association, and to present and former members of the Board of Directors for all of the assistance and support that has made possible any of the achievements of my nine-year tenure as your President.

During these years a large number of physical improvements have been made to the facilities and grounds. To a great extent, this has been made possible through the far-seeing decision of the Board just before my assuming the presidency to sell an eleven-acre parcel of land to the local school board. The large sum of money realized from that sale provided seed-money which along with generous contributions from the membership has made possible the upgrading of the hotel and dining room, the construction of new youth facilities, the expansion of the facilities for campers, and the construction of a new English nursery. Alongside these accomplishments, we have been able to put new steel roofs on many of the camp-owned buildings. For these and many other achievements, I am especially grateful to Larry Holley, of fragrant memory, and David Minger, former and present chairs of the Buildings and Grounds committee, and Steve Skinner, our much appreciated facilities manager, along with several key volunteers whose names I will not mention for fear of overlooking someone. But you know who you are.

But as satisfying as these tangible things are, the intangibles are of even greater importance. Attendance has held steady or moved gently upwards in almost all services since 2008. There has been an increase in the number of younger families attending. The amount of giving has increased very significantly. Creative afternoon programming has offered a variety of activities for recreation, fellowship, and learning. And in most years, the movement of the Spirit has been very evident among all categories of attenders, from infants to senior adults. May this only increase in coming years, for in the end this is why we exist.

For the last several years, our practice has been to hold five Board meetings per year (the constitution mandates at least three). Not counting the one during campmeeting in which we have distributed the missionary funds and organized the Board for the coming year, the first has typically been devoted to receiving and discussing reports from the just-completed campmeeting. The second has been for planning, both for the coming year and for the longer term. The third has been devoted to adopting the budget for the coming year. The fourth and fifth meetings have dealt with on-going business and with preparation for the up-coming campmeeting. During the past year, the most notable actions of your Board to which I would call your attention are the following: the establishment of credit-card contribution policies, and social media and e-mail policies; the redesign of the website, something that is continuing to go forward (Publicity chair David Price has done a great deal of work on these); the implementation of our policies for the sale of camp-owned cottages; technical support for the ongoing writing of our history by Dr. David Baggett; and steps to make the secretary's position more workable (special thanks to Heather Sprague for volunteering here). With all of these, there has been the on-going business that can consume more time than one might imagine. This year, as in previous years, the attendance of Board members has been outstanding. There have been meetings with 100% attendance, and in most cases, above 80%. That is a great record.

There are several issues that face you and your Board in the future. One of those is the reroofing of the Tabernacle. This is of course a major expense for which all of us, I am sure, will "step up to the plate," as it were. In that regard, let me report that there is a new building inspector in Eaton Rapids, who is enforcing the building code very rigorously, and we were concerned that we might be required to remove all present roofing material before moving forward, something that would dramatically increase the cost. But he has looked at the structure and sees no problem with putting new roofing over the old, so we were very thankful for that. Since many of you are cottage holders, let me here remind you of an announcement that I believe was made in the cottage-holders meeting: the building inspector is enforcing the requirement that a building permit must be obtained before doing any work on cottages, including replacement of roofing.

Another issue that you face is how to widen the reach of the campmeeting. I hope that your new president will be more successful than I have been in enlisting the support of pastors, something that has been a key to the success of the campmeeting in the past. But this widened reach will require a creative and cooperative effort on the part of the entire membership.

A final issue that I want to call to your attention is the continuing temptation to dilute the message which we exist to proclaim. This has been true for every holiness campmeeting that has ever existed. We exist to proclaim to the world and the church the full message of salvation, that not only is Christ's power sufficient to save a person from the guilt and condemnation of sin, but also from its power. How desperately the Church and the world need to know that God can deliver us from self-serving and self-centeredness, that he can enable us to live lives that are truly an expression of the holiness of God, in moral purity, in spiritual power, and in self-giving love. May Eaton Rapids campmeeting never become simply a place for "spiritual uplift," or worse, for Christian recreation. We do not need any more of those places. But we desperately need places where the Holy Spirit can transform men and women, boys and girls, into the living image of Jesus Christ.

Before I close, I want to give special thanks to those who have served me and the Association on the executive committee during these nine years. They are Kathleen Ray, who has been my Vice President and program director whose creativity, enthusiasm, and plain hard work have meant so very much. Then there is John Werner, who, as secretary, has kept track of all the essential administrative data that are vital to keeping the wheels turning. His untiring attention to detail and wise counsel have been priceless. Carol Johnson, David Minger, and now Mark Shapton have, as treasurer, shouldered the complicated task of keeping track of our finances. The fact that we have "killed" one after another in these years has been testimony to the extreme difficulty of the task. But each one has stepped in at the critical hour and has given selflessly to insure that we had the information necessary to make good financial decisions. Finally, there is my special assistant, William Shapton, who right at the outset stepped into the vacancy for a director of food service, and has carried that often thankless task faithfully and uncomplainingly all these years. Whatever measure of success God has granted me has been almost solely due to the kind and selfless efforts of these persons (and many others, I might add). It is not modesty on my part when I say that without their above-and-beyond labors of love, I would have certainly failed. Thanks to you and glory to God.

Finally, I congratulate you on your election last year of the Rev. LaVerne Davenport as your president for the next three years. I am confident that he will provide strong leadership and will take the Association and the campmeeting to new heights during his tenure in office. I wish him God's very best and urge you to give him full support, as I also intend to do.

Postlude

Thy Kingdom Come

A Consecrated Ministry
(2 Corinthians 6:14—7:1)

Bible Study by Bruce Moyer

Friday morning's Bible study finished Moyer's talk on the **Commended Life/Ministry**. In addition to *partnerships* (ministry is not our own program), its *purposes*, and *problems* we victoriously endure (tough circumstances, tough opposition, tough commitments), there are *principles by which it's done* (verses 6-7). Among them are purity, uprightness, how we behave when nobody's looking, knowledge saturated with the Word of God, patience, forbearance, slowness to avenge, kindness, courteousness. It's the Holy Spirit who makes all of this possible. Sincere love for truthful speech, the power of God. In general, this is mostly not about *what we do*, but *who we are*.

A fifth attribute comes from verses 8-10: *perceptions we adopt*. Here we find a list of contrasts (9 of them). Honor vs. dishonor, etc. A sixth attribute: *the practice by which we live*. Paul felt like he loved without being loved in return, yet he continued loving.

Then comes a **Consecrated Ministry** (6:14-7:1). This is an often abused passage, one that people use to push separation to the point of isolation. That's not the intent, but it remains true that whom we fellowship with affects us greatly. Bad company corrupts good character. Several important points to emphasize here:

First, *understanding our responsibilities* (6:14-16). Don't get mismatched, unequally yoked. Remember we're called to a ministry of reconciliation. Not isolated but insulated. Jesus was holy yet a friend of tax collectors and sinners. In verses 15-16, there are 5 questions and contrasts—light and darkness, etc. Loyalty to God first. What shared purpose is there with unbelievers? What fellowship, intimate communion? (Same word as fellowship in Trinity.) What harmony between Christ and Satan? (Language of symphony, beautiful music.) What agreement between temple and idols? (Language of a joint deposit, co-signing a loan.) Love the world but don't compromise with it.

Second, *we are the temple of the living God*. See last part of v. 16. (Recall previously we are called clay pots, then tents, and now temples of the living God.) We're God's sanctuary that God indwells.

Third, *a consecrated life or ministry is begotten of God*, and we may have to forsake certain other relationships.

The Friday 10:30 service saw French preaching from 1 Samuel 1:9-17. Hannah prayed intently for a son, and of course she would get one: Samuel, one of Israel's most important leaders.

Effective Prayer (1 Samuel 1:9-17)
Sermon by Jack French

He then preached a topical message on answers to prayer and their biblical requirements. Why has God awakened people to pray when God already knows the need? Why pray with importunity? Here are central requirements for effective prayer:

   Being a child of God.
   Obedience and rightness before God.
   Right relationships. Prayers are hindered otherwise.
   Commitment to the will of God.
   Fervency: lack of hypocrisy, not casual.
   Pray with biblical motives.
   Don't let the tyranny of the urgent stop us from praying.

At 2 o'clock that afternoon I gave a talk on this history book's development, status, challenges, and anticipated end date. We asked if those present (about thirty) had any questions they'd like to see answered in the book; we asked them questions about the history of the Camp to test their knowledge; we discussed the six-page synopsis of highlights of the book we distributed; we encouraged their contributions by way of anecdotes, pictures, ideas, etc. We also shared some funny stories from the History, talked a bit about the city of Eaton Rapids and camp meetings generally, along with upcoming History Committee events and aspirations, and what they can do to help.

The Friday service featured David Gallimore again, this time preaching from Joshua 24:14-15. By Friday the weather had cooled for several days. From about Monday onward the temperatures had lowered considerably and it was consistently around the 70s and without the stifling humidity that had oppressed the campus at the start. Gallimore was again quite in his inimitable element.

Guiding the Family (Joshua 24:14-15)
Sermon by David Gallimore

Joshua, by the time of this passage, was advanced in years, and he gathered his family around him. The passage is just two verses, so they bear repeating: "Now, therefore, fear the Lord, and serve him in sincerity and in truth; and put away the gods which your fathers served on the other side of the river, and in Egypt, and serve ye the Lord. And if it seem evil unto you to serve the Lord, choose you this day whom ye will serve, whether the gods which your father served that were on the other side of the river, or the gods of Amorites, in whose land ye dwell; but as for me and my house, we will serve the Lord."

We need revival in America, in our churches, in our homes, and in our families. We may have lost influence in many spheres in society, but we retain it in our house. We can be a Joshua to our children. Stand up and tell our families to follow our lead. Kids today are facing much tougher circumstances than their parents did. A good indication of what they're confronted with can be found in popular entertainment. We need to be proactive. Be like Joshua, and lead the way.

Imagine your family going on an airplane trip. What do we need?

First, *a clear destination*. Where's family life headed? Where's marriage headed? Are we enjoying or merely enduring marriage? How about our kids? Hope that it'll all turn out is not a strategy. Be proactive. Are we going in circles, lacking intentionality? Where there is no vision, the people perish. Clearly defined destination. Establish a family altar. We can influence the outcome.

Second, *a flight plan*. Turbulence will come. All sorts of bad weather is bound to come on us all of a sudden. We need a flexible flight plan, one with midair adjustments as necessary. This requires two things: feedback and constant communication with the control tower. Need communication with kids. A big part of this is listening. And of course constant communication with our Strong Tower. The good news is that when we hit turbulence, we don't have to crash. Make the needed adjustments. Marriages are worth saving; pray!

Third, *a working compass* (or, today, GPS). We live in a world that says there are no moral absolutes. This is the way; walk in it. Usually it's not about trying harder, but being intentional and proactive.

A Confronting and Contagious Ministry (2 Corinthians 7—9)
Bible Study by Bruce Moyer

On Saturday morning, it was time to go back to the Bible study: 2 Cor. 7. **A Confronting Ministry**.

First, *a spirit to help* (verse 2). We must be sure we want to be of help. Wrong no one. Don't injure, damage, or corrupt. Exploit nobody building yourself up. Confrontation with condemnation won't help. Paul made it clear his love for them was nonnegotiable. He approached them with great distress, a heavy heart, and many tears. Pray before confronting.

Second, *a spirit of hope* (verses 4, 14-16). Paul was frank to people, and proud of them behind their back. This is a reversal of how it usually goes. Negative words take up lodging in young people's hearts; be careful.

Third, *a spirit of honoring them* (5-7, 13). Accentuate the ways people have been a positive—honoring them, valuing them.

Fourth, *a spirit of honesty* (8-11). Need to come face to face with truth. A previous letter hurt, but only for a little while. The people were not harmed in any way. (To hurt is to grieve, but to harm is to inflict loss or injury.) It's usually not success but sorrow that promotes the most growth. Paul was willing to confront sin, and joyful when they repented.

Moving on now to chapters 8 and 9: **A Contagious Ministry**. Marks of a ministry that is catchy. While these chapters focus on giving, they contain a lot of good principles. Five Marks of a Contagious Ministry/Life:

First, *grace*, an echoing theme throughout the passage. It all begins and ends with grace.

Second, *generosity*. Sowing and reaping generously. It abounded even in their poverty (8:2). Sacrificial living. Generous ministry follows the law of sowing and reaping. Generosity is an act of faith. This turns worldly principles upside down. The world says take care of yourself first. But they gave beyond their ability. Generosity is a matter of the heart. People with 25,000 say they need 5,000 more; those with 50,000 say they need 10,000 more; those with 100,000 say they need 25,000 more. See a pattern here?

Third, *gladness*. Enthusiasm; not the way they gave. They begged for the privilege of sharing. God loves a cheerful giver. Do it with reckless delight.

Fourth, *giving/sharing*.

Fifth, *gratefulness and glory to God*.

God Heals (John 5:1-18)

Healing Service by John Oswalt

Saturday morning's 10:30 service was the annual healing service, and Dr. Oswalt preached from John 5:1-18. Jesus healed in different ways: instantaneously, through a process, through his spittle. He healed based on his knowledge of who the people were. Miraculous signs are designed to teach who Jesus is. Most of his healings came on the Sabbath, which made religious authorities bristle. But all the holy days were designed to point to Jesus.

Instantaneous healing today is still a mark of who Jesus is, but Jesus also heals in other ways—through doctors, sparing life, giving miracles of sufficient grace, and, ultimately, the triumphant crossing.

The man in the passage was blind, paralyzed. Recall that Jesus' miracles are suited to who we are. Jesus focused the man's attention on his own attitudes. He asks him if he really wants to get well. Of course! Right? Not necessarily. What's the answer the man provides? There's nobody to put me in the pool—it wasn't his fault. Did he really want to be healed?

Why wouldn't he want to be healed? Well, who's been feeding him for 38 years? Who's been taking care of him? If we take responsibility, what will it mean? Do we really want to be well? To face the responsibilities that come with health?

Or are there secret sins we hug to ourselves? We're told, quite simply, to stop sinning. Face the reality; if Jesus tells us to stop it, He can enable us to stop. Come to grips with the underlying causes of our maladies. And, on being healed, be obedient. But remember: If God gives us a commandment, He gives us the ability to obey it.

The Bible describes our relationship with God as a *walk*. When God heals, He has a plan. Jesus enabled him to have a clear testimony, for example. Likewise, if He heals us, He has a plan.

Count the Cost (Luke 14:25-33)
Sermon by Jack French

Later that day, Saturday night at 7:30, French spoke again, this time on Luke 14:25-33. The sermon was on Counting the Cost—enduring hardship. We're to hate our family; not in a carnal sense; as a matter of priority, God must come first. All sorts of prices are to be paid—self-pity, envy, personal purity (in thoughts, acts, relationships, etc.), fear of men, and the like. Put God first in every relationship.

Sunday's Morning Watch featured poignant awareness that camp's imminent end was looming, but openness to what God still wanted to do in our midst. Though camp may end, its effects will not.

A Confident and Caring Ministry (2 Corinthians 10-13)
Bible Study by Bruce Moyer

That morning's Bible study covered 2 Cor. 10-13. Chapter 10 revealed what it takes to have **A Confident Ministry**. In this chapter Paul was responding to questions about his ministry. Self-appointed? Teachings not in line with others? Cowardly? Some churches didn't support him. Paul uses language of boasting 21 times in this context. Confident yet humble. Why so confident?

First, *divine arsenal* (1-6), not the weapons of this world. The latter? Perhaps intimidation, legal action, marketing, etc. What are our weapons instead? Meekness of Christ. Sword of Spirit. Truth. The Word. Speaking the truth in love. Prayer. These weapons have divine power to destroy strongholds (big fortresses). Moyer thinks such strongholds pertain to value systems, worldviews, self-centered views. It has to do, he thinks, with philosophy and worldview. The weapons: love, prayer, truth, faith. We demolish arguments and every pretension against the knowledge of God. Demolish warped philosophies. Today: abortion, the gay agenda, etc. They allow us to hold every thought captive, even "fantasies." *Every* thought! God is able to change our thinking.

Second, *divine authority* (verses 7-11). Are people under my ministry living in victory? Leaders versus bosses. To be a *leader* is to use divine authority: let's go, shows how, inspires enthusiasm, helps fix, build people up, *we*. To be a *boss* is to use human authority: go, know, inspires fear, fixes blame, tears people down, *I*.

Third, *divine approval* (18). How can we know we have it? Verse 12: (a) How do we assess our work? Paul's accusers measured themselves by themselves. (b) Am I where God wants me to be? Be content being where God wants you. (13-16) (c) Is God being glorified by ministry? What matters is what God does through us. (17-18)

Then Moyer moved on to Chapters 11-13: **A Caring Ministry**. Paul boasts in the Lord. 4 Marks of a Caring Life:

Godly Jealousy (11:2-3). Earnest concern, devoted zeal. Refuses to tolerate rival. Intimacy with Christ.
An Honest Word. Loves them enough to be truthful.
Authority under Control (13:10; 11:4-5).
A Servant's Heart (12:14-15, 19; 13:4). Five times Paul said he wasn't a burden on anybody. And look at all he's endured! What have we endured? Can we respond like Paul? Serve out of love. (Illustration with son.)

Building on the Rock (Matthew 7:24-29)
Sermon by Jack French

Sunday morning was sunny and cool, and French preached for the last time, this sermon on Matthew 7:24-29, on the importance of building on a solid foundation. Storms will come! Wisdom is to follow the teaching of Christ—not just hear it. Practice what's taught—don't just preach it, promulgate it, debate it, and the like. Practice it.

Navigating Troubling Times (2 Samuel 6:1-11)
Sermon by LaVerne Davenport

The Sunday afternoon service featured the new President of the Association as of the end of this year's encampment, LaVerne Davenport. He began with 2 Sam 6:1-11. The Ark of the Covenant was not to be touched. It was no magic box to ensure victory. Don't forget who you're dealing with! We live in troubled times, filled with racial tensions, grave lack of respect among many, lots of polarization, sexual issues. The trouble is real. What to do?

Know the scriptures. Read great Christian biographies. Strive to live God's way. Earn trust. Remember the difference prayer makes.

Challenges: Are we students? Lovers of God's Word—moving beyond our favorite passages? What's holding us back? Poor time management, laziness, shame over failures? What's our relationship to Christ beyond our relationship with things in the church? And is the fruit really showing? Are we touching lives? Putting faith to action?

The final service—both of this camp meeting and Oswalt's tenure as president—at 7:30 p.m. Sunday evening had the decided feeling of the camp's culmination. Attendance was a bit thinner; a number of campers had left, perhaps with plans to return to work the next day. Offering was taken, prefaced by an exciting announcement that this year's financial goal in terms of gifts and promises (about $74,000) was met earlier in the day. After some worship time once more led by Scott Crecilius, assisted by Hayden Carruth, Jr. (whose veins carry so much ERC history), Oswalt got up to deliver his last sermon at Eaton Rapids for some time to come—an apt closure of this history, the farewell sermon of one of the truly great presidents in ERC history, my teacher, an academician and churchman extraordinaire, the man to whom this book is dedicated.

The closing of a significant chapter, and the start of a new one.

Walk Worthy of Your Calling (Ephesians 4-5)
Sermon by John Oswalt

Oswalt directed us to the book of Ephesians 4:1-3, 17-18; 5:1-2, 8, 15, New Testament passages all, though Oswalt's an Old Testament scholar. "Live worthy of the vocation to which you're called." "Don't walk like the Gentiles." "Be imitators of God, and walk in love." "Walk as children of light," and "Have no fellowship with works of darkness." "Walk carefully, not as fools, but as wise, redeeming the time." "Be filled with the Spirit."

A recurring word: "Walk." Let's talk about walking. Every Jewish male was required to go to the tabernacle, and later the temple, three times a year: Passover, Pentecost, and the Feast of Tabernacles and Day of Atonement. Not just the males. It was a family affair. A wonderful feast time. Deuteronomy tells us they were required to keep their tithe, and buy food for themselves for the feast. Then the feast was over, and they had to walk home. The first three chapters of Ephesians are a feast. We are the saints seated with Christ in the heavenly places—God wants to make us into temples where God lives in His fullness, where the love of Christ is manifest.

But now, walk. For us the feast is over. It's been a rich and enjoyable feast, but now we have to walk home. Right through the Bible is this striking metaphor of life with God: walking. In progress. Going forward. Not walking alone. And toward a destination. God invites every one of us to walk with God, walk home.

Life is not a journey into the far country; it's a journey home.

Paul says we must walk in unity, together. That's a walk worthy of our calling. To live in unity is a walk worthy of our calling, because we're not only walking with the Father, but with one another. And in this calling there is one Savior, only one. One Father. One way of salvation. We're called to maintain the unity of the Spirit. Not "organizational unity." No, we're talking about that sense when we meet one another as brother and sister, that we're in it together.

As Paul describes what kind of people we are: not competitors, not rivals, not enemies. Rather, brothers and sisters. We need to walk together as one, doing everything we can to keep that bond of fellowship in place. Eager to see one another as family—but it's marked by diversity. A diversity of gifts.

The Bible has five lists of gifts. Only prophecy is the common gift. No standard list, therefore. Not all of us have all the gifts, and no one of us is expected to. He gifts each of us for the purpose of the functioning of the body. Jesus is the head, and every part under the leadership of the head carries out its part, so the whole body can move and live.

The question is: What am I able to do? Remember the woman who broke the alabaster perfume on Jesus' feet. *Doing what we can.* What can we do? Don't let the devil say we don't matter. Tell him to shut up, and ask the Lord what our part is in the body.

E. Stanley Jones conducted a retreat that he styled on retreats in India. In the "ashram," there was an hour of sharing—policing the grounds, taking care of the retreat center, etc. And Jones insisted on his gift: cleaning toilets. Walk worthy of our calling. Each of us has different part to play, for the goal…

Verse 13: To Know Him. The goal of our unity is to know Him personally. The second function of the body is that we be rooted and grounded in good doctrine. The unity of the faith is found in the teachings of the Word. Our body functions well when we enable one another to know Christ and be rooted in good doctrine, not blown away by every new idea. And v. 15: to grow up in all things into Him who is the head, Christ. To mature. We know why we're here. To be experiencing the fullness of Christ. Walk as one who is transformed.

Verse 17: Paul insists we should no longer walk as the rest of the Gentiles walk. In order for that to happen, we need to put off old nature and put on new nature. Paul uses a variety of images to capture what he's getting at here. Putting to death, coming to life, exercising faith. Here it's this: take off old set of clothes and put on new. What is the characteristic of the old clothes? It's walking in futility of their mind. We need a transformed way of thinking.

What's the evidence of old thinking: blindness. Futile thinking: My life is mine. I am God. That's futile. We did not make ourselves.

That's what's going on today in our culture. We make up the terms of our existence. Futile.

My needs are primary. I have an absolute right to satisfy my needs any way I choose. Futile.

If I desire something, the only road to happiness is to have that desire met. Futile. 24/7 the tube gives us this message.

What are the characteristics of this new nature? It's not an idea, but a Person. Put on Christ. That's the genius of the Christian faith. Not reducible to doctrine. It's a Person. How to do this?

Turn over your life to Him. Turn over your needs to Him. Turn over your values to Him. Turn over your will to Him.

As Oswalt likes to say: bottom line is I will have my way—old way. New way: You have your way in my life, because mine leads me to the pit, but your way leads to eternal life.

But we can say, "Take my will," and then we discover there's another level. And we have to give that to God, too, and then another. Then another. There must be that climactic way of saying, "I want you to have my life," but then it needs to be worked and walked out, as we discover ever deeper levels.

What are the results of these two sets of clothing? The old? Lying, rage, theft, foul and malicious language, sexual immorality, lewdness, uncleanness, greed, foolish coarse talk; we will do whatever we have to in order to get our way. Not caring about offending anyone; it's about me. It's a downward road. Why is TV situation comedy so incredibly fouler than it was 40 years ago? Why didn't it get less foul? This path leads to corruption and death. At bottom evil is simply banal: simply stupid. Not a high and mighty terrible thing. It's a teenage boy telling dirty bathroom jokes. That's the old man.

Paul says we can't walk there. Because if we do at the least we'll grieve the Holy Spirit, the seal of our salvation. We'll destroy our inheritance. We'll come under the wrath of God.

God is not a raging monster. That's the tragic picture we have, but it's not real. God's heart is broken over sin. If Oswalt's daughter had ruined her life, sure he'd be angry—angry for her because he loves her. God's wrath is also part of the laws of life. Jump off a building and you'll smash into the sidewalk; it's breaking a law of existence. Walking in the old clothing breaks a fundamental law of existence that says we don't belong to ourself.

Results of new nature? Humble, gentle, patient, forbearing, making allowances for faults, binding ourselves together in shalom, not letting anger rule us, kind, tenderhearted, forgiving, walking in love. They're all about other people. Humility is not thinking too little of yourself; it's about not thinking about yourself at all.

"Gentle": meek? Other words have been tried; it's the idea of being non-self-assertive. We don't have to be the center of every conversation. Don't always have to get our way, or our rights. The old nature is turned into self; new nature is turned out, set free, to genuinely care about other people, to be kind.

In our culture: the death of kindness. It's kind of expensive, and people don't have it. Kindness takes thinking about that other person.

It all comes down to summary statement in ch. 5: *Imitate God.* Love as He loves. Not sentimental feelings. Walk in love as Christ loved? Biblically defined: to choose the best for another at whatever cost to oneself. But it takes a will. We don't always want the best for another at first.

The Gentiles walk in the futility of their lives thinking their lives are their own and they can satisfy their desires for themselves, and the results are horrible, all about self. New nature has been set free, to forget about yourself, not to worry about that, and be concerned for others.

Walk. Be transformed. Not rage, but forgiveness. Not greed, but generosity.

Why does Paul say this to Christians? Psychological reason: we can't exercise faith for something we don't know we need. We need to know we've got an old nature. Yes, we want Jesus, but we also want our way. This is what destroys our churches. We've got to believe God to do this thing. It's faith in

Him that's required, that He will do it. If we in our own act of will unbutton that old set of clothes, He'll take them off.

That's what ERC has been preaching for 130 years. We can indeed imitate God, walk in love. It's not throwing a switch, but it has to begin in a place of saying we don't want to live in that old way, consumed by our desires, destroyed by futility of thinking. Then God can begin doing the work.

Walk in the light. Walk worthy of your calling. Walk transformed. Walk in the light.

What are we Christians going to do about the entertainment industry? It's destructive. We laugh at stuff nobody should. Walk in the light. Have no fellowship with the darkness. Have no association with darkness. We can't be a little light and a little dark. Some of the darkness is too horrid to mention in public. We're not exposing the darkness; we're laughing at it.

Quit the direct input of darkness into our head.

Expose the darkness.

Don't have any association with darkness. And in that light, walk carefully. This is in 5:15. See then that you walk carefully. Not as fools. Why is calling someone a fool so serious? The fool has said in his heart there is no God. Walk wisely. Keep remembering: there is a God, and I'm not Him. Remember who you are and who God is. Understand the will of the Lord. The wise person conducts his life in the consciousness of God's will. God's will is 99% clear.

Walk wisely. Don't be a fool. God has a will for your life. Live in it. That good and acceptable and pleasant will of God. Buy back the time; it's precious. Redeem it. It's precious. Walk carefully. Don't dissipate your energies. Drunkenness—but in other ways too, spending our energies in the wrong ways. Keep it focused. By being filled with the Spirit. The Holy Spirit is an exciter, filling us with Himself, enabling us to walk carefully, to walk in light and love, to walk transformed, worthy of our calling. Let your energy be enhanced and empowered by the Spirit.

The result? Look at 5:19. Songs, hymns, spiritual songs, making melody in your heart to God, submitting to one another in the fear of God. Evidence of Holy Spirit? Spiritual mouths. Is your speech a blessing? Our conversation will be a blessing to others, building them up. Giving them clean laughter. And we'll have a musical heart. Grateful spirits, giving thanks always for all things. And submissive wills, wanting God's way above everything else.

How are we going to walk home?

In light of the presidential transition, Oswalt then invited the Davenports forward, and asked us all to come and pray for them. After the people assembled in front of the altar, Oswalt asked for three or four to pray for the Davenports. Prayers of praise and expectancy were uttered. Prayer for holding up the arms of the new president, for God's blessing on him and his wife. Prayers for the new president to have the strength and needed guidance for this new task. Prayers for the Davenports to be given God's vision for this camp meeting. Prayers for the Board, and strength for following God's direction, and to turn this camp meeting into a revival again.

Then Oswalt prayed a final prayer—we've been called to be God's hands and feet. It's hard to know why God would do this, but He has. He prayed God would guide, fill, enable them to see what others don't, to project a vision that would compel the vision of others. He committed and dedicated and entrusted them to God, believing in God for great things as they lead us.

Finally, as is the custom, all the congregation encircled the inside perimeter of the tabernacle, holding hands and singing: "Our Father, which art in heaven, hallowed be thy name. Thy kingdom come, thy will be done, on earth, as it is in heaven. Give us this day our daily bread, and forgive us our debts as we forgive our debtors, and deliver us not into temptation, but deliver us from evil. For thine is the kingdom, and the power, and the glory, forever. Amen."

Conclusion

Back to the Future

1885 to 2015. The years covered in this history. Also years dear to the heart of *Back to the Future* fans: 1885 was when Marty McFly went back to the Wild West, and 2015 the year he went to the future. Coincidence? Of course it is, but still, having looked to the past, perhaps it's time to look to the future as well. What history can teach us about the present and future is at least one of the reasons to study it.

What does the future hold? For some clues and suggestions, let's consider the past, and these lessons:

1) The Primacy of Prayer—the need to maintain a spirit of anticipation, setting distractions aside. It's harder to "get away from it all" nowadays, with cellphones and computers. But it's worth the effort to give spiritual things our exclusive attention at least once in a while.

2) God is the same yesterday, today, and forever—let's pray the best is yet to come. History is still being written; we're still in the middle of the story. We can hope and pray the best days at ERC are not in the past, but still to come.

3) An Emphasis on Biblical Holiness. Happiness will follow, but conceptually it remains secondary. This point is worth dwelling on, because it reminds us of this book's unifying theme.

We live in a day and age when happiness, or something people think is happiness, trumps holiness. Even among many professing evangelical Christians, the emphasis on God's love is more typically geared toward a consideration of what makes us happy over what God calls us to do to please Him.

But God's love for us is transformative; there is joy unspeakable for followers of Christ, but the path to our deepest joy involves transformation, self-denial, the death of certain of our desires, mortifying the flesh, even pain—none of which is possible apart from complete consecration and the operation of God's sanctifying grace within us. Nothing we're called to endure compares with the glory to come, but the biblical teaching is clear: the path to glory involves our willingness to die, to be changed, to be transformed. Our focus has to shift from self to others, and this is a message that ERC has always consistently trumpeted and proclaimed, and if such a message could be heard to resound in the churches of America once more, it could help effect the Copernican moral and spiritual revolution we so desperately need.

Often Philippians 2:4 is translated to say not to look *alone* at one's own interests, or *only* at one's own interests, or to look at the interests of others *also*, which is not the right translation, so why is it there? Kinlaw conjectures that it is "because we twentieth-century Christians don't believe the Lord can deliver us from self-interest, so we insert our assumptions into Scripture."[73]

C. S. Lewis, in his *Reflections on the Psalms*, echoes a similar theme: "It is surely . . . very possible that when God began to reveal himself to men, to show them that He and nothing else is their true goal and the satisfaction of their needs, and that He has a claim upon them simply by being what He is, quite apart from anything He can bestow or deny, it may have been absolutely necessary that his revelation should not begin with any hint of future Beatitude or Perdition. Those are not the right point to begin at. An effective belief in them, coming too soon, may even render almost impossible the development of (so to call it) the appetite for God; personal hopes and fears, too obviously exciting, have got in first."[74]

The point here is subtle but worth reiterating and clarifying. It isn't that Christian holiness is indifferent to matters of personal fulfillment, but rather—as the account of Eaton Rapids Camp Meeting shows—that the way to the deepest fulfillment of which we're capable as human beings is through the cross and a life sanctified from sin. To achieve the most joy, something other than joy needs to be sought—or, to put it another way, one must realize that in God is both Holiness and Joy, that they are inseparable, rightly understood. But to seek happiness, self-realization, or self-actualization apart from intimacy with the Divine and the experience of the Holy is vain idolatry. Eaton Rapids, all throughout its history, has consistently assigned primacy to holiness—understood as a work of grace and a subsequent walk of obedience—recognizing that only then the deepest joys will follow and highest aspirations be realized.

Kinlaw writes, "Self-interest is the supreme characteristic of a sinful person. It has been said that sinfulness is to be 'curved inward upon oneself.' Conversely, the purpose of the redemption offered by Christ is to undo our distorted orientation—to turn us outward, so that we are not interested in ourselves but in the well-being of others . . . . Self-interest is well demonstrated by the question, 'What's in it for me?' Jesus never strived to get something for himself. The Gospels relate no instance in which Jesus' self-interest was his first consideration."

Proclamations of full salvation, the holy life, and its consequent joy has been the message of ERC since its inception, and it's a message that is as timely today as ever—perhaps more timely today than ever before. Whether or not camp meeting as an institution survives, its vital message must continue to be proclaimed, and its vision appropriated at the deepest levels.

---

[73] Dennis Kinlaw, *Mind of Christ*.
[74] C. S. Lewis, *Reflections on the Psalms* (New York: Houghton Mifflin Harcourt, 1964), 40.

And so, with that, this History must come to an end. Dusty records yet untapped still abound: hotel registries, women's auxiliary minutes, treasurer reports, 75-year-old faded receipts, building specifications, dated directories, the finer points of constitutional bylaws, litanies of cottage transactions—a treasure trove undoubtedly filled with still-to-be-found gems. But for now, this particular History must draw to a close.

Jonathan Andersen, who pastors a United Methodist church in Georgia, recently wrote a short piece called "5 Reasons We Need Camp Meetings Now More Than Ever." Although it pertains to camp meetings generally, we thought it would be nice to include here, with his permission, as this written history winds down and we are left with a nagging question about the ongoing relevance of camp meetings today:

> Each summer I do something odd by most American standards: I spend one week with my extended family, we sleep in a crowded cabin with no air conditioner, and we go to worship services three times per day—alongside of hundreds of others—in an open air structure with a sawdust floor. The songs we sing were written long before I was born and the sermons last much longer than fifteen to eighteen minutes.
>
> Each summer I go to camp meeting.
>
> Camp meetings are uniquely American institutions that were developed during the early years of the Second Great Awakening. At the time, they were a new method for evangelism and revival that sprang up all across the country. Camp meetings often provided a place for those who lived in unsettled areas to worship and gather as a community for a short period of time—typically during the late summer. They began with very temporary arrangements such as tents, wagons, and brush arbors to worship under. Over time, these gatherings established more permanent structures and began to draw people from all over the surrounding communities.
>
> Francis Asbury once called camp meetings "a battle ax and weapon of war" that broke down walls of wickedness throughout America. He believed they were a great means of grace. And in 1811, he estimated that these spirit-filled gatherings brought together one-third of the total American population.
>
> More than 200 years later, thousands of people continue to make the pilgrimage each summer to camp meetings that have withstood the test of time.
>
> Here are five reasons why I think we still need them today:
>
> 1. They provide an opportunity for true Sabbath rest.

The first thing most people feel when they attend a camp meeting is that they have passed from busyness to tranquility in just a few small steps. Nestled away from billboards and rush hour traffic, part of the beauty of modern camp meetings is that most have literally been set apart from the world and inherited the simplicity of the times in which they were started.

You'll rarely see a laptop, television, or gaming console. You'll often see porch swings, laughter, and lounging. Many who attend take the week of camp meeting as vacation from work, and when no one else is worrying about being productive or efficient, you won't feel the need to either.

The experience of camp meeting is difficult to describe, but Eugene Peterson's description of Sabbath does a phenomenal job: "uncluttered time and space to distance ourselves from the frenzy of our own activities so we can see what God has been and is doing."

2. They aid in the slow work of cultivating true community.

Today the average worker stays in their job less than five years. The average homeowner sells their home in less than ten years. Sure, in five to ten years, great relationships can be built. But like cast iron skillets, the best relationships are formed slowly over time.

This summer will mark my 26th camp meeting. I've shared the crying years of infancy, the awkward years of middle school, and the growing years of being a young adult with an intergenerational community that hasn't gone anywhere. Each year in this community babies are celebrated, deaths are mourned, people with cancer are cared for, and wayward children who once attended are lifted up in prayer.

Although I sleep in a cabin at camp meeting each night that holds three generations of my family, generations of others have helped them raise me and shape who I am. And they're not all from the same church. As they were in the beginning, camp meetings continue to be a place where Methodists, Baptists, Presbyterians, and others truly come together for the gospel.

3. They are a foundation that helps with recalibration.

Questions like "who am I?," "where am I headed?," and "what's the purpose of all of this?" aren't anything new. Yet in a VUCA world—one that is volatile, uncertain, complex, and ambiguous—these questions are more challenging than ever and it's easy to lose one's bearings. Camp meetings are the antithesis of VUCA. Many of them are now 100+ years old and they exude steadiness, embody regular life-shaping rituals, and offer simplicity.

The altar calls, Sabbath time, and community that surround camp meetings provide just the kinds of opportunities through which one can easily explore the deep questions of life and experience the Holy Spirit move in a powerful way. They also come with the advantage that you can count on them every year.

J. Ellsworth Kalas once preached, "As marvelous as grace is when it invades our life, grace needs many continuing opportunities to invade our lives if we are to go on marching." Camp meetings provide the time and place for this abundant grace to invade.

4. They serve as a reminder that we don't have to make faith up as we go. As Christians we've been called "to contend for the faith that was once and for all entrusted to the saints." Yet as contemporary Americans, we often act as if we can make Christianity up as we go along.

Sitting under old brush arbors and tabernacles, walking with friends where others have walked for many years, sleeping in cabins that have been with families for generations, singing old gospel hymns, and listening to someone preach with the fervor of a second great awakening preacher each serve as a reminder that we're part of something that started well before us. And the fact that camp meetings survive in our world today also serves as a testimony to the unstoppable nature of the gospel.

Countless institutions have closed down since the turn of the 20th century, but for some reason God has preserved camp meetings. I hope they don't end anytime soon.

5. They form Christians in a deep way.

According to James Bryan Smith, spiritual formation is the process, empowered by the Holy Spirit, in which we adopt the narratives of Jesus as the narratives of our lives, adopt the practices of Jesus as the daily rhythms of our lives, and spend time with others doing the same.

Camp meetings are a place where these three things happen in an intentional way for one week each year. Every day preaching, teaching, and conversation take place that help replace false narratives adopted from the world with the true narratives about God that Jesus regularly taught. Throughout the week, countless opportunities arise to spend time alone in prayer, care for broken and hurting people within the community, and encourage others with love. Every moment is spent with other people who have chosen to dedicate their lives to these same tasks.

The fruit of this formation is evident at many camp meetings. Simply visit and ask around, "How has God used camp meeting to shape your life?"[75]

Writing a history like this is a fascinating experience. Among other things, it provides a lesson in historiography. It is natural to think that writing a history involves looking up the relevant facts and arranging them chronologically, and perhaps in some sense that's true; but all sorts of difficult and inevitable questions arise along the way.

For example, what facts are relevant? If a particular historical survey is severely limited in its focus and scope, such a question is easier to answer. But if a study aspires, as this one did, to be fairly comprehensive in touching great numbers of salient features of the whole narrative—from the noumenal to the nitty gritty, from the profound to the provincial, and well-nigh everything in between—it is harder to know what to exclude.

Yet exclude we must, because otherwise the history would have been prohibitively long. It's already probably longer than some would prefer, and shorter than others would like. Much had to be left out, and without a script to follow or a precise algorithm to figure out what should stay and what should go. There were all sorts of judgments along the way, and no doubt the job was done imperfectly—too much of this, not enough of that. For this we ask the reader's forgiveness and indulgence and grace, and we hope that perhaps a future chronicler will revisit this text, and supplement, augment, prune, and in various other ways make it better, more comprehensive, and more accurate.

---

[75] http://seedbed.com/feed/5-reasons-need-camp-meetings-now-ever/. The comments below Jonathan's blog are a joy to read, and a reminder that camp meeting, at the end of the day, is about transformed lives. One sample from many that could have been selected comes from a reader named Maura: "I am now a seminary student because of my campmeeting experience. I was living in St. Louis, teaching, struggling. I never found a church while I was living there, so my faith was weakening. I was not walking close to the Lord, but I am so in love with campmeeting that I attended every summer like always. During that time I felt the Lord stirring in my heart. I prayed fervently that God would do a radical work in my life and that whatever changes needed to be made would happen. I prayed that God would, 'make it blatantly obvious to me what I should do.' God answered my prayer. When I returned home to St. Louis, my relationship with my boyfriend fell apart in a dangerous way, and I saw who he really was. Because of that relationship, I needed to leave St. Louis, and God made that possible. God protected me, and directed me to exactly where I was supposed to be. God provided an opportunity for me to go to seminary, which was a call that had been on my heart for years, but I dismissed because I thought it was impossible to follow. I am so grateful for the time spent in prayer at campmeeting, and the prayers of the saints around me, because I am now happier than I have been in years. I am ministering and learning and growing every day. If you have never felt God move in a dynamic way in your life, you should take the time to attend campmeeting."

In a sense, the challenge we faced was made stiffer by the excellent work of previous camp historians, chroniclers, and collectors of material. There was simply so much excellent material to draw from—Board minutes, personal journals, letters, camp publications, groundbreaking ceremonies, sermons, and such—that, over the 130 consecutive year history, the amount of material gathered was mammoth, rendering it impossible to do it justice. We literally had enough material that we could have written an independent history for each decade of the camp—in fact, we still may do just that. The 150th is in a few decades, after all!

The historical account you hold in your hands could have been considerably longer, needless to say, and continues to grow each year. If important events or figures or anecdotes have been left out, please realize their exclusion was inadvertent, and that later editions can rectify such mistakes. We think it altogether inevitable, albeit unintentional, that we did in fact miss some important people and notable events along the way; please consider the book as it stands, warts and all, a work in progress, able to be extended, corrected, modified, and expanded in the future by the History Committee and camp historians of ERC. More biographies to share, more anecdotes to tell.

Working on this history has been our unadulterated joy and privilege. By turns it has made us feel like spelunkers, private detectives, and archaeologists, discovering new nooks and crannies, coming across unexpected finds and delightful gems, riding the rhythms and vagaries of history, discovering new clues and hints along the journey and how they stitched together to form the mosaic forged by ERC's rich history.

We hope this book contributes to the heritage of Eaton Rapids Camp Meeting; and, even for those of you who may no longer frequent camp meeting or darken the doors of its tabernacle, we hope this story has brought a bit of camp meeting to you and contributed to keeping its vital spirit alive.

Only God knows what the future holds. But if the American Revolution could serve as a precursor to the Second Great Awakening and revivals at Red River and Cane Ridge, and the Civil War could be the prelude to the second great epoch of camp meetings in America, perhaps the current cultural conflicts and ideological fragmentation in which we find ourselves might serve, once more, to engender a spirit of renewal, a national repentance, and the camp meeting tabernacles and sawdust trails of America might be filled to overflowing once again.

Appendix 1

Presidents

1884-1888	James Hamilton
1888-1889	W. H. Thompson
1889 - ?	W. I. Cogshall
1892-1919	Marshall H. Callen
1919-1922	Wallace P. Manning
1922-1926	William G. Nixon
1926-1932	H. D. Skinner
1932-1952	Lloyd H. Nixon
1952-1958	Byron A. Hahn
1958-1963	Warren E. Brown
1963-1971	Clarence Hutchens
1971-1979	Hayden Carruth, Sr.
1979-1982	Howard Coil
1982-1988	Wallace Haines
1988-1995	William R. Shapton
1995-1999	William Doubblestein
1999	David Minger & Clyde Leigh
1999-2005	Clyde Leigh
2006-2015	John Oswalt
2015-	LaVerne Davenport

Appendix 2
Year-by-Year Records—Platform Speakers, Camp Officers, and Workers

1885: June 13 – 21, 1885 was first Camp Meeting at the Lansing Fair Grounds

1885 ERC PLATFORM SPEAKERS: Rev. Sam Jones, NHA. December 1885: James Hamilton, President; F. L. McCoy, Vice President; W. I. Cogshall, Secretary; William F. Sterling, Treasurer. [In some places it lists W. D. Brainerd as Treasurer.]

1886: July 24 – Aug 3. James Hamilton, President; W. I. Cogshall, Secretary; William F. Sterling, Treasurer.

1886 ERC PLATFORM SPEAKER: Rev. Sam Jones, NHA.

1887: James Hamilton, President; W. I. Cogshall, Secretary; William F. Sterling, Treasurer.

1887 ERC PLATFORM SPEAKERS: Rev. William Jones. Rev. Sam Jones (?).[76]

1888: W. H. Thompson, President; Dr. M. M. Callen, Secretary – Central Michigan Camp Meeting Association.

1889: W. I. Cogshall [Niles, MI], President; J. H. Potts [Detroit, MI], Vice President; W. J. Aldrich [Muskegan, MI], 2nd Vice President; W. Washburn [Saginaw, MI], 3rd Vice President; Dr. M. M. Callen [Lansing, MI], Secretary; W. F. Stirling [Eaton Rapids, MI], Treasurer.

1890: W. I. Cogshall, President.

1891: July 23 – Aug 2; W. I. Cogshall, President; L. DeLamarter [Eaton Rapids, MI], Secretary.

---

[76] In a clipping about the 1887 National Camp-Meeting in Eaton Rapids, from late June into July, the following were to be present: Bishop Willard T. Mallalieu, D.D., of New Orleans; Dr. George D. Watson, of Florida; Rev. Sam Small of Atlanta, GA, Mrs. Maggie Van Cott, of Cairo, New York; and Henry Date, of Chicago. The "Hill family" was to assist in the singing under the direction of the Rev. M. M. Callen. "The remarkable meeting of last year gave such a prestige to this gathering, that this year promises a larger attendance and greater results. The spread of scriptural holiness will be steadily kept in mind under the direction of Dr. Watson. It is intended to give the meeting scope also in direct saving results."

1891 ERC PLATFORM SPEAKERS: Bishop W. F. Mallalieu, D.D. (LA); Dr. James Potts (editor Michigan Advocate); David B. Updegraff (The Quaker Methodist); Dr. Joseph H. Smith (IN) [first year on the platform]; Enoch Stubbs (PA); Major Cole; Dr. D. F. Barnes; Dr. J. I. Buell; Dr. R. W. Van Shoick. MUSICIAN: Dr. M. M. Callen. MISSIONARIES: Miss Sarah M. DeLine (Bombay, India).

1892: Dr. Marshall M. Callen [Kalamazoo, MI], President.

1892 ERC PLATFORM SPEAKERS: Dr. Joseph H. Smith (IN)

1893: Dr. Marshall M. Callen [Kalamazoo, MI], President; L. DeLamarter [Eaton Rapids, MI], Secretary.

1893 ERC PLATFORM SPEAKERS: Dr. Joseph H. Smith (IN); Dr. R. N. McKaig (MN); Bishop J. N. Fitzgerald, D.D.; Dr. L. P. Davis; W. F. Sheridan; E. A. Craig; F. L. Thompson. YOUTH: A. J. Luther. CHILDREN: Miss Mattie Lawrence (Eaton Rapids). MUSICIAN: Miss Minnie Jacobs (Union City).

1894: July 26 – Aug 5. Dr. Marshall M. Callen [Kalamazoo, MI], President; L. DeLamarter (Eaton Rapids, MI), Secretary.

1894 ERC PLATFORM SPEAKERS: Dr. Joseph H. Smith (IN); Dr. George D. Watson (FL); Bishop Mallalieu; Evangelist F. A. Morehouse; Dr. E. W. Ryan; Dr. J. H. Potts; Dr. Levi Master. YOUTH: George C. Cutter (Ionia). CHILDREN: Mattie M. Decker (Deaconess from Grand Rapids).

1895: July 25 – Aug 4. Dr. Marshall M. Callen, [Kalamazoo, MI] President; DeLamarter, Secretary.

1895 ERC PLATFORM SPEAKERS: Dr. Joseph H. Smith; Dr. R. N. McKaig (MN); Dr. Samuel W. Horner; Dr. L. P. Davis; Dr. J. C. Floyd; A. M. Gould; Bishop Dr. W. X. Ninde (China and Japan). CHILDREN/YOUTH: M/M H. C. Scripps

1896: Dr. Marshall M. Callen [Kalamazoo, MI], President.

1896 ERC PLATFORM SPEAKERS: Dr. Joseph H. Smith (IN); Dr. George D. Watson (FL); Bishop Mallalieu; Evangelist F. A. Morehouse; Dr. E. W. Ryan; Dr. J. H. Potts; Dr. Levi Master. YOUTH: George C. Cutter (Ionia). CHILDREN: Mattie M. Decker (Deaconess from Grand Rapids).

1897: July 22 – Aug 1. Dr. Marshall M. Callen [Kalamazoo, MI], President; W. D. Brainerd [Eaton Rapids, MI], Secretary.

1897 ERC PLATFORM SPEAKERS: Dr. Joseph H. Smith; Isaac Naylor; Dr. M. C. B. Mason; Dr. J. H. Potts (Detroit); C. T. Allen (Detroit); W. M. Puffer (Lansing); James Hamilton (St. Joseph); P. J. Maveety and Ernest O. Sellers (Missionary Day Service Leader). YOUTH: W. E. Sheridan (Pontiac). CHILDREN: Mamie Boynton (Eaton Rapids). MUSICIANS: Ernest O. Sellers (Moody Institute, Chicago); Edith King (Jackson).

1898: July 28 – Aug 7. Dr. Marshall M. Callen [Kalamazoo, MI], President; W. D. Brainerd (Eaton Rapids, MI), Secretary

1898 ERC PLATFORM SPEAKERS: Dr. Joseph H. Smith (CA) [In charge of The School of the Prophets, an Evangelistic Institute for all attending ERC]; C. S. Nusbaum (KS); Bishop Ninde; President Ashley of Albion College; Dr. J. L. Berry (IL); Joshua Stansfield (Detroit); W. I. Cogshall (Coldwater); W.

M. Puffer (Lansing); P. J. Maveety (Jackson). YOUTH: Herman C. Scripps (Detroit). CHILDREN: Mrs. H. C. Scripps. MUSICIANS: Miss Birdie Blodgett (Eaton Rapids); "Dr. Marshall Callen will direct the singing."

1899: July 27 – Aug 6. Dr. Marshall M. Callen [Kalamazoo, MI], President; W. D. Brainerd [Eaton Rapids, MI], Secretary.

1899 ERC PLATFORM SPEAKERS: Dr. Joseph H. Smith; C. S. Nusbaum (KS); H. W. Kerr (Detroit); G. B. Johns (Milford) [The Singing Evangelists]; Dr. J. H. Potts; Dr. L. DeLamarter (Muskegon); C. W. Baldwin (Port Huron); D. D. Martin (Battle Creek); Dr. W. M. Puffer (Lansing); P. J. Maveety (Albion). YOUTH: Dr. J. F. Berry; H. C. Scripps. CHILDREN: Mrs. H. C. Scripps. MUSICIANS: H. W. Kerr and G. B. Johns (Milford) – The Singing Evangelists; Ella C. Parks (Battle Creek).

1900: Aug 2 – Aug 12. Dr. Marshall M. Callen [Kalamazoo, MI], President; W. D. Brainerd [Eaton Rapids, MI], Secretary.

1900 ERC PLATFORM SPEAKERS: Dr. Joseph H. Smith; Dr. R. N. McKaig (MN); Dr. Manley S. Hard (PA); Dr. J. P. Ashley (Albion); Dr. I. E. Springer (Detroit). MUSICIANS: Dunham and Baker (OH); Hattie Reynolds (Jackson).

1901: July 25 – Aug 5. Dr. Marshall M. Callen [Eaton Rapids, MI], President; W. D. Brainerd [Eaton Rapids, MI], Secretary; Joseph Carr [Eaton Rapids, MI], Treasurer.

1901 ERC PLATFORM SPEAKERS: Dr. Joseph H. Smith; Dr. E. S. Dunham (OH); L. H. Baker; Dr. C. W. Winchester (NY); Dr. George Elliot (Detroit); Dr. C. T. Allen (Detroit); Dr. D. F. Barnes; Dr. J. C. Floyd. CHILDREN: Mrs. A. B. Morse (St. Joseph). YOUTH: L. H. Baker. MUSICIANS: L. H. Baker; Edith King (Jackson).

1902: July 24 – Aug 4. Dr. Marshall M. Callen [Kalamazoo, MI], President.

1902 ERC PLATFORM SPEAKERS: Dr. Joseph H. Smith. YOUTH: C. F. English.

1903: July 23 – Aug 3. Dr. Marshall M. Callen [Kalamazoo, MI], President; Dr. Louis DeLamarter [Lansing, MI], 1st Vice President; E. S. Ninde [Ann Arbor, MI], 2nd Vice President; C. T. Allen [Ypsilanti, MI], 3rd Vice President; W. D. Brainerd [Eaton Rapids, MI], Secretary.

1903 ERC PLATFORM SPEAKERS: Dr. Joseph H. Smith [The School of Prophets]; C. F. English; Bishop Dr. E. E. Hoss (TN); Dr. W. F. Oldham (IL); W. G. Howson (London, Ontario); Dr. Louis DeLamarter; Dr. E. B. Bancroft. CHILDREN: Mrs. H. C. Scripps (Albion). MUSICIANS: C. F. English (Homer); Beulah Green (Eaton Rapids).

1904: July 28 – Aug 7. Dr. Marshall M. Callen [Kalamazoo, MI], President; Dr. Louis DeLamarter [Lansing, MI], 1st Vice President; E. S. Ninde [Ann Arbor, MI], 2nd Vice President; C. T. Allen [Ypsilanti, MI], 3rd Vice President; R. E. Meader [Eaton Rapids, MI], Assistant Secretary; W. D. Brainerd [Eaton Rapids, MI], Secretary; Joseph Carr [Eaton Rapids, MI], Treasurer.

1904 ERC PLATFORM SPEAKERS: Dr. Joseph H. Smith; Dr. C. W. Winchester (President of Taylor University); Dr. M. C. B. Mason; Bishop W.

F. Oldham, D.D.; Bishop W. F. Mallalieu, D.D.; Dr. J. P. Brushingham (IL); Dr. C. H. Morrison (KY); YOUTH: C. F. English.

1905: July 27 – Aug 6. Dr. Marshall M. Callen [Kalamazoo, MI], President; Dr. D. D. Martin [Albion, MI], 1st Vice President; Dr. John Sweet [Detroit, MI], 2nd Vice President; Dr. E. W. Ryan [Detroit, MI], 3rd Vice President; A. A. Geiger, Secretary [Jackson, MI]; D. E. Reed, Assistant Secretary [Albion, MI]; M. D. Crawford, Treasurer [Eaton Rapids, MI].

1905 ERC PLATFORM SPEAKERS: Bishop Willard F. Mallalieu; Bishop Luther B. Wilson (TN); Dr. Joseph H. Smith [The School of Prophets]; Dr. C. J. Fowler (President of National Holiness Association); F. E. Morehouse (Jackson); Charles F. English; U. V. Silloway (Grand Rapids); Harold Sayles (IL); Will Colegrove (Grand Rapids); H. O. Wills (Detroit); Charles B. Kolb (OH); Melvin E. Trotter (of City Mission Fame); Bishop Isaac W. Joyce; J. W. Hallenbeck (Marshall). YOUTH: Ms. Deborah Davis (MO); David Reed and Charles F. English. MUSICIANS: Charles F. English (OH) and Melvin J. Hill (IN); Taylor University Quartette; Mr. Peter Quartelle (Grand Rapids); Mr. William Wilson (Grand Rapids). SPECIAL APPEARANCE: Melvin E. Trotter (Grand Rapids). CHILDREN: Mrs. Mae Murray; Mrs. Helen Scripps.

1906: July 26 – Aug 5. [21st ANNUAL] Dr. Marshall M. Callen [Kalamazoo, MI], President; Dr. D. D. Martin [Albion, MI], 1st Vice President; Dr. L. A. Beeks [Elkhart, IN], 2nd Vice President; S. W. Bird [Stoney Creek, MI], 3rd Vice President; A. A. Geiger [Jackson, MI], Secretary; W. D. Brainerd [Eaton Rapids, MI], Assistant Secretary; M. D. Crawford [Eaton Rapids, MI], Treasurer.

1906 ERC PLATFORM SPEAKERS: Dr. Joseph H. Smith [The School of Prophets]; Dr. C. H. Fowler (MA); Dr. Theodore S. Henderson (NY); Dr. C. W. Ruth (IN); Bishop J. W. Hamilton (CA); Bishop Henry Spellmyer (OH); Bishop W. F. Oldham (Singapore); Bishop J. F. Berry (NY); Bishop W. F. McDowell (IL); Dr. F. E. Day (Albion); Dr. J. T. R. Lathrup (Grand Rapids); C. E. Allen (Flint); David E. Reed (Detroit). YOUTH: Ms. Iva D. Vennard (MO); David E. Reed. CHILDREN: M/M A. O. Carman (Homer). MISSIONARIES: Dr. Lucy Gaynor (WFMS – China); Nellie Snider (WHMS). MUSICIANS: The Albion College Quartette; J. A. Oakes (Albion).

1907: July 25 – Aug 4. Dr. Marshall M. Callen [Kalamazoo, MI], President; Dr. D. D. Martin [Albion, MI], 1st Vice President; Dr. L. A. Beeks [Elkhart, IN], 2nd Vice President; S. W. Bird [Stoney Creek, MI], 3rd Vice President; A. A. Geiger [Jackson, MI], Secretary; W. D. Brainerd [Eaton Rapids, MI], Assistant Secretary; M. D. Crawford [Eaton Rapids, MI], Treasurer.

1907 ERC PLATFORM SPEAKERS: Dr. Joseph H. Smith [The School of Prophets]; Dr. C. J. Fowler (MA); Dr. C. W. Ruth (IN); Dr. I. E. Springer (Saline, MI); Dr. P. J. Maveety; Dr. F. A. Chapman (Coldwater); Dr. I. A. Beeks (IN); Dr. J. C. Floyd (OH); Dr. E. F. Walker (CA). MUSICIANS: R. E. Akin; Albion College Quartet; George Bennard, TSA (Reed City). YOUTH: Ms. Iva D. Vennard (MO). CHILDREN: M/M A. O. Carman

(Homer). MISSIONARY: Dr. George Elliot (IL). BOOKSTORE: H. R. E. Quant (Ganges) ran the bookstore.

1908: July 23 – Aug 2. Dr. Marshall M. Callen [Kalamazoo, MI], President; Dr. D. D. Martin [Albion, MI], 1st Vice President; Dr. L. A. Beeks [Elkhart, IN], 2nd Vice President; S. W. Bird [Dexter, MI], 3rd Vice President; A. A. Geiger [Jackson, MI], Secretary; M. D. Crawford [Eaton Rapids, MI], Treasurer.

1908 ERC PLATFORM SPEAKERS: Dr. Joseph H. Smith [The School of Prophets] (MS); Dr. C. J. Fowler (MA); C. W. English (OH); Dr. E. F. Walker (CA); G. F. Oliver (President of Sychar Holiness Camp Meeting Association). YOUTH: Ms. Iva D. Vennard (MO). CHILDREN: Mrs. Joseph Smith. MUSICIAN: George Bennard.

1909: July 22 – Aug 2. Dr. Marshall M. Callen [Kalamazoo, MI], President; Dr. W. P. French [Lansing, MI], 1st Vice President; Dr. F. D. Leete [Detroit, MI], 2nd Vice President; S. W. Bird [Ypsilanti, MI], 3rd Vice President; A. A. Geiger [Marshall, MI], Secretary; M. D. Crawford [Eaton Rapids, MI], Treasurer.

1909 ERC PLATFORM SPEAKERS: C. W. English (OH); Dr. Joseph H. Smith (MS); Dr. E. F. Walker (CA); Hart and Magann (IL); Bishop D. H. Moore (OH); Dr. M. C. B. Mason (OH); E. A. Armstrong (Albion) [The School of the Prophets] MUSICIAN: A. S. Magann (Fairbury, IL); George Bennard. YOUTH: Ms. Iva D. Vennard and C. W. English (OH). CHILDREN: David E. Reed. MISSIONARY: Miss Nellie Snider.

1910: July 28 – Aug 7. [25th ANNIVERSARY YEAR] Dr. Marshall M. Callen [Kalamazoo, MI], President; Dr. W.P. French [Lansing, MI], 1st Vice President; Dr. F. D. Leete [Detroit, MI], 2nd Vice President; S. W. Bird [Davison, MI], 3rd Vice President; A. A. Geiger [Marshall, MI], Secretary; M. D. Crawford [Eaton Rapids, MI], Treasurer.

1910 ERC PLATFORM SPEAKERS: Dr. Joseph Smith [The School of Prophets] (MS); Dr. E. F. Walker (CA); Dr. H. C. Morrison (KY). YOUTH: Ms. Iva D. Vennard (MO). CHILDREN: The School of Evangelism and Personal Workers Conference with District Superintendents of the Albion, Lansing, Ann Arbor, and Flint Districts of the Methodist Episcopal Church; Mrs. H. Rebecca Bell Griffith (PA). MUSICIANS: R. E. Akin; Emma Perrine; George Bennard.

1911: July 27 – Aug 6. Dr. Marshall M. Callen [Ionia, MI], President; Dr. W. P. French [Lansing, MI], 1st Vice President; Dr. F. D. Leets [Detroit, MI], 2nd Vice President; Dr. I. E. Springer [Detroit, MI], 3rd Vice President; George A. Brown [Battle Creek, MI], Secretary; W. D. Brainerd [Eaton Rapids, MI], Assistant Secretary; M. D. Crawford [Eaton Rapids, MI], Treasurer.

1911 ERC PLATFORM SPEAKERS: Dr. Joseph H. Smith (MS); Dr. E. F. Walker (CA); Dr. H. C. Morrison (KY); C. B. Allen (CO). YOUTH: Ms. Iva D. Vennard (MO). MUSICIAN: Frank Arthur (Ypsilanti); George Bennard; Emma Perrine. CHILDREN: Miss Mary Morey (Jackson). MISSIONARIES: Miss Sue Wang (Ching Kiang, China).

1912: July 25 – Aug 4. Dr. Marshall M. Callen [Ionia, MI], President; J. W. Lawrence (Lansing, MI), 1st Vice President; Dr. F. D. Leete (Detroit, MI), 2nd Vice President; Dr. W. P. French (Lansing, MI), 3rd Vice President; George A. Brown (Kalamazoo, MI), Secretary; M. D. Crawford (Eaton Rapids, MI), Treasurer.

1912 ERC PLATFORM SPEAKERS: Dr. B. Carradine (MO); J. L. Brasher (AL); Dr. Joseph Smith [The School of Prophets] (MS); Dr. E. F. Walker (CA). YOUTH: Ms. Iva D. Vennard. CHILDREN: David Reed (Albion). MUSICIANS: George Bennard; Frank Arthur; Emma Perrine. SUNDAY SCHOOL: W. W. Robinson (Detroit) and E. E. Horner (Eaton Rapids). BOOKSTORE: H. R. E. Quant (Jackson).

1913: July 24 – Aug 3. [The Twenty Eighth Annual Meeting] Dr. Marshall M. Callen [Ionia, MI], President.

1913 ERC PLATFORM SPEAKERS: Dr. E. F. Walker (CA); William H. Huff (IO); I. H. Hodge (KS); Dr. Joseph H. Smith (MS) [The School of the Prophets]; Dr. Beverly Carradine (MO); C. H. Babcock (VA). YOUTH: Mrs. Iva D. Vennard (IL). CHILDREN: Harriet Miller (Grand Rapids). BOOKSTORE: Managed by A. A. Geiger (Marshall).

1914: July 23 – August 2. Dr. Marshall M. Callen [Ionia, MI], President; Dr. W. G. Nixon [Pontiac, MI], 1st Vice President; G. H. Whitney [Tecumseh, MI], 2nd Vice President; W. P. French [Kalamazoo, MI], 3rd Vice President; George A. Brown [Kalamazoo, MI], Secretary; M. D. Crawford [Eaton Rapids, MI], Treasurer.

1914 ERC PLATFORM SPEAKERS: Will H. Huff (IO); C. H. Babcock (VA); C. D. Hestwood (KS); Dr. E. F. Walker (CA); Isaac Hodge (KS); Dr. Joseph H. Smith (CA); Dr. Frederick S. Goodrich (Albion). MUSICIANS: Isaac Hodge; George Bennard.

1915: July 22 – Aug 1. [30th Annual Meeting] Dr. Marshall M. Callen [Cadillac, MI], President; Dr. W. G. Nixon [Pontiac, MI], 1st Vice President; O. W. Willits [Medina, MI], 2nd Vice President; E. A. Armstrong [Big Rapids, MI], 3rd Vice President; George A. Brown [Kalamazoo, MI], Secretary; H. V. Wade [Carson City, MI], Assistant Secretary; Wilber Fowler [Eaton Rapids, MI], Treasurer.

1915 ERC PLATFORM SPEAKERS: Dr. Joseph H. Smith (CA); Bishop Dr. William Burt (NY); Dr. C. D. Hestwood (KS); W. G. Nixon (Pontiac); Dr. S. A. Danford (ND); Dr. P. J. McVeety (OH). YOUTH: Miss D. Willia Caffray (WI). CHILDREN: Mrs. Joseph H. Smith (Jennie). MUSICIANS: J. Wilbur Hestwood (son of Dr. Hestwood). BOOKSTORE: Managed by A. A. Geiger (Sturgis). [Copy of the 1915 Brochure is in the Secretary's Record Book]

1916: July 27 – Aug 6. Dr. Marshall M. Callen [Cadillac, MI], President; Dr. W. G. Nixon [Detroit, MI], 1st Vice President; E. A. Cross [Linden, MI], 2nd Vice President; W. A. Exner [Athens, MI], 3rd Vice President; H. V. Wade [Lansing, MI], Secretary; Wilbur Fowler [Eaton Rapids, MI], Treasurer.

1916 ERC PLATFORM SPEAKERS: Mr. Long (Taylor University); Dr. S. A. Danford (ND); E. Stanley Jones (India); Dr. Joseph H. Smith (CA); Dr. Henry Clay Morrison (KY); Dr. James M. Taylor; Dr. Sheridon.

MUSICIANS: Mr. C. B. Mott (Albion); Dr. M.M. Callen; Miss Emma Perrine; George Bennard. YOUTH: Miss D. Willia Caffray (WI). CHILDREN: Mrs. Joseph H. (Jennie) Smith. MISSIONARIES: Bishop Lewis (China). BOOKSTORE: David E. Reed (Albion). [Copy of the 1916 Brochure is in the Secretary's Record Book]

1917: July 26 – Aug 6. Dr. Marshall M. Callen [Cadillac, MI], President; Dr. W. G. Nixon [Pontiac, MI], 1st Vice President; E. A. Cross [Highland Park, MI], 2nd Vice President; W. A. Exner [Bellaire, MI], 3rd Vice President; E. L. Ford [Litchfield, MI], Secretary; Wilbur Fowler [Eaton Rapids, MI], Treasurer.

1917 ERC PLATFORM SPEAKERS: Dr. Joseph H. Smith (PA); Bishop Dr. W. F. Oldham (South America); Dr. G. W. Ridout (IO); Dr. S. A. Danford (ND); C. J. Fowler (President of National Holiness Association); Dr. George W. Oliver (IL); Mel Trotter (Grand Rapids); Dr. Hugh Kennedy; Dr. W. F. Kendrick. MUSICIANS: Mr. C. B. Mott (Albion); Dr. M. M. Callen; Miss Emma Perrine; George Bennard. YOUTH: Miss D. Willia Caffray (WI). CHILDREN: Mrs. Joseph H. (Jennie) Smith. MISSIONARIES: Bishop Lewis (China). BOOKSTORE: H. R. E. Quant (Jackson) [Copy of the 1917 Brochure is in the Secretary's Record Book].

1918: July 25 – Aug 4. Dr. Marshall M. Callen [Marshall, MI], President; Dr. W. G. Nixon [Pontiac, MI], 1st Vice President; G. H. Whitney [Chelsea, MI], 2nd Vice President; W. F. Kendrick [Kalamazoo, MI], 3rd Vice President; E. L. Ford [Litchfield, MI], Secretary; Wilbur Fowler [Eaton Rapids, MI], Treasurer.

1918 ERC PLATFORM SPEAKERS: Dr. Joseph H. Smith; Bishop Dr. Theodore S. Henderson; Dr. S. A. Danford; Dr. J. G. Morrison; Dr. Monroe Vayhinger; Dr. Hugh Kennedy. YOUTH: Mrs. S. A. Danford. MUSICIANS: Mr. C. H. Mott (Albion); Miss Emma Perrine. BOOKSTORE: H. R. E. Quant (Jackson). [Copy of the 1918 Brochure is in the Secretary's Record Book]

1919: July 24 – Aug 3. Wallace P. Manning [Albion, MI], Acting President; Eugene Moore [Ypsilanti, MI], 1st Vice President; G. H. Whitney [Chelsea, MI], 2nd Vice President; W. F. Kendrick [Kalamazoo, MI], 3rd Vice President; E. L. Ford [Litchfield, MI], Secretary; Wilbur Fowler [Eaton Rapids, MI], Treasurer.

1919 ERC PLATFORM SPEAKERS: Dr. Joseph Smith (CA); Dr. J. G. Morrison (ND); Joseph Owen (AL). MUSICIANS: M/M C. C. Crammond; Male Quartet from Taylor University; Emma Perrine; Lloyd H. Nixon. CHILDREN: M/M C. C. Crammond. BOOKSTORE: Under the management of Walter Quant. [Copy of the 1919 Brochure is in the Secretary's Record Book]

1920: July 22 – Aug 1. [35th ANNUAL SESSION] Wallace P. Manning [Albion, MI], President; H. D. Skinner [Jackson, MI], 1st Vice President; James Chapman [Bay City, MI], 2nd Vice President; George A. Brown [Coloma, MI], 3rd Vice President; E. L. Ford [Litchfield, MI], Secretary; Wilbur Fowler [Eaton Rapids, MI], Treasurer.

1920 ERC PLATFORM SPEAKERS: Bishop Theodore Henderson (Detroit); Arthur Moore (GA); Joseph Owen (AL); Dr. Joseph H. Smith (CA). MISSIONARIES: Bishop Frederick Leete (GA). YOUTH: Dr. William G. Nixon (Detroit). CHILDREN: David E. Reed (Albion). MUSICIANS: Lloyd H, Nixon (IN); Charles Boswell (PA).

1921: July 28 – Aug 7. Wallace P. Manning [Albion, MI], President; Dr. W. G. Nixon [Detroit, MI], 1st Vice President; F. H. Clapp [Albion, MI], 2nd Vice President; James Chapman [Bay City, MI], 3rd Vice President; E. L. Ford [Linchfield, MI], Secretary; Wilbur Fowler [Eaton Rapids, MI].

1921 ERC PLATFORM SPEAKERS: Bishop Theodore Henderson (Detroit); Dr. Joseph Smith (CA); Joseph Owen (AL); Arthur Moore (TX). YOUTH: Rev. Fern Wheeler (Charlotte); assisted by Verna Fenstermacher and Gladys Kline. CHILDREN: David E. Reed (Albion). MUSICIANS: Lloyd H. Nixon (Augusta); Miss Emma Perrine. BOOKSTORE: Under the management of Walter Quant.

1922: July 27 – Aug 6. W. P. Manning [Albion, MI], President; Dr. William G. Nixon [Detroit, MI], 1st Vice President; F. H. Clapp [Albion, MI], 2nd Vice President; John C. Willetts [St. Joseph, MI], 3rd Vice President; E. L. Ford [Litchfield, MI], Secretary; M. D. Crawford [Eaton Rapids, MI], Treasurer.

1922 ERC PLATFORM SPEAKERS: Dr. John Paul (KY); Bishop Theodore S. Henderson (Detroit); Dr. Joseph H. Smith (CA) [preacher for the School of Prophets]; Dr. C. D. Hestwood (KS). BOOKSTORE: Managed by David E. Reed (Albion). YOUTH/MUSIC: Lloyd H. Nixon (Jonesville); Howard Skinner, Jr (Muskegon); Emma Perrine (Tekonsha). CHILDREN: David E. Reed (Albion).

1923: Dr. William G. Nixon [Detroit, MI], President.

1923 ERC PLATFORM SPEAKERS: Dr. Joseph H. Smith (CA), MUSICIANS: Lloyd H. Nixon. BOOKSTORE: Managed by David E. Reed.

1924: July 24 – Aug 3. Dr. William G. Nixon [Detroit, MI], President; H. D. Skinner [Grand Rapids, MI], 1st Vice President; H. R. E. Quant [Charlevoix, MI], 2nd Vice President; Mrs. Bertha Bush [Delton, MI], 3rd Vice President; Miss Fern C. Wheeler [Charlotte, MI], Secretary; M. D. Crawford [Eaton Rapids, MI], Treasurer.

1924 ERC PLATFORM SPEAKERS: Dr. Joseph H. Smith (CA); E. Stanley Jones (India); Dr. John Paul (IO); E. M. Dunaway (GA); Bud Robinson. CHILDREN: Blanche Shepard Francis. MUSICIANS: Lloyd H. Nixon; Howard Skinner; Mrs. Blanche Shepard Francis. BOOKSTORE: Managed by David Reed.

1925: July 24 – Aug 2. Dr. William G. Nixon [Detroit, MI], President; H. D. Skinner [Muskegon, MI], 1st Vice President; H. R. E. Quant [Charlevoix, MI], 2nd Vice President; Mrs. Bertha Bush [Delton, MI], 3rd Vice President; Miss Fern C. Wheeler [Charlotte, MI], Secretary; M. D. Crawford [Eaton Rapids, MI], Treasurer.

1925 ERC PLATFORM SPEAKERS: Bishop Thomas Nicholson (Detroit); Dr. John Brasher (IO); Dr. Joseph H. Smith (CA); C. W. Ruth (IN); Thomas Henderson (OH); Dr. John Paul (IN). MUSICIANS: Lloyd H. Nixon

(Lowell); Howard Skinner (Muskegon). YOUTH: Dr. Iva Durham Vennard (IL). BOOKSTORE: Managed by David Reed.

1926: July 23 – Aug 1. Dr. William G. Nixon [Detroit, MI], President; H. D. Skinner [Muskegon, MI], 1st Vice President; H. R. E. Quant [Charlevoix, MI], 2nd Vice President; Mrs. Bertha Bush [Delton, MI], 3rd Vice President; Miss Fern C. Wheeler [Charlotte, MI], Secretary; M. D. Crawford [Eaton Rapids, MI], Treasurer.

1926 ERC PLATFORM SPEAKERS: Dr. Joseph H. Smith (CA) (Pres of the National Association for the Promotion of Holiness); Guy Wilson (MA); Raymond Browning (NC); W. G. Nixon (Detroit). MUSICIANS: Lloyd H. Nixon (Lowell); Howard Skinner (Grand Haven). CHILDREN: Blanche Shepherd Francis. BOOKSTORE: Under the management of the Golden Rule Book Shop (David E. Reed) of Albion, MI. [Copy of 1926 Brochure is in the Secretary's Record Book]

1927: July 29 – Aug 7. Howard D. Skinner [Muskegan, MI], 1st Vice President; H. R. E. Quant [Charlevoix, MI], 2nd Vice President; Mrs. Bertha Bush [Delton, MI], 3rd Vice President; Miss Fern Wheeler [Charlotte, MI], Secretary; M. D. Crawford [Eaton Rapids, MI], Treasurer.

1927 ERC PLATFORM SPEAKERS: Dr. John Paul (IN); Dr. Joseph H. Smith (CA); Dr. Will Huff (IO); Dr. S. H. Turbeville (IO). MUSICIANS: Lloyd H. Nixon (Lowell); Howard Skinner (Muskegon). YOUTH/CHILDREN: Rev. Blanche Shepherd Francis. MISSIONARIES: Dr. Rockwell Clancy (India). BOOKSTORE: Managed by David Reed, Golden Rule Bookstore, Albion.

1928: July 27 – Aug 5. Howard D. Skinner [Muskegon, MI], President; Charter Member; Lloyd H. Nixon [Grand Rapids, MI], 1st Vice President; J. C. Willetts [Holland, MI], 2nd Vice President; Mrs. Bertha Bush [Delton, MI], 3rd Vice President; Fern C. Wheeler [Charlotte, MI], Secretary; M. D. Crawford [Eaton Rapids, MI], Treasurer.

1928 ERC PLATFORM SPEAKERS: Dr. Joseph H. Smith (CA); Dr. Will Huff (IO); Bishop William F. Oldham (OH); Dr. John Thomas (KY); Dr. S. H. Turbeville (IO); Guy Wilson (MA). YOUTH: Mrs. Emily Thomas (KY). CHILDREN: David E. Reed (Albion). MISSIONARIES: Woodford Taylor (National Holiness Association of North China). MUSICIANS: Lloyd H. Nixon; Howard Skinner; The Atkinson Quartette (IN); The Yinger Quartette #2 (Grand Rapids). BOOKSTORE: Managed by David Reed.

1929: July 24 – Aug 4. Howard D. Skinner [Muskegon, MI], President; Lloyd Nixon [Grand Rapids, MI], 1st Vice President; J. C. Willits [Holland, MI], 2nd Vice President; Mrs. Bertha Bush [Delton, MI], 3rd Vice President; Fern C. Wheeler [Charlotte, MI], Secretary; M. D. Crawford [Eaton Rapids, MI], Treasurer.

1929 ERC PLATFORM SPEAKERS: Dr. Paul Rees (CA); Dr. Joseph H. Smith (CA); C. H. Babcock (CA); Raymond Browning (NC); Colonel S. L. Brengle (The Apostle of Holiness of the Salvation Army); Iva D. Vennard (IL). MUSICIANS: Lloyd Nixon (Grand Rapids); Prof. Howard Skinner, Jr. (FL). YOUTH: Dr. D. Willia Caffray (South America; India; China; Africa). CHILDREN: Miss Mary Vennard (IL). BOOKSTORE: David Reed.

1930: July 25 – Aug 3. [45th ANNUAL MEETING] Howard D. Skinner [Muskegon, MI], President.

1930 ERC PLATFORM SPEAKERS: Dr. Paul Rees (CA); Dr. Joseph H. Smith (CA); J. L. Brasher (AL). YOUTH: Dr. D. Willia Caffray (South America; India; China; Africa). MISSIONARIES: Dr. D. Willia Caffray. CHILDREN: Miss Mary Vennard (IL). MUSICIANS: Lloyd H. Nixon (Grand Rapids); H. Morse Skinner (FL). BOOKSTORE: David Reed.

1931: July 24 – Aug 2. H. D. Skinner [Muskegon, MI], President.

1931 ERC PLATFORM SPEAKERS: Dr. Joseph H. Smith (CA); Joseph Owen (IO); John Thomas (IL). YOUTH: Dr. Iva D. Vennard (IL). MISSIONARIES: Dr. Iva D. Vennard (IL). CHILDREN: Mary Vennard (IL). MUSICIANS: Lloyd Nixon (St. Joseph); Howard M Skinner (FL). BOOKSTORE: Managed by David Reed.

1932: H. D. Skinner [Muskegon, MI], President (resigned).

1932 ERC PLATFORM SPEAKERS: Dr. Joseph H. Smith; John H. Paul; Lloyd H. Nixon. MUSICIANS: Howard Skinner; Lloyd H. Nixon. YOUTH: Byron A. Hahn. MISSIONARIES: Dr. Howard Musser. BOOKSTORE: Managed by David Reed.

1933: July 27 – Aug 6. Dr. Lloyd H. Nixon [St. Joseph, MI], President; H. D. Skinner [White Pigeon, MI], 1st Vice President; George Brown [Leslie, MI], 2nd Vice President; Mrs. Bertha Bush [Delton, MI], 3rd Vice President; R.V. Birdsall [Portland, MI], Secretary; Byron A. Hahn [Lansing, MI], Treasurer.

1933 ERC PLATFORM SPEAKERS: Joseph Owen (IO); John Thomas (KY); Dr. Joseph H. Smith (CA); Lloyd H. Nixon (St. Joseph). MUSICIANS: Professor and Mrs. Howard Skinner (IL); Professor N. B. Vandall (OH); Lloyd H. Nixon (St. Joseph). YOUTH: Byron Hahn (Lansing). CHILDREN: Mary Vennard Waite (IL). BOOKSTORE: Managed by David Reed. MISSIONARY SPEAKER: Dr. E. Stanley Jones (India, China, South America).

1934: July 26 – Aug 5. Dr. Lloyd H. Nixon [Battle Creek, MI], President; H. D. Skinner [White Pigeon, MI], 1st Vice President; George Brown [Leslie, MI], 2nd Vice President; Mrs. Bertha Bush [Delton, MI], 3rd Vice President; R. V. Birdsall [Lansing, MI], Secretary; Byron A. Hahn [Jackson, MI], Treasurer.

1934 ERC PLATFORM SPEAKERS: Dr. Peter Wiseman (Ottawa, Canada); Paul S. Rees (MO); Dr. S. H. Tubeville (IN). MUSICIANS: Howard and Ada Skinner (IL). YOUTH: Byron A. Hahn (Jackson, MI). CHILDREN: Mrs. Mary Vennard Waite (IL) [Children's Meetings held in the Austin Memorial Tabernacle]. MISSIONARY SPEAKER: Miss Lela G. McConnell (KY). BOOKSTORE: Managed by David Reed.

1935: July 25 – Aug 4. [Golden Jubilee Year]. Dr. Lloyd H. Nixon [Pontiac, MI], President.

1935 ERC PLATFORM SPEAKERS: Dr. John Brasher (IO); Dr. Joseph H. Smith (CA); Paul Reese (MN). YOUTH: Byron Hahn (Jackson). CHILDREN: Mary Vennard Waite (IL). MUSICIANS: Professor and Mrs.

Howard Skinner (IL); Dr. Savage (Pontiac). BOOKSTORE: Managed by David Reed.

1936: July 23 – Aug 2. Dr. Lloyd H. Nixon [Battle Creek, MI], President; H. D. Skinner [Jackson, MI], 1st Vice President; George Brown [White Pigeon, MI], 2nd Vice President; Mrs. Bertha Bush [Delton, MI], 3rd Vice President; R. V. Birdsall [Lansing, MI], Secretary; Byron A. Hahn [Jackson, MI], Treasurer.

1936 ERC PLATFORM SPEAKERS: Dr. Peter Wiseman (Dean – Theology of Lorne Park College, Port Credit, Ontario); Dr. Z. T. Johnson (KY); John Thomas (KY); Bishop J. Waskom Pickett (Methodist Episcopal Church of India). MUSICIANS: Walter L. Mullett (OH); Gladys Watson. MISSIONARIES: Bishop J. Waskom Pickett (India). CHILDREN: Leah Brown. YOUTH: Byron Hahn (Jackson). BOOKSTORE: Managed by David Reed.

1937: Dr. Lloyd H. Nixon [Battle Creek, MI], President.

1937 ERC PLATFORM SPEAKERS: Dr. George Vallentyne (MN); Dr. John Owen. BOOKSTORE: Under the Management of Helen Riggs Brown.

1938: July 28 – Aug 7. [54th Encampment] Dr. Lloyd H. Nixon [Albion, MI], President; Byron A. Hahn [Alma, MI], 1st Vice President; Warren Brown [Portland, MI], 2nd Vice President; Mrs. Bertha Bush [Delton, MI], 3rd Vice President; R. V. Birdsall [Lansing, MI], Secretary; H. V. Wade [Grand Rapids, MI], Treasurer.

1938 ERC PLATFORM SPEAKERS: Dr. Henry C. Morrison (KY); Dr. S. H. Turbeville (IN); Dr. John Owen; Dr. George G. Vallentyne (MN); MUSICIANS: Professor/Mrs. Byron Crouse. CHILDREN: Leah Brown. YOUTH: Hugh Townley (Detroit).

1939: July 27 – Aug 6. [55th ENCAMPMENT] Dr. Lloyd H. Nixon [Albion, MI], President; Byron A. Hahn [Alma, MI], 1st Vice President; Warren Brown [Marshall, MI], 2nd Vice President; Mrs. Bertha Bush [Delton, MI], 3rd Vice President; R. V. Birdsall [Lansing, MI], Secretary; H. V. Wade [Lansing, MI], Treasurer.

1939 ERC PLATFORM SPEAKERS: Dr. John R. Church (NC); Dr. William Kirby (CA); Dr. Harry Jessop (IL). MUSICIANS: Walter Mullett; Esther Prosser. MISSIONARIES: Dr. Iva Durham Vennard (IL). YOUTH: Miss Janie Bradford. CHILDREN: Leah Brown.

1940: July 25 – Aug 4. [1884 – 1940: FIFTY SIXTH ENCAMPMENT] Dr. Lloyd H. Nixon [Albion, MI], President; Byron A. Hahn [Alma, MI], 1st Vice President; Warren Brown [Marshall, MI], 2nd Vice President; Mrs. Bertha Bush [Delton, MI], 3rd Vice President; R. V. Birdsall [Cadillac, MI], Secretary; H. V. Wade [Lansing, MI], Treasurer.

1940 ERC PLATFORM SPEAKERS: Dr. A. Wesley Pugh (IN); Dr. C. W. Butler (IO); John Thomas. YOUTH: Miss Janie Bradford. CHILDREN: Miss Jean Pound. MUSICIANS: M/M Byron J. Crouse; Esther Prosser. MISSIONARIES: Dr. Iva D. Vennard.

1941: July 24 – Aug 3. [The 57th Encampment] Dr. Lloyd H. Nixon [Albion, MI], President; Byron A. Hahn [Alma, MI], 1st Vice President; Warren

Brown [Marshall, MI], 2nd Vice President; Mrs. Bertha Bush [Delton, MI], 3rd Vice President; R. V. Birdsall [Cadillac, MI], Secretary; H. V. Wade [Lansing, MI], Treasurer.

1941 ERC PLATFORM SPEAKERS: Dr. Henry C. Morrison (Founder/President of Asbury Theological Seminary; Wilmore, KY); Dr. John R. Church (NC); Dr. Warren G. McIntyre. MUSICIANS: M/M Ira Wood; Esther Prosser; Isabelle Nixon. CHILDREN: Miss Jean Pound. YOUTH: Byron Hahn (Alma). MISSIONARIES: Miss Leila McConnell (KY).

1942: July 23 – Aug 2. [FOR 58 EVENTFUL YEARS] Dr. Lloyd H. Nixon [Albion, MI], President; Byron A. Hahn [Alma, MI], 1st Vice President; Warren Brown [Marshall, MI], 2nd Vice President; Mrs. Bertha Bush [Delton, MI], 3rd Vice President; R. V. Birdsall [Grand Rapids, MI], Secretary; H. V. Wade [Lansing, MI], Treasurer.

1942 ERC PLATFORM SPEAKERS: Dr. John L. Brasher; Dr. Paul Rees (MN); Dr. Harry Jessop (IL). MUSICIANS: M/M Ira Wood; Miss Esther Prosser. YOUTH: Byron Hahn (Alma, MI). CHILDREN: Mrs. Ira Wood. MISSIONARIES: Dr. Iva Vennard (IL). BOOKSTORE: Managed by Mrs. Warren (Helen) Brown.

1943: Dr. Lloyd H. Nixon [Pontiac, MI], President.

1943 ERC PLATFORM SPEAKERS: Bishop Arthur Moore; Dr. Joseph Owen. MUSICIAN: M/M E. Clay Milby.

1944: July 27 – Aug 6. Dr. Lloyd H. Nixon [Pontiac, MI], President; Byron A. Hahn [Big Rapids, MI], 1st Vice President; Warren Brown [Marshall, MI], 2nd Vice President; Mrs. Bertha Bush [Delton, MI], 3rd Vice President; Harold Jacobs [Decatur, MI], Secretary; Paul Schanzlin, Cassapolis, MI], Treasurer.

1944 ERC PLATFORM SPEAKERS: Dr. Joseph Owen (TN); Dr. E. R. Overly (KY); Dr. Ira Mason Hargett (KY). MUSICIANS: Harry Blackburn (Indian Springs Camp Meeting, Georgia); Esther Prosser Webb; William Cox. YOUTH/CHILDREN: M/M William Cox.

1945: July 27 – Aug 5. Dr. Lloyd H. Nixon [Pontiac, MI], President; Byron A. Hahn [Big Rapids, MI], 1st Vice President; Warren Brown [Marshall, MI], 2nd Vice President; Mrs. Bertha Bush [Delton, MI], 3rd Vice President; Harold Jacobs [Decatur, MI], Secretary; Paul Schanzlin, [Cassopolis, MI], Treasurer.

1945 ERC PLATFORM SPEAKERS: Dr. S. H. Turbeville (IN); Dr. Gideon Williamson (MA); Dr. Harry E. Jessop (IL). YOUTH: Wallace Haines (The Chicago Evangelistic Institute). CHILDREN: Miss Leah Brown. MUSICIANS: M/M E. Clay Milby; Esther Prosser Webb. MISSIONARIES: Miss Marjorie A. Burt (KY).

1946: July 25 – Aug 4. Dr. Lloyd H. Nixon [Pontiac, MI], President; Byron A. Hahn [Big Rapids, MI], 1st Vice President; Warren Brown [Marshall, MI], 2nd Vice President; Mrs. Bertha Bush [Delton, MI], 3rd Vice President; Milford E. Bowen [Cedar Springs, MI], Acting Secretary; Paul Schanzlin [Cassopolis, MI], Treasurer.

1946 ERC PLATFORM SPEAKERS: Dr. George Vallentyne (MN); Dr. E. R. Overley (KY); Dr. I. M. Hargett (KY). MUSICIANS: Professor Kenneth Wells; Esther Prosser Webb. YOUTH: Wallace Haines (IL); Herbert Wiggins. CHILDREN: Miss Marjorie Hawkins (Dundee); Miss Leah Brown.

1947: July 24 – Aug 3; Dr. Lloyd H. Nixon [Pontiac, MI], President.

1947 ERC PLATFORM SPEAKERS: Dr. S. H. Tubeville (IN); Dr. Paul Rees (MN); Dr. C. W. Butler (OH); William Wiseman (PA). MUSICIANS: Professor Kenneth Wells (IL); Esther Prosser Webb. CHILDREN: M/M Roderick McDonald (Big Rapids). YOUTH: Herbert Wiggins (IL) and William Meadows.

1948: July 22 – Aug 1; Dr. Lloyd H. Nixon [Pontiac, MI], President; Warren E. Brown [Marshall, MI], 1st Vice President; Clair J. Snell [Jackson, MI], 2nd Vice President; Mrs. Bertha Bush [Delton, MI], 3rd Vice President; Milford E. Bowen [Cedar Springs, MI], Secretary; Ray V. Birdsall [Eagle, MI], Treasurer.

1948 ERC PLATFORM SPEAKERS: Dr. John Paul (IN); Dr. Harry Jessop (IL); William Wiseman (PA). YOUTH: Miss Irene Wiseman (KY); William Meadows. CHILDREN: M/M Roderick MacDonald. MUSICIANS: Charles Shepherd (KY) and Irene Wiseman (KY); Leah Brown.

1949: July 28 – Aug 7 [65th Year]; Dr. Lloyd H. Nixon [Flint, MI], President; Dr. Byron A. Hahn [Sturgis, MI], 1st Vice President; Warren E. Brown [Marshall, MI], 2nd Vice President; Clair J. Snell [Jackson, MI], 3rd Vice President; Milford E. Bowen [Cedar Springs, MI], Secretary; Ray V. Birdsall [Eagle, MI], Treasurer.

1949 ERC PLATFORM SPEAKERS: Dr. I. M. Hargett (KY); Morton Dorsey; Dr. Horace Sprague (IN). MUSICIANS: Charles Shepherd (KY). YOUTH: Russell and Evelyn Nachtrieb (Pontiac).

1950: July 27 – Aug 6. [**66th YEAR**] Dr. Lloyd. H. Nixon [Flint, MI], President; Dr. Byron A. Hahn [Sturgis, MI], 1st Vice President; Warren E. Brown [Marshall, MI], 2nd Vice President; Clair J. Snell [Jackson, MI], 3rd Vice President; Milford E. Bowen [Lawrence, MI], Secretary; Ray Birdsall [Eagle, MI], Treasurer.

1950 ERC PLATFORM SPEAKERS: Dr. S. H. Turbeville (FL); Dr. Clyde Meredith (IN); Dr. C. I. Armstrong (NY). MUSICIANS: Charles Sheppard (KY); Leah Brown; Margaret Fogel. CHILDREN/YOUTH: M/M C. S. Thompson, Jr. (KY). MISSIONARIES: George Warner (NMS).

1951: July 26 – Aug 5. Dr. Lloyd H. Nixon [Flint, MI], President; Dr. Byron A. Hahn [Sturgis, MI], 1st Vice President; Clair J. Snell [Jackson, MI], 2nd Vice President; Wallace Haines [Zephyr Hills, FL], 3rd Vice President; Milford E. Bowen [Lawrence, MI], Secretary; Ray Birdsall [Eagle, MI], Treasurer.

1951 ERC PLATFORM SPEAKERS: James Gibson; L. S. Hoover; Morton Dorsey. YOUTH: William and Ruth Cox (Urundi, South Africa). MUSICIANS: M/M Clay Milby; Leah Brown; Flint Citadel Band. BOOKSTORE: Clair J. Snell, Manager.

1952: July 24 – Aug 3. [67th YEAR] Dr. Lloyd H. Nixon [Flint, MI], President; Dr. Byron A. Hahn [Sturgis, MI], 1st Vice President; Warren Brown [Lansing, MI], 2nd Vice President; Clair J. Snell [Jackson, MI], 3rd Vice President; Milford E. Bowen [Lawrence, MI], Secretary; Ray Birdsall [Eagle, MI], Treasurer.

1952 ERC PLATFORM SPEAKERS: T. H. Gaddis; Dr. Paul S. Rees; George E. Failing (Houghton, NY); H. E. Burrge (Herrin, IL). MISSIONARIES: M/M George Belknap (The National Society); Lelah McConnell (KY); William Gillam (OMS -Columbia, SA). MUSICIANS: The Gaddis Moser Evangelistic Party (T. H. Gaddis and the Moser Sisters - Bertha Moser; Rachel Moser-Gaddis; Elma Moser); Flint Citadel Band; Quartets from Taylor University; Asbury College and The Chicago Evangelistic Institute; Warren Brown; Leah Brown (in the Austin Tabernacle); Moser Sisters.

1953: July 23 – Aug 2; Dr. Byron Hahn [Sturgis, MI], Acting President; Clair J. Snell [Hart, MI], 2nd Vice President; Warren E. Brown [Lansing, MI], 3rd Vice President; M. E. Bowen [Lawrence, MI], Secretary; Ray V. Birdsall [Lansing, MI], Treasurer.

1953 ERC PLATFORM SPEAKERS: Dr. Ira M. Hargett (KY); B. C. Gamble; Dr. Claude A. Watson, J.D. (CA). YOUTH: Donald Strobe; Mrs. Warren (Helen) Brown. MUSICIANS: "The Singing Sheppards" – Charles and Jeanette Sheppard; Leah Brown.

1954: July 22 – Aug 1; Dr. Byron A. Hahn [Sturgis, MI], President; Warren E. Brown [Lansing, MI], 1st Vice President; Clair J. Snell [Hart, MI], 2nd Vice President; Mrs. Lloyd H. Nixon [Pontiac, MI], 3rd Vice President; Milford E. Bowen [Lawrence, MI], Secretary; Ray V. Birdsall [Lansing, MI], Treasurer.

1954 ERC PLATFORM SPEAKERS: Dr. J. C. McPheeters (KY); Dr. Harold B. Kuhn (KY); Dee W. Cobb. YOUTH: Mrs. Warren (Helen) Brown, Harold Jacobs, and Donald Strobe. CHILDREN: Mrs. Russell (Jane) Jaberg (IN). MUSICIANS: M/M/ Dee W. Cobb; Leah Brown. MISSIONARIES: M/M John Kunkle (Bolivia, SA, National Holiness Missionary Society).

1955: July 28 – Aug 7; Dr. Byron A. Hahn [Sturgis, MI], President; Warren E. Brown [Lansing, MI], 1st Vice President; Clair J. Snell [Hart, MI], 2nd Vice President; Mrs. Lloyd H. Nixon [deceased], 3rd Vice President; H. James Birdsall [Carson City, MI], Secretary; Milford E. Bowen [Lawrence, MI], Treasurer.

1955 ERC PLATFORM SPEAKERS: Dr. H. M. Couchenour (IL); Dr. James Gibson (KY); Dr. Claude A. Watson, J.D. (CA). YOUTH: Donald Sailor (White Pigeon) and Harold Jacobs (Lansing). CHILDREN: Mrs. Russell (Jane) Jaberg (IN). MUSICIANS: William Stone (Constantine); Leah Brown; Mrs. James Birdsall. MISSIONARIES: M/M Maron Garrison (The Methodist Church in Southern Asia, Bombay Annual Conference, India). BOOKSTORE: Dickson's Bible and Book House of Detroit, MI.

1956: July 26 – Aug 5. Dr. Byron A. Hahn [Sturgis, MI], President; Warren E. Brown [Lansing, MI], 1st Vice President; Clair J. Snell [Reading, MI], 2nd Vice President; Paul Conklin [Lansing, MI], 3rd Vice President; H. James

Birdsall [Carson City, MI], Secretary; Milford E. Bowen, Sr. [Lawrence, MI], Treasurer.

1956 ERC PLATFORM SPEAKERS: Rev. Helen Riggs Brown; Dr. John R. Church; Dr. Delbert R. Rose; Walter L. Mullett. YOUTH: Donald Sailor; Harold Jacobs. CHILDREN: Mrs. Russell (Jane) Jaberg (IN). MUSICIANS: "The Singing Shepherds" - Charles and Jeanette Shepherd; Leah Brown; Mrs. James Birdsall. MISSIONARIES: Miss Marjorie Burt (KY).

1957: July 25 – Aug 4; Dr. Byron A. Hahn [Sturgis, MI], President; Warren E. Brown [Lansing, MI], 1st Vice President; Clair J. Snell [Reading, MI], 2nd Vice President; Paul Conklin [Lansing, MI], 3rd Vice President; H. James Birdsall [Carson City, MI], Secretary; Milford E. Bowen, Sr. [Lawrence, MI], Treasurer.

1957 ERC PLATFORM SPEAKERS: Dr. Heber Burge (IL); Dr. George Failing (Wesleyan Methodist Church Associate Sunday School Editor); David E. Wilson; Dr. Glenn Frye (Jackson). YOUTH: Donald Sailor (White Pigeon). CHILDREN: Mrs. George Failing. MUSICIANS: Clay Milby; Leah Brown; Mrs. James Birdsall. MISSIONARIES: The Oriental Missionary Society.

1958: July 24 – Aug 3; Dr. Byron A. Hahn [Sturgis, MI], President; Warren Brown [Lansing, MI], 1st Vice President; Clair J. Snell [Reading, MI], 2nd Vice President; Paul Conklin [Lansing, MI], 3rd Vice President; H. James Birdsall [Carson City, MI], Secretary; Milford E. Bowen, Sr. [Bellevue, MI], Treasurer.

1958 ERC PLATFORM SPEAKERS: Dr. C. I. Armstrong (WGM); Dr. B. C. Gamble. YOUTH: Donald Sailor (White Pigeon, MI). CHILDREN: Mrs. John Bullock (Leslie). MUSICIANS: "The Singing Sheppards" – Charles and Jeanette Sheppard; Leah Brown. BOOKSTORE: From Dickson's Bible and Book House from Detroit.

1959: July 23 – Aug 2. Warren E. Brown [Lansing, MI], Acting President; Clair J. Snell, 2nd Vice President; Paul Conklin [Lansing, MI], 3rd Vice President; H. James Birdsall [Carson City, MI], Secretary; Milford E. Bowen, Sr. [Bellevue, MI], Treasurer.

1959 ERC PLATFORM SPEAKERS: Bishop Marshall R. Reed (Bishop - Michigan Area UMC); Dr. Joseph T. Edwards (Director of Evangelism - Michigan Area UMC); Dee W. Cobb (MI); Dr. Paul Kindschi (MN). MUSICIANS: M/M Franklin Lusk (IN); Leah Brown; Mrs. James Birdsall. MISSIONARIES: Miss Lela McConnell (KY). YOUTH: Donald Sailor. CHILDREN: Mrs. John W. Bullock

1960: July 28 – Aug 7 [75th Diamond Anniversary Year] Warren E. Brown [Lansing, MI], President; G. Russell Nachtrieb [Detroit, MI], 1st Vice President; Clarence Hutchens, [Grand Rapids, MI] 2nd Vice President; Paul Conklin [Lansing, MI], 3rd Vice President; Milford E. Bowen [Bellevue, MI], Treasurer; H. James Birdsall [Muskegon, MI], Secretary.

1960 ERC PLATFORM SPEAKERS: Dr. Paul F. Elliot (Pres – Owosso Bible College); Dr. C. I. Armstrong (WGM); Dr. Stimson R. Smalley (IL). MUSICIANS: Dr. Glen Johnson (TX); Leah Brown; Mrs. James Birdsall. YOUTH: Clarence Hutchens; John Bullock; Mrs. Lee Shapton.

1961: July 27 – Aug 7; Warren E. Brown [Lansing, MI], President; Russell Nachtrieb [Detroit, MI], 1st Vice President; Clarence Hutchens [Grand Rapids, MI], 2nd Vice President; Paul Conklin [Lansing, MI], 3rd Vice President; Mable McKiddie [Lansing, MI], Secretary; Milford E. Bowen, [Bellevue, MI], Treasurer.

1961 ERC PLATFORM SPEAKERS: Dr. Heber Burge (IL); Dr. Andrew Gallman (MS); Dr. Paul Kindschi (IN). MUSICIANS: M/M Jack Bierce (IN); Leah Brown. YOUTH: John Maes (East Lansing, MI); Clarence Hutchens. CHILDREN: Ardeth Chilson (IO).

1962: Warren E. Brown [Lansing, MI] President; G. Russell Nachtrieb [Detroit, MI], 1st Vice President; Clarence Hutchens [Grand Rapids, MI], 2nd Vice President; Paul Conklin [Lansing, MI], 3rd Vice President; Milford E. Bowen [Bellevue, MI], Treasurer; Miss Mabel McKiddie [Lansing, MI], Secretary.

1962 ERC PLATFORM SPEAKERS: H. B. (Jim) Jones (NC); Dr. William M. Arnett (KY). MISSIONARIES: Richard Adkins (Kenya – WGM). MUSICIANS: Dr. Glen Johnson; Leah Brown.

1963: July 25-Aug 4. Clarence Hutchens [Lansing, MI], Acting President; Miss Mabel McKiddie [Lansing, MI], Secretary; Milford Bowen [Bellevue, MI], Treasurer.

1963 ERC PLATFORM SPEAKERS: Dr. Philip Hinerman (MN); Delbert R. Rose (KY). MUSICIANS: M/M Jewarren Bunting (Lansing); Leah Brown. CHILDREN AND YOUTH: M/M Norman Clothier.

1964: Clarence Hutchens [Ithaca, MI], President; James Birdsall [Muskegon, MI], Vice President; Miss Mabel McKiddie [Lansing, MI], Secretary; Milford Brown [Bellevue, MI], Treasurer.

1964 ERC PLATFORM SPEAKERS: Dr. C. Phillip Hinerman (MN); Dr. J. Sutherland Logan (IO); Dr. G. Ernest Thomas (Birmingham, MI); Dr. Walter H. Judd (Washington, DC). YOUTH/CHILDREN: Maurice Glasgow; M/M Norman Clothier. MUSICIANS: Prof. Marvin Dean (Taylor University); The Earl Nelson Singers. BOOKSTORE: Managed by Paul Conklin through Dickson's Bible and Book Stores in Detroit, MI.

1965: July 15 – 25. [The 80th Year Celebration – Enduring Tradition] Clarence Hutchens [Ithaca, MI], President; James Birdsall [Muskegon, MI], Vice President; Miss Mabel McKiddie [Lansing, MI], Secretary; Milford Brown [Bellevue, MI], Treasurer.

1965 ERC PLATFORM SPEAKERS: Dr. Dennis Kinlaw (KY); Dr. Dr. Floyd George (NY); Dr. Harry Denman (UMC); Senator Frank Carlson. MISSIONARIES: Lela McConnell (KY); Paul Rees (World Vision, Inc). MUSICIANS: Dr. Glen Johnson (TX); Leah Brown. YOUTH: E. Louis Mahigel; David Showers; John Bullock; Maurice Glasgow. CHILDREN: Carole Waldron (MN).

1966: July 21-31. Clarence Hutchens [Ithaca, MI], President; James Birdsall [Muskegon, MI], Vice President; Milford Bowen [Battle Creek, MI], Treasurer; Maurice Glasgow [Eaton Rapids, MI], Secretary.

1966 ERC PLATFORM SPEAKERS: H. B. "Jim" Jones (NC); Dr. William Arnett (KY); Richard Adkins (WGM – Kenya). MUSICIANS: Dr. Glen Johnson (TX); Leah Brown; Harbor Lights Quartette. CHILDREN: Miss Gertrude Cooper. YOUTH: Dr. Glen Johnson.

1967: July 20-30. Clarence Hutchens [Ithaca, MI], President; James Birdsall [Muskegon, MI], Vice President; Maurice Glasgow [Eaton Rapids, MI], Secretary; Milford Bowen [Battle Creek, MI], Treasurer.

1967 ERC PLATFORM SPEAKERS: Tommy Tyson (NC); Dr. Stimson R. Smalley (IL). CHILDREN: Miss Gertrude Cooper. MUSICIANS: The Singing Sheppards – Charles and Jeanette Sheppard; Leah Brown.

1968: July 18 – 28. Clarence Hutchens [Lansing, MI], President; James Birdsall [Muskegon, MI], Vice President; Maurice Glasgow [Eaton Rapids, MI], Secretary; Milford Bowen [Battle Creek, MI], Treasurer.

1968 ERC PLATFORM SPEAKERS: Dr. Merne A. Harris (IO); Dr. Philip Hinerman (MN). YOUTH: Ross Tracy and Eugene Moore. MUSICIANS: Dr. Glen Johnson (TX); Leah Brown. MISSIONARIES: William Cox (WGM-Burundi); Fred Maitland (UMC – Brazil).

1969: July 17-27. Clarence Hutchens [Lansing, MI], President; James Birdsall [Muskegon, MI], Vice President; Maurice Glasgow [Eaton Rapids, MI], Secretary; Milford Bowen [Battle Creek, MI], Treasurer.

1969 ERC PLATFORM SPEAKERS: George Morris; Philip Hinerman (MN); Dr. Kenneth Kinghorn (KY). MUSICIANS: Murk Family Musicale (IL); Dr. Glen Johnson (TX); Leah Brown; Mrs. James Birdsall. MISSIONARIES: Richard Barker (WGM – Japan); Paul Haines (OMS – Korea).

1970: July 16-26. [85th Anniversary Year] Clarence Hutchens [Lansing, MI], President; James Birdsall [Muskegon, MI], Vice President; Maurice Glasgow [Eaton Rapids, MI], Secretary; Cecile Davis [Eaton Rapids, MI], Treasurer.

1970 ERC PLATFORM SPEAKERS: Tommy Tyson (NC); Andrew Gallman (KY); Merne Harris (IO). MUSICIANS: Dr. Glen Johnson (TX); Leah Brown. YOUTH: Ross Tracy (Belding UMC). CHILDREN: Beth Nixon Carruth; Mrs. Kell; Katie and Carol Jones. MISSIONARIES: Fred Maitland (Brazil - UMC); William Cox (Burundi, Africa - WGM).

1971: July 15-25. Clarence Hutchens, President; Dr. Hayden Carruth, Sr., President-Elect.

1971 ERC PLATFORM SPEAKERS: Dr. J. Harold Greenlee (Medillin, Columbia, South America); Paul Leaming (CO); Dr. David Seamands (KY). MUSICIANS: Dr. Glen Johnson (AZ); Leah Brown. YOUTH: Ed Richmond. CHILDREN: Beth Nixon Carruth. MISSIONARIES: Dr. O. Carl Brown (WGM); Fred Maitland (UMC); Dr. Harold Greenlee (OMS).

1972: July 20-30. Dr. Hayden Carruth, Sr. [Ann Arbor, MI], President; James Birdsall [Grand Ledge, MI], Vice President; Mrs. Charles Cookingham [Milan, MI], Secretary; Mrs. Donald Davis [Eaton Rapids, MI], Treasurer.

1972 ERC PLATFORM SPEAKERS: Tommy Tyson (NC); Dr. Kenneth Kinghorn (KY); Herbert L. Bowdoin ("The Methodist Hour" Founder; UMC Pastor). MISSIONARIES: Mardy Picazo (OMS); Dr. Harold Sloan (Irish Methodism); Wallace Haines (International Christian Leadership).

CHILDREN: Kay Starks; Gay Sommerfeld; Mrs. Markey; Mrs. Doerfler; Beth Nixon Carruth; Alice Camber; Helen Arnold. YOUTH: Steve Harper; Ed Richmond. MUSICIANS: "The Musical Pedes" - Wayne and Barbara Pede (Mary Jane; Beverly; Steve).

1973: July 19 -29. Dr. Hayden Carruth, Sr. [Ann Arbor, MI], President; James Birdsall [Grand Ledge, MI], Vice President; Louise Cookingham [Milan, MI], Secretary; Cecile Davis [Eaton Rapids, MI], Treasurer.

1973 ERC PLATFORM SPEAKERS: Dennis Kinlaw (KY); Maurice Stevens (KY); Paul Leaming (CO). CHILDREN: Beth Nixon Carruth; Mrs. Markey; Mrs. Doerphler; Kay Starks; Gay Sommerfeld; Helen Arnold; Alice Camber. YOUTH: Steve Harper; Ed Richmond. MUSICIANS: "The Musical Pedes" - Wayne and Barbara Pede (Mary Jane; Beverly; Steve).

1974: July 18 – 28. Dr. Hayden Carruth, Sr. [Ann Arbor, MI], President; John Bullock [New Buffalo, MI], Vice President; Louise Cookingham [Mt. Morris, MI], Secretary; Cecile Davis [Eaton Rapids, MI], Treasurer.

1974 ERC PLATFORM SPEAKERS: Tommy Tyson (NC); Dr. William Baggett Coker (KY); H. Eddie Fox (Board of Discipleship in the UMC). MUSICIANS: Professor William Goold (KY); Leah Brown; Mary Jane Pede. YOUTH: Jerrold Russell (TN); Beth Nixon Carruth. CHILDREN: Beth Nixon Carruth; Mrs. Markey; Mrs. Doerphler; Kay Starks; Gay Sommerfeld; Helen Arnold; Alice Camber. BOOKSTORE: Logos Bookstore, Ann Arbor, MI.

1975: July 17 – 27. Dr. Hayden Carruth, Sr. [Ann Arbor, MI], President; John Bullock [New Buffalo, MI], Vice President; Louise Cookingham [Mt. Morris, MI], Secretary; Cecile Davis [Eaton Rapids, MI], Treasurer.

1975 ERC PLATFORM SPEAKERS: Dr. Phillip Hinerman (MN); Dr. Kenneth Kinghorn (KY); Dr. Les Woodson (KY). MUSICIANS: Professor William Goold (KY); Leah Brown. YOUTH: Roger Cunningham (KY); Beth Nixon Carruth. CHILDREN: Beth Nixon Carruth; Mrs. Markey; Mrs. Doerphler; Kay Starks; Gay Sommerfeld; Alice Camber; Helen Arnold. BOOKSTORE: Logos Bookstore, Ann Arbor, MI.

1976: July 15 – 25. Dr. Hayden Carruth, Sr. [Ann Arbor, MI], President; John Bullock [New Buffalo, MI], Vice President; Louise Cookingham [Mt. Morris, MI], Secretary; Maxine Topliff [Eaton Rapids, MI], Treasurer.

1976 ERC PLATFORM SPEAKERS: Dr. Samuel Kamaleson (CA); Dr. Roy Putnam (NC); Dr. Victor Hamilton (KY). MUSICIANS: Gordon Vandemark; Leah Brown; Eleanor Peck. YOUTH: Paul Sweet (KY); Beth Nixon Carruth. CHILDREN: Beth Nixon Carruth; Kay Starks; Gay Sommerfeld; Alice Camber; Helen Arnold. BOOKSTORE: Logos Bookstore, Ann Arbor, MI.

1977: July 21 — 31. Dr. Hayden Carruth, Sr, President; Ron Houk, Vice President; Peg Gilpin, Secretary; Maxine Topliff, Treasurer.

1977 ERC PLATFORM SPEAKERS: Dr. Ira Gallaway (IL); Dr. Jimmie Buskirk (OK); Dr. John Oswalt (KY); Dr. Philip Hinerman (MN). MUSICIANS: Gordon Vandemark, Leah Brown, and Mardelle Bates. MISSIONARIES: Billy Davis (UMC); M/M Devee Brown (WGM); Mardy

Picazo (OMS); YOUTH: Paul Sweet (KY); Beth Nixon Carruth. CHILDREN: Beth Nixon Carruth; Kay Starks; Gay Sommerfeld; Jo Vredevo; Helen Arnold; Alice Camber. BOOKSTORE: Logos Bookstore, Ann Arbor, MI.

1978: July 20 – 30. Dr. Hayden Carruth, Sr., President; Ron Houk, Vice President; Rose Belcher, Secretary; Maxine Topliff, Treasurer.

1978 ERC PLATFORM SPEAKERS: Dr. Paul Rees (World Vision Magazine); Dr. Paul Mickey (NC); Jack Williams (PA and IN); Jim Daniel (National Blind Golfer's Assoc); Donald Scavella, Sr. (Detroit). MISSIONARIES: Richard Brunk (WGM); M/M Richard Buckta (OMS). MUSICIANS: Gordon Vandemark, Leah Brown, Ruth Tennant. CHILDREN: Beth Nixon Carruth; Gay Sommerfeld; Kay Starks; Alice Camber; Helen Arnold. YOUTH: Hayden Carruth, Jr.; Beth Nixon Carruth. BOOKSTORE: Logos Bookstore, Ann Arbor, MI.

1979: July 19 – 29. Dr. Hayden Carruth, Sr, President; Howard Coil, President Elect.

1978 ERC PLATFORM SPEAKERS: Tommy Tyson (NC); Dr. Kenneth Kinghorn (KY); Steve Harper (NC). MUSICIANS: Gordon Vandemark; Leah Brown; Ruth Tennant. MISSIONARIES: Dr. Wallace Haines; Robert Erny (OMS); Richard/Barbara Barker (WGM). YOUTH: Hayden Carruth, Jr. (KY); Beth Nixon Carruth. CHILDREN: Beth Nixon Carruth; Kay Starks; Gay Sommerfeld; Alice Camber; Helen Arnold. BOOKSTORE: Logos Bookstore, Ann Arbor, MI.

1980: July 17–27. Howard Coil, President; Elmer Faust, Vice President; Charlene Minger, Secretary; Joan Glasgow, Treasurer.

1980 ERC PLAFORM SPEAKERS: Dr. Dennis Kinlaw (KY); Dr. Samuel Kamaleson (CA); Dr. Merne Harris (IO) MUSICIANS: Jack Rains (CA); Leah Brown; Ruth Tennant. MISSIONARIES: Virgil Maybray (Good News); Dr. Edwin Kilbourne (OMS); Phil Mangas (Men for Missions International, OMS International). YOUTH: Tommy Martin; Beth Nixon Carruth. CHILDREN: Judy Vandemark; Kay Starks; Gay Sommerfeld; Alice Camber; Helen Arnold. BOOKSTORE: Logos Bookstore, Ann Arbor, MI.

1981: July 16 – 26. Howard Coil, President; Elmer Faust, Vice President; Gene Hutchens, Secretary; Joan Glasgow, Treasurer.

1981 ERC PLATFORM SPEAKERS: Dr. John Oswalt (KY); Jack Williams (IN); Larry Shelton (WA). MUSICIANS: Gordon Vandemark, Leah Brown, Ruth Tennant. MISSIONARIES: Dr. Thomas Hermiz (WGM); M/M Roger Skinner (OMS); M/M Elwynn Hulett (UMB). YOUTH: Tommy Martin; Beth Nixon Carruth. CHILDREN: Judy Vandemark; Kay Starks; Gay Sommerfeld; Alice Camber; Helen Arnold. BOOKSTORE: Logos Bookstore, Ann Arbor, MI.

1982: July 15 – 25. Howard Coil, President; Dr. Wallace Haines, President-Elect.

1982 ERC PLATFORM SPEAKERS: Dr. John Bergland (NC); Dr. Eddie Fox (UMC); Col. Bramwell Tillsley (London, England). MISSIONARIES: Lena Eschtruth (Glen) (UMC-KY); Paul Haines (Florence) (OMS); Ralph Haupers

(Lorraine) (Wycliffe Bible Translators). MUSICIANS: Gordon Vandemark; Leah Brown; Ruth Tennant. YOUTH: Tommy Martin (KY); Beth Nixon Carruth. CHILDREN: Judy Vandemark; Carol Shaffer; Gay Sommerfeld; Helen Arnold; Alice Camber. BOOKSTORE: Logos Bookstore, Ann Arbor, MI.

1983: July 21 – 31. Dr. Wallace Haines [England], President.

1983 ERC PLATFORM SPEAKERS: Dr. William Coker (Wilmore, KY); Dr. Richard Halverson (Chaplain of the United States Senate); Dr. William Quick (Detroit, MI); Dr. O. Gerald Trigg (CO); MUSICIANS: Gordon Vandemark; Leah Brown; Ruth Tennant. YOUTH: David Robbins (KY); Beth Nixon Carruth; Joelee Bateman. MISSIONARIES: Miss Mary Joiner (OMS); David Kushman (WGM); Jerry Russell (UMB of Global Ministries). CHILDREN: Judy Vandemark; Carol Shaffer; Gay Sommerfeld; Kay Starks; Helen Arnold; Alice Camber. BOOKSTORE: Logos Bookstore, Ann Arbor, MI.

1984: July 19 – 29. Dr. Wallace Haines [England], President.

1984 ERC PLATFORM SPEAKERS: Dr. Steve Harper (KY); Dr. Lawrence Lacour (OK); Bishop Carl Saunders (AL); Dr. O. Dean Martin (FL). MUSICIANS: Gordon Vandemark; Leah Brown; Ruth Tennant. MISSIONARIES: Dr. and Mrs. Harold Greenlee (OMS); Jack and Ariene Seeley (WGM); David Parker (UMC). YOUTH: Matt Friedman (KY); Beth Nixon Carruth; Joelee Bateman. CHILDREN: Judy Vandemark; Joelee Bateman; Gay Sommerfeld; Kay Starks; Alice Camber; Helen Arnold. BOOKSTORE: Logos Bookstore, Ann Arbor, MI.

1985: July 18-28 [100th Centennial Anniversary]. Dr. Wallace Haines [England], President.

1985 ERC PLATFORM SPEAKERS: Dr. Maurice Boyd (London, Ontario); Dr. Donald English (London, England); Dr. Dennis Kinlaw (KY); Senator Mark Hatfield (Washington, DC). MUSICIANS: Gordon Vandemark; Leah Brown; Ruth Tennant. MISSIONARIES: Paul Haines (OMS); Manfred Kohl (WVI); Kenneth and Carol Lister (WGM). YOUTH: Ron Colwell (KY); Beth Nixon Carruth; Joelee Bateman. CHILDREN: Gay Sommerfeld, Kay Starks, Alice Camber; Helen Arnold; Joelee Bateman; Judy Vandemark. BOOKSTORE: Logos Bookstore, Ann Arbor, MI.

1986: July 17 – 27. Dr. Wallace Haines, President; Ron Houk, Vice President; Gene Hutchens, Secretary; Virginia Tague, Treasurer.

1986 ERC PLATFORM SPEAKERS: Bishop Judith Craig (East Ohio Conference of UMC); Dr. John Oswalt (KY); Dr. William Ellington (Fuller Theological Seminary); Dr. Harold McElvany (IL). MISSIONARIES: Harry Lee (China); Doris Garrett (Philippines); Leon and Vicki Reich (Indonesia). YOUTH: Larry Sachau (Lansing, MI); Will Clegg; Joelee Bateman. CHILDREN: Carol Shaffer; Gay Sommerfeld; Alice Camber; Helen Arnold; Joelee Bateman. MUSICIANS: Gordon Vandemark; Leah Brown; Ruth Tennant.

1987: July 16 – 26. Dr. Wallace Haines, President; Dr. William Shapton, Vice President; Joelee Bateman, Secretary; Virginia Tague, Treasurer.

1987 ERC PLATFORM SPEAKERS: Dr. Joe Harding (WA); Dr. Elsworth Kalas (OH); Dr. O. Dean Martin (FL) [Did not come, due to having brain cancer] MUSICIANS: Gordon Vandemark; Leah Brown; Ruth Tennant. MISSIONARIES: Darlene and Terry Rueger (Malang - OMS); Bob and Pat Linton (Arizona-WGM). YOUTH: Will Clegg; Joelee Bateman. CHILDREN: Carol Shaffer; Gay Sommerfeld; Alice Camber; Helen Arnold; Joelee Bateman.

1988: July 21 – 31. Dr. Wallace Haines, President; Dr. William Shapton, President-Elect.

1988 ERC PLATFORM SPEAKERS: Dr. Leonard Sweet (OH); Barbara Brokhoff (FL); Dr. Alvern Vom Steeg (CA); Dr. Richard Halverson (Washington, DC). MUSICIANS: Scott McPherson (KY); Leah Brown; Barbara Pede. MISSIONARIES: Paul and Florence Haines (Korea - OMS); John and Kendra Enright (Zaire - UMCB); Bruce and Vickie Fivecoat (Tanzania – WGM). YOUTH: Will Clegg. CHILDREN: Carol Shaffer; Gay Sommerfeld; Joelee Bateman; Alice Camber; Helen Arnold.

1989: July 20 – 30. Dr. William R. Shapton, President; Bill Doubblestein, Vice President; Joelee Bateman, Secretary; Virginia Tague, Treasurer.

1989 ERC PLATFORM SPEAKERS: Dr. Rodney Wilmoth (NE); John E. Hendricks (Spring Arbor, MI); Dr. Riley B. Case (IN). MUSICIANS: Dr. William Goold (KY); Leah Brown; Barbara Pede. MISSIONARIES: Kemp Edwards (Tokyo – OMS); Dr. H. T. Maglin (The Mission Society for United Methodists – Zaire and Kenya); Grant Neals (Hong Kong – OMS); Rick Newberry (Red Bird Missionary Conference - President of Beulah Holiness Camp); Eugene and Elaine Lain (OMS – Wilmore, KY). YOUTH: Will Clegg. CHILDREN: Carol Shaffer; Gay Sommerfeld; Joni Clegg; Alice Camber; Helen Arnold; Joelee Bateman.

1990: July 19 – 29. Dr. William R. Shapton, President; Bill Doubblestein, Vice President; Joyce Richmond, Secretary; Virginia Tague, Treasurer.

1990 ERC PLATFORM SPEAKERS: Bradford Dinsmore, Jr. (FL); Dr. Steve Harper (KY); Dr. Alvern Vom Steeg (CA). YOUTH: Matt Kreh; Mike and Deb Long; Will Clegg. MISSIONARIES: Rick Newbury (Pres – Beulah Holiness Camp); Ernest and Sue Steury (WGM – Kenya); William Reincheld (Director of Field Ministries for the Mission Society for United Methodists). MUSICIANS: Scott McPherson; Gerard Faber; Ruth Tennant McLean. CHILDREN: Gay Sommerfeld; Carol Shaffer, Joni Clegg; Helen Arnold; Cathy Minger; Alice Camber; Gene and Elaine Lain (Haiti).

1991: July 18 – 28. Dr. William R. Shapton [Houghton, MI], Pres.

1991 ERC PLATFORM SPEAKERS: Dr. John Oswalt (KY); Barbara Brokhoff (FL); Dr. Leonard Sweet (OH). MISSIONARIES: Todd Wymer (OMS); Dick McClain (The Mission Society for United Methodists); Larry Cochran (Missionary World Service and Evangelism). MUSICIANS: Dr. William Goold (KY); Gerard Farber; CHILDREN: Cathy Minger; Mary Jane Peterson; Joni Clegg. YOUTH: Greg Wood (KY); Scott Mahan (Ypsilanti, MI); Ron and Nancy Kuhlman (OH).

1992: July 16 – 26. Dr. William R. Shapton [Houghton, MI], President.

1992 ERC PLATFORM SPEAKERS: Dr. Ira Gallaway (CO) [Cancelled]; John Mark Nysewander (Francis Asbury Society); Dr. Lawson Stone (KY); Jack Williams (IN). CHILDREN: Cathy Minger; Mary Jane Peterson; Sandi Helms; Cynthia Roberts; Diane Sammons; Jenny Holdread; Mary and Scott Crecelius; Alice Camber; Helen Arnold. YOUTH: Trent Bushnell (Lansing, MI); Scott Mahan (Ypsilanti, MI); Nancy and Ron Kuhlman (OH). MUSICIANS: Scott McPherson (OH); Gerard Faber; Ruth Tenant McLean. MISSIONARIES: David Greenlee (Operation Mobilization); Earl and Dorothy Bowen (World Missionary Service); Steve Sleeper (Bethany Christian Mission Center, KY).

1993: July 15 – 25. Dr. William R. Shapton [Houghton, MI], President.

1993 ERC PLATFORM SPEAKERS: Dr. Samuel Kamaleson (CA); Douglas Crossman (MA); Dr. Philip Granger; David Clardie. CHILDREN: Cathy Minger; Alice Camber; Helen Arnold. YOUTH: Trent Bushnell (Lansing); Scott Mahan (Ypsilanti, MI); Ron and Nancy Kuhlman. MUSICIANS: Dr. William Goold; Gerard Faber; Ruth Tennant McLean.

1994: July 21 — 31. Dr. William Shapton, President; William Doubblestein, President - Elect.

1994 ERC PLATFORM SPEAKERS: Roy Johansen (Norway/Sweden); George Morris (IL); Tommy Tyson (NC). MUSICIANS: Scott McPherson; Gerard Faber; Ruth Tennant McLean. YOUTH: Matt Kreh (Lansing); Hayden and Evan Carruth; Ron and Nancy Kuhlman. CHILDREN: Create Ministries; Alice Camber; Helen Arnold.

1995: July 20 – 30. [110th ANNUAL MEETING] Dr. William Doubblestein, President Elect.

1995 ERC PLATFORM SPEAKERS: David Clardie (MI); Dr. David Thompson (KY); Dr. Lawson Stone (KY). YOUTH: Matt Kreh (Lansing); Hayden and Evan Carruth (Adrian); Ron and Nancy Kuhlman (OH). MUSICIANS: Dr. William Goold; Gerard Faber; Ruth Tennant McLain. CHILDREN: Beverly Sloothak; Out of the Box Ministries; Alice Camber; Helen Arnold. SPECIAL EVENT: Charles D. Killian (KY) as John Wesley and Francis Asbury special presentation.

1996: July 18-28. Dr. William H. Doubblestein [Byron Center, MI], President.

1996 ERC PLATFORM SPEAKERS: Larry Cochran (Pres-Go International); Dr. Steve Harper (Ex Dir – A Foundation for Theological Education); Dr. Robert Mulholland (KY). MUSICIANS: Scott McPherson; Gerard Faber; Ruth Tennant McLean; The Capitalairres (Opening Concert). MISSIONARIES: Bill and Nancy Kidwell (OMS – Russia); Kenneth and Carolyn Wade (WGM – Kenya); Lt. Colonel William Roberts (TSA). YOUTH: Wade Melton; Hayden and Evan Carruth; Ron and Nancy Kuhlman. CHILDREN: Beverly Sloothak; Alice Camber; Helen Arnold.

1997: July 17 – 27. William H. Doubblestein [Byron Center, MI], President.

1997 ERC PLATFORM SPEAKERS: Bob Nelson (KY); Dr. Elsworth Kalas (KY); Dr. Dennis Kinlaw (KY). MUSICIANS: Randy Vandemark; Gerard Faber; Ruth Tennant McLean; Allison Durham (Opening Concert). MISSIONARIES: Dr. Wes Griffin (Assoc Director of World Methodist

Evangelism); James Ogan (OMS – Latin America); Kevin and Becky Zirkle (WGM – Tokyo). YOUTH: Wade Melton; Hayden and Evan Carruth; Ron and Nancy Kuhlman. CHILDREN: Beverly Sloothak; Helen Arnold; Alice Camber.

1998: July 16-26. William H. Doubblestein [Byron Center, MI], President.

1998 ERC PLATFORM SPEAKERS: Philip Brooks (OH); Dr. John Oswalt (KY); Wade Panse (Eaton Rapids); Barbara Brokhoff (FL). MUSICIANS: Scott McPherson (KS); Gerald Faber; Ruth Tennant McLean; Nancy Williams (Opening Concert w/ Scott McPherson). YOUTH: Nathan Emmelheinz; David Price; Joelee Bateman. CHILDREN: Beverly Sloothak; Alice Camber; Helen Arnold. MISSIONARIES: Art and Nancy Butler (AZ); Larry Cochran (Go International); Dr. Margaret Brabon (OMS – Medelin, Columbia, South America).

1999: July 15 – 25. William H. Doubblestein; David Minger; Clyde Leigh – (all Presidents throughout the year.)

1999 ERC PLATFORM SPEAKERS: Roy Jahansen (Norway, Sweden); Dr. David Gyerston (KY); Dr. Roderick Barnett (WV); Dr. William Ury (MS). MUSICIANS: Randy Vandemark (OH); Ron and Linda Sprunger (Ashland Theological Seminary). YOUTH: Nathan Emmelheinz; Carol Stafford; Hosanna (Marion, IN). CHILDREN: Beverly Sloothak; Alice Camber; Helen Arnold.

2000: July 20 – 30. Clyde Leigh [Grand Rapids, MI], Pres.

2000 ERC PLATFORM SPEAKERS: Dr. Gary Cockerill (MS); Dr. Donald Riggs (IN); Dr. Lawson Stone (KY). MUSICIANS: Scott McPherson. MISSIONARIES: Treasure Berens (WGM); Nathan and Heather Emmelhainz (Northern Ireland); Dr. Don Riggs (OMS). YOUTH: Jonathon Arnold; Joelee Bateman; Nathan Emmelhainz. CHILDREN: Beverly Sloothak; Alice Camber; Helen Arnold.

2001: Jul 19 – 29. Clyde Leigh [Grand Rapids, MI], President.

2001 ERC PLATFORM SPEAKERS: Roy Lauter (KY); Dr. Alex Deasley (Nazarene Theological Seminary); Dr. Grad Tanner (Francis Asbury Society). MUSICIANS: Scott Gulledge (Spring Arbor, MI); Cory Williams; Elizabeth Claar. YOUTH: Carol Stafford; Ken Reitz; Nathan Emmelheinz; James Ballard. CHILDREN: Beverly Sloothak; Mary Jane Davenport; Alice Camber; Helen Arnold.

2002: July 18 – 28. Clyde Leigh [Grand Rapids, MI], President.

2002 ERC PLATFORM SPEAKERS: Dr. Randall Davey (Fairview Village Church of the Nazarene); Dr. Bruce Moyer (IO); Dr. Bill Ury (MS). MUSICIANS: Scott Dunham (KS); Elizabeth Claar; Carol Zink. YOUTH: Ben Elliot (MS); Nathan Sparks; Ken Reitz. CHILDREN: Beverly Sloothak; Mary Jane Davenport; Alice Camber; Helen Arnold.

2003: July 17 – 27. Clyde Leigh [Grand Rapids, MI], President.

2003 ERC PLATFORM SPEAKERS: Roy Johannsen (Norway, Sweden); Dr. Sam Kamaleson (CA); Dr. David Thompson (KY). MUSICIANS: Dr. Dennis Crocker (KS); Betty Uithoven; Carol Zink. YOUTH: Ken Reitz; Ben Elliot (Alberta, Canada) [Cancelled] James Ballard [stepped up].

CHILDREN: Beverly Sloothak; Mary Jane Davenport; Alice Camber; Helen Arnold.
2004: July 15 – 25. Clyde Leigh [Grand Rapids, MI], President.
2004 ERC PLATFORM SPEAKERS: Dr. Alex Deasley (KS); Dr. Bruce Moyer (IO); Dr. Roy Lauter (KY). MUSICIANS: Scott Dunham (KS); Carol Zink; Elizabeth Claar. YOUTH: Ken Reitz; James Ballard. CHILDREN: Beverly Sloothak; Mary Jane Davenport; Alice Camber; Helen Arnold.
2005: July 21 – 31. Clyde Leigh [Grand Rapids, MI], President.
2005 ERC PLATFORM SPEAKERS: Dr. Sam Kamaleson (CA); Dr. John Oswalt (MS); Paul Blair (Cancelled); Dr. Ken Kinghorn (KY). MUSICIANS: Dr. Dennis Crocker (KS); Elizabeth Claar; Carol Zink. YOUTH: James Ballard; Ken Reitz; Jason Robey. CHILDREN: Beverly Sloothak; Mary Jane Davenport; Alice Camber; Helen Arnold.
2006: July 20 – 30. Dr. John Oswalt [Jackson, MS]. President Pro-Tem.
2006 ERC PLATFORM SPEAKERS: Dr. Stacy Minger (KY); Dr. David Bauer (OH); Larry Cochran (GO International); Rev. Scott Dunham. MUSICIANS: Scott Dunham (KS); Carol Zink; Elizabeth Claar. YOUTH: Michael Barber (Covenant Theological Seminary); Jason Robey (Covenant Theological Seminary). CHILDREN: Beverly Sloothak; Mary Jane Davenport; Alice Camber.
2007: July 19 – 29. Dr. John Oswalt [Jackson, MS], President.
2007 ERC PLATFORM SPEAKERS: Dr. Sam Kamaleson (CA); Dr. Lawson Stone (KY); Dr. Bruce Moyer (IO). MUSICIANS: Dr. Dennis Crocker (KS); Elizabeth Claar; Carol Zink. YOUTH: Shane Chellis (MO); Hayden Carruth, Jr.; LaVerne Davenport; Kathleen Ray. CHILDREN: Beverly Sloothak; Mary Jane Davenport; Alice Camber.
2008: July 18 – 28. Dr. John Oswalt [Jackson, MS], President.
2007 ERC PLATFROM SPEAKERS: Daniel Tipton; Dr. John Oswalt; Rev. Todd Eckhardt. MUSICIANS: The Jacobys; Burt Kettinger; Carol Zink; Elizabeth Claar. YOUTH: Shane Chellis (Mansfield, MO); Hayden Carruth, Jr.; LaVerne Davenport; Kathleen Ray. CHILDREN: Beverly Sloothak; Mary Jane Davenport; Alice Camber.
2009: July 16 – 26. Dr. John Oswalt [Jackson, MS], President.
2009 ERC PLATFORM SPEAKERS: Dr. David Bauer (Wilmore, KY); Dr. Eldred Kelley (WGM); Tom Adkins (Georgia UMC); Dr. Roy Lauter (Wilmore, KY). MUSICIANS: Dr. Dennis Crocker (Didn't Come); Scott Crecilius; Elizabeth Claar; Carol Zink. YOUTH: Shane Chellis; Will Weatherhead; Hayden and Sylvia Carruth; Kathleen Ray; Laverne Davenport. CHILDREN: Beverly Sloothak; Mary Jane Davenport.
2010: July 15 – 25. 125thANNIVERSARY YEAR Dr. John Oswalt, President; Kathleen Ray, Vice President; John Werner, Secretary; Dave Minger, Treasurer.
2010 ERC PLATFORM SPEAKERS: Dr. Allan Coppedge (KY); Dr. Bill Ury (MS); Dr. Gary Cockerell (MS); Jack French. YOUTH: Shane Chellis (MO); Scott Engebretson; Kathleen Ray; Hayden and Sylvia Carruth; LaVerne

Davenport. MUSICIANS: Scott Crecilius; Elizabeth Claar; Carol Zink. CHILDREN: Beverly Sloothak; Mary Jane Davenport.

2011: July 18 – 28. Dr. John Oswalt [Jackson, MS], President.

2011 ERC PLATFROM SPEAKERS: Dr. Lawson Stone; Rev. Todd Eckhardt; Dr. Bruce Moyer. MUSICIANS: Scott Crecilius; Carol Zink; Elizabeth Claar. YOUTH: Shane Chellis (MO).

2012: July 16 – 26. Dr. John Oswalt [Jackson, MS], President.

2012 ERC PLATFORM SPEAKERS: Dr. Victor Hamilton; Rev. Tom Atkins; Rev. Jack French. MUSICIANS: Scott Crecilius; Elizabeth Claar; Carol Zink; Hayden Carruth, Jr.

2013: July 15 – 25. Dr. John Oswalt, President; Kathleen Ray, Vice President; John Werner, Secretary; Dave Minger, Treasurer.

2013 ERC PLATFORM SPEAKERS: Stanley Key; Dr. William Ury; Dr. Christopher Bounds; Stacy Minger. MUSICIANS: Scott Crecilius;

2014: July 18 – 27. Dr. John Oswalt, President; Kathleen Ray, Vice President; John Werner, Secretary; Dave Minger, Treasurer.

2014 ERC PLATFORM SPEAKERS: Dr. Lawson Stone; Rev. Todd Eckhardt; Dr. Eldred Kelley. YOUTH MUSICIANS: Scott Crecilius; Carol Zink; Becky Wilson; Hayden Carruth; Rufus Harris (concert).

2015: July 17 – 26. Dr. John Oswalt, President; LaVerne Davenport, President-Elect; Kathleen Ray, Vice President; John Werner, Secretary; Dave Minger, Treasurer.

2015 ERC PLATFORM SPEAKERS: Dr. Bruce Moyer; Rev. David Gallimore (GA); Rev. Jack French.

Appendix 3

"The Victory Life, How to Keep in the Will of God" (I Thessalonians 3:12-13)

Sermon by Rev. W. G. Nixon, President of ERC, 1926

The will of God for every Christian is expressed in the next chapter: "For this is the will of God, even your sanctification, that ye may abstain from fornication."

This may not be your desire; it is not the desire of your worldly friends. But it is certainly the climax of God's desire for every child of his. This "second blessing, properly so called," as John Wesley said, is not an end in itself but a means to an end, that climaxes with the coming of Jesus. And the very God of peace sanctify you wholly: and I pray God your whole Spirit and soul and body be preserved blameless unto the coming of our Lord Jesus Christ (ch. 5:23).

God regenerates a soul in order to sanctify it and he sanctifies the soul in order to keep it justified, and the soul that lives in the experience of full salvation is ready at any moment to be glorified.

My earnest desire in this message is to show the newly sanctified soul how to retain this experience in the life in holiness. We must remember that sanctification is a process, an instantaneous work of grace, while holiness is the life lived every day after this crisis experience.

I offer here five helps to enable one to keep in the will of God.

I. Learn to Distinguish between the Carnal Man and the Natural Man

This is very important and the more so because the devil will not do this. He will make some pull of temptation on you and then turn and insist that it came from a desire of your carnal heart. Now sanctification kills the carnal nature, the sin principle. The old man, the tendency to evil; but it does not destroy a single God-given faculty, or power, or appetite of a normal human body.

Temptation usually appeals to some one of the five senses for gratification. There are but few purely spiritual temptations.

James gives us the genesis of temptation: "Let no man say when he is tempted, I am tempted of God: for God cannot be tempted of evil, neither tempteth he any man: but every man is tempted when he is drawn away of his own lust and enticed." James 1:12-13. Or as I believe the better marginal reading: "When he is drawn away of his own desires and enticed."

To have a temptation there must be the "drawing away" of some natural appetite or passion of the soul or body, usually the latter. Let me illustrate by the temptation of Jesus in the wilderness. He had been forty days without food. He had lost weight; he was emaciated and oh so hungry. Then it was that the devil suggested that he turn the stones into bread. By the suggestion, desire was aroused for bread. There was a pull on his appetite and a temptation to work a miracle on his own behalf. He refused the temptation and trusted God for bread as he expects us now to do and lo an angelic host came fluttering through the blue and spread a table for him in the wilderness.

Permit me to lay down a rule that applies to temptation. "The first natural movement of any God-given appetite or passion of the life is not a sin."

Suppose a business man arises too late to have his breakfast and catches a car for his office. So he goes without his breakfast. Reaching the heart of the city he leaves the street car and passes a fruit stand on his way to his office. He sees there luscious sun-kissed apples, pears, and peaches. His mouth waters for the fruit, as men say, that is, the saliva begins to flow. A normal passion or appetite has been aroused. Everything is normal so far. Just then the keeper of the stand turns his back and the devil says: "Help yourself. No one is looking." Now there is a real temptation on. The business man spurns it, saying, I will not satisfy my hunger by being a thief. There is no sin in being tempted. The sin is in yielding to the temptation. This application applies in sex relationships, and in all life's experiences. "The first natural movement of any God-given appetite or passion is not a sin." The sin is in the wrong use of appetites and passions.

II. Learn to Keep the Natural Man Under Control

Paul tells us that the priceless knowledge of the glory of God in a personal religious experience has its abode in a fleshly tabernacle. Here are his words: "God, who commanded the light to shine out of darkness, hath shined in our hearts, to give the light of the knowledge of the glory of God in the face of Jesus Christ, but we have this treasure in earthen vessels, that the excellency of the power may be of God and not of us." II Cor. 4:6-7. So then grace tabernacles in a soul that inhabits a body that is subject to external appeals and temptations.

The subjective battle of every soul shifts to be in keeping with his relation to God.

The sinner battles against God. He puts the fists of his soul in the face of the Almighty and defies Deity. He turns away from the Savior and says: "I will not let this man Christ Jesus reign over me." It is a losing battle but so he fights. "Saul! Saul!! It is hard for thee to kick against the pricks."

For the truly saved man the subjective battle shifts. He finds something within him that was against the true spiritual life in his soul. Something that will not obey God. This is the carnal nature, the body of sin. The old man, the root of bitterness.

Now the subjective battle of a newly saved soul is to suppress, to restrain, to control the carnal nature and, just as one thinks he has succeeded, the Old Man slips from under and asserts himself for "the carnal mind is not subject to the law of God, neither indeed can be." God himself cannot convert the carnal mind, but, thank God the Holy Ghost can kill, destroy carnality.

For the truly sanctified man the subjective battle changes again. He must now watch his step, watch his deeds, watch his thoughts. The great apostle Paul gives this exhortation and testimony: "Every man that striveth for the mastery is temperate in all things. Now they do it to obtain a corruptible crown; but we an incorruptible. I therefore so run not as uncertainly. So fight I, not as one that beateth the air: But I keep under my body and bring it into subjection: lest by any means, when I have preached to others, I myself should be a castaway!" I Cor. 9:25-27.

I must therefore keep my body under. The body the servant of the spirit. I must keep my body clean. I must keep my body fit. I must not defile it with cigarettes or tobacco in any form. I must keep my body clothed and modestly attractive, and hear me: The indwelling Holy Ghost will make a woman's face more beautiful than all the concoctions of the apothecary shop. I must do all I can to keep my body well.

If disease overtakes me, I will call on God for help, take the remedies prescribed by my physician unless I have absolute assurance that God will heal me, and when well again, by cheerful moods, by physical exercise do my best to keep my body well.

At the best our bodies are frail, often subject to pain and nervousness. What will I do if yielding to a temptation from without in an unguarded moment I speak hastily or harshly or do a wrong deed? This is what I will do. I will ask God to forgive me and see to it that no seed of carnality get into my soul, and then on first opportunity and as publicly as the offense ask forgiveness of the one I wronged and go on in unbroken fellowship. My friends, the emergency promise of I John 2:1 is as much for the sanctified as for the converted. "If any man sin we have an advocate with the father Jesus Christ the righteous and he is the propitiation for our sins, and not for ours only but also for the sins of the whole world." What an emergency break is to an automobile. What an extinguisher is in time of fire. This promise is for the sanctified if surprised into sin.

III. Learn to Keep Love the Dominant Note of the Life

Can this be done by trying? No. Does an apple tree in May days struggle and groan and keep awake nights to put forth leaf and blossom? No. It is a matter of right relationship of the tree to the soil and the air, and it grows without trying. Does a mother try to love a new born baby? No. She loved her ere she saw the light of day and coming up out of the valley of death with a baby at her breast she loves without trying. Motherhood is love. It is a matter of relationship. My text asks that "the Lord make you to increase and abound in love one toward another and toward all men even as we do toward you." And Paul tells us in Rom 5:5 that "the love of God is shed abroad in our hearts by the Holy Ghost which is given unto us."

Beware of faultfinding, censoriousness, sourness, bitterness. Exalt the good, pity the bad, have compassionate love for everybody. Love that sacrifices. Love that runs errands. Love that suffers. Love that hopes. Divine love shed abroad by the Holy Ghost in the soul. Love that weeps at the altar crying: "Spare thy people, O Lord, and give not thine heritage to reproach." Joel 2:17. Love that seeks the erring. Love that comforts the sorrowing. Love that breaks in tears of pity over a lost world. Oh! God possess in perpetual mood of love.

IV. Learn to Keep Character Building the Greatest Subjective Task

The purpose of abounding love is "to the end he may stablish your hearts unblamable in holiness before God." The heart is the citadel of selfhood whose greatest asset is character. Whenever I see a mighty oak a hundred years old putting its fists against a north wind I feel like taking off my hat and saying in the language of the poet: "A little of thy steadfastness,/ Rounded by leafy gracefulness,/ Old Oak give me;/ That the world's blasts about me blow,/ And I yield gently to and fro:/ While my stout hearted trunk below,/ And firm set roots unshaken be."

You can grow a corn stalk in three months but it will take a hundred years of storm and sun to grow an oak. Lord give us something of the fibre of the oak. Note the expression, "stablish." Get settled, rooted, grounded. How? By grace that "He may stablish you." Note it is one's heart, not his head, that is to be stablished. And note also that God is to be the judge of character. It is to be before him, not before the people. The story is told how in one of Mr. Apdedraff's meetings a lady was graciously sanctified and told the preacher that she was going home to convince her community of the reality of her experience. The wise soul winner said, "Sister, with a soul as white as snow and wings as white as those of an angel, there are those with so bad a case of color blindness that they would shoot you for a blackbird." Is God less exacting than man? No. But God has better eyesight. "Man looketh on the outward appearance. The Lord looketh on the heart." To Abraham God said: "Walk thou before me and be thou perfect." A pure heart, pure motives, pure living as in the sight of God will please him even when it does not please those about us.

God's intention in perfecting the saints is to so establish us that we henceforth be no more children tossed to and fro and carried about with every wind of doctrine by the sleight of men and cunning craftiness whereby they lie in wait to deceive. Eph 4:14.

V. Learn to Keep Alive the Blessed Hope of Christ's Second Coming

This truth is in my scripture "to the end he may stablish your hearts…unto the coming of our Lord Jesus Christ with all his saints." It is the clear teaching of the scriptures that Jesus will come back to earth again. "In like manner as he went." He will come through the blue attended by saints; probably the martyr saints who went, battle scarred, into glory, will return with the Savior as he comes for his Bride. I do not know when this will be. The event may find me alive on the earth—I would be glad to escape a grave yard. It may find one under the clods of the valley. It matters little. The early church believing in the soon appearing of Jesus began to worry about their dead whom they had recently laid in burying grounds. Paul reassured them saying: "The Lord himself shall descend from heaven with a shout, with the voice of the archangel, and with the trump of God: and the dead in Christ shall rise first. Then we which are alive and remain shall be caught up together with them in the clouds to meet the Lord in the air. And so shall we ever be with the Lord. Wherefore comfort one another with these words." I Thess. 4:16-18.

Whether this second coming is premillennial or post-millenial is of little importance. Whether we who are now alive go by what Joseph H. Smith calls the "valley route or the air route" is of minor concern. The thing of paramount importance is that we be ready to meet him when he comes. I am convinced that the normal attitude of every Christian in every age of the world's life is to keep the blessed hope of his coming and to so live as to be ready if he should come today.

Dear friend, are you now ready to meet him? You answer, "Yes, through obedience and faith in his shed blood, I believe I am ready."

These plain advices are calculated, under the blessing of God, to help you to keep in his blessed will until his coming again.

Bibliography

Adams, Doug. *Meeeting House to Camp Meeting Saratoga: Resource Publications Asbury Grove Directory.* Salem, MA: Newcomb & Gauss, Printers, 1905.

Baker, Sheridan. *Living Waters; Being Bible Expositions and Addresses Given at Different Camp-Meetings and to Ministers and Christian Workers on Various Other Occasions.* Introduced with the author's experience in spreading holiness. 3rd ed., corr. and enl. Boston: McDonald and Gill, Office of the Christian Witness, 1889.

Beard, Christine. *The Boston Globe Meeting Ground at Asbury Grove (March 1, 1998).*

———. *History of Asbury Grove* (http://www.asburygrove.org) August 9, 2009.

Blanchard, Charles L. "A Study of the Modern Camp Meeting." (Unpublished thesis presented to the faculty of the Louisville Presbyterian Theological Seminary.) May, 1962.

Boardman, William E. *The Higher Christian Life* (Boston: Henry Hoyt, 1858).

Brown, Kenneth O. *Holy Ground: A Study of the American Camp Meeting* (New York: Garland Publishing, Inc., 1992).

———. *Holy Ground, Too, The Camp Meeting Family Tree* (Hazleton: Holiness Archives, 1997).

———. Inskip, McDonald, Fowler: *"Wholly and Forever Thine"* (Hazleton: Holiness Archives, 2000).

Bruce, Dickson D., Jr. *And They All Sang Hallelujah.* Knoxville, TN: The University of Tennessee Press, 1974.

Cartwright, Peter. Autobiography *of Peter Cartwright, the Backwoods Preacher*, ed. W. P. Strickland. New York, 1857.

Cary, W. W. "Sychar an Holiness Camp Meeting." Louisville: The Pentecostal Publishing Company, n.d.

Coleman, Robert E. *The Master Plan of Evangelism.* Old Tappan, New Jersey: Fleming H. Revell Company, 1963).

Dayton, Donald W. *Discovering An Evangelical Heritage.* New York: Harper & Row, 1976.

Dayton, Donald W., David W. Faupel, and David D. Bundy. *The Higher Christian Life: A Bibliographic Overview.* New York & London: Garland Publishing, 1985.

Dieter, Melvin Easterday. *The Holiness Revival of the Nineteenth Century.* Metuchen, New Jersey: The Scarecrow Press, Inc., 1980.

Eltscher, Susan M. *Women in the Wesleyan and United Methodist Traditions: A Bibliography.* Madison, N.J.: General Commission on Archives and History, United Methodist Church, 1991.

Forney, Christian Henry. *History of the Churches of God in the United States of America Harrisburg: Board or Directors of the Publishing House and Book Rooms of the Churches of God,* 1914.

Gorham, Reverend B. W. *Camp Meeting Manual.* Boston: H. V. Degen, 1854.

Grider, J. Kenneth. *A Wesleyan-Holiness Theology.*

Grimes, John Franklin. *The Romance of the American Camp Meeting.* Cincinnati: The Caxton Press, 1922.

Heyrman, Christine, *Southern Cross: The Beginnings of the Bible Belt.* New York: Knopf, 1997.

Johnson, Charles A. *The Frontier Camp Meeting* (Dallas: Southern Methodist University Press, 1955).

Jones, Charles Edwin. Black Holiness: *A Guide to the Study of Black Participation in Wesleyan Perfectionist and Glossolalic Pentecostal Movements.* Metuchen, N.J. & London: American Theological Library Association and The Scarecrow Press, 1987.

———. *A Guide to the Study of the Holiness Movement.* Metuchen, New Jersey: The Scarecrow Press and the American Theological Library Association, 1974.

———. *Perfectionist Persuasion: The Holiness Movement and American Methodism,* 1867-1936 (Metuchen, New Jersey: The Scarecrow Press, Inc., 1974).

Kostlevy, William. *Historical Dictionary of the Holiness Movement.* (Lanham, Md.: Scarecrow Press: 2001.

———. *Holiness Manuscripts: A Guide to Sources Documenting the Wesleyan Holiness Movement in the United States and Canada.* Metuchen, N. J.: The American Theological Library Association and the Scarecrow Press, Inc., 1994.

Lawrence, Harold, *A Feast of Tabernacles: Georgia Campgrounds and Campmeetings* (Tignall, Ga.: Boyd Publishing, 1990).

Lee, Jesse. *A Short History of Methodists in the United States* (Baltimore: Magill and Clime, 1810).

Mannoia, Kevin W. and Don Thorsen. "The Holiness Manifesto" (William B. Eerdmans Publishing, 2008).

Matthews, Donald G. *Religion in the Old South* (Chicago: University of Chicago Press, 1977).

McDonald, William and John E. Searles. *The Life of Rev. John S. Inskip, President of the National Association for the Promotion of Holiness* (Chicago: The Christian Witness Co., 1885).

Mead, A. P. *Manna in the Wilderness; or the Grove and Its Altar Offering, and Thrilling Incidents.* Containing a history of the origin and rise of camp meetings and an account of a Wyoming Camp Meeting. Philadelphia, 1859.

Miller, William Charles. *Holiness Works: A Bibliography.* Kansas City: Nazarene Publishing House for Nazarene Theological Seminary, 1986.

Osborn, Mrs. W. B. *Pioneer Days of Ocean Grove*. New York: Methodist Book Concern, n.d.

Owen, Christopher. *The Sacred Flame of Love: Methodism and Society in Nineteenth-Century Georgia* (Athens: University of Georgia Press, 1998).

Richardson, Faith. *History of the New England Conference of the United Methodist Church, 1796–1995* (http://www.neumc.org/pages/detail/74),1992.

Scott, Harvey. *Religion, Theology, and Morals* (Kessinger Publishing, 2007).

Smith, Hannah Whitall. *The Unselfishness of God, and How I Discovered It: A Spiritual Autobiography* (New York: Fleming H. Resell Co., 1903).

Smith, Joseph Henry. *Things Behind and Things Before in the Holiness Movement* (Chicago: Evangelistic Institute Press, 1916).

Smith, Logan Pearsall, ed. *Philadelphia Quaker: The Letters of Hannah Whitall Smith* (New York: Harcourt, Brace and Co., 1950).

Smith, Timothy L. *Revivalism and Social Reform* (New York: Abingdon Press, 1957).

———. Called *Unto Holiness: The Story of the Nazarenes—The Formative Years,* (Nazarene Publishing House, 1962).

Spencer, Carol. *"Holiness: The Soul of Quakerism"* (Paternoster. Milton Keynes, 2007).

Stanley, Susie C. *Wesleyan/Holiness Women Clergy: A Preliminary Bibliography*. Portland, Oregon: Western Evangelical Seminary, 1994.

Sweet, William W. *Revivalism in America*. New York: Harper & Brothers, 1939.

———. *The Story of Religion in America*. New York: Harper & Brothers, 1939.

———. *The American Churches—An Interpretation*. London: The Epworth Press, 1974.

The Double Cure, or Echoes from National Camp Meetings (Boston and Chicago: The Christian Witness Company, 1894). (Sermons by representative leaders of the National Holiness Association.)

Turner, Kristen D. *A Guide to Materials on Women in the United Methodist Church Archives*. Madison, N.J.: General Commission on Archives and History, United Methodist Church, 1995.

Vincent, Hebron. *History of Wesleyan Grove, Martha's Vineyard, Camp Meeting* (Boston: G. C. Rand & Avery, 1858).

Wallace, Rev. Adam. *A Modern Pentecost.* Embracing a record of the Sixteenth National Camp Meeting for Promotion of Holiness, held at Landisville, Pennsylvania, July 23 to August 1, 1873. Philadelphia: Methodist Home Journal Publishing House, 1873.

Weiss, Ellen. *City in the Woods* (Boston: Northeastern University Press, 1998).

White, Charles Edward. *The Beauty of Holiness: Phoebe Palmer as Theologian, Revivalist, Feminist, and Humanitarian* (Zondervan/Francis Asbury Press, 1986).

Williams, David S. *From Mounds to Megachurches: Georgia's Religious Heritage* (Athens: University of Georgia Press, 2008).

Wood, J. A. *Perfect Love* (Chicago: The Christian Witness Company, 1909).

―――. *Purity and Maturity* (Philadelphia: National Publishing Association for the Promotion of Holiness, 1876).

www.ingramcontent.com/pod-product-compliance
Lightning Source LLC
Chambersburg PA
CBHW032000220426
43664CB00005B/85